AF560065

THE FOUNDATIONS OF THE COMPOSITE CULTURE IN INDIA

THE FOUNDATIONS OF THE COMPOSITE CULTURE IN INDIA

MALIK MOHAMED

THE FOUNDATIONS OF THE COMPOSITE CULTURE IN INDIA
Malik Mohamed

First Published, 2007
Reprinted 2016
Reprinted 2018

ISBN 978-93-50028-390-7

Published by
AAKAR BOOKS
28 E Pocket IV, Mayur Vihar Phase I, Delhi 110 091
Phone: 011 2279 5505 Telefax: 011 2279 5641
aakarbooks@gmail.com; www.aakarbooks.com

Typeset at
Arpit Printographers, Delhi 110 032

Printed at
D.K. Fine Art Press, Delhi 110 052

Contents

Preface

From time immemorial, India has been the meeting place of diverse races and civilizations. India is a vast country surrounded by natural barriers and there are considerable variations in terrain and clime within her borders. Geographical factors have, to some extent, influenced unity in diversity, but there is some basic element in India's genius, something in its 'genetic code', as it were, which has always moved towards an underlying unity despite apparent diversity.

In the dim twilight of history, the migration of primordial hordes of ethnic groups, mostly from the central, south-central and north-eastern parts of Asia that have descended wave upon wave into the fertile Indo-Gangetic plains moving southwards to the alluvial Deccan plateau inhabited by the earliest known indigenous people, provided the first pattern of inter-ethnic mixture in this mighty generous land that was to become one of the biggest crucibles of race and culture in human history.

The Aryans appeared on the Indian scene as conquerors around 1600 B.C. Perhaps they came from Eurasia via Iran. In the beginning they had neither a settled life nor were they literate. Gradually they settled, took to agriculture, and territorial states began to emerge from a tribal society. They first spread over the north of India and then penetrated into the south. One of the most wonderful civilizations of the world was founded by them. The Indo-Aryan fusion is the first major metamorphasis of Indian culture.

The civilization that the conquering Arabs brought from peninsular Arabia had a great integrating tendency, which, besides other factors, facilitated its acceptance and expansion. This speedy and quick expansion, much of which was undertaken at the invitation of the overburdened local masses and internal schisms, demanded of the Arabs a liberal and adjusting attitude towards the people of the lands they were occupying.

Contrary to popular impression, the Arab conquest of Sind in A.D. 712 by Mohammed-bin-Kasim was not the first point of contact between the Arabs and Indians, except from the military point of view. Long before this invasion, Arab traders had come into contact with the people of Malabar in South India. Apart from the above inroads of a civil nature into the life of the people of India, there were also military incursions by different races coming from different regions at different times during the medieval period, notable amongst them being the Arabs, the Turks, the Afghans and the Mughals. They ruled over India, settled here, and made it their homeland, like the earlier invaders and rulers, but unlike the later ones.

It must be remembered that the Arabs, even before coming to India had contacts with India and an understanding of Indian sciences and religious thought (Hinduism). They had only praise for India. Another point to be remembered is that Sufism, which was born in Iran had some influence on Indian thought (Vedanta), especially on yoga and Buddhism.

The coming of the Muslims to India meant the meeting of two vitally strong civilizations, each different from the other in many fundamental ways. But, amazingly, they came close to each other in religious thought and other modes of outlook, leading to an almost complete fusion of the two cultures. Sir John Marshall has rightly observed : "Seldom in the history of mankind has the spectacle been witnessed of two civilizations, so vast and so strongly developed, yet so radically dissimilar as the Muhammadan and Hindu, meeting and mingling together".

Humanistic tendencies were plentiful within the Islamic fabric and these were exploited by the Sufis, especially that group which believed in the unity of existence. They studied the Hindu religion with avidity and idol-worship was explained as worshipping a certain attribute of God. There were efforts by both Hindus and Muslims (Sufis) to find equivalence between Vedanta and Sufism.

Prince Dara Shikoh attempted to show that Sufism and Vedanta were the same process and had similar ideals. The *Wahdatul–Wujud* of the Sufis and Advaita more or less coincided and this led Dara to compose his *Majmaul–Bahrain*—the confluence of two oceans—to demonstrate that the two oceans, Islam and Hinduism do merge.

When the Hindu society was regimented and stratified into social classes based on religious sanction and lacked simple formulae of faith, well-defined dogmas and rituals and democratic theories of social organisation as well, "Islam appeared upon the scene with formulae of faith, well defined dogmas and rites and democratic theories of social organisation".

The Muslim rulers also brought about the best and the most harmonious relations between the Hindus and Muslims. During the Sultanate as well as the Mughal period, religion was more or less a matter of personal faith and not a source of strife in society. The state was not theocratic and the Ulemas were not allowed to interfere in state matters. Liberalism and not orthodoxy governed the public or private life of the rulers.

All Muslims, mostly converts from the lower classes of the Indian society, owed their loyalties only towards this country. Thus medieval India was an age of enlightenment, elevation eloquence, peace, progress, prosperity and communal harmony.

The cross-fertilization of Islam and Hinduism led to the Bhakti and Sufi movements. The Bhakti cult emphasised the fundamental equality of all religions and the unity of God, preached simple devotion and faith as the means of salvation, protested against excessive ritualism and formalities of religion, and condemned the caste system.

The Bhakti movement was the consequence of Hindu tolerance in theology, religion and metaphysics and the Islamic sense of equality in social practice. Hindu tolerance was displayed vividly amongst the Sufis and the Sufi and Bhakti movements proved an anchor for all those who felt alienated from orthodox Islam and Hinduism.

In terms of cultural depth and intensity and wider social repercussions, the most profound influences on civilization are those of the ancient Indo–Aryan and the medieval Indo–Muslim segments. The Indo–Aryans contributed to the flowering of Vedic cultural streams which, over the centuries, have continued to fertilize the body politic of this ancient land. The Indo–Muslim stands have weaved into the texture of India's national existence a rich design of 'composite culture' by intertwining the threads of the Bhakti Marg (Bhakti movement) with the Islamic Sufi (movement) ideals, thereby creating a new inter-cultural synthesis, in which the values of man and social ethics reflected a new ethos. I have pointed out in my study that the second cultural metamorphosis (which took place after the first Indo–Aryan cultural metamorphosis) is the most effective one in formulating the composite culture of India.

As the contributions of Sufi saints and their impact on Indian society and culture are so great, I have felt it necessary to provide eleborate details of the Sufi ideals and Sufi institutions in the present study.

Other factors which have contributed to the Hindu–Muslim mingling throughout the medieval period have been dealt with in some chapters as the foundations of the composite culture of India. In particular, the efforts made by Muslim rulers towards unity and harmony have been elaborately pointed out in one chapter. Solid historical evidences are presented to pinpoint the religious liberalism and magnanimity of the Muslim rulers to refute historical distortions created by the British historians as part of the British policy of 'divide and rule' during their reign and after by the Indian communal historians having vested interests.

In this, I have been greatly benefited by the book *Harmony of Heritage : An insight into Medieval India* written by Dr. Ajeet Jawed. It is a valuable research work which throws light into the 'little known dimensions of Muslim rule'.

After the death of Aurangzeb in 1707 and the weakening of

the Mughal empire, the British traders who came to India as merchants of a company started meddling with Indian political affairs. By playing one ruler against another and acquiring economic and political advantages thereafter, they acquired the position of dictating their terms. Their first victory was over Nawab Siraj-ud-Daula in 1757 and the train of success continued till 1857, when their home country directly enslaved India.

Finding that they could rule this country only by dividing Hindus and Muslims on the basis of religion, the British adopted the policy of 'divide and rule'. They applied many techniques to achieve their aim. They engaged their historians to rewrite Indian history and text books. British historians have laid emphasis on differences and portrayed the relations between Hindus and Muslims in pictures bearing most prominently the marks of violence, conquest, rapine and religious bigotry. They have depicted Muslims as destroyers of Hindu culture and tradition, despoilers of Hindu temples and palaces and brutal idol-breakers who have offered to their Hindu victims the terrible alternative of conversion or the sword. Their motivation was not hidden, but expressed in clear words. British historians and their hired Indian historians did not lag behind in presenting a communal view of Indian history.

The British were bent upon implementing their policy of divide and rule through many designs. Even in the case of language, it was the British who put the 'Muslim' label on Urdu. The British rulers often generated hostility between Hindus and Muslims where it did not exist and followed policies which would further accentuate differences. They paved the way for religious nationalism, which took an ugly shape in the course of time. This led to hate-campaigns between Hindus and Muslims. Religious nationalism finally led to the 'two-nation' theory. Thus, the Britishers did great harm to the Hindu–Muslim unity which had prevailed for many centuries.

The thrust-point in my present book throughout is Hindu–Muslim unity, which was formulated due to historical, social and cultural factors during the course of some ten centuries and which was the dawn of the composite culture in India.

In preparing this book and collecting material for its various chapters, I have been greatly benefited from the scholarly works of Dr. Tarachand, Dr. K.A. Nizami, Dr. B.N. Pande, Dr. Rafiq Zakaria, Dr. Asghar Ali Engineer, Dr. Rasheeduddin Khan and some others, who are pioneers in this field and to whom I acknowledge my sincere gratitude. To my great advantage, I am to point out that some foreign scholars, who have done valuable work concerning different sections of my present work. To them also, this work owes a lot.

Finally, I thank my publisher Mr. K.K. Saxena of Aakar Books for undertaking the publication of this book in the shortest time possible.

The composite culture of India, rightly understood, can contribute significantly to the cause of national integration. The integrity of our nation is being threatened by various political, religious and theoretical forces. The compositeness of a culture leaves room for, if not directly promotes, the peculiarities and richness of local and regional cultures.

I hope my present work will be received well both by academics, students and the reading public in understanding the various facets of the foundations of the composite culture in India.

Malik Mohamed

1

The Assimilating Charcteristics of Indian Culture

From time immemorial, India has been the meeting place of diverse races and civilizations. India is a vast country surrounded by natural barriers, with considerable variations of terrain and clime within her borders. Geographical factors have, to some extent, influenced unity in diversity, but there is some basic element in India's genius, something in its 'genetic code' as it were, which has always moved towards an underlying unity despite apparent diversity. True, India in the past achieved political unity of spirit or mind in a broad sense after initial difficulties. This is a unique feature of India's chequered history. Ours is perhaps the oldest civilization of the world with an uninterrupted history (with the possible exception of China). Most of the old civilizations are dead and gone. We have not only survived the vicissitudes of time but maintained, developed and enriched a continuous culture. To quote Iqbal, *'Yunan-o-Misr-o-Roma sab mit gaye jehan se, Ab tak magar hai baqi nam-o-nishan hamara'* (Greece, Egypt, Rome, all have vanished from the world. But our name and symbol still exist). Further, as Iqbal says, there is 'something' which precludes our existence from getting effaced: *'Kuchh bat hai ke hasti, mitti nahin hamari'*. This 'something' is everything: this is the secret of our vitality, the secret of our wisdom. The history of Indian civilization and culture is a story of unity and synthesis, of adaptation and development, of fusion of old traditions with new values.[1]

Our culture is like a mighty river fed by many tributaries, the mainstream flowing on and on. The Hindustani expression for fusion, *Ganga-Jamuni*, comes from this concept of unity. Our culture is also compared to a great cauldron to which different ingredients have been added from time to time to produce a lustrous compound; above all, the seething cauldron has never cooled and is always ready to accept new ideas without losing its pristine identity. There are other comparisons too: a rich tapestry interwoven with colourful warp and woof, a garden in which flowers of different hues and fragrances bloom, a mosaic with chips of different colours exhibiting a distinctive pattern, which probably led the poet Rabindranath Tagore to invoke the image of India as a confluence, a meeting place of many races and cultures.

Wave after wave of peoples of different races poured into the Indian subcontinent, settled here, and made it their homeland, barring a few exceptions. We do not know much about the earliest inhabitants—perhaps they were Dasas or Dasyus—but the earliest invaders were those who founded the Indus Valley civilization of about 3000 BC. They had urban settlements in Punjab, Sind and other places. They were literate, although their script has not yet been deciphered. Their civilization resembled the Sumerian civilization of Mesopotamia (Iraq).

The Aryans appeared on the Indian scene as conquerors around 1600 BC. Perhaps they came from Eurasia via Iran. In the beginning they had neither a settled life nor were they literate. Gradually they settled, took to agriculture, and territorial states began to emerge from a tribal society. They first spread over the north of India and then penetrated into the south. One of the most wonderful civilizations of the world was founded by them. The *Rigveda* is perhaps the oldest extant literary work of the world. The great epics, *Ramayana* and *Mahabharata*, can be traced back to roughly 1000 BC. Jainism and Buddhism were born in the sixth century BC. Empires arose and fell. The North Indian population mixed and mingled with the South Indians. Despite this mixture, it appears, the North Indian blood is predominantly Aryan and certain regions of the South are Dravidian in character. Be that as is may, throughout the length and breadth of India the predominent strain of Indian culture is Aryan.[2]

In the age of Buddha, when the Magadh rulers held their sway in North India, there was some political instability in the north-western region. Taking advantage of this, the Achaeminian rulers of Iran expanded their empire. The Iranian emperor Cyrus occupied a portion of Gandhara, west of the Indus, in the mid-sixth century BC. A little later (in 516 BC) his grandson, Darius, sent a naval expedition which resulted in the annexation of the Indus valley and the Punjab. This area constituted a province or *satrapy* of Iran. It was the most fertile and populous part of the empire. Indian subjects were also enrolled in the Iranian army. Darius's successor, Xerxes, employed Indians in his long war against the Greeks. It appears that north-western India continued to be a part of the Iranian empire till Alexander's invasion.

In the fourth century BC, the Iranians and the Greeks struggled for the supremacy of the world. Under the leadership of Alexander the Great, the Iranians were finally defeated by the Greeks. After conquering Asia Minor, Iraq, Iran and Afghanistan, Alexander marched to India in 326 BC. We are all familiar with how he defeated Ambhi of Taxila and Porus, whose kingdom lay between the Jhelum and Chenab. We also know how he was impressed by the valour of Porus. He marched up to the Beas and wanted to advance further but his soldiers were unwilling to do so. Alexander left behind one of his generals, Seleukos, as his successor in India. Chandragupta fought against Seleukos and won the hand of a Greek princess.

The period which began in about 200 BC is notable for the intimate and widespread contact between Central Asia and India. A series of invasions took place from about this time. The first to attack were the Bactrian Greeks. Bactria lay south of the Oxus in Afghanistan and the Greeks who ruled there are known as Bactrian Greeks. They occupied a large part of north-western India and perhaps pushed forward as far as Ayodhya and Pataliputra. The most famous ruler was Menander, who was converted to Buddhism by Nagasena or Nagarjuna.

The Bactrian Greeks were followed by the Sakas. They did not meet with much effective resistance from the rulers and peoples of India except for the legendary Vikramaditya, the ruler of Ujjain. There were different branches of Sakas who ruled different parts of India, like Punjab, Mathura, Western India and the upper Deccan. The areas under the Indus Valley and western India came to be styled as Scythia by Greek geographers. The most famous Saka ruler in India was Rudradaman.

The Sakas were followed by the Parthians. Parthia was the area in Iran adjacent to Bactria in Afghanistan. The Parthians moved from Iran into India. The most famous Parthian king was Gondopherms, who ruled over north-western India in the first century A.D. St. Thomas is said to have come to India during his reign to propagate Christianity.[3]

Then came the turn of the Kushans. The Kushans were one of five clans into which the Yuechi tribe was divided. They were a nomadic tribe from the steppes of north-central Asia, living in the neighbourhood of China. The most famous of them was Kanishka, who ruled in the first century A.D. His empire extended from the Oxus to the Ganges, from Khorasan in Central Asia to Varanasi in Uttar Pradesh. This included parts of five modern states—the (former) USSR, Iran, Afghanistan, Pakistan and India. Kanishka started the Saka era in A.D. 78, now adopted by the Government of India with some modifications. He extended his whole-hearted support to Buddhism and held a Buddhist Council in Kashmir.

Towards the fall of the Gupta empire, in the fifth century BC, the Huns invaded India. They were ferocious barbarians who came from the steppes of Central Asia. Hordes of them spread into the Roman empire in the west and the Gupta empire in the east. Their early incursions into India were repulsed by Skanda Gupta, but they renewed their attacks after his death. Towards the close of the fifth century and early in the sixth century, the Huns established their supremacy over the Punjab and Western India. The invasion by white Huns or

Hephathalites took place about this time, bringing in its train the Gurjaras and Jats.

Well before the second millennium BC, that is, even before the advent of the Aryans, India had a high civilization of its own, popularly described as Dravidian. We have evidence of an even earlier state of culture than the Dravidian. What we now call the classical civilization of India is a fusion of Dravidian and Aryan culture, a fusion which took centuries to achieve and which was by no means a smooth or easy one. To start with, the advent of the Aryans meant a severe cultural decline, which lasted for many centuries. Only when Aryan culture was fertilized by the indigenous culture did it begin to advance to form the classical civilization of India. Culturally speaking, it was like the victory of the conquered over the conquerors.

The Indus Valley civilization was the oldest on Indian soil. When the Aryans came, they merged some of the features of the older culture into their own. In Harappa and Mohenjodaro, numerous terracota figurines of women have been found, in one of whom a plant is shown coming out of the womb of a woman. This represents the goddess of earth. In early Vedic religion, there is hardly any mention of a goddess. Durga, Kali, etc. are deities that appear in the sixth century A.D. The Sakti cult in modern Hinduism is obviously an adaptation from the Harappan culture. Simlarly, a Mohenjodaro seal shows a male, horned god with animals around. The Siva cult with its attendant phallus worship is an adaptation of the above. The early Aryans worshipped the forces of nature and personified them in their myths and hymns. After they settled in India, the Vedic gods were gradually replaced by the trinity—Brahma, Vishnu and Mahesha—who retained some of the features of the earlier gods. The trinity have their individual identities, but there are also some overlapping features among them. Siva, for instance, evolved from the Vedic Rudra to which certain pre-Aryan elements were added. The dark features ascribed to Vishnu are obviously a non-Aryan concept. The trinity constitute the Supreme Being, and Siva and Vishnu are the great gods of classical Hinduism.

A bewildering variety of sects or religions developed from

the classical trinity. The devotees of each tried to ascribe to their deity attractive features from different sources. It must be emphasized that Hinduism is both a way of life and a highly organized social and religious system, quite free from any dogmatic assertions concerning the nature of God; the core of religion is never felt to depend on the existence or non-existence of God, or on whether there is one God or many. It is perfectly possible to be a good Hindu whether one's personal views incline towards monotheism or polytheism or even atheism. The classical Hindus did not think of religious truth in dogmatic terms: dogmas cannot be eternal but only transitory, the truth transcends dogmas and all verbal definitions. The unity of religious outlook in India is based on a philosophic spirit which recognizes the value of both form and spirit, of outward ritual and inner essence. Quite early in their history, the Aryans held that every creed contains an element of truth, for it is the product of man's vision at different levels about the same truth, about the same reality.

Al-Biruni, who came to India in the eleventh century, observed: "On the whole, there is very little disputing about theological topics amongst themselves (the Hindus); at the most, they fight with words, but they will never stake their soul or body or property on religious controversy". Absence of religious persecution is the inevitable concomitant to the absence of dogma in classical Hinduism; but one may not lose sight of the central core of the Hindu religion. One of the undisputed beliefs is the doctrine of transmigration of soul or rebirth, which practically all sects and philosophical systems accept, not so much as a revealed dogma but as a self-evident fact of existence. The doctrine itself presupposes the further doctrine that the condition into which the individual soul is reborn is itself the result of good or bad actions performed in former lives. This leads to the law of *Karma* as well as the caste system of ancient India.

When the Aryans settled in India, there were different races under different stages of civilization. The Aryan attempt was to adjust and integrate the different elements of society. Perfect equality and perfect democracy were out of question at that time of human civilization. In the context of heterogeneity of blood, colour and language, of custom and belief, the achievement of a homogenous social and political entity seemed almost impossible. The institution of caste was devised initially on the basis of division of labour and functions; but subsequently it degenerated into a rigid system. The fact that along with the inclusion of Dravidian gods into the Aryan pantheon,[4] Dravidian priests were accepted as Brahmans in Hindu society is testimony to the elasticity of the system as well as to the spirit of accommodation and adjustment.

From the historical perspective, there are considerations in favour of a system which sought to integrate many different races into one social whole and find room for different stages of civilization within one cultural unity. At least in origin the institution of caste was a device for different races and individuals to live together in harmony.

The Iranians had invaded India in the sixth century BC and their rule in north-western India lasted for about 200 years. They brought into India a form of writing which came to be known as the Kharosthi script: it was written from right to left, like Arabic. Some Ashokan inscriptions in north-west India were written in this script in the third century BC. This script continued to be used in that region till the third century A.D.

Alexander's invasion in 326 BC provided the first occasion for ancient Europe to come into close contact with ancient India. The Greeks were influenced by the philosophy and religion of India and the Indians in turn were influenced by Greek sciences and arts.

The coming of the Bactrians, Parthians, Sakas, Kushans and Huns led to contact with the West and a close relationship with Central Asia. They settled in India for good and completely identified themselves with its culture and religion. They became an integral part of Indian society. Since most of them came as conquerors they were absorbed in Indian society as a warrior class or Kshatriyas. In no other period of ancient Indian history were foreigners assimilated into Indian society on such a large scale as they were in post-Mauryan times. The lawgiver, Manu, admitted the foreigners as second-class Kshatriyas who had fallen from their duties, and thus paved the way for their complete absorption without any discrimination in the course of time. Some of the foreign rulers themselves were converted to Buddhism, Saivism or Vaishnavism. The origin of Mahayana Buddhism is also traced to the influence of foreigners. The original form of Buddhism is too puritanical and abstract for ordinary mortals; the foreigners wanted something more concrete and intelligible which could satisfy their religious cravings. Hence they developed a new form of Buddhism, called Mahayana, in which the image of the Buddha came to be worshipped. The doors of this sect were of course open to all sections of people.

Despite the tremendous popularity of Buddhism in and outside India, Vedic culture was not materially affected inasmuch as the teachings of Buddha were not hostile to the essence of dharma of the Vedic Brahma. Buddha wanted to establish *sangha,* a casteless unified society on the basis of ethical principles such as non-violence, truthfulness, abstinence, forgiveness, compassion and goodwill. Buddhism did not accept the rigidity of the Brahmanical rituals or animal slaughter, or *varnasrama*. Buddhism and Jainism had a natural impact on the prevailing Indian thought, but such influence only enriched the traditional Indian culture. Even the Bactrian Greeks in Gandhara and Sakala, the Huns and Scythians at Mathura, influenced the sculpturing of the Surya images, and of Buddhist monasteries, *stupas,* as well as the cave temples of Ajanta and Ellora, which became specimens of great architecture. Such influences further enriched the heritage of Indian culture.

After the advent of the Aryans in the upper reaches of Sapta Sarasvati in about 2000 BC, the *Rigvedic* hymns indicate that the seers again and again prefer the contemplation of the One, the Indivisible, all-pervading Brahman, to the multiplicity of gods, which are only separate members of the one soul.

The fundamental unity of Bharatvarsa is instilled in the Indian mind by the ancient *Puranas, dharma sastras*, temples, pageants and pilgrimages. This Bharatvarsa is not a mere geographical integration. It is a historical cultural synthesis. India's approach to politics is essentially metaphysical, her ideal is the building up of a cultural state through prosperity and discipline rather than an empire by the might of arms. Even in the midst of bitter struggles with foreign peoples establishing themselves on the Indian soil, the genius of Indian culture was maintained; its spirit of assimilation, comprehension, and synthesis was able to meet the challenge of diversity and conflict. In short, the Indo–Aryan fusion is the first major metamorphosis of Indian culture.

The second metamorphosis of Indian culture took place with the emergence of Islam in the subcontinent. The civilization that the conquering Arabs brought from peninsular Arabia had a great integrating tendency, which, besides other factors, facilitated its acceptance and expansion. Within the short span of a century, the Arabs had traversed from Spain and the Atlantic in the West to India in the East and from the steppes of Central Asia in the North to the highlands of Sudan and Somalia in the South. This rapid expansion, much of which was undertaken at the invitation of the overburdened local masses and the internal schisms within the Byzantine Christian Church, demanded of the Arabs a liberal and adjusting attitude towards the people of the lands they were occupying.

Besides, both the Byzantians and Sassanids had flourishing cultures and civilizations and storehouses of knowledge, wisdom and the experience of ages which had influenced the peninsular Arabs for a few centuries before Islam, but came into closer and wider contact with them when the latter ran over the larger part of the two ancient empires. Nascent Islam had within itself inexhaustible eclectic tendencies and an insatiable hunger for the knowledge of the unknown. The seeds of syncretism and integration lay in the basic formulation of Islam that it was not a new faith but a continuation and repetition of the ancient message to humanity of the unity of God and His creation. It granted recognition and authenticity to all religions and all revealed books that had preceded it, and accepted all men of God as true guides from God.

The coming of Muslims to India meant the meeting of two vitally strong civilizations, each different from the other in many fundamental ways. The result was that by and large neither did the ruled accept the religion of the rulers, (unlike what had happened in most countries of West and Central Asia and North Africa), nor were the rulers completely absorbed into the society of the ruled, unlike what had happened with the Indo-Greeks, Sakas and Huns. Although complete merging of the two religions did not take place, it is amazing how close they came to each other in religious thought and other modes of outlook, leading to an almost complete fusion of the two cultures.

In language and literature, in arts and architecture, in music and painting, in dance and drama, in economic and political life, in social habits and customs; in short, in every walk of life, a near homogeneity was achieved. Sir John Marshall has observed: 'Seldom in the history of mankind has the spectacle been witnessed of two civilizations, so vast and so strongly developed, yet so radically dissimilar as the Muhammadan and Hindu, meeting and mingling together.' Of the early phase of the coming of the Muslims, Al-Biruni had said in the eleventh century: 'The Hindus totally differ from us in religion, as we believe in nothing in which they believe, and vice-versa'. In the course of about five hundred years, the scene changed completely—the process of cultural assimilation had gone so far that Babar in the sixteenth century characterized it as a unique mode of life, to which he gave the name of the Hindustani way.

After initial hesitation the Hindus and Muslims began to respect each other's religion and to show reverence to each other's saints. The Muslims evinced keen interest in the *Upanishads,* the *Gita, Vedanta* and yoga, and the Hindus were deeply impressed by the Islamic spirit of equality and brotherhood, its simplicity of rituals and its insistence on monotheism. Occasionally this led to the common worship of '*satyapir*' or 'true saint'. The cross-fertilization of Islam and Hinduism led to the Bhakti and Sufi movements. The Bhakti cult emphasized the fundamental equality of all religions and the unity of God, preached simple devotion and faith as the means of salvation, protested against excessive ritualism and formalities of religion, and condemned the caste system.

Sufism is a mystic cult popularly regarded as an offshoot of Islam, although some of its principles and practices are contrary to Islamic tenets. Sufism had bridged the gulf and spread the message of peace among various segments of society. Nothing could better prove or show the different stages through which Hindu–Muslim relations grew than Sufism or the Bhakti movement. Yusuf Husain has rightly pointed out: 'The Bhakti movement of medieval India represents the first effective impingement of Islamic culture and outlook'.[5] There was an exchange of ideas and values between the two communities with a very clear message of unity in diversity. The amalgam was expedited due to many common points in the socio-religious fabric of Indo–Muslim culture. The Sufis had left behind a rich cultural heritage. The most salutary effect of Sufism on Indian society was a social synthesis. Sufism had both a lasting impact on the medieval society and a wider appeal to all the cross-sections of the society.

Unlike Hinduism in India or Islam in Arabia, Islam in India was intrusive in character. It came over an already established civilization and could establish itself only gradually and by slow degrees over the already deeply entrenched indigenous traditions. Already in the course of its journey through Persia and Turkestan, the Islamic faith had acquired certain accretions so that the version of Islam which had been introduced into India was quite different from what it had been in its original heartland. On arrival in India, it had been further diluted through conversion to its fold of large groups of local converts who were bound to bring their pre-conversion beliefs and practices into the faith. Thus, it was almost inevitable that the religious tradition of the Muslims in India should comprise two distinct elements : one ultimate and formal, derived from the Islamic texts; the other proximate and local, validated by custom.

The integration of the two elements to a point that they should come to co-exist as complementary and integral parts of a single common religious system was presumably conditioned by the constraints of Islam's own struggle for survival in an alien environment. As a distinct religious tradition characterized by a vigorous iconoclastic zeal on the part of those who were responsible for first introducing Islam into India, the intruding Islamic tradition would probably have liked to conquer the indigenous religious traditions wholesale. However, this could not be possible for Islam to achieve because the indigenous mores and traditions were already an integral part of the life of the people and their total displacement could be achieved only at the cost of Islam's own rejection.

It seems plausible that the resistance and resilience shown by the indigenous traditions encouraged Islam in India to accept and retain the local cultural traditions but adapt them to its own requirements and needs by putting an Islamic content into them. This seems to be the logical modus operandi whereby presumably Islam was eventually successful in establishing its integrity and at the same time stabilizing itself on the otherwise religiously clustered Indian scene.

In terms of cultural depth and intensity and wider social repercussions, the two most profound influences on the making of a distinct Indian civilization are those of the ancient Indo–Aryan and the medieval Indo–Muslim segments. The Indo–Aryans contributed to the flowering of Vedic cultural streams which, over the centuries have continued to fertilize the body politic of the ancient land, and even today remain the subsoil of acculturation. The Indo–Muslim strands have weaved into the texture of India's national existence a rich design of 'composite culture', by intertwining the threads of the *Bhakti marg* with the Islamic Sufi (mystic) traditions, the Indian social customs with the Turko–Iranian mores of collective life, thereby creating a new inter-cultural synthesis, in which the values of man and social ethics reflected a new ethos.

The second metamorphosis of Indian culture leading to the ushering in of composite culture should be recognised as a product of the encounter between streams of Hindu traditions (the *Vedanta* and *Bhagavad Gita*) and the stream of Islamic consciousness.

Let us at this juncture briefly examine the nature of Hinduism as a belief pattern and the essence of the Muslim Sufi traditions in India. Let us analyze the connotation of the term 'Hinduism' as to whether it is only a religion and a belief system or something different.

Hinduism is no religion in the Semetic sense of the word; that is, if the paradigm of West Asian belief systems, the Judaic–Christian–Islamic combine is acknowledged as the normative form. It is something more and different than religion. It is a mix of customs, traditions, social behaviour, rituals, metaphysical speculations, cultural and value orientations. There is no duality of orthodoxy and heresy in Hinduism, because there is no defined and closed faith, no established church based on the foundations of a divine scripture revealed by a 'divine being' to divinely ordained prophet/s. This gives Hinduism a flexibility and resilience and a traditional base wide enough to cover the syndrome of Indian culture.

That is why sometimes the revivalism of Hinduism takes the form of revivalism of ancient culture, symbols, values, idiom and traditional pattern of living. It does not take the particular form of the revival of a faith because there is no such ordained, integral and defined faith to be revived. Hinduism's religious content has generally been referred to as Brahmanism, while the term Hindu (adapted from Sindhu, i.e. the inhabitants in, around and beyond, to the east of River Indus/Sindhu), which was used by the ancient Persians, Greeks and later by the Arabs and Central Asian people, referred essentially to the ethnic geographic identity of the inhabitants. In this sense, irrespective of belief and religion, language or culture, every Indian is considered 'Hindi' by the Arabs, the Iranians and the Turks.

Noted anthropologist Shri K.S. Singh observes that Hinduism is a historical process that has articulated the pluraties of all types, structural, ideological and processional. It has been an ongoing, ever-growing process reaching out and subsuming traditions, structures and substrata at different historical levels without destroying their identity. 'The various components have been in a stage of vibrant interaction with one another within an ever-widening framework of deeply felt cultural identity over the historical period. Thus Hinduism does not have any of the elements of a structured religion. In fact it is loosely structured which explains why it has been resilent and tenacious enough to survive and expand.'[6]

In *The Discovery of India* Jawaharlal Nehru writes :[7]

"The word 'Hindu' does not occur at all in our ancient literature. The first reference to it in an Indian book is, I am told, in a *Tantrik* work of the eighth century A.D., where 'Hindu' means a people and not the followers of a particular religion. But it is clear that the word is a very old one as it occurs in the *Avesta* and in old Persian. It was used then and for thousand years or more later by the peoples of Western and Central Asia for India, or rather for the people living on the other side of the Indus river. The word is clearly derived from *Sindhu*, the old, as well as the present Indian name for the Indus. From this *Sindhu* came the words Hindu and Hindustan, as well as Indos and India. The famous Chinese pilgrim I-tsing, who came to India in the seventh century A.D., writes in his record of travels that the 'northern tribes', that is the people of Central Asia, called India 'Hindu' (Hsin-tu) but, he adds, 'this is not at all a common name. . . and the most suitable name for India is the Noble Land (*Aryadesha*)'. The use of the word 'Hindu' in connection with a particular religion is of very later occurrence."

The old inclusive term for religion in India was *Arya dharma*. *Dharma* really means something more than religion. It is from a root word which means 'to hold together'. It is the inmost constitution of a thing, the law of its inner being. It is an ethical concept which includes the moral code, righteousness, and the whole range of man's duties and responsibilities. *Arya dharma* would include all the faiths (Vedic and non-Vedic) that originated in India; it was used by Buddhists and Jains as well as by those who accepted the *Vedas*. Buddha always called his way to salvation the *Arya Path*.

The philosophy of Hinduism has developed in the last 4000 years, in six well-recognized periods of time: (i) 2500 to 600 BC —the Vedic period; (ii) 600/500 BC to A.D. 200—the Epic period; (iii) A.D. 200 to 800—the Sutra period; (iv) A.D. 800 to 1300 – the Scholastic period; (v) A.D. 1300 to 1700—the period of the great Bhakti saints; and (vi) A.D. 1800 to 1950—the period of reform movements and philosophical revivalism.

There are two aspects of Hindu tradition: (i) the emancipation of the soul (*moksha*), which is the highest goal of human action in Hindu thought, the quest for a morally good life. For this the Hindu tradition recognizes three paths: (i) *Karma Marg* (ii) *Jnana Marg* and (iii) *Bhakti Marg*. *Karma Marg* literally means the 'path of action'—actually path of conformism to doctrines, acceptance of destiny and resignation to moral fate within the framework of fourfold caste system (*varna*) and fourfold stages of life (*asrama*) that is *Varnasama dharma* (predestined order of life).

Jnana Marg literally means the 'path of knowledge', as epitomized in the *Upanishads* and the Sutra literature dealing with discussions regarding cosmic origin, human destiny, good and evil, the nature of the ultimate reality and its relation to the individual, etc.; and (iii) *Bhakti Marg*, literally the 'path of devotion', that helps the 'devotee' to attain salvation through love of a personal god and compassion towards fellowmen. This path is sometimes referred to as the emotional aspect of faith, in contradiction to the 'intellectual' or 'conative' aspects, as implied respectively in the *Jnana Marg* and the *Karma marg*. The biggest sources of inspiration for the *Bhakti Marg* are the *Bhagavad Gita*, the 'Narayaniya section of the *Santiparvam* of the *Mahabharata* and the *Bodhisattva* and *Amitabha* concepts in Mahayana Buddhism.

The second aspect that needs to be stressed is that there has been a persistent dichotomy in Hindu society reflective of more than mere class cleavage of differentiation of status groups in any society. The existence of two distinct social strata or two levels of consciousness, one higher and the other lower, one smaller and the other more populous, the one as 'closed' custodians of traditional knowledge and philosophy, of social ideas and institutions, and the other on the lower rung of the social and cultural ladder, comprising the general mass of people with their folk culture and regional traditions, had almost permanently bifurcated the continental Hindu society vertically.

Brahmanical social exclusiveness, monopoly of knowledge, refusal to allow the lower caste even the learning of the Sanskrit language, discrimination in rituals and social intercourse, and adherence to the practice of endogamy, all of which represented a sort of operational socio-cultural apartheid, had kept Hindu society divided into compartments, and its castes and *jatis* almost counterposed to each other. Inequality and segregation were permitted and even sanctified by *dharma shastra* as well as by the laws of Manu, which dominated the scene for centuries.

We have discussed at length, the most important inherent characteristics of Indian culture, that is assimilation and synthesis. Now let us look into some of its other salient features.

The most outstanding feature of Indian culture is its tradition of tolerance.[8] This tradition of tolerance is not merely an attitude of indifference to others. It is a fundamental postulate of Hindu thought that every way of life has its own contribution to make to human welfare. It is this positive approach to other groups and communities—this convinced eschewal of the doctrine that one's own way is right—which gives to the Indian doctrine of toleration its special significance.

It is a wide tolerance, a feeling that others may be equally right in the methods they follow, that is the essence of Hindu teaching. This has coloured Hindu life to such an extent that it may truly be considered the differentiating mark of Indian culture, a respect for the faith and beliefs of others and a generous charity in understanding the approach of other people to the problems of life. It is this sense of tolerance and charity that gives harmony to the inner life of an Indian of culture; for a while he is firm in his own faith, he is prepared to approach other faiths with an open mind.

The result of this tolerance has been to add to the richness and variety of Indian life. The Hindu religion provides perhaps the best illustration of this fact. While the basic tenets and even the outward forms of this great religion have remained unchanged through many centuries, the interplay of forces generated by the toleration of other religions has led to a continuous re-interpretation of its doctrines and a readjustment of its approach to the problems of life.

The process by which Buddhism was absorbed into the body of what may be called the mother church is one outstanding example. Though the religion of the Buddha vanished from

India over a thousand years ago, its teachings have become closely interwoven with Hinduism. The impact of Islam was perhaps responsible for the re-emphasis of monotheistic teachings in medieval India. The religious revivals of the 14th, 15th and 16th centuries, which put new vigour into the old body of Hinduism were in the main the result of this impact.

Another main characteristic of Indian culture is its universal outlook. Whatever the limitations of Hindu social practices and the narrowness of Indian institutions, Indian thought has never accepted geographical, racial and other considerations as affecting ultimate values. They have held on to truths which they consider to be of universal validity. This universality of approach is responsible for the unique characteristic of Hindu civilization, its readiness to assimilate what is of value in other civilizations. There was never any refusal to learn from others, or any resistance to ideas, on the ground of their being foreign.[9]

Hindu thought has, therefore, encouraged a continuous synthesis, even when it had to deal with philosophies like those of Christianity and Islam. Saints and teachers, who combined Hindu and Islamic teachings, for example, were freely accepted as religious leaders, at a time when the two religions were confronting each other.

It is the fundamental belief of Hinduism that every human being has in him a spark of the divine; that it is in the nature of man that he can, by right conduct and by right knowledge, attain illumination and reach Godhead directly. It may also be noted that this is the basic doctrine of Buddhism, that Buddhahood can be attained by each one by a process of spiritual evolution.

This doctrine of the divinity in man may appear to be merely a metaphysical hypothesis incapable of positive proof. Its validity is not the point at issue. The fact which is of importance to us is that it is accepted as a cardinal article of faith by every Indian, and consequently it has certain social results which are of great importance. The belief that every sentient being carries within himself a spark of the divine is the origin of the conception of the inalienable worth of the individual and its corollary of the limitation of the absolutism of external forces.

Of the specific features of Indian culture, one is a cosmic vision. The quality of man is judged by the quality of his mind and spirit, the quality and depth of his perceptions, not by the quantity of his possessions, much less by the size of the arsenal of arms and weapons at his disposal. A culture is judged similarly. "What is that by knowing which everything in this universe is known?" *(Mundaka Upanishad,* 1.1.3) was the question that our ancient seers raised, the answer to which they searched tirelessly.

In Indian thought, heaven, the earth and the underworld mingle effortlessly, and no great barriers are erected to prevent passage from one to the other. The Indian mind felt *free* to wander in thought through such wide and uncharted expanses. Similarly, man has been seen as an *integral part* of the total reality, the supreme reality. An evolutionary ascent to higher levels of awareness and actualization till the oneness of cosmic reality is perceived: this was seen as the goal and purpose of life.

Thought, reason, knowledge, have an honoured place in Indian tradition, so much so that knowledge is seen as a means of liberation, not only in the here and now, but capable of the final liberation of men as well. Other cultures, for example, the Graeco–Roman, had also given a high status to reason. But to push this beyond being merely an instrument of human progress to make it the medium for total and final liberation; this is unique to India.

Our ancient seekers sought God and the ultimate meaning of life with relentless desire. The philosophical formulations of the nature and description of this ultimate reality, this *paramatman* are many. From the perspective of the inner dynamic of a culture and its depth, these variations offer proof of the quality of the ancient Indian, and remain lasting monuments of Indian metaphysical thought.

For the ancients, life was to be lived and enjoyed! There was full involvement in life and its manifold activities. Hence, there were many occasions for joyful celebration. Against the oft-repeated picture presented of the ancient Indian drawing within himself and away from life and its expressions, the actual picture that emerges from ancient literature is of life that was vibrant. There was a *naturalness* about the ancient Indian, a sense of buoyancy, far removed from the ascetical puritanism attributed to him. To him, life was meaningful, not a myth or *maya*. In the articulation of the four fundamental interests or pursuits of man, this grounding in reality is obvious. The *purushartha* path leads from economic security.

As we have observed briefly, the meeting of the two religions —Islam and Hinduism on Indian soil—influenced both Muslim–Hindu cultures extensively. Thus, the role of religion in influencing culture is an obvious phenomenon. A discussion of the role of religion and culture as integrated components will help us in clearly understanding the natural process of cultural synthesis which took place on account of the coming closer of Islam and Hinduism with mutual understanding of and absorbing elements from each other.

Dr. John Marshall has rightly observed, "Seldom in the history of mankind as the spectacle been witnessed of two civilizations, so vast and so strongly developed, yet so radically dissimilar as the Muslims (Islam) and Hindus (Hinduism) meeting and mingling together. The very contrasts which existed between them, the wide divergences in their cultures and their religions, make the history of their impact peculiarly instructive".

Of all contacts that India had with alien cultures, the advent of Islam into the country had the biggest impact on its culture. The process of amalgamation started long back, even before the natural settling of Islam in India.

As religion and culture are inseparable aspects, the meeting of Hinduism and Islam on Indian soil was a major historical event in giving shape and dimension to the cultural synthesis shaping India's composite culture. Religion played an important role in giving shape to culture, hence the relationship between religion and culture needs to be discussed in detail.

The Relationship Between Religion and Culture

Religion is a way of life; it is an interpretation of life and faith and hope of life. These are the most important areas of individuals' personal belief systems which control their actions and, consequently, the process of social change. Religion is considered as a way of life when religious precepts and practices become part of living itself. Religion influences every aspect of an individual's life and every aspect of human behaviour. When we encounter religion as a way of life we see religion as vibrant at the social, individual and transcendental levels. Religion at the social level refers to its various aspects which affect and control group behaviour and an individual's relation with other individuals. It is religion which gives meaning to our traditions, conventions, customs, etc. and controls human social interaction. Religion, as Gandhi saw it, expresses itself only through the ordinary activities of life.

If religion changes, there will be corresponding changes in culture too. Religious identity thereby determines cultural identity. If religion is the core of culture, changing the core amounts to drastic changes in culture. Ultimately, losing one's religion amounts to losing one's cultural identity.

One may claim to retain one's own cultural identity in spite of the fact that one has lost one's religion. Hence, strictly speaking, changing religion, while claiming to adhere to the same culture, is impossible. The practices of one religion differ from the practices of another. Therefore, change from one religion amounts to adopting a new way of life determined by the new religion.

Religion is generally understood as a system of belief in something which humans consider to be beyond themselves and which binds them together so as to organize their lives into some kind of socio-religious community. Therefore, religion is considered as an important factor in a society or culture.[10]

A.K. Saran holds that a traditional human being did not distinguish himself/herself from nature and the Creator. Humans and nature are part and parcel of the divine.[11] This view was also true of many societies and cultures where religion is the sole determinant of culture. Zen Buddhism, Islam, Christianity (to some extent) and the various tribal societies are examples of social groups where religion plays a vital role in determining the way of life of the people. It becomes the overall authority in determining the meaning, purpose and end of life.

Though religion is not identical with culture, it is one of its most important elements, which determines the way of life of the people. It is something that binds people together and gives meaning and purpose to their lives. Religion is both a response to a human's total environment and an exploration of its frontiers. It is human life in its ultimate context, struggling for meaning. However, religion does not exist separate from other aspects of culture. Religious behaviour patterns influence and are influenced by what happens in the rest of culture.

S. Abid Husain, in *The National Culture of India,* says : "Religion in its wider sense coincides with, and goes beyond culture, and in its narrower sense forms an important part of it". His argument is that religion signifies the inner experience which reveals to the mind the real meaning and purpose of life; it is the very soul of culture. When it is used for external form in which the inner experience has crystallized itself, it is only part of it. He says : "Religion as the inner realization of the highest truth can never be opposed to culture; but positive religion, when it has degenerated into mere form without substance, is often in conflict with cultural life."[12]

Michael C. Howard, in *Contemporary Cultural Anthropology*'[13] maintains that religion is not merely a matter of belief, it also involves institutionalized patterns of behaviour—rituals, ceremonies and the like—which express and reinforce religious belief.

Traditions, customs and practices, thereby are religion-oriented and prescribed mostly by religion. This is true especially in many societies. In Islamic societies religion plays a dominant role in determining the life of the people. Zen Buddhism once upon a time acted as a moulding factor of Japanese culture. This phenomenon was also seen in Christian communities in the West and in tribal cultures. In other words, in the traditional thought religion and culture are not different; they form what is known as a 'unity'.[14]

Culture is a product of society in the sense that it cannot exist without society—at least not without a special group. When culture is defined as a system of beliefs, rules, customs, traditions, skills and practices, it gives us the impression of something static and self contained. No doubt, cultures have traditions embodying forms of life. Traditions are practices, signifying repetitive reproduction of knowledge and values. However, cultural traditions are open-ended, dynamic 'systems' of meaning.

Culture as a complex whole, therefore, consists of the way we think, do and everything we have as a member of a society which helps its people as a socially organised human group. If culture is a 'way of life' of the people, then many things will come under it, as we have seen, e.g. behaviour patterns, traditions, customs, practices, habits, moral laws, belief systems, rituals and so on. In other words, culture appears, as pointed out earlier, to be all-pervasive.

Speaking generically of 'culture', several elements form its parts: religion, beliefs, behaviour patterns, institutions, language, customs, the arts, ceremonies, works of art, inventions, technology, traditions, other products of human work and thought, and the entire way of life. Cultural features are generally measured as expressed in a particular community or period of time.

Culture and religion are systems of values, which are intrinsically connected. A value is a behavioural concept related to an individual or a group or society. In the determination of human behaviour, the most important factor is a person's specific value awareness. One's choice of a course of action is dependent on value alternatives; we prefer one course of action to another on the assumption that our choice will help us to realize our inherent values at a comparatively higher level. Both culture and religion cannot have significant meanings apart from value. Both refer to the ways of life for achieving some valuable ends.

Culture is based on certain foundations like empirical facts, social customs and values. Value as foundation plays a vital role in the determination of culture. Culture is not just the sum total of artifacts and behaviour patterns which can be regarded as events of some sort. Beyond the world of facts, there is the world of values. In fact, we have good evidence that value statements were discussed by humankind long before the dawn of science.

Some thinkers consider religion as one of the aspects of culture, just like language, art, etc. whereas others identify religion with culture itself because it determines the way of life of the people.

Religion, of course, does not exist separately from other aspects of culture. Religious behaviour patterns influence and are influenced by what happens in the rest of the culture. Religion and marriage, for example, are interrelated and interconnected, each influencing the other. The same is true of with religion and government, religion and education, religion and the economic life of individuals, religion and art, religion and all aspects of culture. But religion does not play the same role in all societies. The type of relationship among the various elements in a culture is almost unlimited. Each culture has certain aspects which are emphasized above others. In some cultures government is more important than religion, while in others the reverse is true. In this way religion is influenced by and influences the rest of culture. But it is just one part of the 'complex whole'. An understanding of this interactive relationship is necessary if we are to understand religion fully. Religion can be meaningfully studied only by an analysis of culture and society of which religion is a part. Thereby we can portray the relation between religion and culture from the functional point of view, especially when both religion and culture have a moral code of their own which in the process tries to regulate the behaviour patterns of the people.[15]

There is a common running theme in almost all considerations of culture, that it is a 'way of life' of people living in a particular society in a particular time. Culture has several elements within it and acts as a system or framework of meaning, behaviour and symbols for human beings; it also means the way humans conduct their lives within this broad system and orient themselves towards it. It is the whole way of life—material, intellectual and spiritual—of a given society. Thus humans are born into a cultural framework and are inescapably caught up within it.

Cultural properties are acquired properties by individual members of the group or society through interactivities. In the process of 'interactivity', certain values are attached to certain things, which then can be considered as being cultural products or traits. In other words, we can say that the meaning of the notion of culture consists in the behaviour or functional patterns of the individual or group or society. This is the reason why culture may be more properly understood as a 'way of life'. The cultural way of life is built up by the people of the society, individually or collectively, through interpersonal relationship whereby they promote their cultural life and transmit its values from one generation to another. Thus an individual or group or society can be judged on the basis of behaviour or function patterns of the cultural values which form the standard or norms of the culture.

At the heart of culture could be certain values, standards, or ideals which may not find full (or even partial) expression in real life. By sheer force of unpredictable and uncontrollable historical events, the community may be coerced into adopting certain life styles, certain ways of coping with material emergencies, which in the course of time may produce taboos, rituals and even traditions not intended at the time of the initial adoption of those life styles.

William A. Haviland, a cultural anthropologist, maintains that "Culture consists of abstract values, beliefs and perceptions of the world that lie behind peoples' behaviour and which that behaviour reflects. These are shared by the members of a society, and when acted upon they produce behaviour considered acceptable within that society".[16]

A culture is that aspect of the life of a community which signifies an ongoing quest for achieving the goal or aim of society. It would be better to call it a 'preferred way of life' rather than 'the way of life'. This preferred way of life includes how we think, do and behave as members of society for achieving some ends. It includes both the material and non-material aspects of culture. The non-material aspects of culture consist of the subjective aspects, the objective mental aspects and the ideal aspects. The subjective aspects represent the subject's commitments, feelings and what one owes to his/her own culture. The objective-mental aspect represents the belief system, principles, collective institutions, moral law, art, etc. which are handed down from generation to generation. The ideal aspects represent the norms, standards of perfection and the ultimate values of social life. Culture finds expression in actual life and activities. It stands for values and activities which contribute to the enrichment of human life. It consists of those values and norms in which man and woman is born and grows up as a social being. Culture creates social consciousness and creativity.

Culture and religion are a system of values. Religion cannot exist without culture. Removed from the cultural context, religion becomes mere blind faith in God and fanatic attachment with a set of rituals, beliefs, priest craft, etc. Religion in this form has played havoc in the past. People of different faiths are ample proof of the fact that once we separate religion from culture, it is bound to become the most dangerous phenomenon of humankind. A person of culture is characterized by extreme sensitivity. A sensitive person is conscious not only of his/her social and physical environment, but is quick in his/her reactions to whatever happens around him/her.

Culture and religion are closely related: culture gives religion its language, and culture acquires its meaning from religion. Religion determines the way of life of the people. It plays a vital role in prescribing meanings to most cultural activities. Festivals, for instance, will not be meaningful bereft of the religious meanings attached to them. Culture is all-inclusive, consisting of several components. Religion, though considered an element of culture, claims to be all-pervasive and includes many things just as culture does. In this way, one is tempted to think that culture is identical with religion. However, they are not so; religion is not merely one of the important elements of culture, it is in fact the core which determines the way of life of the people.

In culture and religion, various actions and interactions are noticed, for they are the ways of life. Values, on the other hand are the basic ingredients of human actions which require underlying norms or principles to guide them. These norms are the values or the ideal objects that guide human life. In this way, cultural values overlap religious values and vice versa.

The relation between culture and religion can be viewed from several perspectives for the sake of clarity. Both culture and religion provide moral codes of conduct which regulate the behaviour patterns of people. Hence, in the everyday mode of functioning, culture and religion are closely knit. In its invisible institutional aspect, religion may be viewed as a segment of culture alongside others such as family, economic order, political order, etc. At this level we have the church, temple, etc. existing alongside the local governments, schools, museums, etc. Another more profound dimension of culture is also closely related to religion, whether or not it is institutionally expressed or acknowledged. This includes marriage, festivals, governing a clan, and so on, which have religious connotations and meanings. Lastly, any culture embodies norms and values, and religion is one of the value determinants.[17]

Although both culture and religion concentrate on values which guide the behaviour of individuals, groups and societies, the two are not the same. Since the meaning of culture is different from its constitutent elements, or from what it manifests, it cannot be identified with any one of its elements.

The relation between culture and religion, therefore, is important, especially when both refer to almost one and the same thing, that is, the way of life of the people and more important, when religion is considered as a central component of integrative value system. Religion can be one of the most important and distinctive means for maintaining life values. Religion is not a phenomenon apart and distinct from mundane life nor is it a philosophical enquiry. It only emphasizes and preserves those values accepted by the majority of a group at the given time. Religion is a storehouse of values.

Traditionally, religion and culture are not separated. Religion is seen as the way of life of the people just as culture is. This definition immediately raised the question whether the concept of religion is the same as the concept of culture, for both can be viewed as the way of life of people. If religion is seen as a set of beliefs, practices of patterns of behaviour or as an institution, it pervades the whole gamut of life. It is thus both a response to man's total environment and an exploration into its frontiers;

moreover, it participates in the polarities of life just as culture does.

In *Notes Towards the Definition of Culture,* Eliot states that no culture can appear or develop except in relation to religion. In fact, he goes so far as to say that the religion of the people and their culture are nearly identical. Religion, he says, is essentially far more an unconscious matter than a conscious one. It must primarily be a matter of behaviour and habit, integrated with its social life, its business and pleasures.

REFERENCES AND NOTES

1. Mohideen, M. *The Elements of Composite Culture*. In "Composite Culture of India and National Integration". Ed. Dr. Rasheeduddin Khan, p. 84.
2. Ibid., p. 86.
3. Ibid., p. 87.
4. R.G. Bhandarkar gives a detailed account of the fusion of Aryan and Dravidian gods in his book *Vaishnavism, Saivism and Other Minor Sects*.
5. Husain, Dr. Yusuf. *National Culture of India*. p. 37.
6. "Hinduism and Tribal Religion". In *Culture, Religion and Philosophy*. Ed. N.K. Das. New Delhi: Rawat Publications, pp. 106–107.
7. Nehru, Pandit Jawaharlal. *The Discovery of India*, p. 228.
8. Panikkar, K.M. *Essential Features of Indian Culture*, pp. 5–7.
9. Ibid., p. 11.
10. Pohlong, Dr. Basil. *Culture and Religion : A Conceptual Study*, p. 10.
11. Saran, A.K. "The Traditional of Man". In *Language, Tradition and Modern Civilization*. Ed. R.C. Gandhi.
12. Hussain, S. Abid. *The National Culture of India*, p. 3.
13. *Encyclopedia of Cultural Anthropology*, Vol. 3. Eds. D. Levinson and M. Ember.
14. Polhlong, Dr. Basil. *Culture and Religion : A Conceptual Study*, p.15.
15. Ibid., p. 19.
16. Haviland, William A. *Cultural Anthropology*, p. 511.
17. Pohlong, Dr. Basil. *Culture and Religion : A Conceptual Study*, Introduction, p. xvii.

2

Early Arab Contacts and the Advent of Islam in India

Early Arab efforts to understand Indian and Hindu Culture

When Sind was a province of the caliphate, for a brief period between A.D. 718 and 800, some direct rendering of Sanskrit learning into Arabic took place. The Arab interest in Hindu sciences, especially in medicine and astronomy, was parallel to their interest in Greek learning. Hindu physicians were invited to Baghdad, where the house of the Barmakids—converts to Islam from Buddhism and ministers to the Abbasids—was all-powerful and to some extent still interested in the culture from which it had seceded. Al-Kindi's account of India was based partly on the evidence of the envoy sent by Yahya al-Barmaki to India to procure Indian medicines and to report on Indian religion and customs. An Arab physician, Ibn al-Tanukhi, visited India in the ninth century to study medicine. A number of Sanskrit treatises on medicines, poisons and snakes was translated into Arabic.

Even before the translation of Ptolemy's *Almegest*, three Indian works on astronomy were rendered into Arabic, the most famous of them being Brahmagupta's *Siddhanta*, given in Arabic the convenient name *Sindhind*, translated by al-Fazari and Ya'qub ibn Tariq, both of whom worked in collaboration with a Brahman scholar. The other two works on Hindu astronomy were Brahmagupta's *Khandkhadayaka* and the *Aryabhata*. Digests and commentaries of the *Siddhanta* continued to be written until the eleventh century in the Arab world.

Hindu mathematics left a more lasting impression on the Arab sciences. In the reign of al-Ma'mun (A.D. 813–33), the mathematician al-Khwarizmi (A.D. 780–840) adapted Sanskrit numerals to Arabic orthography. An assessment of Hindu influence on mathematics can be made from the work of al-Nasawi (A.D. 980–1040). Some mathematical and astronomical terms were borrowed by Arabic from Sanskrit.

Among other Sanskrit works translated into Arabic were the ethical writings of Canakya (Shanaq) and the *Hitopadesa*, and works ranging from logic to magic catalogued by Ibn Nadim. *Panchatantra*, better known to the Muslim world as *Kalila wa Dimna*, was translated via a Sassanid old Persian version into Arabic by Ibn al-Muqaffa. The fascinating story of Sindbad, later incorporated into *The Arabian Nights* was partly of Indian origin. Among the Hindu religious epics, parts of the *Mahabharata* were rendered into Arabic by Abu Salih ibn Shu'ayb and later by Abu'l Hasan 'Ali Jabali.

In Arab writings Buddha is referred to as the prophet of Samaniya. Works dealing directly or obliquely with the life and teaching of Buddha mentioned by Ibn Nadim as having been translated from Pehlevi into Arabic are: *Kitab al-Budd, Kitab Balawhar wa Budhasaf*, and *Kitab Budhasaf mufrad*. Al-Nubakhti's *Kitab al-ara-i wa'l adyan-i Madhahib al-Hind*, mentioned by al-Mas'udi, seems to have been the earliest study of Hindu sects. Even the superficial contact with Hindu sciences came to an early end as the political grip of Baghdad over the remote province of Sind loosened.

Sulayman the merchant, who visited India about A.D. 851, wrote of curious Hindu customs like trial by ordeal, or the cremation of the dead or burning alive of widows, and praised Hindu proficiency in medicine, astronomy, and philosophy. Abu Zayd Hasan al-Sayrafi, who continued his account after his own visit (c.916) showed interest in Hindu ascetics and yogis and commented on the spread of Buddhism from India to China.

Al-Mas'udi (d.956) who visited India wrote about it in detail, sketching briefly Hindu religious beliefs, including metempsychosis, reconstructing Hindu history from Hindu legends, complimenting Hindus on their achievements in sciences as the cleverest among 'dark people'.

In the same century, al-Baghdadi appears to be more interested in Hindu culture and describes, though not accurately, Hindu sects, divides idol-worship into categories of the worship of images of God, the avatars, demons and Bodhisattavas, regarding 'Budd' as the genus, idols as the species; and gives a picturesque account of the four-handed idol of Shiva and of the sun and moon-worshipping cults and the yogis. In an interesting treatise on the superiority of Blacks over Whites, al-Jahiz regards Hindus as the chief representatives of dark-skinned people, remarkable for their achievements in astronomy, medicine, architecture and the fine arts, for their invention of chess and their taste for perfumes.

Hindu religion and its sects were commented upon by al-Shahrastani (A.D. 1086–1153) who regards Hinduism a great religion with a variety of shades of faith and sects. He points out the confusion in the writings of some Muslims who mixed up Brahmans with the followers of Abraham. He notes that the Hindu rationalistic pantheism is critical of Muslim ritual and faith. He describes briefly the various Buddhist and Hindu sects, and is appreciative of the meditation of Hindu ascetics who separate imagination from their physical environment, achieving considerable self-subjugation 'so that when meditation becomes emancipated from this world, the next world is revealed to it'. He is, however, critical of the adoration of idols, which he regards as attributing divinity to the image, and as there is no Divine sanction for using idols as intermediaries, the Hindus are not, in his view, likely to go beyond their idols to God.

By this time Islam was already established in north-western India as a powerful state and Al-Biruni's famous work on Hindu religion and sciences had been written a little earlier.

Al-Biruni and India : The first attempt to understand India

Abu Rayhan al-Biruni marks the culmination and fulfilment of the Arab tradition of intellectual curiosity and objective analysis of Hindu religion and sciences.

The first Muslim thinker who paid significant attention to Indian culture was also the most thorough and profound of all. Abu Raihan al-Biruni (A.D. 973–1050), one of the great luminaries of mediaeval Islamic science, was born in Khwarazm. When his native place was overrun by Mahinud-bin-Sabuktigin in A.D. 1017, he was brought to Ghazna and later accompanied Mahmud on some of his military expeditions to India. He studied with Indian sages and made great efforts to collect Indian books. In this way he acquired there a first-hand knowledge of Indian civilization and subsequently wrote his outstanding account of India under the title: *Tahqiq ma li-l Hind min maqula maqbula fial aql aw mardhula.* While al-Biruni cannot be considered an Indian Muslim in the full sense of the word, he visited the country and his importance is so substantial, that his views of India and its civilization cannot be ignored in this context. He clearly writes as a Muslim, is in many places critical of Hindu beliefs, and the information provided by him may serve those who want to engage in polemics with the Hindus. Yet his basic approach is that of a scholar and the *Tahqiq* is avowedly informative, descriptive, and non-polemical. His critical attitude to idolatry is tempered by the statement that this type of worship is designed for the benefit of the uneducated, common people who are impressed only by the concrete (*mahsus*), and fail to appreciate the abstract *(ma 'qul).* In order to cater to the religious needs of their uneducated adherents, the Jews, the Christians, and the Manicheans introduced 'pictorial representation' *(taswir)* into their houses of prayer. Islam is different in this respect and did not make such concessions to the common people's predilection for concrete objects of worship; yet even a Muslim who does not belong to the educated part of his community would express his adoration, should he be presented with a picture of the Prophet, of Mecca, or of the Ka'ba (al-Biruni 195:84; Sachau 1964: 1,111). Hinduism therefore is not substantially different from the other faiths: the Hindu idols were constructed only for the benefit of the common people whose understanding is limited. The absurd beliefs (*khurafat*) which al-Biruni relates in his work belong also to the common people only, because those who march on the path of liberation, or those who study philosophy and theology, and those who desire abstract truth which they call *sara*, are entirely free from worshipping anything but God alone, and would never dream of worshipping an image manufactured to represent him.

In this way al-Biruni reaches the conclusion that the elites of all communities, including the Hindus, worship Allah alone. On the other hand, all uneducated people, without regard to their religious affiliation, need concrete objects of worship, and their religious leadership frequently takes their susceptibilities into account.

Al-Biruni's acquaintance with India and its culture and sciences began from the time he was brought to the court of Ghazni by Sultan Mahmud, along with other scholars. Before coming to Ghazni, Biruni had little knowledge of Indian sciences, and what he knew about Indian astronomy and mathematics was derived from the writings of men like Ibrahim-bin-Habib al-Fazari, Yaqub-bin-Tariq and Muhammad-bin-Musa-al-Khwarazmi. But in his *India*, Biruni tells us that what he had learnt from these scholars about Indian sciences had generally been incorrect and inadequate. In his famous work, *Athar al-baqiya,* composed during the last decade of the 4th century A.D., which deals with the histories and chronologies of ancient peoples of the world, Biruni refers not more than two or three times to the calendars of the Hindus, their festivals and ceremonies, and ceremonies.

After coming to Ghazni, Biruni found the opportunity for which he had been waiting. He travelled through the Punjab and Sindh, and stayed in Peshawar, Multan and Lahore. In these travels he devoted himself to the study of Sanskrit, collected works on Indian sciences, received instructions from Indian masters, engaged himself in discussions with Hindu scholars; and thus, to the best of his capacity, learned about their scientific theories, religious views and social customs and institutions. In his *India* he tells us about the difficulties he had to face during this period of intellectual pursuit:

'I have found it very hard to work my way into the subject, although I have a great liking for it, in which respect I stand quite alone in my time, and although I do not spare either trouble or money in collecting Sanskrit books from places where I supposed they were likely to be found, and in procuring for myself, even from very remote places, Hindu scholars who understand them and are able to teach me.'

Biruni passed thirteen years of his life (A.D. 988–1001) in the service and company of Mahmud. He accompanied the Sultan on most of his expeditions and watched with his own eyes the destructions caused by the invading forces in Indian cities. Biruni could hardly reconcile himself to this situation. On the other hand, the King's company gave him a chance to travel through India, a country full of wonders. The rich and highly developed culture of the land at once engaged his attention. As may be judged from the number of the works that he produced on subjects dealing with India, and in view of the extensive knowledge that he acquired through his studies and from the Hindu masters that he could meet, this was the most fruitful period of Biruni's life. His *India*, which is definitely the best manifestation of his scientific mind, is also a product of this period. This is an encyclopaedic work, which contains much valuable information about various aspects of Indian culture and civilization and about Indian sciences, and by his insight into Hindu philosophy, theology and jurisprudence. The scientific method used in *India* is sound and comprehensive. In the year A.D. 1007, Biruni prepared a list of his works, which contains more than a hundred titles.

He made use of some of the mutilated Arabicised forms of Sanskrit works like *Sindhind* (Siddhanta) *Kandakhadayaka*. In addition to these works composed originally, or translated from Sanskrit, Biruni in *India* speaks of other works on Indian religions, philosophy and astronomy, and translates copiously from them.

It may be mentioned here that Biruni was not merely making an effort to introduce Indian sciences and philosophy to the Islamic world. His endeavours to make Greek thoughts and sciences known to Indian scholars are equally admirable. It is quite obvious that Biruni discussed scientific and philosophical matters with Indian intellectuals, or, perhaps, corresponded with them on these subjects.

After extensive travels in the western regions of India, and after he had devoted a full thirteen years to the study of Indian sciences religions and philosophical schools in the original language, Biruni set himself to the writing of *India*. No civilized nation by that time, or even centuries after, produced on the socio-religious life of an alien people such a work, which is matchless by virtue of the extent of its scope, the diversity of its subjects, the comparative method adopted in it, and above all, the deep and unbiased insight of the author. *India*, indeed, shall always remain wonder of the world of learning.

The work consists of a short introduction and eighty long chapters. It begins with a vivid description of the Hindu conceptions of God and the universe, followed by chapters on geography, history and legends of India, Further on, the author takes up the subject of Hindu rituals, festivals, religious ceremonies and the sacred days of the years to give a resume of Indian prosody and of the fundamentals of the Hindu law, jurisprudence and social practices.

In the introduction of *India,* Biruni discusses the importance of truthful reports and the causes of false narrations. He makes a critical review of the opinions held by the Muslims about other religions. In the eighth chapter Biruni tells us about the Hindu trinity of Brahma, Narayana and Rudra, the unity of the three in Vishnu, and compares it with the Christian trinity, and with the Greek ideas about Zeus.

He discusses the various types of marriage prevalent in India, and their comparison with the socio-religious ceremonies observed by the pagan Arabs, Jews and Iranians. Most of the information about India in this chapter is derived from the *Mahabharata* and the *Vishnu-purana*.

India is not merely a description of the scientific and religious views of the Hindus, their morals and manners, and their social organisation. Biruni has endeavoured to discuss these points comparatively and on a global scale; and though he is fully aware of differences which exist between the religious and social views of the Hindus and the Muslims, their customs, languages and ways of thinking, his judgements are not influenced by parochial predilections.

In his observations, Biruni is not simply a narrator, but very often gives his own critical and independent views on philosophical or scientific doctrines and argues the value and validity of his observations. He tries to be unbiased and unprejudiced, and does not allow his own religious attitudes and convictions to colour his judgments. When he sees something wrong or absurd he openly decries it, be it a Muslim belief or a Hindu practice.

Biruni was not a Sufi, but like all great mystics he recognized the fact that the divine truth may be revealed in all places and to all communities, and not in a particular place or to a selected group of people. He was aware of the fact that the beliefs, ideals and values of the Hindus were greatly different from those of the Muslims, Christians and Zoroastrians.

As against the Muslim theologians, to whom the religion of the Hindus was false, and the bigots who believed that idol-worshippers should be killed or converted, Biruni asserts that the Hindu sages are under the grace of God and are true in their beliefs and practices. He then supports his statement with quotations from the *Book of Patanjali* and the *Bhagvadgita*. But, unlike his master, Biruni pays due respect to the religious and philosophical writings of the Hindus and quotes copiously from them in his work, sometimes supporting their contents with Quranic verses.

According to Biruni, the true representatives of the Hindu religion are the philosophers, Brahmans and their sages, who believe in one God. But the Hindu masses, who worship idols do it out of sheer ignorance, for they can hardly see beyond the sensible form and appearance of the object of their worship. Biruni does not make a hasty judgment about the practices of the Hindu masses.

In the eleventh chapter of *India,* Biruni discusses the grounds of idol-worship among the masses, and says that the common man by his nature leans towards the sensible world and has an aversion to abstract ideas.

Biruni devoted himself to discovering the intellectual achievements of the Hindus, to introduce their cultural values and philosophical ideas to the Muslim world, and thus, to create an atmosphere of understanding between the two people.

Some of the Muslim historians and scholars living in the eighth and ninth centuries A.D., such as Masudi in his *Muruj al-dhahb*, Mutahhar-bin-Tahir al-Maqdasi in *al-Bad wa'l ta'rikh* and Ibn al-Nadim in *al-Fihrist* had made occasional references to Hindu beliefs, while some others like al-Nawbakhti in his *Kitab al-ara wa'l diyanat*, Abu'l-Qasim Balki in his *Uyun al-masa'il wa'l jawabat*, Zarqan, the Mu' tazalite, in his *Kitab al-maqalat*, and Iranshahri in his book on religions, had discussed them more elaborately.

In the beginning of his *India*, Biruni speaks about the Muslims' ignorance of other people's religious and intellectual life, and makes a detailed analysis of its causes and consequences with typical clarity.

While discussing astrology, astronomical computations and mathematics, Biruni often quotes the four standard authors: Brahmagupta, Aryabhata, Varahamihira and Vitesvara, along with the commentaries written on their works. He has also made a thorough study of the *Pulisa-siddhanta*. In writing about the geography, mythological and religious history of India, he makes use of the *Mahabharata, Ramayana, Manu-smriti* and some important *Puranas*, which provide valuable information on these subjects. In his discussions of the Indian sciences, that spread over the greater part of his work, Biruni has exhibited deep insight and comprehensive knowledge.

In an age when everyone around him had an eye on Indian cities and temples for the sake of rich booties, and while others regarded the Hindus as idol-worshipers who should be killed or converted, Biruni had come to India in search of treasures of wisdom, and endeavoured to open the eyes of the Muslims to the cultural heritage of the Hindus and to their scientific achievements. In this regard he was unique in his own age, and his equals are few in the history of mankind.

To sum up, Al-Biruni's main contribution lies in his unprejudiced study of Hindu religion, which did not appear to him to be mere idol-worship, as it did to most Muslims during the first 500 years of Muslim rule in India between Mahmud of Ghazna and Akbar. He regarded the essence of Hindu religion as a form of monotheism and the Hindu idol-worship as merely the manifestation of the dark and ignorant passions of the crowd. He was the first to introduce the study of the *Bhagavad Gita* to the Muslim world, the first Muslim to study the *Puranas* and to translate *Patanjali* and *Samkhya* into a Muslim language. He was critical of the caste system, but observant of the escape possible from it in the sublime path of Vedantic mysticism. In considerable detail he outlined the principles of Hindu sciences, astronomy, geography, mathematics, and medicine. He observed that the Hindus had not worked out their astronomical notions as scientifically as the Greeks, but acknowledged piecemeal Hindu influences on Arab writers like Abu Ma'shar. He wrote on the Sanskrit language and Hindu dialects and the multiplicity of their vocabulary, and paid tribute to the boundless literature of the Hindus and their cultivation of arts.

Amir Khusrau is perhaps the first Indian Muslim to show an assertive pride in his Indian origin. He came from a family of Turkish descent, but his mother was probably an Indian. His patriotism is argued in terms of mathematical exactitudes. There are seven arguments to prove that India is the Earthly Paradise; first, that India was the country to which Adam was exiled from the Garden of Eden; second, that the peacock, which is a bird of Paradise, is found in India; third, that the serpent was also exiled from Eden and came to India and made it is home; fourth, that Adam was unhappy in every other land except India; fifth, that whereas the flowers of India are fragrant, those of Persia and elsewhere are not; sixth, that the Prophet is reported to have said that the joys of this world are not for true believers but for pagans, who will enjoy heavenly bliss on earth and not in the life hereafter, therefore the paradise of India has been given to the unbelieving Hindus; and seventh, that India is a paradise because its ruler is his patron Qutb al-din Mubarak. More mathematical exactitudes follow. There are ten arguments to prove the superiority of India over 'Khurasan' (the vague Muslim homelands outside the subcontinent): India's climate is not cold like that of 'Khurasan'; people die of cold, not of heat; in a warm climate requirements of clothes are few and living is cheap; India is evergreen while spring comes to 'Khurasan' only for a few weeks; India's flowers have colour and scent, 'Khurasan's' only colour; Indian flowers remain fragrant even after they fade; Khurasanis cannot grow bananas; on the other hand Khurasani fruits can be grown in India; India has a rare fruit; banana; and a rare leaf, *pan* (betel). Reading these arguments one wonders how far Khusrau is serious. They occur in *Nuh Sipihr*, which was a command performance, written for Qutb al-din Mubarak whose favourite, Khusrau Khan was a convert from Hinduism, and all-powerful at the court. Perhaps it was politic and fashionable at that juncture to praise India.

Yet there is genuine absorption of Indian environmental beauty in the creative activity of Khusrau. He praises Delhi for its mosques, its ravishing Hindu beauties, its splendour and scholarship, in which 'it surpassed Bukhara and Khwarizm and even Baghdad slashed in two halves by the sword of the Tigris', and because it is the capital of his patron. He takes pleasure in writing sensually of India's fauna and flora in contradiction to the tradition of Indo-Persian poetry. In his poetic diction, especially in *Ashiqa*, he blends Hindi words musically and harmoniously. And yet he uses them sparingly and only when they are unavoidable. For the amusement of his friends he wrote mixed Persian and Hindi (pre-Urdu) verses.

Positive attitudes to India and favourable evaluations of its religious traditions received strong support during the reign of the Mughal emperor Akbar, whose well-known policies were exceedingly propitious for their development. Even if we treat Badayuni's hostile descriptions with the necessary circumspection, it is clear that Akbar's policies created an atmosphere in which belief in the exclusive truth of Islam was substantially undermined. The willingness of Akbar to admit Hindu sages into his presence and to listen to their religious discourses implied that their views were worthy of consideration. Abul Fazl's desire to discuss spiritual issues with sages who belong to religions other than Islam points in the same direction. The classical conviction that Islam is the only true religion lost its axiomatic nature, and the way was opened for the development of conciliatory attitudes towards Hinduism. These attitudes are clear in Abul Fazl's *Ain-i Akbari*. Like Al-Biruni before him, Abul Fazl asserted that the Hindus one and all believe in the unity of God and that the reverence that they pay to images of stone is only an aid to fix the mind and keep the thoughts from wandering. The intention of this exposition was to refute the equation between Hinduism and polytheism, hoping that the Muslim hostility towards the Hindus would thereby be reduced. This revision of attitudes towards the Hindus also resulted in the reassessment of certain historical personalities:

Muslim interest in India—particularly in Indian sciences, viz. religion, astronomy, astrology, medicine, mathematics—presents today a great historical phenomenon revolving back to as early as the first half of the eighth century A.D. The meteoric rise of Islam beyond the Arabian peninsula into Syria, Iraq, Egypt and Persia within a decade of the death of the holy Prophet, brought the sturdy Arabs into contact with some of the most ancient civilisations the world had ever seen. The Arab warrior, with a fanatical zeal conquered new lands, the Arab administrative genius incorporated them into the Dar-ul-Islam, but in the wake of the two came slowly and imperceptibly the Arab mind, to study and understand the cultural and the intellectual achievements of those whom they had conquered. Gradually, within a century, the process of cultural contact with the outside world proved a great civilising force which culminated in the Arab renaissance movement at the great centre of Islamic learning at Baghdad, founded by Al-Mansur in A.D. 725.

Indian thought reached the early Islamic world through diverse channels. The Magian, imbued both in Indian and Persian philosophy and learning, embraced Islam during al-Mansur's reign. He brought with him the knowledge of Indian and Buddhistic religions, customs and traditions. The great family of Bramak ministers who ruled the Islamic world for more than half a century (A.D. 716–766), were perhaps the greatest Indianists whose interest in Indian learning was unbounded. Though the Bramarks were Indian Buddhists in origin converted to Islam, and it is probable, that Khalid-bin-Bramark might have been 'induced by family traditions' to introduce Indian sciences into the Islamic world.

Indian sciences had already aroused Muslim interest to such an extent that during the next few centuries we find Arab historians, scholars, geographers and travellers visiting India to obtain first-hand information about her people, geography, religion, sciences and social customs. The process of cultural contact between the Arabs and the Indians was a part of the great Arab renaissance movement; though academic in character, it was, nonetheless, a spontaneous effort of the Muslims to acquire knowledge of the sciences of other peoples of the world.

From the second century A.H. onwards, Arab historians, geographers and travellers reflected the increasing interest of the Muslim intellectual world in India. Muhammadan literature on Indian religious beliefs before Al-Biruni's time, as compared with works on Indian sciences, is negligible.

In the exposition of the religious and philosophical doctrines of the Hindus, Abul Fazl stands almost alone after Al-Biruni. A genuine spirit of enquiry and love for knowledge vibrates through his detailed descriptions of Indian sciences, 'religious cults and philosophical schools of thought. He is comparable with Al-Biruni in many respects. Both had associated with the leaders of contemporary Indian religious thought and scholars of Sanskrit literature, and both were equally fond of comparing Hindu philosophy with Muslim and Greek doctrines. Al-Biruni's *Kitab al-Hind* seems to be spontaneous and outspoken in criticism, unfettered by any political objective, while Abul Fazl, who wrote the *Ain-i-Akbari* at Akbar's command, kept in view not only the Muslim intelligentsia of the time but also the fact that his readers included the Persianised Hindu court nobility.

In his Preface, he observes that it was his main idea to bring into open evidence the system of philosophy, the degrees of self-discipline of the Hindus, in order that 'hostility towards them might abate and the temporal sword be stayed awhile from the shedding of blood, that discussions within and without be turned into peace and the thornbrake of strife and enmity bloom into a garden of concord'. Incidentally, he outlines the causes which lead to contention and hostility between the Hindus and the Muslims.

Abul Fazl's pursuit of Indian religious thought seems predominantly intellectual. Among the eighteen sciences discussed by him are the *Vedas*, the *Puranas*, the *Dharma-Sastras* or the Institutes of the Law. His account also deals with the Indian *sangeet* or music and dancing, and *rajniti* or the science of statecraft.

Abul Fazl also gives an account of the practical modes of life of the Hindus, which include the Four Periods of Religious Life, the worship of the Deity, the Divine worship (*Isvarapuja*), the Sacrifice (*yajna*), the Alms-giving (*dana*), the ceremonies in honour of the deceased ancestors (*sraddha*) and the Incarnations of the Deity.

Among the translations of Abul Fazl only two have survived: a prose Persian version of the *Bhagwad Gita* and a modernised version of the Indian *Panchatantra* with some additional chapters.

The most significant Muslim religious thinker representing the conciliatory trend towards Hinduism seems to have been the Mughal prince Dara Shikoh (1615). In contradiction to Amir Khusrau, who only condescendingly admits that the Hindus maintain some correct beliefs, Dara Shikoh considers the Hindu tradition as an essential tool for understanding the religious truth and, indeed, for the real understanding of the *Quran*. Dara Shikoh's philosophy of religion is well explained in the introduction to his Persian translation of the *Upanishads*, entitled *Sirr-i-Akbar* (The greatest secret). His basic assumption is that religious truth is one. It is included in the *Vedas*, the *Upanishads*, the *Taurat* (Bible), the *Injil* (New Testament), the *Zabur* (Psalms), and the *Quran*. All these are heavenly books and contain the ultimate religious truth of monotheism (*tauhid*). Yet the degree of clarity and intelligibility with which this truth is expounded in them is not uniform. Turning first to the *Quran*, Dara Shikoh maintains that most of its contents is not formulated in an explicit manner. It is full of allegories (*akthar marmuz ast*) that are understood only by a few. The character of the Bible, the New Testament, and of the Psalms is similar: the truth is not explained in a sufficiently detailed and complete fashion.

Being unable to attain his goal of full religious understanding with the help of these four books, Dara Shikoh turned to the religious thought of India. He noted that according to the *Quran*, no nation was left without prophetic mission (Sura 35:22), and India cannot be an exception to the universality of divine guidance. Indeed, the question of *tauhid* was extensively discussed in that country. Ancient Indian sages never rejected it and never condemned its upholders. Furthermore, the four *Vedas*, which are heavenly books, had been in India before all other books of the same kind. They were revealed to ancient prophets; the greatest among these was Brahma, who according to Dara Shikoh is identical with Adam. The quintessence of the *Vedas* are the *Upanishads*, which are a treasure of monotheism.

Dara Shikoh creates an intimate connection between the *Quran* and the *Upanishads* by saying that they are hinted at in Sura 56:77-80. Verily it is a noble *Quran* in a protected book; none but the purified shall touch it, a revelation from the Lord of the world *(innahu la-quran karim fikitab maknim la yamassuhu illa al-mutahharun tanzil min rabb al-alamin)*. The crucial question with regard to this verse is the interpretation of *kiab maknun*. Classical Islamic commentators normally prefer to consider this phrase as a reference to the preserved tablet *(al-lauh al-mahfuz)* in which the original text of the *Quran* was inscribed by Allah. Less frequently they take it to mean the actual copy of the book or the *Taurat* and the *Injil*. Dara Shikoh does not accept any of these exegetical attempts. Without offering any substantiation of his view, he rejects the idea that *kitab maknun* refers to the *Taurat*, the *Injil* or the *Zabur*. Subsequently he argues that the word *tanzil* (revelation, sending down) used in the verse precludes the possibility that the phrase refers to the preserved tablet. The reason implied here is that the preserved tablet was never revealed or sent down. Having eliminated all other possibilities, Dara Shikoh concludes that *kitab maknun* refers to the *Upanishads*. In his view, the *Quran* called the *Upanishads* hidden or protected, because the Indian sages did their best to conceal them from the Muslims. The *Upanishads*, which undoubtedly are the earliest heavenly books and provided Dara Shikoh with answers to all his questions, are not only compatible with the *Quran* but also serve as its commentary. This is according to the principle that divine speech is its own exegesis: Whatever is expressed concisely in one book is detailed in another. The concise formulation of one book can therefore be elucidated and understood by the detailed exposition found elsewhere.

Is some of his works, Dara Shikoh also expressed high appreciation of the religious achievements of the Hindus. In the preface to *Majma al-bahrain*, he asserts that there is no fundamental difference between Islam and Hinduism. Elsewhere he ascribes to Hindu idolatry a positive, and even essential role in the development of religious consciousness: the idols are necessary for those who are not yet aware of the inner meaning of religion and therefore need a concrete representation of the deity; as soon as they come to know the batin, they dispense with the idols.

Dara Shikoh's view of the relationship between the Hindu religious literature and the *Quran* seems to be his most significant contribution to Islamic thought. The idea that one must use the Hindu scripture in order to attain the real meaning of the *Quran* is hitting at the very core of the conviction that Islam is a self-sufficient system that is in no need of ideas extraneous to it. It seems to have been deviant enough to put Dara Shikoh beyond the pale of medieval Indian Islam.

The 18th-century Naqshbandi Sufi Mirza Mazhar Jan-i Jahan (died in 1781) also expressed relatively conciliatory views of the Hindus, but he did not go as far as Dara Shikoh in recognising the legitimacy and validity of the Hindu religion after the emergence of Islam. Like Dara Shikoh, Jan-i Jahan accepted the antiquity and divine origin of the *Vedas* which, he thought, had been revealed at the beginning of creation. All Hindu sects agree that God is one, hold that the world is created, and believe in resurrection and retribution. Their idolatry does not involve association of partners with God; it rather resembles some *dhikr* ceremonies of the Sufis who meditate on the person of the *pir* in order to gain some spiritual benefits but refrain from carving out a concrete representation of him. The Hindus make representations of certain angels, concentrate their thought on them, thereby creating a link with the entities represented by them, and reaping some spiritual benefits. They even prostrate themselves in front of them, but this is only a prostration of greeting (*sajda-yi tahiyyat*) and not a prostration of worship (*sajda-yi ubudiyyat*). All this bears no resemblance to the idolatry of the pre-Islamic Arabs, who thought that the idols were powerful in themselves and not mere instruments of the divine power. Arab idolatry was, therefore, an association of partners with God. Its Indian variety is different and serves only as a means that enables the worshippers to forge a spiritual link with the deity. This deity is totally different from its concrete representation.

Like Dara Shikoh before him, Jan-i Jahan also thought that India was favoured with the divine gift of prophecy. Krishna and Rama Chandra fulfilled in his view prophetic tasks, and their title of avatar is to be understood as comparable—in Islamic terms—with messenger (*rasul*) prophet (*nabi*), or saint (*wali*). This being so, the Hindu religion was in the past a true divine faith, and it was incumbent upon the Indians to follow the prophets who had been sent to their country. With the advent of Muhammad, however, a fundamental change took place in this regard; all former religions were abrogated by Islam, and since that time nobody was justified in refraining from embracing it.

Thus, the crucial failure of Jan-i Jahan's view of Hinduism is the distinction he made between the Hindus who lived prior to the mission of Muhammad and those of the Islamic era. Those who have lived since the coming of Islam without joining its fold are infidels, even if their beliefs are different from those of the *jahili* Arabs and are not polytheistic. There is no contradiction between this and Jan-i Jahan's statement, according to which all Hindu sects agree on the unity of God: even a monotheist who does not acknowledge the prophethood of Muhammad is an infidel.

The thinkers, whose attitudes have been discussed here are representatives of the conciliatory approach to Hinduism in Indo-Muslim thought. While there are valid reasons to characterise them in this way, we must also not lose sight of important differences between them. Al-Biruni differs from the rest by being first and foremost a scholar who speaks about the various religions, including Islam, with a considerable degree of detachment. As such, he is able to discern in the religions compared features that may easily escape a person whose starting point is his own personal faith. His analysis of religious attitudes characteristic of comparable social groups in various religious communicates is a case in point.

Both Dara Shikoh and Jan-i Jahan are primarily religious thinkers, but they differ substantially from each other. While the relationship between Islam and Hinduism is for Dara Shikoh an all-pervasive concern, it is only one detail in Jan-i Jahan's religious world view. The nature of both thinkers' attitude to Hinduism is also not identical. Dara Shikoh ascribes to the Hindu scriptures a legitimacy not less than that of the *Quran*. In a certain sense the *Upanishads* are even superior to all other heavenly books, because the divine message is expressed in them in the most explicit fashion. They are therefore essential for understanding the less clear statements of the *Quran*. In saying this, Dara Shikoh abandons the cherished Islamic conviction that Islam is, in the eyes of Allah, the only true faith (Sura 3:19) and that the *Quran* is a clear, readily understandable book. It is precisely on this point that he differs from Jan-i Jahan. While the tenor of Jan-i Jahan's discourse about the Hindus is relatively moderate and he speaks favourably about some ancient Hindu religious figures, he strongly believes that Hinduism was valid only in the pre-Islamic past. Islam abrogated all other faiths and has been the only true religion since its emergence. All people who are now not Muslims are therefore infidels. In contradistinction to Dara Shikoh and despite the conciliatory tone of his discourse, Jan-i Jahan assiduously maintains the exclusive validity of Islam and does not deviate from the mediaeval *ijma* on this manner. His inclusion among the exponents of the conciliatory trends is due only to the fact that he displays some sympathy for the Hindu religion in its pre-Islamic past and that he expresses his views on Hinduism without the acrimony frequently encountered in mediaeval Indo-Muslim writings.

The Arab praise for India

It may be conceded at once that the Arab conquest of Sind was an insignificant event in the history of Islam, from the political point of view. But the effects of this conquest upon Muslim culture were profound and far-reaching. When the Arabs came to India, they were astonished at the superiority of its civilisation. The sublimity of Indian philosophical ideas and the richness of the Indian intellect were a strange revelation to them. The cardinal doctrine of Muslim theology, that there is one God, was already known to the Indian saints and philosophers. The Arabs found that in the nobler arts which enhance the dignity of man, the Indians far excelled them. The Indian musician, the mason and the painter were as much admired by the Arabs as the philosopher and the man of learning.

Tabari records that Khalifa Harun once sent for an Indian physician to cure him of an obstinate and painful disease. The Arabs learnt from the Indians a great deal in the practical art of administration. The employment of Brahman officials on a large scale was due to their better knowledge, experience and fitness for efficiently discharging the duties of administration. A great many of the elements of Arabian culture, which afterwards had such a marvellous effect upon European civilisation, were borrowed from India. Arab scholars sat at the feet of Buddhist monks and Brahman pandits to learn philosophy, astronomy, mathematics, medicine, chemistry and other subjects of study. The court at Baghdad extended its patronage to Indian scholarship. During the Khilafat of Mansur (A.D. 750–774), Arab scholars returned from India to Baghdad carrying with them two books, the *Brahma Siddhanta* of Brahmagupta and his *Khand Khadyaka*. These works were translated by Al Fazari into Arabic with the help of Indian scholars. It was from these two works that the Arabs learnt the first principles of scientific astronomy. There is ample reason to endorse Havell's view that it was India, not Greece, that taught Islam in the impressionable years of its youth, formed its philosophy and esoteric religious ideals, and inspired its most characteristic expressions in literature, art and architecture.

Arab authors have accepted in unambiguous terms the superiority of Indian achievements. Thus Al-Jahiz (A.D. 869) writes : 'The Hindus excel in astrology and mathematics. They have a special Indian script. They excel in medicine and possess some wonderful secrets of that art, in particular those remedies that are of the greatest use in the most dangerous diseases. They have developed to a perfection their arts like sculpture, painting and architecture. They are the inventors of chess. They make good swords and know all the tricks of fencing. They know charms that can remove poison and pain from the body. Their music is pleasant and they have all sorts of dances. From India we received that book called *Khalilah-wa-Dimnah*. These people have judgement and are brave. In some virtues they surpass the Chinese.'

Yaquibi (A.D. 895) observes : 'The Hindus are superior to all other nations in intelligence and thoughtfulness. They are more exact in astronomy and astrology than any other people. The *Brahma Siddhanta* is a good proof of their intellectual powers; by this book the Greeks and the Persians have also profited.'

Al-Idrisi (A.D. 1154), speaking of the accomplishments of the Hindus, says : 'The Hindus are by nature inclined to justice and never depart from it in their actions. Their good faith, honesty and faithfulness to their promises are well known and they are so famous for these qualities that people flock to their country from every side'.

Another Arab historian, Quazi S'aid, observes : 'The Hindus have always been considered by all other people as the custodians of learning and wisdom. Their knowledge of God ascertains His unity and purity. To kill or injure an animal is a sin with them'.

Influence of Buddhism on Islam

Long before the Muslim scholars translated Hindu works into Arabic or Persian, and before the Muslim travellers brought news from India, the Muslims had some glimpses of India's religious conceptions through Persian literature and also through Buddhistic influence that still lingered in some of the most remote parts of Iran. The word *'bud'* or *'but'* had long ago degenerated into the sense of idol worship and conveyed no other meaning. Buzasaf, that is, Bodhisattva, was known to them as the founder of Buddhism. Not long ago Buddhism had flourished in Balk, Transoxiana, Khurasan, Turkistan and Persia, and to some extent also in Iraq, before the Muslims conquered them. After these countries were converted to Islam, the Buddhist priests did not at once stop their preaching. The rosary is one of the objects that the Muslims inherited from the Buddhists. The Sufi doctrine of Fana is the Nirvana of the Buddhists. The whole Sufi system of spiritual *Muqamat* (Stations) or *chakras* that the seeker after illumination realises on his way to 'exinction', is Buddhistic.

The inhabitants of Balk and Bukhara had displayed a strong tendency to revert to their old Buddhist habits of thought. Abu Nasr Ahmad-bin-Narshakhi (A.D. 943) relates in his history of Bukhara: 'Every time the people of Bukhara were conquered, they accepted Islam, and no soon than the Arabs retired, they gave it up again'.

A good number of thinkers amongst Muslims, especially in the Abbasid reign, was more or less directly influenced by Buddhism. Ibn Muqaffah (A.D. 760) translated the *Kalilah-wa-Damnah* from Pahlavi to Arabic. In his introduction to *Kalilah-wa-Damnah,* he describes an ascetic when he is absorbed in meditation; 'for he is still contented, unambitious, satisfied, free from cares, has renounced the world, has escaped from evils, is devoid of greed, is pure, independent, protected against sorrow, above jealousy, manifests pure love, does none any harm and remains himself unmolested.'

Explaining the philosophical aspect of idol worship, Abul Fazl says : 'The inhabitants of this land are religious, affectionate, hospitable, genial and frank. They are fond of scientific pursuits, inclined to austerity of life, seekers after justice, contended, industrious, capable in affairs, loyal, truthful and constant. The true worth of this people shines most in the day of adversity and its soldiers know no retreat from the field....They, one and all, believe in the unity of God, and as to the reverence they pay to the images of stones and wood and the like, which simpletons regard as idolatry, it is not so. The writer of these pages has exhaustively discussed the subject with many enlightened and upright men, and it became evident that these images of some chosen souls nearest in approach to the throne of God are fashioned as aids to fix the mind and keep the thoughts from wandering, while the worship of God alone is required as indispensible.'

The most eminent scholar was Abu Rihan Al-Biruni who compiled a comprehensive treatise on Hindus, religions and philosophies as early as the 11th century. Throughout the Middle Ages, the Muslims took enormous pains to acquaint themselves with the religious literature of the Hindus. They translated almost all the important texts into Persian—the *Vedas*, the *Upanishads*, the *Mahabarat*, the *Ramayana*, the *Dharma Sastra, the Puranas*, the *Yoga Vasistha*, the *Yoga Sastra, Vedanta Sastra*, etc.

Among later writers may be mentioned the name of Mirza Jan Janan Mazhar (b. 1699). Mazhar wrote about the Hindu worship of idols : 'Idol worship, the process is similar to the Dhikr, contemplative ritual, which is prescribed for Muslim Sufis.'

Mahmud Sha-bistari (A.D. 1317), the well-known writer of *Gulshan-i-Raz*, writing on the theme of idol worship, explains the difference and similarity between it and Islam : 'The idol is the expression of love and unity in this world, and to wear the sacred thread is to take the resolve of service. As both faith and unfaith are founded in existence, unity of God is the essence of idol worship. As things are the expression of existence, one out of them must at least be the idol. If the Muslim knew what the idol is, then he would not go astray in his faith. The latter did not see in the idol anything but external creation, and for this reason he became kafir in the eyes of the law. If thou too would not see that reality is hidden in the idol thou wilt also be not known as a Muslim according to the law.'

Islamic mysticism originated and grew in two regions of the Muslim world—ancient Khorasan and Mesopotamia. In both these regions, seekers of truth and enlightenment among the Muslims came in close contact with Indian mystics. The whole of Khorasan was studded with Buddhist monasteries and Hindu temples at the time of the Muslim conquest, as is testified by Hiuen Tsiang who had passed through these lands barely seventy years earlier. In Mesopotamia, Junda Shapur, Damascus and Baghdad were centres of learning where Hindu scholars taught Indian science and Hindu ascetics (yogis) held debates with Muslim scholars. The Pramukhas of the Nava Vihara of Transoxiana became the prime ministers (Baramakas) of the Abbasid Caliphs and they invited Hindu doctors, astronomers and scientists to Baghdad and encouraged the translation of Sanskrit treatises into Arabic. Thus it was that the philosophy of pantheism and the practical discipline of yoga passed into the Sufi circles of the Middle East.

Pre-Muslim Hindu Culture

At this juncture, it will not be out of place to understand the religious conditions prevailing in India at the time of the advent of Islam in India.

The Hindus treat their religion from the point of view of emancipation (*moksa*) for the attainment of which they recognise three paths—the paths of action (*karman*), of knowledge (*jnana*), and of devotion (*bhakti*). It must, however, be remembered that the three paths are not mutually exclusive and do not necessarily imply antagonism; as a matter of fact, practically all the sects recognise their value and enjoin them on their followers. But it is interesting to note that the religious importance of the path of action exclusively was greatest in the earliest times, that of the path of knowledge grew later and that of the path of devotion last. The three have existed side by side but while the influence of the first two has waned, that of *Bhakti-Marga* has increased.

The path of action is the one principally laid down by the *Vedas*, developed and systematised in the *Brahmanas*, *Kalpa-Satras*, and *Karma-Mimamsa* and popularised by *Dharma-Sastras*, *Mahabharata* and the *Puranas*.

Whatever historical strata Vedic thought may contain, in its mature form it is a well-rounded philosophic-religious system. In this system one supreme being stands forth as the ultimate reality. It is conceived of as the One (*ekam*), the Person (*purusa*), the Creator *(visvakarman, prajapati)*, the Absolute (*tad*), Brahmana transcendent.[1]

The universe is the theatre of God's will, every being—living and non-living—is moved by His eternal order and all action and movement is bound in one chain of law. Not only are natural phenomena—day and night, sun and moon, rivers and oceans— and the gods—*Agni, Soma, Brhaspati, Indra, Aditi* and *Varuna,* under the sway of law, but the very act of worship—rite and sacrifice—which man offers to the gods, obeys the all-comprehending, all-encompassing rule of cosmic law. In fact, before the severe majesty of law even the power of the gods pales into insignificance.

Sacrifice is the symbol of this universal order; it is even the source of Prajapati's power, for when He exhausts it in creation, the gods replenish his pristine vigour with sacrifice. Through sacrifice the gods display their activity in rain and storm and the rising of the sun. Sacrifice is thus the instrument by which the will of God is fulfilled. Man is the creature of God dependent upon His will, seeking to understand and interpret that will, and naturally moulding his actions in imitation of his gods. Sacrifice is, therefore, the means of attaining prosperity here and blessedness hereafter.

The pathway of eternal bliss is that of action, which means sacrifice performed with faith and accompanied with prayer. Sacrifices are manifold—they are obligatory and regular (*nitya*) obligatory but occasional *(naimittika)*, and optional *(kamya).*

But sacrifice, although symbolic of cosmic law and hence efficacious in bringing about the desired ends, is not the whole of human action. Man's life, therefore, is mapped out and man's place in society fixed. Rules are laid down for the governance of each part of the fourfold station of life *(asrama)* and fourfold classification of society *(varna)*. The permanence of these duties becomes the essential part of the religion of action *(varnasrama dharma)*.

Yet another development of this conception takes place in the *Bhagavadgita* where it is taught that salvation may be won through the path of action, and action is interpreted as performance of duty without attachment to fruits.

This then was the speculative basis of the religion of *Karman*. But in popular practice it means more or less the offering of sacrifice to the gods and the observance of the domestic rites. In the *Vedas,* the gods were the earliest products of creation. They were semi-anthropomorphised forces of nature, their functions were scarcely differentiated and therefore they easily melted into one another:

'They call him Indra, Mitra, Varuna, Agni, and he is the heavenly winged Garutman'.[2]

But later they acquired more definite personalities. On the eve of the advent of the Muslims in India, the significance and numbers of the ancient deities had greatly changed. Most of them had disappeared from the popular pantheon, the importance of others had enormously varied, and a number of new ones had risen in favour. As beings of a higher order, they played an important role in the universe and the life of man.

The Vedic pantheon was peopled with gods that lived in the heavens or in the atmosphere or upon earth, their number was reckoned as thirty-three, but those to whom the greatest number of hymns were devoted were *Indra, Agni,* and *Soma*. *Varuna* was the most exalted, and *Prajapati* was the lord of creation, *Vishnu* and *Rudra-Siva* received meagre attention. In older epic mythology *Brahma* presided over the deities as creator and beneficent ancestor of all, while *Agni, Yama, Varuna, Kubera* and *Indra* were most often invoked. Later, *Siva* and *Vishnu* attained the predominant position and joined with *Brahma,* formed the great Trinity.

For the seventh and eighth centuries there is a considerable amount of contemporary evidence to show what the state of popular worship was. This evidence consists of the accounts of the Chinese travellers, the Sanskrit dramas, the inscriptions and coins of Indian rulers, and the descriptions of the Arab writers. They disclose that while the non-Vedic religions, Buddhism and Jainism were on the decline, the old Vedic religion had greatly changed, the worship of *Siva* was the predominant religion of India, the cult of *Sakti* was rising into importance and *Vishnu* and other deities were held in popular esteem on a descending scale.

In the narratives of Fa-Hien one finds that in the 5th century, when the traveller came to India, the north-western portion of the country from Kabul and Khotan to Mathura was still loyal to Buddhism *(Hinayana)*, in the Madhya Desa the assimilation of Buddhism and Hinduism was rapidly proceeding. When Hiuen-Tsiang visited India two hundred years later he found Hinduism vigorously established by the side of Buddhism. Hiuen-Tsiang's narrative is full of references to the prevalence of Saiva worship, especially in *Pasupata* form. In Makran there were hundreds of *Deva* temple and very many professed the *Pasupatas* cult, and in the city there was a large temple to *Mahesvara* which was held in great reverence by the *Pasupatas*. In Kashmir the *Kritiyas* had overthrown Buddhism and established heresy (probably Saivism), in the Punjab from the Indus to the Sutlej there were numerous heretics, in Jalandhar all the heretics belonged to the *Pasupatas*. In Kanauj there was a splendid temple and more than ten thousand adherents of the sects, the majority being devotees of *Siva*. They covered their bodies with ashes, and by the practice of all sorts of austerities they sought to escape from birth and death.

The Arabs, who during the course of the seventh and eighth centuries had made many descents upon the coast of Gujarat, the Gulf of Cambay and the Malabar Coast, acquired information regarding Hindu sects which was embodied in their books of religion compiled in the ninth and later centuries. These references shed interesting light on Indian religious and social customs. The Arabs' attention was naturally attracted to what was peculiar and strange to them, but was usual in the country. Thus, for instance, Sulaiman mentions the ascetics who lived on herbs and fruits and who rarely communicated with the rest of the world, and other who wore nothing but panther skins round their loins and performed severe penances; Abu Zaid al Hasan Sirafi saw wandering monks who carried round their neck a cord to which a human cranium was attached, out of which they ate their food. Undoubtedly he refers to *Kapalikas*, a Saiva sect.

It appears that *Siva* worship prevailed over the greater part of India about the seventh and eighth centuries, but along with it the worship of other gods was also practised though not so extensively; among them Vishnu was the most important. The early Muslim accounts are too vague as regards non-Saiva sects to permit any legitimate inference concerning the prevalence of Vaisnavism. The evidence as a whole seems to indicate that northern India of the seventh and eighth centuries was not Vaisnavite but Saivite, although subsequently, in the time of Al-Biruni their relative position had been reversed.

The followers of the path of action *(Karma marga)* were found in all the sects and among the devotees of all the gods. Their worship consisted in addressing prayers to the gods before the images at home or in the temple, in performing prescribed rites—(domestic and public) in offering sacrifices (rarely human, in some cases bloody), but more often consisting of corn and milk and fruits. Fasts, pilgrimages, charity, penances and ascetic exercise were part of the good deeds which won the favour of the gods.

The three principal sectarian Hindu philosophical systems are *Vaisnava* (or *Satvata* or *Pancaratra* or *Bhagvata*), *Saiva* and *Tantrika*. The history of the various systems included under the three sects goes back to very early times.

In the *Pancaratra* system *Vishnu* is the transcendent absolute reality, Laksmi is the energy, residing in him as Iness in I or moonshine in the moon. *Laksmi* has a twofold aspect: as *Kriyasakti*, she represents Vishnu's will-to-be, and is independent of space and time, as *Bhuti-sakti* it is the matrix of the universe.

The *Saiva* system was founded by Lakulin or Lakulisa about the second century B.C. Later it was divided into a number of schools forming two groups: (i) Saivas, Pasupatas, Kapilikas and Kalamukhas; (ii) Spanda Sastra, Pratyabhijna Sastra and Siva Siddhantas, (Kashmir). The philosophic basis of the Saiva systems of the first group was the recognition of three principles, the lord (*pati*), the individual (*pasu*), and the fetters (*pasa*). Siva is the Lord who is endowed with a body made of the five powers of creation, protection, destruction, concealment and benefaction.

The Pasupatas aimed at a mystic union reached by pious mutterings, meditation and the cessation of all action, so that a state of mere feeling (*sanivid*) was attained. The Kapalikas and Kalamukhas carried things to disgusting extremes. They went about wearing garlands of skulls, armed with clubs and lances, carrying wine pots, eating ashes, and performing bloody rites.

The third path for the attainment of liberation is that of devotion and faith *(Bhakti Marga)*. *Bhakti* has been defined as 'the worship of a personal deity in a spirit of love', as personal faith in a personal God, love for him as for a human being, the dedication of everything to his service, and the attainment of 'moksa' by this means rather than by knowledge, or sacrifice, or works, as an affection fixed upon the Lord after acquiring knowledge of the attributes of the adorable one. *Bhakti* is the emotional aspect of religion, its roots lie in the feeling or affective side of human consciousness, as those of *jnana* lie in the cognitive or intellectual, and those of *karma* in the conative or willing. In this sense, the stream of *Bhakti* which began as a little trickle in the Vedic times went out with the advance of history as a mighty flood sweeping over the whole land.

The earliest written text of the school of devotion is the *Bhagavad Gita*. Krishna teaches that it is by unswerving devotion to Him alone that He is reached. God is so pleased that He accepts all that is offered to him with devotion—a leaf, a flower, a fruit, water. 'Devotion implies the dedication of all actions of Him, for the devotees live and have their being in God.' God extends His ineffable grace to His devotees, for even the sinful worshippers are promised that they will be accounted righteous provided they worship with undivided heart, and that they will never perish. In the sight of God all devotees are equal whether they are born in sin or not, and to whatever caste or sect they may belong. Devotion is the means of the mystic vision and the unitive state. The devotee is dear to God, surpassingly dear to him, for God is the father, the husband, the mother, and the friend.

Bhakti had a parallel development in other systems besides the *Pancaratra Agawa*, but the most important contribution among them was that of *Buddhism* of the *Mahayana* School. Now

Mahayana Bhakti centred round Buddha and the *Bodhisattvas*. Buddhism emphasised the democratic side of religion, the spiritual enfranchisement of *sudras* and women, and the preaching of religion through the medium of the popular languages, that is, the vernaculars. It also provided examples for the organisation of monastic orders.[3]

Religious, Social and Political Conditions at the time of the advent of the Muslims in the North

When the empire of Harsa fell, the north broke up into small principalities. Rajput clans starting from their original homes in the West spread north and east, establishing the chieftaincies in the Himalayan regions, in the plains watered by the Ganges and the Jumna, and in the wide stretch of territory broken up by the Vindhya and Kaimur ranges between Gujarat and Orissa. Even those who had no title to the name of Rajput constructed imaginary pedigrees and affiliated themselves to the dominating race. The Rajputs thus were masters of the destinies of India from the Panjab to the Deccan and from the Arabian Sea to Bengal before the Muslims appeared upon the scene.

Under their sway great changes came upon the social life and culture of northern India. The ancient seats of culture and regions of a busy and humming life changed. Magadha was no longer the cradle of the empire; Pataliputra and Gaya were in ruins, and in their walled cities there were few inhabitants.

In religious matters a vast transformation took place. The India of Harsha was still mainly Buddhist or Saivite. India in the 11th century, as Al-Biruni saw it, was quite different. Buddhism or a mixture of Buddhism and Saktism or Tantrism was confined to one corner of the country, namely, Bengal; Jainism maintained its existence in the extreme west, Gujarat and Rajputana; but the dominant creed of India was Hinduism. The transformation was due to the ascendancy of the Brahmans in the social life of India, an ascendancy which began in the Gupta period and was completed when the foreign immigrants were received into the Hindu social system. The Brahmans transformed the Scythians, the Huns, the Sakas and other foreigners, and the Gonds and Bhils and other indigenes into

Rajputs; and the Rajputs paid the price of their elevation from barbarism to civilisation by accepting and confirming their claims of superiority. Vaisnavism, at one time a heterodox system, had very early been appropriated by the Brahmans as peculiarly their own. Siva's worship was, however, the religion of the common folk or semi-Hinduised peoples. The first recommended itself to them because the priest played such an important part in it, the latter's ritual might be performed without a priest. The Rajputs themselves were attached to Siva, they built numerous temples in Gujarat, Rajputana and Bundelkhund, dedicated to him, but in deference to the views of their benefactors paid worship to Vishnu and erected his temples and created endowments for their maintenance. The Guptas had encouraged Vishnu worship, they had set up pillars to Vishnu and proclaimed themselves in their title admirers of Bhagwat.

Although the devotional religion of the *Bhagwata Purana* opened the way for the spiritual emancipation of the individual, it did not remove the chains of social slavery, it still demanded that the followers of Bhagwata, 'forsaking all desires should act in consonance with their castes'. Nor did it hold an uncompromising position regarding the external forms of worship. It regarded yoga, knowledge, virtue, study of the *Vedas*, asceticism, charity, sacrifice, vows, worship of deities, mantras (spells), journey to sacred shrines, self-control, as inferior to the companionship of the devotees, yet not quite dispensable to devotion. It prescribed the worship of idols and symbols, and meditation upon the image of God according to yogic methods.

The *Bhagwata Purana* marked the transition from the ancient religion of books to the medieval religion of Bhakti. But the influence of the emotional elements in the faith was not strong enough to counteract effectually the growing rigidity of caste or the growing power of the priest. The period of Rajput ascendancy was one of division and conflict. Society was enfeebled by feudal, anarchy and clannish pretensions on the one side and by religious dissensions and priestly selfishness on the other.

Upon this scene of petty Rajput feuds and glorious Rajput art, burst the avalanche of the Muslim conquest. The Muslim advance from across Baluchistan into Sind, in the eighth century, was held up by the inhospitality of the country and the difficulties in maintaining communications with far-off Baghdad, especially when rebel chiefs blocked the ways which led from the centre of the Caliphate to its outlying territories. Nearly three centuries passed till attacks were resumed but now they proceeded from a different quarter. Subuktagin and Mahmud undertook their annual forays from the north-west. Their effect was not great, some temples were plundered and a few cities were sacked, the Hindu-Shahiya dynasty and with it the Hindu dominion disappeared from the Panjab, otherwise things remained as heretofore. Permanent conquest in India was not the aim of the Ghaznavides, who looked for empire towards the west. Another century passed, during which the disturbances created in Central and Western Asia by the rise of the Turks turned the attention of the Ghori rulers of Afghanistan definitely in the direction of the east.

The thirteenth century had hardly begun when the conquest of northern India was completed. Within a quarter of a century the Muslim armies had overrun the country from the Panjab to Assam and from Kashmir to the Vindhyas. The Rajput princes offered scarcely any resistance, they were all taken by utter surprise. Each one fought singly, bravely, but no one showed any particular foresight, and collectively they showed complete lack of cohesion and power of combination.

The Muslim conquest had a tremendous effect upon the evolution of Indian culture. Superficially, it upset everything: the Hindu religion received a terrible blow, the state patronage of the priest and Pandit ceased, the Hindu monuments were destroyed, literature received no royal encouragement and languished; to all outward appearances political conquest was synonymous with cultural death. Fundamentally, it had a different effect. The Muslim kings displaced the Hindu Rajas in the important principalities. Delhi, Kanauj, Gwalior, Anhilwada, Deogir and Gaur passed into their hands; not so the outlying countries.

The Advent of the Muslims in India

The history of commercial intercourse between India and the Western countries—Arabia, Palestine, and Egypt—goes back to very ancient times. King Solomon obtained his gold from Ophir (modern Beypur), as well as silver, ivory, apes and peacocks. The Greeks imported rice, ginger and cinnamon from the Malabar Coast. The coins of all the Roman emperors from Augustus (d. A.D. 14) to Zeno (d. A.D. 491) are found in southern Indian, attesting to the ample commerce which India had with the west. The Persians manifested the same commercial activity as the Romans. In the middle of the sixth century, commerce reached its greatest activity. The Arabs naturally took a very active part in the commerce between the Orient and the Occident.

The rise of Islam in the beginning of the seventh century and the unification of the Arab tribes under a centralised state gave a tremendous impetus to the movement of expansion which was going on since pre-Islamic days. Muslim armies rapidly conquered Syria and Persia and began to hover on the outskirts of India. Muslim merchants immediately entered into the inheritance of Peursian maritime trade and Arab fleets began to scour the Indian seas.

The first Muslim fleet appeared in Indian waters in A.D. 636 during the Caliphate of Umar. During this period the land approaches to India were explored and a great deal of information collected, ultimately leading to the conquest of Sindh in the eighth century by Muhammad-bin-Qasim. Meanwhile, commerce by sea continued, and Muslims made their settlements in three towns along the South Indian Coast and in Ceylon. The Muslim Arabs first settled on the Malabar Coast about the end of the seventh century. From the seventh century onwards it is well known that Persian and Arab traders settled in large numbers at the different ports on the western coast of India and married women of the country. These settlements were specially large and important in Malabar where from very early times it seems to have been the policy to afford every encouragement to traders at the ports.

In the eighth century the Arab fleets attacked Broach and the ports on the Kathiawad coast. Their trade and settlements continued to flourish. Thenceforth Muslim influence grew rapidly. For over a hundred years the Muslims had been established on the Malabar coast. They were welcomed as traders, and, apparently, facilities were given to them to settle and acquire lands and openly practise their religion. They must have entered upon missionary efforts soon after settling down, for Islam is essentially a missionary religion and every Musalman is a missionary of his faith. Many were undoubtedly held in respectful esteem. Before the ninth century was far advanced they had spread over the whole of the western coast of India and had created a stir among the Hindu populace, as much by their peculiar beliefs and worship as by the zeal with which they professed and advocated them.

The south of India was then greatly agitated by the conflict of religions, for Neo-Hinduism was struggling with Buddhism and Jainism for the upper hand. Politically, too, it was a period of unsettlement and upheavals. The Cheras were losing power and new dynasties were rising. Naturally, the mind of the people was perturbed and they were prone to accept new ideas, from whatever quarter they came. Islam appeared upon the scene with a simple formula of faith, well-defined dogmas and rites, and democratic theories of social organisation. It produced a tremendous effect, and, before the first quarter of the ninth century was over, the last of the Cheraman Perumal Kings of Malabar, who reigned at Kodungallur had become a convert to the new religion. After his conversion the king left Malabar for Arabia and landed at Shahr where he died four years later. He sent from there Malik ibn Dinar, Sharf ibn Malik, Malik ibn Habib and their family to Malabar with a letter of instructions regarding the government of his dominions and the reception of the Muslims. They were treated hospitably and were permitted to build mosques. As a consequence mosques were erected at eleven places on the Malabar Coast.

The conversion of the king must have produced a deep impression upon the mind of the people. The memory of the event is still kept fresh in Malabar. For instance, at the installation of the Zamorin, it is the practice to have him shaved and dressed like a Musalman, and crowned by a Mappilla. The Musalmans evidently had acquired great importance at this period. They were designated by the name of Mappillas which means either 'a great child or a bridegroom' and was considered a title of honour. A Musalman could be seated by the side of a Nambutiri Brahman while a Nayar could not. The religious leader of the Mappillas, the Thangal, was allowed to ride a palanquin alongside the Zamorin.

Under the patronage and encouragement of the Zamorin, the Arab merchants settled in large numbers in his dominions, and not only materially increased his power and wealth by their trade but directly supported him in his campaigns of aggrandisement.

The Zamorin thought so highly of the Muslims that he definitely encouraged conversion in order to man the Arab ships on which he depended for his aggrandisement. He gave the order that in every family of fishermen (*makkuvans*) in his dominion one or more of the male members should be brought up as Muslims.

In the following centuries the influence of Islam continued to wax. Well-known traveller Ibn Battuta (fourteenth century) in his itinerary from Cambay along the western coast touched at all the ports. He met his co-religionists everywhere and found them in a flourishing condition. He notice that the Musalmans were the most highly considered people in that country. Mangalore had a population of four thousand Musalmans, among them merchants from Fars and Yemen. The chief merchant at Calicut was a Muslim.

The traditions enshrined in the *Keralolpatti* and the legends of the Muslim inhabitants, the evidence of inscriptions and of Muslim historians and travellers and the continuity of Arab commerce with India from early times all lead to one conclusion, that the Muslims appeared on the Indian coast not long after the death of the Prophet and swiftly gained a status of privilege and influence among the Hindu rulers of Malabar.

The Muslims inherited the legacy of the pagan Arabs. The usual route from the ports of Arabia or the Persian Gulf to China passed through the seven seas among which were the Gulf of Palk and the Bay of Bengal. Numerous voyagers must have passed along this way and a great deal of commercial intercourse must have been kept up between the Muslim lands and India.

Their principal settlement on the east coast was Kayalpatanam in Tinnevelly district, near the mouth of the Tamraparni river, where even today the Labbes form the majority of the population. The Musalmans started their religious propaganda as soon as they had settled down in some numbers. Many of the Islamic communities of the south trace their origin to these times. The Ravuttans of Madura and Trichinopoly believe that they were persuaded to change their religion by Nathad Vali whose tomb exists at Trichinopoly and bears the date of his death, A.D. 1039. The legend about Nathad is that he was a Sayyid prince who held territory in Turkey, but abandoned his state and became an ascetic and missionary of Islam. He wandered through Arabia, Persia and Northern India until he reached the city of Trisura, modern Trichinopoly. Here he settled down and passed the remaining years of his life in prayer and works of charity, converting a large number of Hindus to Islam.

In Madura, the Muslims made their entrance in A.D. 1050 under the leadership of Malik-ul-Muluk, who was accompanied by a great saint, Hazrat 'Aliyar Shah Sahib. The rulers of the eastern coast pursued an enlightened policy towards the merchants who visited their coast. The Coromandel Coast became the *mabar* (passage) of the Muslim traders.

According to Dr. Tarachand, historical account shows that the Musalmans made their advent in South India on the western coast as early as the eighth century if not earlier, and in the tenth century on the eastern coast; that they soon spread over the whole coast and in a comparatively short time acquired great influence both in politics and society. On the one hand their leaders became ministers, admirals, ambassadors and farmers of revenue and on the other, they made many converts, propagated their religious ideas, established mosques and erected tombs which became centres of the activities of their saints and missionaries. It may, therefore, be premised without overstraining facts that if, in the development of the Hindu religion in the south, any foreign elements are found which make their appearance after the seventh century, and which cannot be accounted for by the natural development of Hinduism itself, they may, with much probability be ascribed to the influence of Islam, provided, of course, that they are not alien to its genius[5].

In northern India, Muslims began their encroachment during the Caliphate of Umar, making their earliest attempts on the ports of the northern coast, and when Persia and Makran had been annexed to the empire they invaded Sindh. During the seventh century many raids were made on the borders of Baluchistan and Sindh and the land routes were thoroughly explored. Finally, in the time of Caliph Walid, Hajjaj, who was Governor of Iraq, organised an expedition which was sent under the leadership of the young and brilliant Muhammad-bin-Qasim. He overcame all difficulties, defeated the Hindu rulers of Sindh, overran the whole Indus Valley, and made the provinces of Multan and Sindh appendages of the empire.

Already, before the invasions of Mahmud of Ghazna had opened the gates of India wide for the Muslims to enter, they had attained in western India an influential position, which they used to spread their religion among the people. They were considerably encouraged in the pursuit of their aims by the favour of the Hindu rulers themselves. The story related by Muhamad Ufl throws a great deal of light upon the relations of Hindu princes and Muslim traders. When the Hindus of Cambay attacked the Muslim merchants, Siddh Raj (109–1143) held an enquiry into the whole affair, punished the aggressors and gave the Musalmans money to build a new mosque. Some Hindu Rajas appear to have employed Muslim mercenaries. The ruler of Somnath, for instance, had a number of Muslim officers, and the Kasbatis of Ahmadabad trace their descent from the Khorasani soldiers of the Vaghela chiefs.

The Muslim saints went wherever the Muslim army led or the traders settled. After the invasions of Mahmud, numerous Muslim men of learning and religion poured into India.

The arrival of Islam in India antedates Muslim rule, and the mere fact of its acceptance and the esteem shown towards its teachings proves that it has comparatively little to do with the proselytising efforts of Islamic conquerors than with the aforementioned essential tenets of Islam. It has been argued that in terms of cultural depth, intensity, and wider repercussions, the two most profound influences on the making of a distinct Indian civilisation are those of the ancient Indo-Aryan and the medieval Indo-Muslim segments. Nevertheless, force, in the form of military might and battle, has played its part in the making of Indian history and civilisation, but in the working out of a new synthesis of the indigenous Hindu and the exogenous Muslim or, from the Hindu point of view, the Hinduism orthodox and the heterodox Islam, it has been the cumulative will of accommodation of both groups that has finally transformed the mighty rivers of these two cultures into a magnificent stream of Indian national life. Muslim Sufism and Hindu Vedanta teachings have jointly contributed to the great inter-religious understanding now prevalent all over India, to the extent that, nowadays, Islam is an integral part of the social and cultural life of the subcontinent.

Sufism, as a moral and spiritual way of life, with its universal appeal found in India an exceptionally congenial ground for its growth and spread. The Indian mind, from the earliest days, has had a strong tendency towards mysticism, to the extent that some scholars have claimed, obviously with a bit of exaggeration, that almost all the mystical tenets that have developed in other religions and philosophical schools find their clearest expressions in the Vedic and Upanishadic literature of ancient India. None the less, the universalistic outlook of Hindu thought and also of Sufism, the pantheistic monism of the Advaita Vedanta and the expression of *wahadat al-wujud* of the Sufis, the self-manifestation of the Divine Being, which is called *pratibhasa* in Vedantic terms and *tajalli* or *zuhur* in Sufi concepts, the Unity of all Being, expounded in such Upanishadic passages as: all variations are matters of mere words and names and in the pantheistic philosophy of Ibn Arabi and his followers, the immanence of the Divine.

As noted earlier, the mystical ideas of Islam and the Sufi way of life were so appealing to the Indian mind that even the Hindu Brahmans were not unaffected by their influence. It has been observed that in the fifteenth and sixteenth centuries, some Brahmans had taken to such heterodox ways of wearing a beard, walking with a big stick, reading the Persian language, and reciting the *Mathnawi*.

Meanwhile, Muslim Sufi saints were, in general, highly respected by the non-Muslim population, and the Hindus often treated them with a deep sense of trust and veneration. Some of the Muslim Sufis had acquainted themselves with Hindu religious thought and mystical ideas and attracted large numbers of Hindus to their *khanqahs*.

As regards the impact of Hindu thought on Islamic mysticism and Sufi *tariqat*, this fact is obviously revealed in the large number of translations of Indian philosophical works, including fifty *Upanishads*, into Persian. Since the eighth centry A.D., Muslim scholars and historians have been engaged in studying different aspects of Hindu thought and sciences, a task remarkably carried forward by Biruni, the famous Iranian scholar and Indologist. Nevertheless, the mass of literature produced in the Persian language by Hindu and Muslim writers about Hindu religious thought and practice still has to receive the attention it deserves.

The diffusion of Islam in India had once awakened the Hindu masses to a number of facts, never before so vividly known to them. Islam's arguments against image worship and polytheism, its strong condemnation of caste discrimination, and its idea that all are equal before the Divine Grace and none can be deprived of loving and worshipping God, which was of great attraction to the low castes and outcast population have all contributed to the spiritual development of Indian society and culture.

The Conflicting Nature of two Cultures and Conciliatory efforts for fusion

'For twelve long centuries,' comments Murray Titus, 'Islam has been in contact with Hinduism in India. The history of medieval and modern India is to a very considerable extent a history of Hindu–Muslim religio-cultural tensions, interspersed with movements or individual efforts at understanding, harmony and even composite development'. As a religio-cultural force, Islam is in most respects the 'very antithesis of Hinduism'. Hinduism is a large aggregate of belief, developed in the course of many centuries, evolving from the sacrificial hymns of the *Vedas* to the philosophical speculation of the *Upanishads*, the discipline of Yoga, the metaphysical subtleties of *Vedanta* and the passionate devotion of Bhakti. Islam, on the other hand, is bound by an austere central discipline, revolving round the *Quran*, and whatever speculation it has evolved or borrowed from external sources has been more or less adjusted to these two primary sources of religious authority. Psychologically, Hinduism tends to be melancholy, sentimental and philosophical; Islam tends to be ardent and austere.[6] Hindu genius flowers in the concrete and the iconographic; the Muslim mind is on the whole atomistic, abstract, geometrical and iconoclastic.

Islamic civilisation in its Arab, Persian and Turkish varieties, had developed in geographical environments very different from the sub-tropical forests of India, teeming with life, and fertility exposed to the mortal challenges of nature's exuberance, which affixed their stamp upon the Hindu mind and shaped the course of much of Hindu religion and mysticism. Islam in India continued to retain throughout the centuries, despite secondary Indian environmental and ethnic influences, its original foreign character. The Indian Muslim remained, as Jadunath Sarkar has put it, on the whole 'an intellectual exotic' who felt that 'he was in India, but not of it'.[7] Nostalgically he preserved as much of the original intellectual and psychological heritage of the original form of his culture as he could. Sociologically he considered himself as belonging to the Muslim umma, the great Muslim community which extended far beyond the Indian frontiers. He was a member simply by virtue of being a Muslim. It remained for him the main unifying religio-political factor amidst the diversity of the Muslim peoples.

The exclusiveness of the umma has been partly religious and partly instinctive. The instinct of self-preservation has been channelled in the Muslim umma through the principle known as *ijma*, the consensus of the community, which is not a counting of votes, but a slowly accumulating pressure of opinion over a long period of time.

The non-proselytising and non-egalitarian resilience of Hinduism, could, on the other hand, 'suck in' and assimilate other faiths absorbing them into its own ever-growing, ever-changing spiritual complex, and fitting the former adherents of other faiths into its caste structure. 'Hinduism,' observes Basham, 'can absorb new ideas, and can even if need be find room for new gods; moreover, every passage in the Hindu sacred texts is open to figurative interpretation, so that it is possible for different schools of Hinduism to hold diametrically opposed doctrines without serious antagonism. Islam on the other hand cannot adapt or compromise.'[9] Hinduism succeeded in India in re-assimilating the seceding Buddhist religion, and quickly absorbed into its own ranks the Greeks, the Sakas, the Kushanas and the Huns who invaded the subcontinent from time to time. Islam alone, rigidly monotheistic, iconoclastic and religio-culturally insular, resisted Hinduism's assimilative pull.

The Hindu has been a spiritual anarchist,[10] his faith being intensely personal and individualistic. Inherently the trend of Brahmanical Hinduism has been to accept all worship and to reject none, to bridge the gap between popular fetishism and learned Vedantism, to ensure that the superstitious cults of the illiterate masses remain in at least oblique touch with the metaphysical speculation of the higher intellectual order, and thus to crystallise an ascending hierarchy of religious faith corresponding to the socio-economic scale of caste-structure. This spiritually and materially hierarchical view of religion and society is diametrically opposed to the religio-social egalitarianism in Islam.

In the long history of Hindu–Muslim co-existence in India, 'the principle of repulsion has been more obviously at work than the principle of attraction'. Even Tarachand, a passionate advocate of the theory of composite growth of Hindu–Muslim culture, has to concede: 'While the Hindu mind was primarily concerned with what is true, the Moslem was exercised over what is right. The Hindu emphasised the private and personal aspect of religious experience, the Moslem its incorporation in the collective body of the faithful. The Hindu was inclined to gloss over the short-comings of his social customs, the Moslem was annoyed with them. On the other hand, the intolerance of the Moslem and the memory of the past distressed the Hindu. The Hindu felt no kinship with the Arab past which the Moslem hugged to his bosom. The Moslem did not feel at home in Vedic India. While consciousness of group developed, and the element of territoriality was prominent in both, the content of the two did not quite coincide and fuse. The mutual interaction of the two communities and the mutual influences in manners, ceremonies, superstition, mysticism and a common economic life "touched merely the fringe and the external element" of their existence; neither the Hindus nor the Muslims imbibed, even to the least degree, the chief characteristic features of the other's culture which may be regarded as their greatest contribution to human civilization'; and in the set pattern of their respective behaviour in India, 'the Hindus combined catholicity in religious outlook with bigotry in social ethics, while the Muslims displayed an equal bigotry in religious ideas with catholicity in social behaviour.'[11]

The Processes of Muslim Arrival

The Muslims arrived in India in three distinct movements: first as traders and missionaries to India's southern coasts; then in the expanding wave of the Umayyad conquests which carried them to the Rhone, the Syr Darya and the Indus; and finally like the Greeks, the Sakas and the Huns, in a more organised-cum-immigration movement of the Central Asian Turks and Afghans.

Muslim Arabs arrived on India's coast in the wake of their pagan ancestors who had carried on a tradition of maritime trade across the Arabian Sea since nearly the dawn of history. With the establishment of Muslim rule in India, the ruling elite conceived its population as a pluralistic society in which the non-Muslim was distinct from the Muslim and required a different social contract.

Theoretically the justification for the Turco–Afghan conquest of India was *Jihad*, religious war against the infidels. Had India been under Muslim rule the justification, as indeed in the later Muslim invasions, would have been punishment for the sin of pride or treachery. But the theory of *jihad* could very well be exploited for military and political expansion, though its motivating forces must have been originally economic. *Jihad* had a meaning and a significance in the medieval Islam very different from its original conception in Quranic revelation.[12]

'It is doubtful if any one of these invasions extending over about eight or nine hundred years was a purely religious invasion undertaken by religious fanatics enthusiasts for spreading Islam. Like all conquests they were actuated by temporal and material motives rather than by religious zeal.'[13]

For several centuries, except for the pagan Turks who were in any case accepting Islam in increasing numbers, the main adversaries of Dar al-Islam on all fronts were the Christian 'people of the Book' who were not 'infidels'. Mahmud of Ghanza's invasion of what was regarded as pagan India was therefore a sensational novelty at the end of the tenth century. The sacritege of Somnath and the destruction of its temple came to be considered a specially pious exploit because of its analogy in the past with the destruction of idols of the pagan Arabia by the Prophet. This led to invention of popular legends, giving Mahmud's invasions a status of sanctity; and it explains the idealisation of Mahmud by Nizam al-Mulk Tusi, and the ideal treatment he has received from early Sufi poets like Sanai and Attar, not to mention such collectors of anecdotes as Awfi.

After the conquest of India by Muhammad ibn Sam Ghuri in the twelfth century, one finds a fixed formula of casus belli which holds good until the end of the seventeenth century. Muslim invaders or Muslim rulers in India, if they are engaged in hostilities against a Muslim kingdom, justify their aggression by asserting either their right to the contested territory or the treachery or inefficiency of the invaded Muslim ruler. But if the invasion is against a Hindu kingdom no such moral self-justification is considered necessary. *Jihad* is considered to be justification enough and is immediately blessed by countries, ulama and the intelligentsia, as it brings to them greater opportunities of career, wealth and advancement. The lip-service to *jihad* is occasionally accompanied by a minor demonstration such as the destruction of a temple, the panegyric of the court-poet or the compliment of the court-historian; but once the territory is conquered and incorporated as a Muslim province or protectorate, a tolerant and pragmatic co-existence develops.

Jaziya (poll-tax payable by non-Muslims and guaranteeing in turn the protection of their lives, rights and property) was levied for the first time in India by Mohammad-bin-Qasim, and graded into three categories according to income; Brahmans were exempted from it and appointed tax-collectors, whose advice to their flock was either to submit to the Muslim law of administration and pay the poll-tax or else to migrate elsewhere in Hindu India.

In the Delhi Sultanate, the policy regarding the levy of *jaziya* varied from sultan to sultan. 'Ala-ud-din Khilji substituted the levy of *jaziya* by a policy of taxation on land produce and livestock to control the economic prosperity of the Hindus as their increasing wealth 'fostered disaffection and rebellion'. *Ghiyas-ud-din Tughluq,* on the other hand followed a more balanced policy of taxation, the object of which was neither to allow the accumulation of wealth in the hands of the Hindus nor to reduce them to poverty and destitution which would cause loss of revenue to the state. The imposition of *jaziya* in strict accordance with the Muslim canon law by Firoz Tughluq is a distinct departure from the normal policy of the Sultanate; though on the other hand he abolished all those taxes which were not specifically sanctioned by the canon law, and levied only four legal taxes : *kharaj, zakat, jaziya,* and *khums* or one-fifth of the total spoils of war or produce of the mines. The remarkable feature of Firuz Tughluq's policy was its imposition on Brahmans, who should have been exempted according to the classical Muslim theory but whom he regarded as holding 'the keys to the chamber of idolatry'.

Akbar's abolition of *jaziya* was in consonance with his general policy of liberalism and of legal equality of all citizens, but it is quite possible that his decision may have been confirmed by such scholars of Muslim law of Fathullah Shirazi and others who must have been familiar with precedents in Islamic history and jurisprudence with causes where *jaziya* had been waived in the case of participation of non-Muslim communities in the Muslim state's military or civil services. This seems to have been the main reason for its continued suspension under Jahangir and Shah Jahan, when Islam had reasserted itself as the state religion. This again seems to explain the discontent that followed Aurangzeb's re-imposition of it; for by that time as it would appear from the letter of a Hindu noble, probably Shivaji, that not only the Muslim, but even the Hindu elite was well aware that *jaziya* was in any case not payable until the *dhimmis* could be fully protected by the Muslim state : 'In strict justice by jaziya is not at all lawful. From the point of view of administration it can be right only if a beautiful woman wearing gold ornaments can pass from one part of the country to another without fear or molestation'.

It is interesting that in some particular cases, the institution of *jaziya* inspired some Hindu rulers to impose upon Muslims a similar discriminatory tax, *Turushkadand* (fine on Muslims) which was a kind of counter-*jaziya*. It will also be interesting to trace how far the Maratha institution of *chauth* or the extortion of one-fourth of the gross revenue of a vanquished Muslim (or by analogy non-Muslim) province or state was on exaggerated reflection of the aggressive reaction to the former Muslim institution of *jaziya*. The pilgrimage tax collected by some Muslim rulers in India from the Hindus had no sanction in the Muslim canon law.

Conversion and Apostasy

Unlike Brahmanical Hinduism, and like Christianity, Islam is a proselytising religion, although Quranic injunctions discourage forcible conversion. The injunction that proselytisation has to be conducted by persuasion and preaching and not by force is stressed in several 'Meccan' verses. The underlying emphasis behind this tolerance is the Quranic concept of the equal power of God over good and evil; it is by His will that evil and unbelief exist as the antithesis of goodness and faith. The same position is reiterated in the *'Medina' suras* after Islam had acquired more material power; and the epitome of the Quranic approach is the oft-quoted verse: 'Let there be no compulsion in religion'.

In the conversion of large masses of Indians to Islam the use of force was the exception rather than the rule. The conversion to Islam of over one-fourth of the *subcontinent*'s population is due to a number of causes. To begin with, Islam spread more rapidly in those areas where Buddhism had lingered until the time of its arrival, as in some north-western and eastern parts of the peninsula. On the Indian coasts proselytisation by Muslim traders and settlers was not regarded as a serious challenge by the Hindu rajas, who imposed no restrictions on conversions to Islam which were in those areas, in any case, on a minor scale. Brahmanical Hinduism offered a much more solid resistance to the spread of Islam, but its Achilles' heel was the caste system. For the lower Hindu castes acceptance of Islam meant an escape from the degraded status they had in the Hindu society to at least theoretical equality with the ruling community; it also meant in the pre-Mughal India better chances of state appointment.

Inter-marriages with Hindu women began with the Arab occupation of Sind as no Muslim women had accompanied the army of Muhammad-bin-Qasim. The practice in India of the Arabs, Turks, Persians, and Afghans of marrying Hindu women was in line with the general Muslim practice elsewhere. Such marriages took place in all classes of society. While through Hindu wives or concubines Hindu influences and customs crept into Indian Islam, Islam itself penetrated into the families of these women.

The Muslim rulers, on the whole, partly for reasons of policy and partly from genuine tolerance, adopted a general attitude of neutrality to the problem of conversion; though some of them exercised political persuasion from time to time, such as the promise of immunity if an adversary at bay accepted Islam. Muhammad-bin-Tughluq, though strongly opposed to forced conversions, considered the peaceful propagation of Islam by the Sufis as a more meritorious virtue than their esoteric concentration on the spiritual advancement of individual human souls. Firoz Tughluq was one of the very few Muslim rulers who showed any enthusiasm for proselytising. He declared: 'I encouraged my infidel subjects to embrace the religion of the Prophet, and I proclaimed that everyone who repeated the creed and became a Musulman should be exempt from the *jaziya'*.... Information of this came to the ears of the people at large, and great numbers of Hindus presented themselves, and were admitted to the honour of Islam. Patronage to the converts to Islam was extended by Sikandar Lodi. Aurangzeb's policy was to offer them rewards or prospects of service, a policy which was contrary to that of Akbar who had granted equality of the right of conversion or reconversion to Hindus as well, but not very different from that of Jahangir, who was opposed to forcible conversion but encouraged peaceful encouragement of converts.

Summing up, in India as in the rest of the world, it is not in the cruelties of the persecutor or the fury of the fanatic that we should look for evidence of the missionary spirit of Islam, any more than in the exploits of that mythical personage, the Muslim warrior with sword in one hand and Quran in the other—but in the quiet, unobtrusive labours of the preacher and the trader.[14]

Among the preachers of Islam in India the Sufi training was more ascetic was closer to the masses of the people than the theologian, who was generally a fanatic and lacked character and spiritual sensitiveness. In city, town and village the Sufi formed himself into a pivot of an inner circle of Muslim disciples and an outer circle of non-Muslims, mainly low-caste Hindus, whom he attracted by his spirituality and humanity. The outer circle was gradually sucked into Islam by an indirect rather than a direct appeal which began with the non-Muslim's admiration for the individual Sufi, and continued through his observation of Muslim egalitarianism in the inner circle. The exoteric conversion often followed the esoteric. There was a cross-section of Hindus converted to Islam by the Sufis, who did not practise their new religion openly because of the fear of caste or social ostracism in their original environment on which they were economically dependent.

REFERENCES AND NOTES

1. Tarachand, Dr. *Influence of Islam on Indian Culture*, pp. 3-4.
2. Ibid., p.5.
3. Ibid., p.21.
4. —
5. Ibid., p.34.
6. Thomas, F.W. *Mutual Influence of Muhammadans and Hindus in India*. Cambridge University, 1892 : p.12.
7. Sarkar, Jadunath. *A History of Aurangzeb*. Calcutta, pp.487–8.
8. Gible, H.R.A. *Modern Trends in Islam*. Chicago, 1945 : p.11.
9. Basham, A.L. *The Indian Sub-continent in Historical Perspective*. London, 1958.
10. Tarachand, Dr. *Influence of Islam on Indian Culture*. Allahabad, 1936: p.234.
11. Majumdar, R.C. *The History and Culture of the Indian People*. Bombay, 1960 : pp. 616–617.
12. Arnold, T.W. *The Preaching of Islam*. London, pp. 347–352.
13. Prasad, Rajendra. *India Divided*. Bombay, 1946 : p.69.
14. Arnold, T.W. *The Preaching of Islam*. London, p.4.

3

In Search of Equivalence : Interaction between Sufism and Hinduism

Sufism before its arrival in India

Sufism is a complex phenomenon; it is like a stream which gathers volume by the joining of tributaries from many lands. Its original source is the Quran and the life of Prophet Muhammad. Christianity and new-Platonism added a large contribution to it. Hinduism and Buddhism supplied a number of ideas, and the religions of ancient Persia, Zorastrianism, Jainism etc. brought to it their share.

Prophet Muhammad was a mystic, and the mystical note sound clearly in the utterances of the Quran. They teach absolute dependence and renunciation. God is spoken of as the light of the heavens and earth. God says concerning the believers, 'He loves them and they love Him' and therefore He bears the beautiful name of lover (*wudud*). Again, the Quran says, 'Those who walk meekly on the earth, and when the ignorant speak to them answer, 'Peace shall be rewarded with the highest place in Paradise'. Then from the earliest times there were among the Muslim devotees who were continually engaged in reading the Quran, and the penitens (*Bakkaun*) who kept fasts and made orisons. These ascetics developed the ordinary rites by works of supererogation, their prayers were more numerous and more highly spiritualised, their fasts more continuous and severe. Naturally their ethics and mode of living were held as examples of saintly life, and their services utilised in the roles of preachers, arbiters ambassadors and leaders.[1]

In the third century of the Hijra (ninth century A.D.), Islamic civilisation, its theology, philosophy and science came deeply under Hellenistic influence. The Arab absorption of Aristotelianism was channelled through the neo-Platonic commentaries of Porphyry and Proclus. The neo-Platonic influence quickened the Christian and the Islamic mystical systems in an identical manner. About A.D. 850 (Pseudo) all Muslim speculative systems which were influenced by Greek philosophy reacted powerfully to Sufism; such as those of the Murjites who set faith above work and emphasised Divine love, the Qadarites who affirmed and Jabrites who denied that men are responsible for their actions, the Mutazilites who built a theological system on the basis of reason, and the Asharites who formulated the metaphysical and doctrinal systems that underline the creed of orthodox Islam.

When the Muslims came into contact with the Christians, these tendencies were accentuated—in liturgical matters, meditation and repetition of God's name and prayer (*dhikr*); and in ethical, complete detachment from the affairs of personal interest, utter dependence upon God (*tawakkul*), rejection of material goods (*fuqr*), indifference towards suffering or sickness, praise or blame.

The ninth century A.D. also marks the strong impress of Christian mysticism on Sufism. Ascetic and quietistic trends of early Sufism were bound to accept and accentuate similar Christian elements as it came in contact with Christian mystical doctrines in North Africa and Syria.

Contact with Christianity, rather than with Hinduism or Buddhism, led Sufism from the ninth to the twelfth century in the direction of analytical emphasis on asceticism–an emphasis which begins with Dhu'l Nun and culminates in Ibn al-Arabi (1164–1240). Ascetic solitude was stressed by Dhu'l Nun. Hunger as an element of ascetic discipline was traced by Nizam al-din Awhya to an (apocryphal) remark of Jesus. Ibn al-Arabi bases the structure of Sufi hierarchy on four elements of aceticism: first, which is of two kinds, silence of the tongue and of the heart, and which leads to the gnosis of God; second, solitude *(al-uzlah)* which ensures the silence of the tongue and leads to the knowledge of the world; third; hunger *(al-ju)* which leads to the knowledge of the real nature of Satan; and fourth, wakefulness *(al-sahar)* which can be of the eye or of the heart and which leads to the knowledge of the soul. Much of Ibn al-Arabi's syncretism is of Christian origin, gathered during his travels to and fro between Spain and North Africa and his contacts with Spanish, Byzantine, and Syrian Christian mysticism.

The neo-Platonists strengthened the feeling of contempt for the world and supported the leanings towards divine life by their doctrines of emanation and of dynamic pantheism. The neo-Platonic ideas passed into Islam when, in the beginning of the ninth century, Greek words were translated into Arabic.

The third foreign source of Muslim mystics was Indian. It stands to reason that if things of material use like Indian steel and sword, and Indian gold and precious stones, and if things of artistic value like the pointed arch and the bulbous dome, reached Persia and Iraq, Indian philosophical ideas should have travelled there also. Many Indians held posts in the financial department at Basra under the early Umayyads. Caliph Muawiya is reported to have planted a colony of them in Syria.

Then the Arabs familiarised themselves from early times with Indian literature and sciences. They translated Buddhist works in the second century of the Hijra, for instance, *Kitabal-Bud*, and *Bilawhar wa Budasif*; treatises on astronomy and medicine called Sindhind (*Siddhanta*) and *Shushrud (Susruta).* They were exceedingly keen on informing themselves of the customs, manners, science and religions of the people with whom they came into contact. Al-Kindi wrote a book on Indian religions. Al-Ashari, Al-Biruni Shahrastani and many others devoted chapters in their books to the descriation and discussion Indian religious and philosophic systems.

Sufism seems to have come into contact with Hindu and Buddhist mystical ideas at a later stage, and after most of its principal features had been developed either in its original Islamic tradition or by the infiltration of neo-Platonic and

Christian elements. Early translation from Sanskrit into Arabic under the Abbasids do not seem to have included any works of Hindu mysticism. The earliest contacts between Sufism and Buddhism took place in the north-west Persian and Central Asian marches of the Caliphate. Analogies can be done between the 'noble path' of the Buddhists and mystic path *(tarka)* of the Sufis, between the Sufi concentration *(muraqaba)* and the Buddhist *dhyana*. The Sufi robe, regarded by the Sufis themselves as a heritage from the practice of the Prophet, is regarded by Goldziher as a borrowing of Buddhist and by Nicholson of Christian origin. Goldziher also regards the Sufi interpretation of Divine Unity (*tawhid*) as fundamentally different from the Islamic monotheistic conception of God, and as borrowed from Indian theosophy.

The conceptions of Divine Unity and *fana* (annihilation), which inexplicably appear first in the utterances of Abu Yazid of Bistam, a mystic of heterodox views and of Zoroastrian ancestry, have been explained as of Upanishadic and Vedantic origin.

The doctrine of *fana* (annihilation), even if derived from Indo–Buddhist sources, cannot be completely identified with *nirvana*. Both terms imply the passing away of individuality, but while *nirvana* is purely negative, *fana* is accompanied by *baqa*, ever-lasting life in God. The rapture of the Sufi who has lost himself in ecstatic contemplation of divine beauty is entirely opposed to the passionless serenity of the *Arahat*.

The legend of Buddha entered Muslim literature as a type of saintly man, and Muslim hagiologists assimilated the stories of Ibn Adham to the Buddhist legend. No wonder then that the conception of *nirvana*, the discipline of the eightfold path, the practice of yoga and the acquaintance of miraculous powers were appropriated in Islam under the name of *fana, tariqa* or *suluk, maraqabah* and *karamat* or *mujjza*.

Two periods may be distinguished in the history of Sufism: the first from the earliest times to the beginning of the ninth century, and the second from the ninth century onwards. During the first period, Sufism was merely tendencious and possessed no system; during the second, it developed metaphysical systems and the organisation of monastic orders. The name Sufi was first applied to Abu Hashim of Kufa who died in A.D. 778. But the Sufi writers among the early mystics were Imam Jafar Sadiq, Hasan al Basri, Ibrahim ibn Adham (d. A.D. 777), Rabia, al Adawiya, and Habib Ajmi.

The chief characteristic of their belief was the submission of the human will to God. They were seekers more of piety and other worldliness than of divine knowledge, with an exaggerated consciousness of sin and an overwhelming dread of divine retribution, yet they had early developed emotional and ecstatic features and negated the externalia of religion.

Among Rabia al Adawiya's sayings there are many which show emotional tendencies. She is reported to have said that the love of God had so taken possession of her soul that there was no room left even for the love of the Prophet, much less of hatred for the devil. The fear of death and of the day of judgment was expressed in many ways. Rabia says, 'O my soul! How long wilt thou sleep to rise no more, till the call shall summon thee on the day of resurrection'.

The second period of Sufism began in the ninth century. The calm monotheistic question of the first, having absorbed Shiah theories and foreign notions, blossomed in a surprisingly short time into full-fledged pantheistic mysticism. The Sufis of the period fall into several groups, men of similar temperaments clustering together around some pious leaders. These groups eventually evolved several orders and different systems, according to the differences of emphasis on particular doctrines, details or organisation, and philosophical schemes.

The man who produced the greatest stir in the Islamic world by his boldness of his doctrines was Husain bin Mansur al Hallaj. His theories were later explained in the systems of Ibn al Arabi and Abdul Karim Jili and in the poetry of Ibn al Faridh and Abu Said Ibn Abul Khair and their influence spread to far-off countries including India. The story of Mansur's life is well known. He started his career as an ordinary Sufi under the guidance of such well-known shaikhs (preceptors) as Tushtari and Junaid. But afterwards he threw away the Sufi garments and put on worldly clothes. He began to preach as an apostle of

God and offended the Jurists—for apostleship was a breach of traditions—and the government, because, it savoured of Shiah legitimism. He travelled to many lands, among them India, and visited Mecca thrice. At last his activities became so obnoxious that he was arrested. He was kept in prison for a long time, tortured and finally executed in A.D. 922. As saints used the language of Muslim Sufism, it is necessary to briefly explain Mansur's mystical system, for his terms became the current coinage of Sufism.[2]

Mansur conceived of the revelation of God with man as the infusion of the divine into the human soul; in Hindu terms, the illumination where 'I become that which I love, and that which I love becomes mine. We are two spirits, infused in one body, to see me is to see Him, to see Him is to see us.' Apparently Mansur was not a thorough-going monist in spite of his declaration, 'I am God', *(anal Haq),* for, according to him there was still some difference of level or potential between the Absolute and His image.

There were many schools of mystic speculation, but two are of special importance: those who regard the ultimate reality as light *(nur)* and those who regard it as thought. The chief exponent of the first was Shaikh Shahab-Uddin Suhrawardi (d. 1209), and of the second Ibn al-Arabi (d. 1241). Shaikh Shahab-Uddin was denounced by the Qazis and executed by the order of Saladin. He wrote a number of works on what is called *Hikmat al Ishraq* (illuminative philosophy). In his philosophy the ultimate principle of all existence is Light *(Nur-i-Qahir),* whose essential nature consists in perpetual illumination. The light is self-existent, self-manifesting, indefinable.

The human soul is the highest dwelling place of the abstract illumination, which enters the body of man (which is not composed of light) through the medium of the animal soul which is midway between not-light and light. The human soul longs for greater and greater illumination in order to gain complete freedom from the world of form or not-light, this is realised through knowledge and action.

The Sufi concept of 'peace with all' *(sulh-i kul)* which is a dominant feature of the Indian Sufism of the later seventeenth and eighteenth century seems to have been borrowed much earlier from Mahayana Buddhism rather than directly from Yogic Hinduism. Some of the *ziyarats* or tombs or relics of the Sufis in Central Asia are situated on the ruins of Buddhist stupas. Some of the old popular Buddhist beliefs and cults seem to have lingered in Transoxian Islam.

The Naqsdbandi order's practice of *tasawwur-i shayikh,* or concentration on the mental image of the preceptor in the early stages of the initiate's education, seems also to have been a borrowing from Buddhism, traceable ultimately to post-Vedic substitution-meditation in early Hinduism. Balk, which had been a Buddhist monastic centre in Central Asia, later became the home of a number of eminent Sufis. The use of the rosary is either a Christian or an Indo-Buddhist borrowing. On a higher plane, Buddhist ascetic meditation and intellectual abstraction left their mark on Sufism. But, as Nicholson reminds us, the features which the two systems have in common only accentuate the fundamental difference between them. In spirit they are poles apart. The Buddhist moralises himself; the Sufi becomes moral only through knowing and loving God.

In addition to the actual elements of borrowing from Indian sources into Sufism, there are parallelisms in the two mystical systems which might have been connected, partly connected or unconnected. Al-Biruni noticed the identity of the views of the Hindus, the Greeks and the Muslim Sufis on the 'first causes' pantheistic trends in heterodox Sufism which resembled similar Hindu trends, and the doctrine of metempsychosis as believed in by the Sufis. He points out resemblances between the views expressed in Samkhya and those of the Sufis regarding their allegorical concept of paradise.

Ibn al Arabi (d. 1241) is one of the greatest authorities on Sufi philosophy. He regarded both nature and man as mirrors which displayed God himself. 'God manifiests Himself in every atom of creation; He is revealed in every intelligible object and concealed from every intelligence except the intelligence of those who say that the universe is His form inasmuch as He stands in the same relation to phenomenal objects as the spirit to the body'. Regarding the relation of God and man he says, 'man is the form of God, and God is the spirit of man'. By means of man God beholds the objects which He has created.

One is struck by the apparently unconnected resemblances in such animistic remarks of Ibn al-Arabi as when he regards every worshipped object as a manifestation of God, in spite of its name of a stone or a tree or an animal or a man or an angel and the underlying essence of Hindu polytheism, or Ibn al-Arbi's symbolisation of sexual and profane love as a stage leading towards love divine, and the same philosophical concept underlying the practices of Hindu Krishna and Shakti cults, which derive from such scriptural premises as the Upanishadic comparison of the bliss of Brahman with unconscious sleep in the arms of a beloved woman.

Apparently unconnected parallels of the doctrines of the *Upanishads* are found in al-Ghazzali's distinction between the worldly and the spiritual, in al-Hujwiri's differentiation between human and divine knowledge, and the doctrine of the descent of the Absolute *(tanzil)* found in some Sufis. Madhva developed in Hindu mysticism a doctrine of phenomenological monism which has striking resemblances with the development of the same doctrine in Indian Sufism in the seventeenth century by Shaikh Ahmad Sirhindi by a process of semi-theological dialectics, apparently without any influence, or even knowledge of the similar speculations of Madhva. In fact the resemblance between the two ends with Madhva's denial that God is the material cause of the world.

Equally striking is the running parallelism between the 'lexique technique' of Hindu and Muslim mysticism, which tempted Dara Shikoh to confound one with the other. In both mystical systems, monism has a similar conceptual terminology; the Reality is Absolute *(mutlaq; param)*, truth of truths *(haqiqat al-haqa'iq; satyasya satyam)* and so on.

On the other hand, there are elements in Hindu religion and in various schools of Hindu mysticism which are the very antithesis of Sufism which is, after all, firmly rooted in Islam. Among such Hindu concepts is the very position of the *Vedas*, a conception of commands, categorical in nature and external in character without the least suggestion of any commander, or the sacrificial nature of Vedic hymns. The Upanishadic quest of the self is fundamentally different from the quest of God of the theistic Sufi. The stress in the *Bhagavad Gita* and by its commentators of different schools on the performance of alloted caste duties, its affirmation of the doctrine of *karma*, and its anthropomorphic belief in the birth of God as man are all opposed to the main trend of Sufism in Islam. Alien to it also are such elements as Ramanuja's view that Isvara grants emancipation from worldly bonds to those who acquire the true knowledge from the study of Hindu scriptures *(sastras)*, or his view that Isvara cannot be proved by inference, but is to be admitted on the authority of sacred Hindu texts, or his acceptance of the Hindu scriptural authority on the division of human society into castes. The doctrine of *karma*, which dominates the entire Hindu mysticism, is even in its Bhakti form in Ramanuja and Nimbarka, the very opposite of the Sufi world view.

Attainment of the knowledge of God was the only end of man, for complete union with Him was not possible as long as the body lasted. The knowledge is gained by faith and contemplation, in which human reason divests itself of its discursive or reflective faculty. The end of knowledge is transcendental consciousness, where the phenomenal vanishes in the presence of the eternal.

The practical inference from this pantheism was that God could be worshipped in innumerable ways, and that all religions obtained truth. For if all things are a manifestation of the Divine substance, God may be worshipped in a star or calf or any other object, and consequently there should be complete tolerance towards all creeds. He says, 'every one praises what he believes, his God is his own creature, and in praising it he praises himself'.

About a century and a half later than Ibn al Arabi lived Abdul Karim al Jili, who wrote a commentary on his predecessor's work, *Futuhat-al-Makkiyah* and an independent treatise on Sufism called 'The Perfect Man' *(Insan al Kamil)*. Jili was an ideal monist. For him all beliefs were thoughts about one reality, and all modes of worship expressive of some aspect of that reality. The differences were due to the variety of names and attributes and all together contributed to the perfection of the whole. Jili was acquainted with the Hindu religion for among the ten principal sects he noted the Brahimna (Brahman). About them he says that they worship God in His absolute aspect. The scriptures of the Brahimna, according to him, were revealed to them not by God but by Abraham (Brahma); they contained five books, the fifth on account of its profoundity was unknown to most of the Brahmans, but those who read it invariably became Moslems. Apparently Jili's fifth book is the *Vedanta,* whose monistic philosophy in the eyes of Jili made it indistinguishable from Islam.

Theoretical Sufism had reached the highest point of its growth; the writers of subsequent times wrote text books for students and popular treatise without adding much of original value. Of these Jami's *Lawaih* in Persian is the best summary of Sufi philosophy and deservingly attained the widest repute. Arabic and Persian poets, who became increasingly imbued with Sufism made it more than the philosophers the religion of the high and the low. Farid ud-Din Attar, Jalal-ud-Din Rumi and Shabistari (d. 1317 or 1320) give the best exposition of Sufi doctrines.

In so far as Sufism is concerned, even if the theory of Abu Yazid's conscious or unconscious assimilation of Upanishadic ideas is accepted, these ideas were completely re-interpreted, explained or reconciled to Islamic orthodoxy by Junayd Baghdadi.

The Islamic principle of Divine Unity was firmly re-emphasised in Sufism in the twelfth century by al-Ghazzali, Abd al-Qadir Jilani and Shihab al-din Suhrawardi. Even earlier, the doctrine of *fana,* which was so close to *Vedanta* in Abu Yazid, had been revolutionised by Junayd for whom it did not mean total extinction but a new life, not indeed as God, but in and through God; *fana* being the death in one's self to live in God. The integration of Sufism with orthodoxy was established by al-Ghazzali's recognition of mystic experience as a valid, even superior proof of the existence of God. A further reconciliation of Sufism with formal Islam was achieved in the doctrines of al-Hallaj, Ibn al-Arabi and Abd al-Karim al-Jili, identifying the pre-eternal essence of Muhammad *(al-haqiqat al-Muhammadiyyah)* with the 'First Intelligence of the Philosophers'.

In India, because of the challenge and the risk of disintegration into Hindu mysticism, Sufism took special care to resolve its differences with orthodoxy. In Islamic religious history the tension between the religious assertion of the transcendence of God and the mystical aspiration for His immanence was perhaps nowhere more thoroughly resolved to a middle of the road position than in India where Islam was propagated mainly by Sufis with a firm emphasis on the observance of the tenets of the sharia.

The integration of religious law and mysticism in India dates back to the advent of Sufism itself in the subcontinent in the eleventh century. Al-Huiwiri equates the three categories of spiritual (esoteric) knowledge, that of the essence and unity of God, of the attributes of God, and of the actions and wisdom of God, with the three categories of the knowledge of the *shari'a*, the *Quran*, the *sunnah* and the *ijma* (consensus).

The Sufi orders that transplanted their hospices in India in the wake of the Ghurid conquest continued the principle of the same close correspondence between the esoteric and exoteric elements of religious life. In the Suhrawardiyah order the surest means of approach to the unique Being of God is the prescribed prayer *(salat)* which unites the created with the Creator. This order believes in the same doctrine of legal purity as that enjoined in the orthodox Islam. And Muhammad is considered as the sum total of all the requirements of exoteric as well as esoteric disciplines.

The relationship between Sufism and Hindu mysticism is multi-positional and ranges from polemical hostility through missionary zeal to tolerant co-existence. In Indian Sufism, anti-Hindu polemics began with Mu in al-din Chishti. Early Sufis in the Punjab and early chishtis devoted themselves to the task of conversion on a large scale. Missionary activity slowed down under Nizam al-din Auliya, not because of any new concept of eclecticism, but because he held that the Hindus were generally excluded from grace and could not be easily converted to Islam, unless they had the opportunity to be in the company of a Muslim saint from some considerable time.

In the performance of miracle, the Sufi hagiographical tradition records cases of competitive spirituality with Hindu yogis. Miracles like flying in the air in competition with a Hindu yogi were attributed to Safi al-din Kaziruni. Miracles of proselytisation were credited to Jalal al-din Bukhari and contests of spiritual strength between Sufis like Muhammadi Bilgrami and Hindu yogis were recorded as late as the eighteenth century.

On the other hand, as missionaries of Islam and as liberal leaders of its spirituality, the Sufis were the first among the Muslim intellectual elite to come in contact with the Hindu masses, and thus indirectly with individual features of Hindu mysticism, especially the yoga. Sayyid Husain Khangsawar, a disciple of Muin al-din Chishti is one of the early Sufis who came to be venerated by some Hindus. Yogis seen to have been attracted to the hospice of Farid al-din Ganj-i shakar, where Nizam al-din Auliya met one of them and was impressed by his classification of human body in two parts, the upper the seat of the spiritual, the lower that of the profane aspect of human nature, and by the yogic principle that one was required to develop truth, benevolence and kindness in the upper part and preserve chastity and purity in the lower.

After Al-Biruni, the first translation of a work on Hindu mysticism by a Muslim, is that of *Amratkund*, by Rukn al-din Samarqandi, first into Arabic, then into Persian. The work is partly philosophic and partly magical. Planned translations of Hindu mystical classics did not begin however, before the reign of Akbar in the second half of the sixteenth century.

In the fourteenth century, at least one feature of the Hindu–Buddhist asceticism, that of wandering in the forests, accentuated the wanderlust of some Indian Sufis. The slightly heterodox Sufi, though an active missionary of Islam, Shara al-din Abu Ali (d. 1323) came to be designated a *qalandar* presumably because of his wanderings. Nasir al-din Chiragh of Delhi and his disciple Gesudaraz also began as wandering dervishes; the former was advised by his preceptor Nizam al-din Auliya to live a spiritual life in towns among people. The most striking case in this category is that of Sharf al-din Yahya Muniri who established the Firdawsiya order in India, which linked itself to the *silsilahs* going back to Junayd al-Baghdadi and Maruf al-Karkhi. He chose after his wanderings a location for his religious exercises close to a spring in Magadha, sacred to the Hindus and the Buddhists, which is now commonly known as Makhdum Kund. Saivism was brought into contact with the Naqshbandi order by Lalla the poetess (Lal Ded) of Kashmir in the fourteenth century. But in its later development in India in the sixteenth and seventeenth centuries Naqshbandi Sufism developed an attitude of uncompromising opposition of Hinduism, especially so in the teachings of Khwaja Baqi-billah and Shaikh Ahmad Sirhindi.

In the fourteenth and fifteenth centuries, as Sufism penetrated into the masses of converts and semi-converts from Hinduism, the Bhakti movement rose as a popular Hindu counter-challenge to the proselytising pull of Sufi humanism. About the same time a number of minor heterodox *(bi-shar)* sects came into being and gained some popular following, though their actual strength and their sphere of operations was very limited. These sects borrowed a number of tantric practices and popular superstitions from the lower forms of Hinduism. In this period heterodox Sufi qalandars from India introduced into other countries of Dar al-Islam the use of coffee, opium and hashish among the heterodox Sufi orders abroad.

The only orthodox Sufi order which seems to have borrowed in India elements directly from yoga, and possibly from other forms of Hindu mysticism was the Shattari, probably linked in its origin with the Bistami order. The followers of the Shattari order lived in forests like the yogis on a frugal diet of fruits and herbs, and subjected themselves to hard physical and spiritual exercises. This syncretic element is also discernible in its liturgical formulae. The Shattari method of *dhikr* (liturgical repetition of the names or attributes of God) implied complete solitude and cleanliness; it began with the Muslim attestation of faith *(kalima)*; but the various formulae of *dhikr* itself could be repeated in Arabic, Persian or Hindi. Some of the expressions of *dhikr* seem to have been borrowed directly from Hindu mysticism. For instance, the formula *ohihi* is reminiscent of the Upanishadic liturgy in which *ha-i* signifies wind, *i* fire, *u* sun, and *au-ho-i* all gods. The physical exercises of the order included and specifically mentioned yogic *asanas* and the *samadhi*. The Shattari mystic was enjoined to be secretive about his mystic practices to avoid the hostility of the theologians. The order gained some popularity in the Gwalior region, the home of its most famous representative Muhammad Ghauth, an ascetic held in esteem by Akbar in his youth. Muhammad Ghauth held Hindu mystics in veneration and his *Bahr al-hayat* is the first treatise written by a Muslim in India on the practices of the yogis.

From the fifteenth century onwards Sufis in India seem to have begun noticing a resemblance between Ibn al-Arabi's formulation of the doctrine of ontological monism and their second-hand information about the prevalence of similar doctrines in the *Vedanta*. But in the seventeenth century, despite the translations of Hindu classics of mysticism from Sanskrit under the patronage of Akbar and his successors, one does not find any cases of specific interest of Sufi orders, other than the Shattari, in either a serious or a superficial study of Hindu mystical doctrines. Apart from Kabir, the only Hindu saint who finds a mention in the Sufi hagiography of this period is Baba Kapur. In the middle of the seventeenth century the Muslim elite sometimes equated *Vedanta* vaguely with Sufism. The eclecticism of Dara Shikoh had behind it the tolerant permission of the official Qadiri order as represented by Shaikh Muhibb-Ullah Allahabadi, who stressed the view that the Prophet of Islam was a blessing for Muslims and non-Muslims alike. A late seventeenth-century Chishti mystic Kalim-Ultah held that mystic training could be given to a Hindu even before his conversion, to attract him to Islam.

All the major Sufi orders in India—the Chishti, the Qadiri and the Naqshbandi—show a similar approach to Hinduism, which begins with hostility, passes through a phase of co-existence and culminates in tolerance and understanding. The Qadiri became perhaps the most tolerant of these in the middle of the seventeenth century under the influence of Dara Shikoh and princess Jahan Ara. The Naqshbandi, so hostile to Hinduism and to any form of syncretism, became liberal in the eighteenth century in the attitude of the poet-saint Mirza Jan-i Janan (1699-1780) who regarded the *Vedas* as divinely inspired and the Hindus, who had their revealed scriptures and prophets like people of the Book as monotheists. In this context he even condoned idolatry among them as a means of concentration on God. Shah Waliullah and his successors including Sayyid Ahmad Barelvi accomplished the absorption of the much-weakened Sufi orders and thus their complete submergence in the orthodoxy, and though much of their reaching was concentrated at the elimination of syncretic borrowings from Hinduism, it is interesting that Wali Ullah's son and immediate successor Shah Abdul Aziz regarded Krishna among the *Auliya* (saints) because of the impact *Bhagavad Gita* made on his mind.

In the copious literature of Sufism all the stages, stations and states have been described with superabundant zest and consummate resourcefulness. The legends of saints overflow with stories illustrative of ascetic contemplative and unitive states, and the language of poetry and symbolism has been exhausted in giving expression to all the emotions—of fear, hope, longing and love—which the mystic experiences.

The Muslim mystic, who sets out upon the path of union *(wasl)* of absorption *(fana)* always needs a spiritual guide, for 'if a man has no teacher, his imam is Satan'. The *pir* or Shaikh is the pivot round which the whole machinery of Sufi monarchism moves. His authority is divine, for the Sufi preceptor has inherited the whole significance of Shiah Imam. In the order to which Sufi belongs he is sovereign. The order provides the companionship of saints which is necessary for spiritual welfare, the Shaikh regulates the conduct of the companions and watches over their spiritual progress. He is a saint who has completed the journey and reached his goal. He has become one with God and therefore his position and status are divine.

The disciple is advised to keep his *murshid* constantly in mind, to become mentally absorbed in him through constant meditation and contemplation of him, to see him in all men and in all things, and to annihilate his self in the *murshid*. From this state of self-absorption in the *murshid*, the master leads him on through several stages at last to absorption in the Deity. Muhammad taught surrender to God (Islam), Sufism surrender to the teacher who is the representative of God upon earth.

The discipline of the seeker is *dhikr*, which ordinarily means remembering God and repeating His name, but which includes all the devotional practice which induce ecstasy and trance. The two kinds are *dhikr i jali* or reciting aloud, and *dhikr i khafi* or reciting mentally. They are very similar to the meditation and the breathing exercises (*pranayama*) of Indian yoga. Shibli pointedly brings out this feature of Sufism in his definition *Tasawwuf* (Sufism) is control of the faculties and observance of the breaths.

Another method of bringing about trance is by song and dance (*sama*). There has been much dispute among theologians as to the lawfulness of music and dancing regarded as religious exercises. Ghazali speaks of them as novelties which had not been received in Islam from the first followers of the Prophet, but which were therefore not forbidden. He himself approves of them for by their means the Sufis 'stir up in themselves greater love towards God, and by means of music, often obtain spiritual visions and ecstasies, their heart becoming in this condition as clean as silver in the flame of a furnace, and attaining a degree of purity which could never be'.

SUFISM IN INDIA

The growth of Sufism in early Islam was inspired by external influences as well as internal urges. Sufis were opposed to formal theologians as well as to the rationalists. The earliest of them aimed at emphasising the mystic elements in the life and teachings of the Prophet Muhammad. They preferred the alleged mystic or esoteric interpretation of the *Quran* to the literal and traced their spiritual descent back to Ali, the son-in-law and cousin of the Prophet. The earlier Sufis had among them both men and women. Hasan Basri, Rabia al-Adawiyah of Basra and Ibrahim. bin Adham belongs to that school of Sufis who attached importance to nothing but love of Almighty, resignation, piety and asceticism. Their teachings are overflowing with love of Eternal Truth, of Eternal Beauty and of Eternal Goodness. No submission to His Will could be interpreted as abject humiliation.[4]

The later Sufism with its endless range of emotional manifestations and imaginative attitudes could, however, not remain unaffected with the mystic and philosophical ideas of other religions and cultures. Spreading rapidly through Syria, Egypt, Mesopotamia and Iran, Sufism became imbued with Hellenistic religious philosophies, Buddhism and to a certain degree with *Vedanta*. By the time Ali bin Usman al-Jullabi-al-Hujwiri wrote his monumental treatise entitled *Kashful-Mahjub,* the Sufis were divided into twelve groups and were named after their Masters.

It is significant that a work like *Kashf ul-Mahjub,* which not only inspired the contemporaries of the author but also continued to be a standard textbook for Sufis for a very long time, was written in Lahore. How much the Buddhist ideologies of Afghanistan and the neighbouring countries as well as the Vedantic thoughts of India influenced Hujwiri and other Sufis in the formative stages of their movement, is now a matter of conjecture, but it is certain that the ideological structure of the Sufis of Ba-Shara school remained basically Islamic though rituals and practices from other sources were freely drawn upon, assimilated and made integral part of Sufism.

Another factor which made later Sufism popular amongst all sections of Muslims particularly those who inhabited the Persian-speaking areas, was the tremendous appeal of the poetry of Sanai, Attar and Rumi. Abul Majd ud-Din bin Adam Sanai of Ghazna was a poet of strong pantheistic tendencies and deep humanitarian outlook. He remained a target of Ghazni throughout his life; they left no stone unturned in getting him and his monumental work *Hadiqat ul-Haqiqah* condemned. His status, however, was later on immensely elevated by Rumi.

Farid-ud-Din Muhammad bin Ibrahim Attar popularised many of the cherished themes of Sufism through his allegorical *masnawis*; the *Asrar Nama* (Book of Secrets) on general Sufic principles, the *Ilahi Nama* (Divine Book) on mystical love.

Jalal ud-Din Rumi was 'surely the greatest mystical poet in the history of mankind'.

The most striking features of the *masnavi*, which covers the entire field of Sufi speculation, are the humanitarian outlook of Rumi and the emphasis which he laid on mitigating the hide-bound prejudices of creeds and catechisms. The Turks, who migrated to India either with the invading forces of the Ghorids or had afterwards to leave their motherland on account of the Mongol ascendancy, could no more look westward for a peaceful living; India was thus left the only place on the earth where they could hope for an honourable existence and which they could call their home. These bands of migrants to India had among them Ulama, Sufis, poets, philosophers, adminstrators, wazirs, soldiers, commanders and men known for their eminence and noble birth.

Gradually the Muslim population in India came to consist of foreign nationals of varied stock and local Muslims, mostly converts from Hinduism. The Turks, in their anxiety to retain their racial identity nurtured prejudices against Indian Muslims, especially low-born ones. In the context of this racial prejudice, the principles of Islamic brotherhood, which the early Turkish rulers in India attempted to put into practice seem to have hardly evoked striking enthusiasm in the caste-ridden Hindu society.

The Ulama, who were the custodians of the interpretation of the Sharia, found themselves in an awkward position at this idea of monarchy. They found no way out of this impasse in the face of the practical, utilitarian policy of the Sultans; so they had to adjust themselves to avoid a crisis.

Even after due compromises and adjustments, the Ulama had no smooth sailing. They fell prey to their own ambitions to consolidate their power and prestige. The Sufis on the one hand and the philosophers and unorthodox thinkers on the other offered them stiff opposition. The division of Ulama into two categories, viz. *Ulama i-Akhirat* or *Ulama i-Rabbani* and *Ulama i-Duniya of Ulama i-Su* was effected with a view to enhancing the prestige of pious, virtuous and selfless Ulama, but it unwittingly provided a weapon against the entire class in the hands of their opponents as well as in the hands of the disgruntled elements of their own groups. No measuring rod for unworldliness, or lust for wealth and power could ever be discovered. Wealth or poverty could never be fixed as standards of piety. Suhrawardi saints rolled in wealth, accepted government service but they could not be dubbed as immoral or impious. Wealth and material prosperity could not therefore be denied to the Ulama. The worldly-minded Alim of one camp could very easily be acclaimed as pious and saintly by the other camp and vice versa; any opposition to the state or to the nobles by them was sufficient to earn them the title of worldly-minded Ulama. Mutual jealousy among the Ulama was not totally absent, and transgressing their own domain of learning and piety, they dabbled in politics and felt no hesitation in extending their prestige through political alliances.

Kings and nobles stood in need of their *fatwas* to suppress their enemies and uproot subversive elements in the state itself; the Ulama in their turn looked towards the kings and nobles for patronage and financial help. They established matrimonial alliances with the kings and nobles. Under strong rulers like Ala ud-Din Khilji and Muhammad-bin-Tughluq, they remained within proper limits but they would quickly retrieve their fallen prestige by turning to their advantage the situation arising out of the accession of weak rulers to the throne or struggle between the nobility and the rulers. They faced serious ups and downs throughout the reigns of Delhi Sultans and the Mughals. *Fatwas* (legal decrees) for the suppression of heresy, unbelief and *bidats* (innovations) were the strongest weapons in their armoury, with which they sought to suppress all and sundry if they opposed them on any issue. In a country like India, with a preponderance of non-Muslim population and a state dependent from its very inception on *Zawabit* and not on the *Shariat*, it was neither unusual nor undesirable that Muslim thinkers and rationalists studied the throughts the institutions and the ideology of Hindus with interest and sympathy and mixed with them freely in social life.

Sufis, on the other hand, were more closely knit as compared with the Ulama who could be played against each other, exploited and suppressed with a little exertion. Of the organised

Sufi orders which played an important role in the religious and cultural history of the country from the beginning of the thirteenth century were the Suhrawardis.

But it was the soil of India which proved fertile for the speedy growth of the Chishti Silsila, for in countries outside India, its growth was stunted in the absence of suitable leadership. Khwaja Muin ud-Din Hasan, came to India in ca 1192, shortly after the defeat and death of Prithvi Raj. After staying for some time at Lahore and Delhi, he finally shifted to Ajmer in 1266, where but for occasional visits to Delhi, he stayed till his death. He died at the advanced age of ninety-seven years. He was humane, gently and quiet in temperament. In Ajmer he was given a cordial welcome by the *darogha* (Commander) of the place. Finding himself exhausted by the strenuous journey, he selected Ajmer for his permanent residence as he probably found the atmosphere of Delhi too suffocating for him to stay there.

The standard authentic works depict him as a man of deep monistic tendencies who could not find any distinction between the lover, the beloved and the love itself. He was neither a missionary nor miracle-monger. He did not work among the masses nor did he write any book. Spurious mystic literature, which appeared in his name as well as in the names of his successors and became popular as early as the fourteenth century, brings to the fore the fact how, with the rise in Muslim population, enthusiastic successors of inferior calibre attempted to bolster up the Chishtiya mission by giving a legendary aura to the achievements and teachings of Khwaja Muin ud-Din Chishti.

'Most of the prominent Hindus of that region were honoured by the robe of faith through the blessings of the traditions of that essence of divine secrets. Most of those who were not converted to the (Muslim) faith would send immense offerings and futuh (gifts) to Hazrat Ishan, so much so that even now those Kafirs are devoted in the same manner.'[5]

Of his disciples, Khwaja Qutb ud-Din Ahmad Musa, a native of Aush, who also had travelled widely and drawn inspiration from various saints of different orders, rose to great eminence. He permanently settled down in Delhi at the instance of his preceptor Khwaja Muin ud-Din Chisti who before his death appointed him as his spiritual successor. Bakhtiyar Kaki died (27 November 1235) under the spell of an ecstatic trance caused by a couplet recited in a sama (dance accompanied by singing) performed by the Sufis to arouse ecstatic feelings.

'From Lahore, Khwaja Muin ud-Din Chishti went to Delhi and then to Ajmer, which was ruled by Rai Prithvi Raj. One cannot think without admiration of this man, almost also, living among people who considered the least contact with a Muslim as defilement. Sometimes he was refused water to drink. In the torrid climate of Rajputana this was the hardest punishment one can imagine. The high-caste priests demanded of the Raja of Ajmer that he should banish the Khwaja, whose influence had begun to make itself felt among the lower classes of the place. The Raja sent the order of expulsion through Ram Deo, head of the priests of Ajmer. Legend relates that in approaching the Khwaja, Ram Deo was so much impressed by his personality that he became, from the moment, a faithful disciple of the Khwaja and spent the rest of his life in the service of the helpless and the down-trodden'.[6] A less credulous estimate is as follows:

'Ajmer was not merely the seat of Chauhan power ; it was a religious centre also where thousands of pilgrims assembled from far and near. Shaikh Muin ud-Din's determination to work out the principles of Islamic mysticism at a place of such political and religious significance show great self-confidence. It cannot, however, be denied that his stay in Ajmer must have been a serious trial for the principles of the Chishti Silsila. On his success or failure in Ajmer depended the future of the Muslim mystic movement in Hindustan'.[7]

He attracted a very large circle of followers drawn from the Muslim population of Delhi. Sultan Shams ud-Din Iltutmish, his nobles and the common people vied with each other in showing reverence to him. The Ulama looked with annoyance at the *sama* parties that he organised. Backed and supported by his friend Qazi Hamid ud-Din Nagori, a saint of Suhrawardi order, these *sama* gatherings went a long way in popularising the Chishti order and in fact became centres of attraction for the Muslims, as the popularity of Sufism in India grew.

Shaikh Hamid ud-Din Sufi, another eminent disciple of Shaikh Muin ud-Din Chishti, was so inclined towards leading a life of seclusion that his preceptor gave his the title of *Sultan ut-Tarikin* (king of anchorites). He settled in Nagor where his life as a village peasant brought him into closer and more frequent contacts with the Hindus who had behind them a rich heritage of the traditions of the yogis given to a life of poverty, resignation and piety. His dietary habits were akin to those of the Hindu saints and he confined himself to a strictly vegetarian food. Hindu or Hindawi was the medium of conversation in his family.

Amongst the disciples of Khwaja Qutb-ud-din Bakhtiyar Kaki, Shaikh Farid ud-Din Masud Ganj i-Shakar was most eminent. Shaikh Farid ud-Din Ganj i-Shakar confined his activities to Hansi and Ajodhan. Overflowing with deep humanitarian outlook, his long sojourns in different parts of India (eastern U.P. Bihar, Rajputana and the Punjab) put him in touch with a number of yogis too, who paid frequent visits to his *jamaat khana*. It was there that Shaikh Nizam-ud-din Auliya came in contact with the yogis whose conversations left indelible marks on his memory and he would often recall them with reverence and admiration.

After the death of Shaikh Farid ud-Din Ganj i-Shakar on 17 October 1265, Shaikh Nizam ud-Din Auliya, the greatest of the later thirteenth and early fourteenth-century Indian saints, succeeded him, though he had to make a hard struggle for obtaining supremacy in the beginning. After his return from Ajodhan he led a comparatively obscure life in poverty and hardship till he finally settled down at Ghiyaspur.

The early Sufis were great missionaries of Islam and had penetrated into the Indian towns where they preached a very high social and moral ideal, if not a superior gospel. Ghori's conquests are being represented as a movement which liberated the caste-ridden and down-trodden, Hindus from the shackles of social discrimination and economic hardship.

A large number of fictitious graves of saints appears to have emerged between thirteenth and fifteenth centuries on account of even closer contacts with the Hindus. Like the particular local deities of Hindus in each village, Muslims contrived to have graves of fictitious saints for their local worship. They exercised immense influence indeed. The fulfilment of vows through prayers at these graves seems to have led many Hindus to embrace Islam. Indeed, inanimate objects such as these graves appear to have played a more important role in conversions than the early saints themselves. The mode of showing veneration to these graves is still very peculiar and differs from place to place. At some places it verges on idolatry. Sultan Sikandar Lodi is said to have banned worship at such graves and Mujaddid Alf i-Sani vehemently opposed these practices. But they are still the objects of great veneration and elicit the devotion of rural Muslims. The beliefs connected with them exercise more influence on them than the *Shariat* itself. Hindus even to this day offer sweets and flowers on such graves. They are the symbols of common culture, heritage and peaceful co-existence of the Muslims and the Hindus in India.

Muslims from all classes were attracted to his discipleship and he was instrumental in bringing about considerable change in their social and moral life. In the *jamaat khana* of Shaikh Farid ud-Din Ganj i-Shakar, where he lived for some time in his youth, he had manifested keen interest in the teachings of yogis.

Shaikh Nizam ud-din Auliya was succeeded by Shaikh Nasiruddin Chiragh of Delhi (Dehlavi) (d. 14 September, 1356) who clung to orthodoxy more strictly than his preceptor. He imposed many limitations on *sama* and tried to render it as less obnoxious to the orthodox as was possible. He attempted to do away with the practice of bowing by touching the head to the ground before the saints as was prevalent during the days of his own preceptors, but permitted kissing the ground with lips. Equally he opposed the veneration of graves, for it often verged on worship, and approved of *tawaf* (circumambulation) of the mausoleums of the saints. He explicitly brought out the importance of yogic breathing exercises over which the most perfect of the yogis, called Sidh, had achieved utmost mastery.

The death of Shaikh Nasiruddin Chiragh of Delhi took away from the domain of Indian Sufism a central figure who possessed a deep humanitarian outlook and commanded more or less universal reverence. The crisis in the mystic field, which was brewing in other countries of the Middle East due to the popularity of the monistic and pantheistic works of Ibn Arabi and his disciples, started to affect the ideology of the Indian Sufis too.

The Suhrawardis in India trace their spiritual descent back to Shaikh Shihab ud-Din Umar bin Abdullah Suhrawardi (1144–1234), the author of the Awarif ul-Maarif which, like *Kashf ul-Mahjub* served as an important textbook of all the Indian Sufis for many centuries. He settled in Baghdad, where he was received at the court of the Caliph al-Nasir. There he rose to great eminence and died at the ripe old age of ninety-two in 1234–1235. Of his disciples who settled down near Delhi, the most important were Shaikh Nur ud-Din Mubarak Ghaznawi (1234–35) who served for some time as Shaikh ul-Islam in the reign of Sultan Shams ud-Din Iltutmish, and Maulana Majd ud-Din who for some time served as Sadr in Iltutmish's reign.

Though Qazi Hamid ud-Din Nagori was a disciple of Shaikh Shihab ud-Din Suhrawardi, he remained more closely associated with Shaikh Qutb-ud-din Bakhtiyar Kaki. He was a man of scholastic attainments and wrote a number of works on Sufism.

The most prominent of Shihab ud-Din Suhrawardi's disciples was Shaikh Baha ud-Din Zakariya who wielded great influence in Multan, its neighbourhood, Sindh, and parts of the Punjab. Sultan Shams ud-Din Iltutmish held him in great esteem and the latter had amassed fabulous wealth which was awfully shocking to many of his contemporaries, but he would retort. There existed very cordial relations between him and Shaikh Farid ud-Din Ganj-i-Shakar.

Both Chishti and Suhrawardi Sufis had carefully imbibed the teachings available in the woks of earlier masters, of Hujwiri, Ghazzali, Shaikh Abdul Qadir Jilani and Shaikh Shihab ud-Din Suhrawardi. The strict adherence of the Chishti and the Suhrawardi orders to orthodox theology dampened all enthusiasm for creative thinking. *Shariat* (Holy Law) and *Tariqat* provided the codes of belief and behaviour for the Chishti and the Suhrawardi saints. They held *Shariat* as the fountain and source of all spiritual progress without caring for the subtle differences of orthodox theology itself.

The characteristic feature of Sufism was the acquisition of knowledge through individual experience; this precluded the possibility of inflexible patterns of rituals, beliefs and ethics. Though the Chishti and Suhrawardi saints in India did not materially deviate from the pattern set by the earlier Sufis, their doctrines did have some distinctive elements. They ruled out logic as a method of getting at the 'Truth'. *Sama* gatherings, where music was played, transported the Chishtis to the realm of unlimited Divine bliss, while the Suhrawardis and the Ulama condemned the practice lock, stock and barrel.

While the popularity of the saints was growing and while many of them shared state patronage, the Ulama expressed their disapproval of the saints. This was partly because of their dissatisfaction with what they thought to be heterodox practices and partly the result of a genuine fear that the rejection of the standards of objective behaviour would adversely affect the position of the Shariat. At the same time the Ulama could not attack all the saints, some of whom enjoyed prestige as theologians. Therefore, the tussle continued between the Ulama and the Sufis though it remained confined within certain limits.

While maintaining the Ulama in position of importance the Sultans and the nobles, in common with the rest of the Muslims, shared the belief that the blessings and the prayers of the saints irrespective of their faith would help them out of difficulty. To the common people, mysticism provided the emotive principle of faith. Their local centres around living or dead Pirs including legendary figures provided local places of pilgrimage and festival; their practices bore a great resemblance to similar practices among non-Muslims and also they provided an escape from the rigours of the routine of the *Shariat*. The stories of the supernatural powers of the saints were readily believed by a gullible audience which did not care to verify or to reject them. This led to the growth of legendary works in the name of the eminent Sufis and continued to be believed as authentic despite vehement protests by their sober disciples. Their importance can in no way be minimised as they exercised immense influence over the masses.

Among the intelligentsia there was an added factor that contributed to the popularisation of the Sufic outlook. In poetry, specially Persian poetry, the concept of love was interchangeable with the concept of divine love, the common intellectual disgust with hypocrisy and formalism of the orthodox Ulama could be freely condemned through the medium of poetry. Moreover, poetry through the symbolism of a Sufic allegory provided new avenues of freedom for intellect and imagination. The idiom of poetry in India as in Persia during the same period became strongly imbued with the spirit of Sufism through the popular sama gatherings which were common amongst most of the Sufis. Sufistic poetry reached quarters which otherwise it would not have.

In view of this popularity of the Sufi saints no government could afford to ignore them. It was inevitable that there should be large sections of disaffected people even amongst the Muslims. The dissatisfied nobles frequently utilised the general disaffection to create trouble.

The practice of yoga and theistic philosophy as developed by Patanjali was known to the Muslims through the excerpts from his works translated in *Kitab ul-Hindi* by *Al-Biruni*. Fresh attempts to study it through the original source were made by Qazi Rukn ud-Din of Samarqand.

The early Chishti and Suhrawardi saints were, however interested only in the studies of the basic texts of their own religion. Whatever knowledge of either *Vedanta* or yoga they acquired was through direct contact with the yogis and Hindu mystics. There was great similarity between Sufi beliefs, organisation and institution and those of the Hindu mystics but the influence of the Hindus, meagre though it was, in the early period was felt among the popular practices rather than in ideology or in any doctrinal reformulations. Shaikh Farid ud-Din Ganj i-Shakar is said to have founded a system of dikr in Hindi, possibly more for the use of those converts who could not adapt themselves to Arabic.

At the same time, as the Hindus and the Muslims lived together, a process of cultural synthesis was inevitable. Many of the Indian Muslims were converts from Hinduism. Even the Turks who had settled down in India in the thirteenth century cherished many cultural traditions of their Buddhist ancestors of Afghanistan. In the growth of this composite cultural and religious tradition, the similarity between popular Hindu practices and the Sufic practices, between the various trends of mystic thoughts amongst the Hindus as well as the Muslims could not remain unnoticed. It was therefore natural that in popular festivals both participated with each other. In praying for the removal of the difficulty, a Hindu would readily go to a Muslim grave or a saint and the common Muslim would approach a Hindu saint. The spirit of tolerance, which the monistic trends amongst the Sufis encouraged, provided an ideological basis for the mixing of the followers of different faiths. In the poetry, the Hindu idiom was easily accepted by the Muslims as cooresponding the Sufic allegory. After all, the position which the orthodox Shariat had prescribed for the non-Muslims was not practicable in India. The liberal trends in Sufism provided a religious justification for the realities of the situation.[8]

Technically, the term *qalandar* applied to those dervishes who generally remained engrossed in a state of *sukr* (mystic intoxication) and confined their religious activities to the obligatory part of religious observances only and did not pay any heed to the formalities of social life and material needs. By the beginning of the thirteenth century, they had, in India, assumed the characteristics of the wandering monks of the Suhrawardi and the Chishri saints. They originally considered the settled *khanqah* life of the saints as a sin and the mystic literature relating to the thirteenth and the fourteenth centuries is full of serious conflicts between the *qalandars* and the Chishti and Suhrawardi saints; often most eminent amongst them were not spared. Some of the Qalandars shaved off their beards, moustaches and eye-brows, some roamed about naked with only a loin-cloth round their waist; a few donned ornaments made of heavy iron rods, called *Alat i-Qalandari* (instruments of *Qalandari*); some of them ate a type of grass, which is not specified in the sources but was apparently hemp. They were generally very temperamental and miracle-mongers. Some of them had great influence with the Sultans and provincial governors, had shared their fortunes and reverses.[9]

Shaikh Sharaf ud-Din Abu Ali Qalandar (d.1324) was originally a theologian but later on, in a moment of mystical ecstasy, threw his books in the river and became a Qalandar. Letters ascribed to him contain exuberant expressions of divine love and his *masnawis* are also in the same vein. He exercised immense influence on later Sufis, and on Qalandars too, who began to cling more and more to orthodoxy. They generally enrolled themselves in the Chishti order but some of them joined the Suhrawardis. However, freedom from the formalities of religion and preference for a life dedicated to divine love and ecstasy remained the cardinal features of that discipline.

To the static Muslim mystic ideologies prevalent in the later twelfth and early thirteenth centuries, a new dynamic outlook come from the monistic and pantheistic doctrines of the Arab mystic Muhi ud-Din Ibn ul-Arabi (Ibn Arabi), styled by his followers as Shaikh ul-Akbar.

Although conforming to the practice of the Muslim faith and professing its beliefs, Ibn Arabi's sole guide was the inner light with which he believed himself illumined in a special way. He held that all Being is essentially one, as it is all a manifestation of the divine substance. The different religions were thus in his opinion identical. Of his works, *al Futuhat ul-Makkiya* (Meccan Victories or Discourses) gives a complete system of mystic knowledge in 560 chapters.

In popular mystic parlance his doctrine of Unity of Being is known as *Wahdat ul-Wujud* or *Tauhid i-Wujudi*. From the time he propounded his doctrine, he had to meet the stubborn opposition of the theologians. Though almost all of his doctrines were vehemently criticised by his opponents, nothing was more obnoxious to the orthodox than the theory, *al-Wujud al-mutlaq asl kulli Wujud* (Absolute Existence is the source of all existence) and the language which he used and the terminology which he coined to express his ideas.

It was, however, Abdul Karim bin Ibrahim al-Jili, the author of *al Insan ul-Kamil fi-marifat il-awakhir wal awwal* (The Man Perfect in Knowledge of the Last and First Things), who presented the pantheistic doctrines more systematically and intelligibly. Ibn Arabi's Futuhat i-Makkiya and Jili's theory of 'Perfect Man' seek to raise the prestige of the Sufis to unimaginable heights, parallel to the 'seal of the prophets' of the 'last of the prophets'.

The credit of popularising the works of Ibn Arabi amongst a vast majority of Muslims, however, goes mainly to his step son Abul Maali Sadr ul-Haq Wa'l Millat Wa'd Din Muhammad of Quniya (d. 1273) who was an eminent Sufi, and a scholar and a teacher of considerable merit. Maulana Jalal ud-Din Rumi was one of his most intimate friends. Ibn Arabi and his followers were tortured and persecuted and had to face refutations of their doctrines. This stimulated creative intellectual activity too.[10]

He issued several *fatwas* against a number of innovations *(bidats)* which had become popular amongst the contemporary Muslims. In one of the *fatwas* he denounced the practice of visiting the tombs of saints and prophets. On account of his works and writings he had to undergo imprisonment a number of times. He died on 26 September 1328. He is said to have written about five hundred treatises, several of which were devoted to refuting and condemning the pantheism of Ibn Arabi and the unorthodox practices of the Sufis. The most effective refutation of the pantheistic doctrines was made by Ala ud-Daula Simnani.

He was a prolific author and himself claims to have blackened one thousand *tabaq* (sheets) for the sake of *tasawwuf*. He was an inveterate opponent of Ibn Arabi's pantheistic theosophy. He believed that none of the followers of different creeds and sects had previously expressed his ideas with such ignominy. 'If it is thoroughly explored' he remarked, 'it would appear that the creeds of the worshippers of physical objects and atheists are better than most of the beliefs of these people'. According to him the goal of union with Reality *(fanafil Haq)* which the pantheists cherished was a very low order of

Mukashifa (mystic revelation), in fact one of the earliest stages in the mystic journey.

His entire approach towards Being and Attributes was that of an orthodox theologian. According to him the *Quran* should be interpreted strictly in accordance with the point of view of the Ulama and Iman i-Rabbani (Godly Immams) and he paid no heed to the commentaries of the Hukama (philosophers) and Mutakallimin (scholastic theologians) who were under the corrupting influence of the intellect. The validity of none of the Quranic verses could in any way be questioned and therefore a full command of *Haquiqat, Tariqat* and *Shariat* was indispensable.

He was vehemently opposed to Ibn Arabi's doctrine of saintship *(Wilayal)* which asserted that 'all Prophets are also saints, but that the saintly aspect of each Prophet is higher than the prophetic aspect'. He did not approve of the quiet and ascetic life of a Sufi. According to him the duties of a Sufi amounted to that of a preacher and a missionary of Islam. As a missionary he encouraged his contemporary Shaikhs to enrol as many disciples as possible quite indiscriminately.

He did not see eye to eye with those who strove to effect some sort of compromise between the kafirs and the Muslims and earnestly longed to engage himself in the battle with the unbelievers. He did not attach any importance to the miracles and supernatural feats of all those saints who did not believe in the Prophet in a formal orthodox manner. Those who took to an ascetic life with a view to acquiring the power to perform miracles and supernatural feats were, in his opinion, not the true seekers after God.

A large number of disciples and orthodox Sunnis rallied round Ala ud-Daula Simnani even during his lifetime. As they were missionaries too, they travelled the greater part of the Muslim world. A group reached India, where they held discussions with Saiyid Muhammad Ashraf Jahangir Simnani. Shaikh Ala ud-Daula's works were a great sources of inspiration to the orthodox Sunnis and narrow-minded Sufis. In popular mystic terminology his doctrines came to be known as *Wahdat ush-Shuhud* or *Tauhid i-Shuhudi* as opposed to the *Wahdat ul-Wujud* or the Tauhid i-Wujudi of Ibn Arabi. Both of these exercised such tremendous influence on subsequent Sufic thought that the Sufi ideology came to be categorised as either the Wujudi or the Shuhudi. Sufis undoubtedly got themselves initiated in different Silsilas but most of them adhered either to the Wujudi or to the Shuhudi ideology.

In India the pantheistic doctrine of Ibn Arabi in their philosophical form gained popularity rather late but monism in its various forms was the basis of the Sufic thoughts of the Suhrawardis as well as of the Chishtis. On account of the influence of Shaikh Nizam-ud-din Auliya, a controversy could not be sparked off in India, for the devotional approach of Nizam ud-Din Auliya regarding the doctrines of Wujud was not basically different from the speculative one of Ibn Arabi.

Among the Indian Sufis and scholars of the later fourteenth and early fifteenth centuries, whose ideas and works in support of the pantheistic mysticism of Ibn Arabi made deep impressions on the minds of the contemporary and later Muslims, as well as on a section of Hindus who had started studying Muslim religion works and mystic thoughts seriously, were Jafer i-Masud Bak, Shaikh Sharaf ud-Din Yahya Manyari and Saiyid Ashraf Jahangir Simnani.

Kufr and Islam both seemed to him as veils between God and His worshippers. A hero amongst the seekers of Divine Being, according to him, was one who was neither a Kafir nor a Muslim. He did not leave the topic of *kufr* undefined. Formal *kufr* was indeed the denial or rejection of the Sharia but the real *kufr* belonged to the worship of Nafs (lower or appetitive soul). The followers of formal religion, according to him, followed the second type of *kufr*. Thus the proselytising efforts of the Muslims were of little importance to him.[11]

In poetry, pantheistic ideas were preached with great exuberance by Ahmad-bin-Mahmud Nakhshabi Sher Khan popularly known as Masud Bak, who was said to have been a relation of Sultan Firoz Shah Tughluq. The former had, under a fit of mystic ecstasy, renounced his wordly riches. Shaikh Abdul Haq Muhaddis Dehlavi says, 'Among the Chishtis, no one has spoken of the secrets of Truth in such an open and unguarded manner, and no one was so given to mystic intoxication (masti) as Masud Bak was'. His prose work on Sufism entiled *Mirat ul-Arifin* contains a clear exposition of the pantheistic doctrines after Ibn Arabi.

Like all the followers of the pantheistic mysticism he wrote, '*Shariat* is learning, *Tariqat* is burning and *Haqiqat* in illuminating. First of all a seeker should acquire the knowledge of the *Shariat*; later on he should burn himself on the path of *Tariqat* and finally kindle the lamp of *Haqiqat* and shut his eyes from his own self'. He likened the *Shariat* to a mirror which was made for seeing the 'Divine Beauty'. According to him, 'a true seeker is one who does not dabble in religious squabbles of the seventy-two sects and considers them all to be the same'.

The efforts of Shaikh Sharf uf-Din Ahmad-bin-Yahya Manyari, who was born in Manyar, a village near Patna, to popularise the pantheistic doctrines of Ibn Arabi were far-reaching in consequence. He originally set out from his village to Delhi with a view to entering the discipleship of Shaikh Nizam-ud-din Auliya but when he reached Delhi, the Shaikh had already passed away. He, therefore, became the disciple of Shaikh Najib ud-Din, an eminent saint of the Firdausi order.

The laws of the *Shariat*, according to him, were elastic and the convenience of Muslims was never to be thrown overboard. Unless something went strictly against the injunction of the *Quran*, the problems confronting the contemporary Muslims were to be interpreted from a practical standpoint. He took a sympathetic view of the practices prevalent amongst the Muslims and did not condemn them for the mere want of previous sanction of some authority. He advised his disciples to refrain from the practices which they did not approve of, but they were not required to compel others to give them up. All sorts of traditions ascribed to the Prophet were not readily believed by him. The betterment of the Muslims was to be given preference over prayers and fasting. He did not fail to recognise the eminence of Yogis and their achievements in the field of ascetic exercises.

According to him, the *Shariat, Tariqat* and *Haqiqat* were inalienable and interdependent. The revelation of Haqiqat did not absolve the seekers of the obligations of the *Shariat*. Even the knowledge, the acquisition of which was indispensable for the proper discharge of the obligations to the *Shariat*, was looked down upon by him, if it was made a source of obtaining access to the doors of kings and nobles and a means of being raised to the post of Qazi or *Mufti*. Marifat could be sought nowhere else but in renunciation.

The task of defending Ibn Arabi's philosophy against the attacks of the Ulama and Sufis, and of reconciling the conflicting views of Ibn Arabi with those of Ala ud-Daula Simnani, and their respective supporters with each other, fell on Mir Saiyid Ashraf Jahangir Simnani (d.1346). He belonged to Simnan and travelling to distant places in the company of Mir Saiyid Ali Hamadani he ultimately reached Bengal where he became the disciple of Shaikh Ala ul-Haq Bangali. In India he had to face opposition of Qazi Shihab ud-Diu Daulatabadi who assailed Ibn Arabi's doctrines from the theologians' point of view and that of Mir Saiyid Muhammad Gesu Daraz, who condemned it from the stand point of the Sufis. He faced the situation most tactfully and did not antagonise any of them. He attributed the hostility of the Sufis towards the doctrines of Ibn Arabi to expediency and emphasised that all the eminent Sufis held no other creed but the one propagated by Ibn Arabi.

Of the early Indian Sufis who launched a tirade against the teachings of Ibn Arabi, the most eminent was Saiyid Muhammad Gesu Daraz, son of Saiyid Yusuf Husaini, known as Saiyid Raja. After receiving immense popularity in the Deccan, he died on 1 November 1422. He was one of the leading disciples of Shaikh Nasiruddin Chiragh. Amongst Chishtis he possessed a peculiar style of expressing the truth. Since the entire framework of the Chishti discipline under which he worked throughout his life was Wujudi, his criticisms were later on glossed over by asserting that he only sought to criticise those expressions of Ibn Arabi which were obnoxious to the orthodox. However, he categorically condemned the works of Ibn Arabi, Farid ud-Din Attar and Jalal ud-Din Rumi as deceitful and their authors as the enemies of Islam.

He advised the Sufis that in no circumstance should the obligations of the *Shariat* be ignored. Mansur al-Hallaj, despite mystic intoxication and lunacy, had performed a hundred *rakats* (genuflexions) of Namaz before he was brought to the gallows. Like Ala ud-Daula Simnani, he emphasised that the status of a prophet was higher than that of a saint, for the latter was commissioned to propagate the divine mission.

No mention of the proselytising activities on the part of the Chishti saints is made in the earlier authentic Malfuzats. But Saiyid Muhammad Gesu Daraz claimed to have held many discussions with Brahmans and tried to convert them to Islam. In this too he seems to have been inspired by the Chihil Majlis, Al-Urwa and the disciples of Ala ud-Daula Simnani who had visited his *khanqah*. However, the framework of the Chishti traditions was too strong for him to break and he could not give up that humane approach which was the cardinal point of the popularity of the Chishtis. He encouraged friendly relations between the followers of all the religions. He could not give up the practice of *sama* and could not even check the recital of Hindawi songs though he tried his best to reform and reconcile it to the *Shariat*. Like other Muslims, he too was highly dissatisfied with his contemporary religious and spiritual environment, and the sincere quest for a true spiritual life was regarded by him as scarce in his days.

The slogan 'back to the Shariat' was not confined only to the theologians and the Sufis opposed to Ibn Arabi; it was raised by some Suhrawardi saints too, such as Makhdum Jahaniyan and Raju Qattal, who had nothing to say against Ibn Arabi, Saiyid Jalal ud-Din Bukhari, popularly known as Makhdum Jahaniyan. He was a disciple of his father and a Khalifa of Shaikh Rukn ud-Din. Sultan Muhammad-bin-Tughluq had appointed him as a Shaikh ul-Islam and put him in charge of Khanqah i-Muhammadi in Siwistan and other *khanqahs* of the adjoining places. Firoz Tughluq, his important nobles and the Ulama had the utmost faith in him.

Similarly Makhdum Jahaniyan considered it heretical on the part of the Muslims to invoke Almighty God with the names which were generally used for common people, viz. *Thakur* (lord), *Dhani* (rich) *Kartar* (master), etc. This shows that the traditions of the early neo-Bhakti movement, which did not differentiate between Rama and Rahim.

The polemics of the Sufis, hostile to the doctrines of the Wahdat ul-Wujud and the 'back to Shariat' slogan, could not, however, check the popularity of Ibn Arabi and the increasing attempts to explore the common grounds, between the Hindus and the Muslims, conducive to the establishment of peaceful and friendly relations between the two.

The popularity of the works of Ibn Arabi, too, went on increasing in India with the passage of time, and mystic circles were practically flooded with the commentaries, which made a detailed exposition of the various aspects of his doctrines. Wahdal ul-Wujud came to be regarded as the dominant system of mystic thoughts. Contacts with yogic and Hindu saints went a long way in popularising pantheistic doctrines. Indian Sufis had started taking more interest in Sanskrit and Hindi. The mystic philosophy of Advaita Vedanta provided wide scope for the development of the pantheistic doctrines.

The execution of Nawahun did not discourage the people, who went on claiming that both Hindusim and Islam were only two different approaches for the achievement of the same goal. Often, some of them were put to death for their convictions but the movement was too strong to be crushed through persecution. The orthodox amongst the Hindus as well as Muslims looked upon this tendency with disgust. It was this atmosphere that fostered the neo-Bhakti movement of the fifteenth century in the northern India, particularly among the linguistic regions of Awadhi, Braj, Gurmukhi and Rajasthani. The appelation of Muwahhid (monist) came to occupy a unique place in the mystic thoughts of the Sufis and this was assigned to the mystics like Kabir.

The Bhakti (devotion) songs of the Vaishnavites excited more mystic ecstasy in the Sufis than the other forms of Hindi and Persian poetry. Their use went on increasing in the fifteenth century though not without strong reactions against these from the orthodox circles. Liberal Sufis were not, however, slow to take up the challenge and they reconciled the entire mythological symbols of the Vaishnavite poetry and other devotional songs with the Muslim orthodox beliefs. Mir Abdul Wahid Bilgrami, an eminent Sufi and the author of Saba Sanabil, a highly technical and popular work of Sufism, went to the extent of writing a treatise entitled *Haqaiq i–Hindi*[12] (November–ecember 1566) in which he sought to reconcile more than fifty symbols of the Vaishnavites and a large number of terms and expressions used in other devotional songs. Krishna and other names used in such verses for him sometimes symbolised Prophet Muhammad, sometimes 'Man' and sometimes the reality of human being *(Haqiqat i-Insan)* in relation to the abstract notion of oneness *(Ahadiyyat)* of Divine essence. *Gopis* (cowherds wives) sometimes symbolised angels, sometimes the human race and sometimes its reality in relation to the *Wahidiyya* (relative unity, i.e. unity in plurality) of the Divine attributes.

The foregoing account gives an idea of the nature of approach and understanding of the Sufis regarding Hindu mythology as well as of their attempts to reconcile the Advaila Vedanta with the Wahdat ul-Wujud. These attempts had no political motives and were started long before Akbar ascended the throne. They appear to have reached fruition in Abdul Wahid Bilgrami Haqaiq i-Hindi. The Hindus too did not fail to obtain mastery over Wahdat ul-Wujud of the Sufis. A Brahman of Sultan Sikandar's reign, who was also a poet, used to give instructions in books of Islamic learning.

The fifteenth century in India also saw the rise of the Shattari Silsila, whose saints had drunk deep at the fountain of the Wahdat ul-Wujud. They indulged in hard ascetic exercises like the yogis and studied yoga and Advaita Vedanta with utmost seriousness. They cultivated Hindi poetry, and some of the highly esteemed Hindi poets like Manjhan rose from amongst them. There was wide scope for development in the Silsila itself. It was known as Ishqiya in Iran and Turan and Bistamiya in Turkey on account of its association with Bayizid Bistami. They preferred to remain in a state of mystic intoxication. Acquisition of divine love had a supreme importance in this Silsila. They derived their epithet Shattari from their claim to making the seekers traverse the mystic path more quickly and swiftly as compared with other Silsilas. They also claimed that they could acquire in their very first step that stage which other dervishes were able to reach only at the last stage of their mystic journey.

The founder of this Silsila in India, Shah Abdullah Shattari, Khurasan as Hazrat i-Ala, had travelled through Khurasan, Iraq and Azarbaijan, before stepping on the soil of India. In India, he travelled as far as Bengal. During his journeys he dressed like a Sultan and his disciples would put on military uniforms. They would march beating their drums and with their banners flying. Wherever he went he would send this message to the saints of that place: 'The dervish has taken to wandering through the would with the view that if anyone has been able to acquire the significance of *Kalma i-Tauhid* better than this dervish, he should teach it to him, otherwise he should obtain the bliss of *Tauhid*'. In Bengal, Shaikh Muhammad, Ala, who was later on known as Shaikh Qazan Shattari, came under his discipleship.

The Shattari Silsila rose to the pinnacle of its popularity on account of Shaikh Muhammad Ghaus (b. 1500–1501). The concept of *Sulh Kul*, monism and the growing belief that essentially *Tauhid i-Wujudi* and Vedantism represent the same truth, became the characteristics of the other trend. The independent provincial governments, in the fifteenth century, generally patronised the policy of peaceful co-existence and harmony between all the sections of their subjects. The Bhakti movement gave the spur to the development of the process of cultural and social rapprochement, nullifying all the efforts of the Shuhudis and other reactionary elements who sought to pander to the communal sentiments. The political changes that were introduced in the wake of the establishment of the Mughul empire and the policy of 'peace with all' as practised by Akbar in every sphere of human activity–political, social, religious and cultural–sharpened the crisis and it was but inevitable that the revivalist movements should grow and clash with the liberal trends of the times in India.

As a matter of fact, the spirit of rapprochement between the various sections of the Indian population had been quite discernible ever since Islam stepped on the Indian soil and more particularly after the establishment of the Turkish rule in India. This process of rapprochement and mutual adjustment suffered temporary setbacks at times, indeed, due to conflicts between the forces supporting orthodoxy and liberalism, between bigotry and the spirit of tolerance. Within Muslim society itself there were small sections which clung fast to orthodoxy and shunned every gesture of reconciliation with other religions groups, while there were also quite a large number of them who condemned the attitude of the bigoted sections and stood for mutual goodwill and tolerance.

These divergent trends–one leaning towards revivalism, the other towards 'peace with all' had their own lists of supporters and opponents from amongst the Muslim community. The prominent Sufi order in the reign of Shah Jahan was that of the Qadiris.

Miyan Mir, his disciples and other eminent pantheists have been dealt with systematically in all the historical works of Shah Jahan's reign, though they usually led a retired life given to prayers, vigils and austerities. They were shy of publicity and least eager to bring the nobles or the rulers under their influence. They did not believe in swelling the ranks of their disciples, but only reluctantly admitted seekers to their fold. On the other hand, nobles as well as a great bulk of Muslim population in India vied with one another in seeking their guidance for their spiritual satisfaction. They often showered blessings on the eager rulers, princes and nobles in the most guarded language but with no motive of extending their influence or obtaining their support for the success of their ideologies.

Other Pantheists

Of the eminent monists and pantheists of Shah Jahan's reign, Shaikh Muhibb-Ullah, Mubariz Hahabadi deserves special mention. He wrote monumental commentaries on Ibn Arabi's works. He belonged to Sadrpur in Awadh. After acquiring a thorough grounding in the traditional forms of contemporary learning, he got initiated into the Sabiriya branch of the Chishtis through Shaikh Abu Said Gangohi. After visiting important Chishti centres and places of pilgrimage, he finally settled down in Allahabad and lived there for about twenty years, till his death on 30 July 1648.

The works of Ibn Arabi, according to him, were thus neither to be interpreted literally nor metaphorically. He regarded Shaikh Ala ud-Daula Simnani and Mir Saiyid Muhammad Gesu Daraz, the opponents of Ibn Arabi's teachings, superior to those commentators who did not seriously follow his works and sought to gloss over them. therefore, after reaching Allahabad, he plunged headlong into a programme of popularising the correct import and significance of Ibn Arabi's works. He had compiled a commentary on Fusus ul-Hikam in Arabic at Sadrpur before settling down in Allahabad.

The main opposition to the entire system of Sufis in general and the *Tauhid i-Wujudi* in particular, in the reign of Shah Jahan, was led by Mulla Mahmud Jaunpuri and his talented disciples. They sought to emphasise the preponderance of rational thinking both over mysticism and dogma. Shaikh Muhibbullah had, therefore, to fight a royal battle against this tendency which dominated an important cultural centre of northern India, like Jaunpur.

Amongst the Sufis who opposed the *Tauhid i-Wujudi* and criticised the works of Ibn Arabi, he mentioned only Ala ud-Daula Simnani and Mir Saiyid Muhammad Gesu Daraz. He accused Ala ud-Daula of not following the true significance of Ibn Arabi's theory of *Wujud i-Mutlaq* and taking it too literally. According to him only those scholars, ascetics and mystics followed Shaikh Ala ud-Daula Simnani who were not able to achieve their ultimate goal of spiritual perfection. He thus labelled all other Sufis who opposed Ibn Arabi as the *Sufi i-Fahil* (ignorant Sufi).

Like some other pantheists of his times, he laid considerable emphasis on the acquisition of mystic knowledge from the Hindus too. In one of his letters he has quoted the Hindu theory of cosmogony but his knowledge of Hindu mysticism seems to be very superficial, though there were considerable opportunities to acquire it at Allahabad. He probably thought himself too old to acquire it or was too busy with his scheme of work to pay attention to it. However, one of his eminent disciples, Shaikh Muhammadi, undertook the study of Hindu mysticism with the pundits systematically after acquiring a perfect grounding in pantheism, under him.

He wrote several letters to satisfy himself. In one of his letters to Dara Shikoh, he urged the need for looking after the peace and prosperity of all the human beings, without any distinction of caste and creed. He informed the Prince, 'The Holy Prophet has been referred to as *Rahmatulli—Alamin*–a blessing to all the worlds and not only to Muslims'. Shah Jahan, in a letter, earnestly requested him to pay a visit to him and quoted the following tradition to convince the Shaikh: 'Obey God and obey the Prophet and all those among you who are in command'. Shaikh Muhibb-Ullah politely declined the Emperor's invitation and wrote to him, 'How can one reach the third stage when one is not able to fulfil the obligations needed for the first two stages?'

The main plank of Miyan Mir's philosophy was that humanity is a sacred trust of the Almighty. Naturally, he possessed a very humane outlook and did not examine contemporary problems from a narrow communal or sectarian point of view. He advised the rulers to look after the prosperity of the country and the subjects, to be compassionate to the people and benevolent to the needy. The magnanimity of his heart and the nobleness of his soul prompted him to address his disciples as comrades; so he never called them disciples. He told Jahangir, 'Your Majesty's existence is indispensable for the protection of the people. Through the blessing of Your Majesty's justice the Fakirs also remain peacefully occupied in their job'. He did not commence his conversation with Shah Jahan when the latter first visited him for a discourse on religion or faith but informed him, 'It is the duty of just kings that they should remain vigilant about their subjects and dominions. The prosperity of his subjects, by seeking to populate new areas and bringing them under cultivation, should be his foremost concern as it makes the soldiery contented and the treasury full'. He considered the ruler to be a perfect specimen of humanity and the chief manifestation of the Almighty. Though he attached great importance to the presence of a ruler on earth, he ranked a Sufi higher than a ruler. 'When a Sufi becomes perfect', he remarked, 'his heart does not care for risks. Nothing harms him. He is himself a ruler. How can he care for others? All the rulers are under him'.

Like other monists and pantheists, Miyan Mir and his followers attached no importance to the external forms of religion, though Miyan Mir and some of them very scrupulously followed the duties enjoined by the *Shariat*, which was regarded by them as the first step to the path of obedience to God. *Tariqat* or the mystic path led the seekers to higher planes of nearness to God and the *Haqiqat* brought the Sufis to their goal, i.e. the stage of being absorbed into Being of the Almighty. To draw a distinction between believers and kafirs, heaven and hell, reward and punishment was frivolous in their eyes, deserving the attention and attachment only of the ignorant. Heaven they defined as union with the Almighty and Hell as separation from Him.

Prayers performed in a mechanical way with no concentration of mind carried no meaning for Miyan Mir and gave him no satisfaction. The seeker was required to banish everything but the Almighty from his mind while offering prayers. Even many of the contemporary saints, according to him, could not come up to this hard test.

Nor did the monists and pantheists of Shah Jahan's reign spare even the mullas and alims from criticism. The saint of Bari, whom Dara Shikoh considered his preceptor, informed the Prince, 'I have killed the *mulla* and the pandit both. With whom then can I study anything?' Dara Shikoh was more frank in his utterances about the self-conceited and ignorant *mullas*. He says: 'Paradise is there where no *mulla* abides'.

Miyan Mir was overcautious in his utterances regarding pantheistic beliefs and was not in favour of inviting unnecessary criticism. During his long stay of about sixty years in Lahore, people from all classes, Ulama, pious people, ascetics and worldly persons, came in contact with him but none could ever find any fault with him. However, he would unequivocally declare his belief in the mystic philosophy of Fusus ul-Hikam and considered the Unity of God beyond the comprehension of ordinary human beings.

The tangible result of the interest in pantheism, which sought to widen the outlook of the Muslims, was that Vedanta, yoga and Indian mysticism came to be studied with added interest by Muslims also. Akbar's reign was a great departure from the preceding ones so far as the translation of Sanskrit works was concerned, in the respect that his translation bureau encouraged a systematic study of the salient features of Hinduism, not for polemics but for creating a better understanding between the two communities. Akbar bequeathed this healthy tradition to his son and successor Jahangir. The salient features of Vedanta appealed to the the inquisitive brain of Jahangir too and he did not find any difficulty in perceiving the similarity between the two.

Much original work to popularise Hindu mythology and thought was done by Abdur Rahman bin Abdur Rasul bin Qasim bin Shah Pudh. Abdur Rahman lived at Dhaniti, a village in the Sarkar of Lucknow, and breathed his last there in 1683. Translated with explanatory notes, a Sanskrit treatise on Hindu cosmogony in 1631-32 was named *Mirat ul-Makhluqat*. It is in the form of a dialogue between Mahadeva and Parvati handed down by Muni Bashisht (Vasishtha). Shaikh Abdur Rahman has explained at some length how the Hindu legends were to be adapted to Muslim ideas; how, for instance, Mahadeva was to be taken as a king of the Jinns, another mythological being to be turned into Adam, a third into Muhammad and so forth. In his abridged translation of the *Gita*, entitled *Mirat ul-Haqaiq*, he sought to emphasise the importance of the doctrine of *Hama Ust* throughout the work.

The points of similarity as brought out by Shaikh Abdur Rahman Chishti may be disputed by the scholars of both the religions but the work distinctly bears the stamp of the spirit of the age in which it was written.

Persian Hindu Writings : Sources for Bringing Sufism Nearer to Hinduism

The mass of literature produced in the Persian language by Hindu and Muslim writers about Hindu religious thought and practice, presents clear examples of how the spiritual values of

Islam and Hinduism could meet, and how the one could try to explain, understand and appreciate the other. The large number of the texts which was translated (and many of them more than once or twice), copies which were made of each of them by Muslim and Hindu transcribers, point to the extensive spread of these Persian-Hindu writings amongst the educated people of India—Hindus and Muslims. It should be noted that this literature was mainly the product of cooperation of Hindu pandits and Muslim scholars.

It was motivated by the idea of creating an atmosphere of mutual understanding between the Hindus and Muslims in India. The idea was anticipated by men like Al-Biruni, whose pioneer work *Indica*, is the earliest serious attempt to introduce Hindu culture to the Muslim world; Sultan Zain al-Abidin of Kashmir, who promoted Sanskrit studies and established a 'bureau' for translating Hindu works; and Qadi Rukn al-Din Samarqandi, who translated the *Amritkunda* into Persian and Arabic. But it was Akbar Shah who felt the vital significance of the idea, developed it into a social and intellectual movement and gave it a decisive form and direction.

Many people of different ranks and vocations, who were concerned with the Hindu–Muslim problem in India, sought to bridge the gap by emphasising the mystical aspects of Islam and Hinduism and to effect an approximation between the two faiths on these grounds. The movement, in its various forms, and in spite of sever opposition of the 'orthodox' leadership, continued to be, at least until the tragic death of Dara Shikoh in his struggles with Aurangzeb, successful and productive; though the spirit did not lose all its force in subsequent ages.

To give an idea of the scope and extent of the Persian works on Indian traditions and translations of Hindu writings, the following details, which have been collected from various available sources, may be useful. These works and translations are numerous and belong to a period of over three hundred years.

Some writings are briefly mentioned here:

1. Ramayana

1. In Persian prose, by Abd al-Qadir Badauni.

2. *Ram wa Sita*, in Persian verse, by Shaikh Sad-allah Panipati 'Massih'.
3. *Mathnawi-i Ramayana*, in verse by Ghirdardas.
4. *Sampurna Ramayana* (complete *Ramayana*) in prose.
5. An abridged prose translation by Candarman b. Sri Ram 'Bidil'.
6. *Nargisistan*, in prose and verse, by the above-mentioned Candarman 'Bidil'.
7. *Amara-prakasa*, a prose version of the *Ramayana*. based on various translations, witten by Amara Singh in 1117 A.H.
8. Tulsidas' Hindi *Ramacarita-manasa* was translated into Persian by Debidas Kayastha.
9. *Ram-nama*, a verse translation by Misra Rabdas 'Qabil' in 1861.
10. *Khulasa-i Ramayan*, an abridged verse translation by Banki Lal 'Zar', in 141 lines.
11. *Adhyatma Ramayana*, an abridged prose version.

II. Mahabharata

1. *Tarjuma-i Mahabharat*, or *Razm-nama*, a prose translation at the instance of Akbar Shah by Abd al-Qadir Badauni. Concerning the Persian translation of the *Mahabharata*, Abul l-Fadl gives the following information: 'The *Mahabharat* which belongs to the ancient books of Hindustan has likewise been translated, from Hindi (Sanskrit) into Persian, under superintendence of Naqib Khan, Mawlana Abdul Qadir of Badaon, and Shaykh Sultan of Thanesar'.
2. The first two *parvas* re-written by the poet Faidi in Persian.
3. *Khulasa-i Mahabharat*, an abridged prose version.
4. *Gulistan-i jannat*, an abridged prose version by Munshi Narayan Daspuri.

III. Bhagavad Gita

1. *Sri Bhagavat*, a verse translation, attributed to the poet Faidi.
2. *Raz-i maghfirat*, a prose translation attributed to Dara Shikoh, in 18 *adhyayas*.

3. *Mirat al-Haqaiq*, a prose version, with Islamic comments and interpretations, by Abd al-Rahman Chishti in 1065/1655
4. *Sri Gita*, in prose, by Munshi Dyaram Khushdil of Kashmir, 11th/17th century
5. *Gita-subodhani*, translated from the Sanskrit commentary Subodhani

IV. Nalopakhyana (Nala and Damayanti)

1. *Nal o Daman*, a free translation of the story in Persian verse by the poet Faidi at the instance of Akbar Shah, in 1003/1594
2. *Hansa-jawahir*, another free translation in verse by Jaisukh Lal 'Zirak'
3. A third verse translation by Fawzi Faidi Dihlawi

V. Bhagavat-purana

1. Translation of the 10th *skandha* of *Bhagavat-purana* in ornate prose, ascribed to Abul-Fadl Allami
2. A prose translation of the whole work (in 12 *skandhas*) attributed to the poet Faidi
3. A prose translation by Raja Manohardas (Todar Mal), the Hindu administrator under the reign of Akbar Shah
4. *Maha-puran*, an abridged version by Chandrasin, son of Kashidas, about 1096 A.H.

VI. Harivamsa

1. *Harbans*, an abridged prose translation of *Harivamsa* by Tahir Muhammad bin Imad al-Din-Sabzivari, at the instance of Akbar Shah, in 1011/1602

VII. Atharva-veda

1. Abd al-Qadir Badauni says (*Muntakkab al tawarikh*, I. P. 212) that he began to translate the *Atharban* in 1575 at the instance of Akbar Shah

   Badauni says, 'In this year (983 A.H./A.D. 1575) a learned Brahman, Shaikh Bhawan had come from Dakhin and turned Muhammadan, when His Majesty gave me the order to translate the Atharban. Several of the precepts of this book resemble the laws of Islam'.

VIII. Upanishads

1. *Sirr-i Akbar*, the Persian translation of 50 Upanisads by Dara Shikoh, with cooperation of Hindu pandits of Banaras in 1067/1657

IX. Yoga-vasistha

1. *Laghu-yoga-Vasistha* (an abridgement of the whole work made by Abhinanda of Kashmir in the 9th century)
2. *Shariq al-ma rifat*, attributed to Faidi, is mainly based on the *Yoga-Vasistha*. To explain Vedantic ideas, the author occasionally quotes Quaranic verses, sayings of the Prophet, or Sufi poetry.
3. *Atwar dar hall-i asrar*, or *Tuhfa-i majlis*, an abridged translation of the *Yoga-Vasistha-sara*, made for Jahangir Shah by Sufi Sharif Qutbjahani

X. Amrita-kunda

1. *Bahr al-Hayat*, translated by Muhammad Ghawth of Gwalior, the spiritual preceptor of Humayun Shah

XI. Prabodhacandrodaya

1. *Gulzar-i Hal*, translation of Krisna Misra's famous philosophical drama, by Wali Ram, Dara Shikoh's secretary, in 1073/1663

XII. Tahqiq al-tanasukh

1. A work in Persian on the Hindu belief in transmigration, Ananda Rau.

XIII. A work on Hindu laws, translated from Sanskrit by Zain al-Din Rasai. The original Sanskrit work was written by Hindu pandits for Warren Hastings

XIV. Haft tamasha, an account of Hindu sects, creeds and traditions, by Muhammad Hasan 'Qatil', a Hindu convert into Islam, about 1230 A.H.

XV. Khiyalat-i Shaida, on Hindu cosmology according to the *Vedas*, by Amara Natha.

XVI. Tuhfat al-Hind, an encyclopaedic work on Indian arts and sciences by Mirza Fakhr al-Din Muhammad

XVII. Muhit-i Marifat, a work on yoga, samkhya and other related subjects, by Sri Maharaj Carandas Sukhadeva ji

XVIII. Hujjat al-Hind, a work in the form of a dialogue

between a parrot and a crane, discussing the Hindu practice of image worship from the Islamic point of view. The work has been written for Ray Karan, governor of Gujarat.

XIX. Riyad al-Madhahib, an account of Hindu sects and castes, by Mathurananth in 1288/1812.

XX. Maqalat-i Hunud, a work on Hindu beliefs, written in 1227 A.H.

XVIII. Abul-Fazl in the introduction to the *Ain-i Akbari* gives extensive accounts of Hindu religious beliefs, philosophical doctrines, social institutions and Indian sciences

XIX. DaraShikoh in this *Majma al-Bahrain* (The Mingling of the Two Oceans) compares Vedantic ideas with Sufi doctrines.

XX. Mufti Ali al-Din Lahuri in several chapters of his *Ibrat-nama.*

The above account—which is by no means final and complete—is confined to the works which are directly related to Hindu religion, philosophy and mysticism. Persian writings and translations dealing with the Indian sciences (medicine, mathematics and astronomy) music, history, romance and moral fables lie beyond the scope of the present study.

Persian translations of Hindu literature and Persian writings on Hindu thought and practice should not be regarded simply as fragments of the past history of Hindu–Muslim relationship. They are of living significance, and reveal an existing human situation which constitutes a part of the history of our age. These writings are, in fact, the meeting place of two different world views, two distinct spheres of language and thought, each trying to know, understand and explain the other. It is here that that the dialogue between Islam and Hinduism actually takes place.

These writings are vivid reflections of how the two great religions, with different traditions and backgrounds, with equal potentialities to resist and to survive, but, at the same time, with the wealth of their spiritual and humanistic values, come together, and without losing their identities, joined hands to build up the Medieval Indian civilisation, with all its richness and all its achievements.[14]

As mentioned above, after the conquest of north India in

the beginning of the thirteenth century, the Muslims turned to the translation of the principal Hindu works in literature and philosophy into their languages, Arabic and Persian. One very important work is *Amratkund*, which deals with the principles of yoga, one of the six schools of Hindu philosophy dedicated to the understanding of reality. The author deals partly with quietism and contemplation and partly with superstitious beliefs, talismans, and amulets. According to the Introduction of the book, the work was originally written in Sanskrit and then translated first into Persian and later into Arabic by Qadi Rukn al-Din Samarqandi, who lived in Lakhnauti during the reign of Sultan Ali Mardani (A.D. 1207–12). The Qadi had heard of this book from a Brahman yogi called Bhujar, who had come to Lakhnauti for religious discussions with the Qadi. He was, however, convinced of the truth of Islam and became a Muslim. Thereafter, he devoted himself to the study of Islamic sciences and acquired such a profound knowledge of Islamic law and jurisprudence that the ulema, the theological scholars, authorised him to deliver *fatwa* or official juridical opinion. This yogi, according to the Introduction of the *Amratkund*, said that there was no difference in the teachings of Brahma, the Hindu creator of the universe, and those of Abraham and Moses. This statement points to a syncretic religious tendency that the teachings of Islam could be reconciled with Hinduism. The same tendency reappeared, two centuries after Samarqandi's book, in the form of the syncretic and tolerant religion of Kabirdas (b. 1398) and his school of thought. The conversion of the yogi to Islam proves clearly that religious persuasion had been a great force in the conversion of Hindus to Islam.

It is very interesting to note that none of the preserved texts of *Amratkund*, in Arabic or Persian, is the same as is attributed to Qadi Rukn al-Din Samarqandi in the Introduction of this book. The yogi told him that Hindu sciences were preserved better in the oral tradition of that race. Then the yogi dictated to him the Sanskrit text of *Amratkund*, which he knew by heart. The author translated it into Arabic and divided it into six chapters.

The Arabic and Persian translations of *Amratkund* should

have been quite well known in the Sufi world. Muhammad al-Misri has in his exposition of Sufism, remarked that *Amratkund* is a very important book for the study of the practices of Hindu yogis which have become an integral part of Indian Sufism.

As an original document of the fourteenth century, *Amratkund* is of great importance for the study of the first contacts between Islam and Hinduism. One of the bases of this contact was mysticism, which gave birth to syncretic religious movements in India during the Middle Ages. In those days, Hindu mysticism had got mixed up with very coarse superstitions, on account of intellectual degeneration and tantric practices, which were in vogue in India when Islam arrived in the interior of the country. The Indian Sufis took over with characteristic facility many yogic practices in the same way as they had welcomed the extreme pantheistic theories of mysticism while formulating their own system. According to orthodox Muslim opinion, these Sufis, who were profoundly influenced by purely Hindu doctrines, were heretics. His liberalism notwithstanding, the author of *Dabistan*, Mohsin Fani, himself believed that these Hinduised Sufis were no longer Muslim.[15]

The Sufi orders in India could have been influenced by Hindu doctrines, to which they were introduced either through translations or through ordinary contact with Hindus. They were quite familiar with Patanjali's system. Al-Biruni's Arabic translation of Yoga-Sutra, *Kitab Patanjal al-Hindi fil Khalas min al-Amthal* was available to them. Among those who have obtained perfect knowledge of yogic practices of respiration and aspiration, we can give the example of Sufi Badi al-din Shah Madar (b. 1051). As legend would have it, he could stop his breath for forty days at a stretch.

The Process of finding equivalence in Bengal

The areas east of the Ganga tended to yield more readily to Muslim development, because of certain explicit restrictions on Brahman settlement and the more general fact that much of that land was insufficiently domesticated for Hindu habitation of a kind favoured elsewhere. In Bengal, opposite religious structures, the ascetic Hindu sanyasi and the Sufi *pir* operated with a kind of exchange equivalence. Doctrine seems often to have had little bearing.

The extensive literatures of pre-colonial Bengal, however, suggest a very different kind of religious experience. The textual evidence of early Bengali Islam, which must be considered potentially idiosyncratic, individualistic, and highly localised, points to very pragmatic applications of doctrine to practice, from the ragged and incomplete to very sophisticated creations. These texts portray the struggle of individuals and their groups—various persuasions of Sufis, but also Sunnis and Shi'is—to understand the Vaishnavas, Saivas, and other Hindus, but never in terms of the gross categories of Hindu and Muslim, which are the stock and trade of syncretistic formulations. These early Bengali Islamic texts document the way authors attempted to make their understanding fit with those they encountered, and that process of understanding became an extended act of translation.

Translation in this context defines a way that religious practitioners seek equivalence among their counterparts. It is this act of translation that offers an alternative interpretive strategy for conceptualising the way these various Sufi communities formulated their understanding of the contours of power in Bengal. Because of the local nature of this religious expression, power that was translated could be effective for everyone, regardless of persuasion. In that dynamic process of translation comes the creative application of doctrine to real life. The results of the encounter of traditions can best be appraised in the process of this interaction.

In his pioneering Bengali literary histories, Muhammad Enamul Haq catalogued Muslim writers from this early period, classifying their works into genres such as *sara-sarayit* (legal and moral codes), *kahini* (historical tales), *srstitattva* (cosmogony), *darsana* (theology and philosophy), *suphitattva* (Sufi metaphysics), *marsiya* (lamentations), *itihasika-kavya* (historical poetry) and *padavali* (lyric poetry). He did much the same for Sufi literature in his *Bange suphi prabhava.* Two other books, called *Agama* and *Jnanasagara,* by one Ali Raja, are important, for they present a sophisticated and systematic theology, grounded in an extensive cosmology that serves to justify the yogic mode of Sufi practice. Ali Raja was a Sufi from the village of Osa Kham. He had for his *murshid* and initiating *diksaguru* the famous Sah Keyamuddin, and in that association he wrote extenstensively: in addition to the two above-mentioned works, a book of meditations put to music, titled *Dhyanamala*. Ali Raja was a fairly prominent member of the Islamic literati around the prosperous region of Chittagong, who left a significant literary and religious legacy. Ali Raja's use of an explicitly non-Muslim vocabulary was in fact a search for equivalence, or an attempt to articulate sophisticated ideas of their own by using the locally available lexicon with its limiting conceptual structure. These texts suddenly come alive as examples of Islamic expansion in an entirely new mode, a linguistic and cultural appropriation, not an Islamic dissipation.

The style of the language used by Ali Raja has been called Musalmani Bengali. Bengali offered a potentially malleable medium for the message of Islam, that is, that the ideas were not so alien that they could not be expressed in the extant vocabulary of the sixteenth, seventeenth, and eighteenth centuries. That Bengali should be so used is paramount to the Islamic conception of its own message, for Islam claims for itself a transnational and universal status. Muslim practitioners argue that the sublime object of their religious world is transportable across all national and cultural boundaries, and that its tenets can be conveyed in any language (in spite of the caveat that the Holy *Quran* can only be in Arabic). The few extant Sufi texts are among the most extensive Islamic Bengali documents of the formative period, capturing the struggle of these early practitioners as they tried to articulate a Muslim vision in the local vernacular, a language that bore the weight of centuries of Hindu adaptation.

The language of the texts composed by the likes of Ali Raja, especially the technical vocabulary, appears largely Hindu, perhaps most obviously in the yogic terminology. But that appearance only disguises from our modern eyes what were thoroughly Islamic conceptions. Most interpreters characterise this language as somehow hybrid in character.

The Muslim writer whose vocabulary was conditioned largely by Hindu ideational constructs attempted to imagine an Islamic ideal in a new literary environment. These texts become, then, historical witnesses to the earliest attempts to think Islamic thoughts in the local language, which is to construct new thoughts for Bengali, ideas that had never previously been explicitly expressed. These Muslim authors did not borrow terms but in a more intellectually astute process, sought the closest terms of equivalence in order to approximate the ideas they wanted to express. These early Bengali Islamic authors 'translated' their concepts into the closest locally available terminology as a step toward articulating a different kind of religious orientation.

All translation is a search for equivalence, but the kind of equivalence sought is dictated by the nature of the concept being translated from the source language and the desired result in the target or receiving language. The process was quickened by the numerous translations of Sanskrit epics and other works that had been commissioned by various royal patrons during the fifteenth through eighteenth centuries, translations such as the *Mahabharata* and *Ramayana*, the stories of the *Bhagavata* and other *Puranas*.

When the first authors of distinctly Islamic texts began to write in the vernacular—something that apparently was considered unnecessary at first—since the language of the courts was generally Persian—considered a more appropriate vehicle for the lofty ideas of Islamic scholarship—most of the Bengali techincal terminology and its concomitant conceptual structures were of Sanskrit origin.

Religious encounter seen as translation, however, is not just an act of utterance followed by the emotional, political, and ideological conflict of conversion. Ultimately, it reveals a movement of accommodation by the receiving or target language and the culture it represents, which, when sufficiently pursued, eventually becomes an act of appropriation, the target language incorporating fully the new terms and concepts that result from this encounter.

The Muslim *pir* and his teaching are not just accepted as legitimate expressions of Bengali religiosity, when appropriated into the language and culture, the image of the *pir* has actually had an effect on analogous, that is, equivalent theological and institutional structures of Hindus by modifying their images of the holy man. This process is especially obvious in the Vaishnava case, where the power of the *pir* was more readily recognised because of strong theological affinities, among other factors. The initial act of this Muslim encounter with a Hindu religious figure leads the authors to search for some kind of parallel or analogue in an effort to find an equivalent term or concept.

Dynamic equivalence not only accounts for overlapping semantic domains, but gives priority to the cultural context, which can begin to account for the different values ascribed to equivalent terms. Ali Raja utilises a *samkhya*-derived terminology to describe the basic dualism that is inherent in all Islamic cosmogonic elements, the syzygies (*yugala*), necessary for discrimination and cognition to arise.

The Vaishnavas, for instance, talk of the descent of god or *avatara*, figures who descend to guide the wayward back to the path of proper conduct *(dharma)*, and as such these figures can easily be conceived of as the dynamic equivalent of the Islamic concept of Prophet or *nabi*. For the obvious reason that only Allah can be divine, a Muslim author would clearly deny as heresy that dimension of the semantic domain that designates divinity for the Vaishnava term *avatara*. But, because prophethood functions in an Islamic environment in a way analogous to that of the *avatara*, i.e. to guide people to the proper religious path, the terms could be established as parallel or equivalent. So, in response to the popular and underlying notion of inspired guidance, which can be found in both *nabi* and *avatara*, authors such as Saiyid Sultan could adopt the term *avatara* to describe the Prophet Muhammad, as he did with some regularity in his monumental work *Nabi Vamsa*.

At the same time, Saiyid Sultan provided sectarian Vaishnavas, Saivas, and Saktas with a different reading of their own traditions in a way that makes them more palatable to a broader audience, and in so doing he permanently altered the conception of *avatara* itself to include this somewhat expanded meaning.

Looking at these texts through the model of translation should, if applied rigorously, demonstrate a different kind of social and religious interaction among the diverse populations of Bengal, not just among different groups of Hindus and Muslims.

Hindu–Muslim Mysticism : A Common Ground for Understanding

Sufism, as a moral and spiritual way of life, and as a current of thought with universal appeal, found in India an exceptionally congenial ground for its growth and spread. The Indian mind, from the earliest phases of its history, had a strong tendency towards mysticism, and almost all the mystical tenets that developed in other religions and philosophical schools, find their clearest expressions in the Vedic and Upanishadic literature of ancient India. The Vedic and Upanishadic *rishis* were the first seers who had realised the unity that underlies all the diversities of forms and expressions. It is, in fact, in the *Rig Veda* that, perhaps for the first time, this realisation is spelled out:

ekam sad vipra bahudha vadanti
agnim yamam matarisoanam ahum

(Rig Veda, I. 164:46)

(The truth is one, the poets give it different names.)

This universalistic outlook, which has always been prominent in Hindu thought and is fully developed in the mystical and religious traditions of medieval India, is also one of the basic features of Sufism, and asserts itself throughout the long process of its development. Since large numbers of both communities shared in its humanistic spirit, mysticism became the catalysing force between the two groups, and paved the way for their mutual understnding.

In fact, there are numerous points of agreement and affinity between the Hindu and Muslim mystical ideas; and not only in higher spheres of philosophical specultations, but also on popular and devotional levels, they present similar tenets and tendencies. The pantheistic monism of the *Advaita-Vedanta* and *Wahdat al-wujud* of the Sufis are different expressions of the same world view, and this is the basis of their conceptions of divinity, man, and the universe. For both of them the Divine Being, which is the sole ground of all that exists, manifests itself as the world, and diversities are nothing but various modes of its appearance. This self-manifestation of the Ultimate Being is spoken of in such Vedantic terms as *vavarta, pratibhasa* and *pratibimba,* which are literally the same as the Sufi concept of *Tajalli, zuhur, aks* and *numud.* The most central idea of the *Advaita-Vedanta,* namely the essential unity of all beings, which is expounded in such Upanishadic passages as *sarvamhyetak Brahma, sarvam khalvidam Brahma* and *neha nanasti kincana,* is also basic to the pantheistic philosophy of Ibn al-Arabi and his followers,and was popularised in the *hama-ust* doctrine of later Sufis. The immanence of the Divine Essence in phenomenal forms which, in the Upanishads, has been referred to in such phraseologies as *sarvabhutatma* and *antaryamin,* and in such passages as *etad atmyam idam sarvam,* is also postulated by the Sufis in their conception of God as the soul of the world.

Just as the Advaita-Vedantists argue that self-knowledge *(atma-jnana)* is concomitant with the realisation of the Supreme Self *(Brahma-vidya),* so also, according to the Muslim mystics, realisation of the Supreme Being ensues from the knowledge of one's own self.

Accordingly, and as examples of mutual agreements between Vedanta and Sufism, one may conveniently compare the idea of *nirguna Brahman* of the former with that of *dhat al-mutlaq* of the latter; *jivatman* with the idea of *ruh.*

Sometimes agreements and similarities are not merely in ideas, but in language and expression as well. *Aham Brahmasmi* and *anal-Haq, sarvam idam Brahma* and *huwal-Haq,* and many others, seem to be exact translations of Upanishadic passages into Sufi terms. Agreements and affinities between the mystical aspects of Islam and Hinduism are not restricted to the higher spheres of theosophical speculations. On the popular level, likewise, there is much in common between Sufism and Bhakti mysticism that developed in Medieval India. Both preached the unity of mankind, believed in the equality of all human beings before the divine grace, condemned image worship, caste distinctions and communal discriminations, and emphasised love and devotional worship of the deity as against formal ritualism and external piety.

Because of all these affinities, and on account of their Catholic and humanistic attitude, as against the so-called 'orthodox' outlook of the 'Ulama', the Sufi saints had an important part to play in creating an atmosphere of mutual trust and understanding between the two communities. They moved about among the masses, lived with them, and preached their message of universal love and brotherhood. Many of them could establish a heartfelt relationship with the Hindu population and gain converts on the basis of spiritual values of their own teachings.

The communal intercourse among the Indian masses and the role of the Sufis in bringing the two groups together have been described by Atindranath Bose in his contribution to *The Cultural Heritage of India* :

'Then Islam knocked on the western gates of India; and the Sufis, inspired by the Islamic idea of equality, came as the torchbearers of a liberal folk philosophy... Their spirit was free from those superstitions and rigidities which caused stagnation among the classical Indian and Islamic schools. Against the sterility of the orthodox systems, the new popular appeals awakened a fresh spiritual fervour and let loose great creative power which so long lay dormant. A new philosophy grew, based on the material of human values. It trusted in the latent divinity of the human soul, in the universality of love, and in the dynamic power of emotion. It released powerful spiritual energy hitherto pent up by social barriers among the dumb millions of the soil....'[17]

The mystical ideas of Islam and the Sufi way of life were so appealing to the Indian mind that even the Brahmans did not remain unaffected by their influence. The Sufis often had the courage to criticise the unfair dealings of the rulers and were ready to persuade them to act fairly and righteously with their subjects.

When Muhammad Tughlaq decided to give to himself the

title of *Adil* (the Just One), Shaikh Shahabud-Din Haq-gu refused to recognise him by this new title, and said, 'Those who are unjust cannot be called the just ones'. The famous Sufi, Nizamud-din Auliya, avoided the company of the kings, and refused to receive Ala ud-Din Shah who had come to see him in his *khanqah*. Similarly, Shah Abdul-Rahim of the Naqshbandi order, in his resolve to avoid the company of the kings, did not accept Aurangzeb's offer of a grant of land, and refused to go to the latter's court. Aurangzeb's approaches to Shaikh Abdul-Latif and Shaikh Burhan did also fail to attract these two mystics to his royal favours. Shaikh Kalimullah Dihlawi and his disciple Shaikh Naizamud-Din Aurangabadi were men of moral and spiritual integrity, had a broad outlook, and attracted both Hindus and Muslims to their *khanqahs*. In his epistles to Shaikh Nizamud-Din, the master instructs his successor to hold fast to the principle of Universal Peace *(Sulh-i Kull)* in his dealings with all communities, to regard Hindus and Muslims as equals in all matters of social life, and to keep the doors of the *khanqah* open to any person from any community who might be willing to associate himself with the Sufis.[18] Sufi hospices were the refuge of both the Hindus and the Muslims who sought the help of the shaikhs or wish to be protected by them.

Hindu saints and yogis studied Hindu philosophy. Dara Shikoh, who had joined the Qadiri order of the Sufis, had great respect for Hindu saints, translated the *Upanishads* into Persian and wrote a treatise on Vedanta in Sanskrit. Islam and Hinduism made such a deep impression on the mind of the Sufi poet that he gave up the idea of continuing his journey and stayed at the sadhu's ashrama for twenty-five days. Rasulvijaya included Hindu gods and *avatars* among Muslim saints and prophets, and his pupil Muhammad Khan was well-versed in Sanskrit and Hindu religious ideas.

Because of their aversion to dogmatic formalism, their freedom from fanatical rigidities, their adherence to voluntary poverty and simplicity, and their ethical and humanistic ideals, the Sufis could easily move and preach among the masses, attract large numbers of Hindus and Muslims to their teachings, and influence their thoughts, manners and social attitudes. Thus, along with the spread of Islam in India, Sufism continued to serve as a major medium of sympathetic inter-relations between the two communities, and brought the brighter side of Islam, its higher values, its principles of universal equality and human brotherhood, and its active realistic outlook, to the view of the Hindu society. The emotional aspect of Sufi poetry with the emphasis it lays on love of God and realisation of God in the heart through love, was of special appeal to the religious feelings of the people; and its effect was greatly enhanced when it was sung with music in Sufi circles. A new channel of sympathy was opened between the two groups when the Sufi poets of Sindh, Punjab, Bengal and other regions began to compose mystical and devotional songs in their local languages. Large numbers of people of all sects and classes flocked around them and listened to their recitations, enjoyed their ethical teachings, and shared in the spiritual atmosphere of these gatherings. How numerous, even in pre-Mughal times, these centres of Sufi training were in India, may be inferred from Qalaqashandi's remark in his *Subh al-asho,* in which he says there were two thousand Sufi hospices in and around Delhi.

The Sufi saints were, in general, highly respected by the non-Muslim population, and the Hindus often treated them with a deep sense of trust and veneration. Sayyid Sultan Ahmad, better known as Sakhi Sarwar (twelfth century) had a large number of Hindus among his followers, and was known to them as Lakhi Data. Similarly, the famous Sufi of the Suhrawardi order, Lal Shahbaz Qalandar, was given the popular name Raj Bharatri by the Hindus who were attracted to him. Maggar *pir* and Khwaja Khidr were two other Sufi saints who had large number of Hindu disciples. The former was given the Hindu name Lal Jas Raj, and the latter was called Zinda *pir* by them.[19]

Baba Farid was another saint who was universally esteemed as a great spiritual guide. The fact that his devotional compositions in the Panjabi language have been included in the *Adi Granth* of the Sikh religion bears evidence to the veneration that was accorded to him by the non-Muslims. Such instances, which are by no means few, point out that contacts between the two communities were close and cordial. Bonds of sympathy and fellowship that developed in this area among the masses were of far-reaching consequences.[20]

Obviously, one cannot think that the advent of Islam in India and its spread to remote parts of the country, its proselytising spirit and the growing number of its adherents, its social institutions, political achievements and cultural richness did not leave any impression on the minds of the Hindu thinkers and religious leaders of the time. The Indian mind has proved to be too sensitive to have remained closed to the ideas that were being preached and promulgated by Muslim preachers. They could not remain inert to this new challenge, nor could they be indifferent to the wholesale conversion of low caste Hindus to the new faith. They were, no doubt, worried about the situation; and seem to have been trying to meet the challenge, not in the crude manner of writing apologies and refutations, but in the ingenious way of counteracting the rival propaganda by re-formulating old religious dogmas and offsetting its basic points by producing their likes and counterparts from within. Those who argue against the influence of Islamic ideas on the religious movements of Medieval India, usually base their views on the ground that all constituent elements of these movements were already present in the ancient scriptures of the Hindus. This argument is beside the point. India has been the richest soil for the rise and growth of ideas, and there is hardly any religious or mystical conception of which one cannot find expressions in the vast literature of the land. But what really matters in this particular case is not the isolated doctrines, but their combinations into new forms; not the idea in their original contexts, but their applications to new circumstances. And the elements that shaped religious movements of Medieval India are not in themselves as important as the spirit which was behind them, the social and historical forces that stimulated them, and the sentiments and attitudes that gave them form and direction.

The diffusion of Islam in India had awakened the Hindu masses to a number of facts that were never before so vividly known to them. Its arguments against image worship and polytheism, its strong condemnation of caste discriminations, and its idea that all are equal before the divine grace and none can be deprived of loving and worshipping God, must have been of great attraction to the low-caste and outcaste population. This was a serious challenge to the Hindu society, and a group of religious leaders and reformers, beginning with Ramananda (fourteenth century) seem to have been engaged in efforts for averting the threat. They had, as we have said, to reformulate religious dogmas and modify them in such a way that they could fulfil the social and spiritual needs of the masses, and, at the same time, might offset and neutralise the attraction of the Muslim propaganda. The rudiments of the movement are, perhaps, to be seen in Ramanuja's reforms (eleventh century), whose teachings and activities were the main source of inspiration for Ramananda and his followers. It is difficult to believe, as some scholars have done, that Shankara's Advaita-Vedanta was affected by the Islamic doctrine of *tawhid*. But the development of philosophical outlook from the absolute monism of Shankaracharya to the qualified monism or *Visistadvaita* of Ramanuja, the duality in unity or *Dvaitadvaita* of Nimbarka (twelfth century), and finally, to the pure dualism or *dvaita* of Madhvacharya (thirteenth century), presents a process of evolution which seems to have been moving towards the same theological position that orthodox Islam has been holding. The shift of emphasis from *jnana* to *bhakti* in God-realisation since Ramanuja's time, and the admission of non-Brahmans and even low-caste people into the religious fold, also point to the same direction. But it was with Ramananda and his followers like Kabir, and later Nanak, Dadu, Rajjab and others that the new Bhakti movement took its final shape and became 'the most characteristic feature of the religious evolution of the period'.[21] The preaching of the Sufis on one hand, and the development of new Bhakti movements on the other, brought the Indian masses together and created an atmosphere in which the two could live and cooperate.

For a very brief period, between the first and the second centuries, there was direct exchange of scientific data between India and Islam through Basra, when Sindh belonged to the Caliphs. From the third century direct contact ends. On account of its complicated idolatry and its chains of entangled causes ad infinitum *(karma, samsara)*, Hinduism had already, at the level of metaphysics, distanced itself from occasional Islam, which attests itself vehemently as a living, alive, menacing, transcendent, and personal God. As for a scientific world, the Arab translators of Hellenist syncretism laid down a very clear doctrine which was closer to Islam, and which was more homogenous and complete than the one being perpetuated in schools in India. This taught the quest of causes and not the actual infinite; one single divinity (not explicitly transcendental), supreme ordinator and prime mover; an astronomic calendar (not heterogenous like the multiple 'astronomical days' of the Hindus. The first serious cases of fecund hybridisation between Islam and Hinduism appeared only on Indian soil, following the arrival of Muslim missionaries, who brought evangelism with them.

The two categories of propagandists—Mystics and Qaramates—led to several manifestations of social hybridisation. A number of low castes who converted to Islam included Hindu customs in their canon law, while certain frivolous observances entered Sunni mysticism. On its part, the syncretic catechism of Qaramates had no difficulty taking over Hindu theogony; its Muslim founders had already adapted themselves to different kinds of monotheism, including Mazdeism, and even Harranian paganism. Thus Ali became, for the Khojas, the tenth *avatar* of Vishnu. Meanwhile, strange syncretic encylopaedias appeared in Persian, such as Mobed Shah's *Dabistan* and *Mazdian Desatir*.

With the encouragement given by Fayzi, Akbar's minister Aboul Fadl's brother (who translated The *Bhagavad Gita* and *Ramayana*), and later by Prince Dara, during the sixteenth and seventeenth centuries many translations of Sanskrit classics appeared in Persian, the language of the Muslim conquerors.

The reaction of the Hindus to certain groups of Muslim men of letters remains insignificant compared to the profound popular work of conversion undertaken by Muslim mystics, which led more and more Hindu masses to embrace Islam. From the sixth to the thirteenth century, the hermitages of

Muslim saints, who were chased from Persia by the invading Mongols, multiplied in north India, and around their venerated tombs, villages were founded by Hindu converts who were attracted to Islam by the austerity and the gentle helpfulness of these hermits. Good examples of these are Moinuddin Chishti at Ajmer, Qoth Kaki at Delhi, Jalal Tabrizi in Bengal; Farid Shakargunj in Punjab, Mohammad Gisoudaraz at Belgaum and Ali Hamadhani and Abdallah Shattari in Kashmir. It is not through war that Islam spread in India, it is through the mystics and their great orders, Chistiyah, Kobrawiyah, Shattariyah and Naqshbandiah. To observe in the local devotion to the Muslim saints of India only 'idolatrous survival' and 'pagan infiltration' is to first, overlook the social reconciliation between the conquerors and the conquered, which can be achieved only by those who give without reclaiming and lend without any hope of return; and second, forget the two liberating notions that the conscience of the converts recognised as their duty: a sovereign and transcendental God and an individual, immortal soul. To these one can add two more: the idea of supernatural grace *(prasada)* and the idea of devotion to a personal God *(bhakti)*.

Since the time of the *Upanishads*, the problem in mysticism has not been the positive unification of the soul through the purification of the heart, but simply a preliminary meditation, which is aimed at the negative exinction of all formation of mental images, of all movements of thought ad extra. The originality of this mysticism consists in its repudiation of all foreign elements, whether metaphysical or ritual. It deliberately avoids any consideration of substance or attribute —the objectivity of the sensible objects or the permanence of personality—of grace or divine transcendence.

The aim of Hindu mysticism is sketched in the school of Nyaya. As the conclusion of a decisive critique of imperfect functioning of the discursive intellect, it is a search for *apavarga*, 'the final emancipation' from sorrow caused by intellectual error. This objective is pinpointed by the *Samkhya* school in the concept of *sattapatti* or the actualisation of the psychological consciousness or pure intuitive realization—'truth without content'.

Patanjali, a follower of the principles of the school of *Samkhya*, has in yoga-sutra given to Hindu mysticism its classical form. The objective he assigns to mystical search is called *asamprajnata samadhi.* Patanjali first explains the four kinds of exercises which should be combined as preliminary training: mastering the senses through abstinence (*yama*), relating intention through vows (*niyama*) and rituals dedicated to some god (*Ishvara*); rendering flexible all the limbs for diverse rigid postures *(asana),* and regulating at will the respiratory reflexes. This ascetic training eliminates foreign phenomena and facilitates the search for the envisaged objective. He who has regulated his breath can concentrate on his thought at will, by first encapsulating the five senses into it through abstraction *(pratyahara).*

Here begins the mystical experiment called 'synergy', remorse or *samyama*. Its first stage is contemplation (*dharana*) where thought comprises only three things: conscious subject (*purusha*), a state of consciousness (*sattva*) and an object (whatever), of which one is conscious (*buddhi*). The second stage is absorption (*dhyana*) where thought is only of two things: a conscious subject and an object which one is conscious of. In the third stage is found psychological ecstacy (*samadhi*), where, through gradual transformation, thought becomes the object itself, of which one has assumed consciousness.

(a) *nirodhaparinama* (for vritti)

(b) *samprajnata samadhi* (for vritti)

(c) *asamprajnata samadhi* (for vritti)

Let us now try to transpose, for the sake of comparison, the terms used by Patanjali into the technical vocabulary of Muslim mysticism.

atman = *nafs*, the 'soul' as well as 'myself'/

manas = *qalb*, the 'heart' as well as the 'intellect'

purusha = *rouh;* in the double sense of 'spirit' in Islam

vritti = *istin irfar;* elucidation, discursive assimilation of the object in thought

sattva = *nazar, royah;* 'the state of consciousness'

buddhi = *manzour;* 'the object of which one becomes

conscious'

Moreover, in Sufism, *fana* is either 'to annihilate (one's thought) in its Object *(fana bil madhkour an al dhikr:)* or 'to annihilate (its Object) in its thought *(fana bi'l dhikr)*. This accords with Sufism, where God is the Real transcendent, and Muslim mysticism cannot make any abstraction from this revealed fact. Once it reaches the threshold of carnal liberation, the Muslim mystic's consciousness can no longer ignore the supremely real Object, the superabundant Truth, which its thoughts reflect. It is necessary to burn an account of it, whether it leads to transfiguration or destruction of the self. This is contrary to Patanjali, in whom the mystical method, denuded of all its metaphysical elements, limits itself to establishing an admirably equiliberated and exact introspective formula for the liberation of the spiritual nature from carnal links, for perfect detachment of consciousness, with regard to all that has been created. The consciousness is suddenly made able to see its thought exercise an extraordinary majesty over all nature (clairvoyance, miracles); but this digression has secondary significance. Patanjali insists that the end of mysticism is not attaining miraculous power but the ability to retain consciousness in the state of complete deprivation.

With characteristic honesty and in opposition to the negations of his masters of the Samkhya school, Patanjali would admit that, in order to stimulate and discipline the vows and acts of devotion, a semi-ritualistic Ishvara, an admired god or a hero, whether historical or imaginary, can be introduced in the beginning of preparatory exercises. But he insists that recourse to this Ishvara should be inoperative during *samadhi;* otherwise this imaginary effigy would become a frivolous idol, and consciousness would indulge in self-admiration. Such is the faithful position of mysticism according to Patanjali. It has no end, it can only have a glimpse of the end in a negative state, obtained by the intermittences of thought at a high frequency, which cleanse the consciousness of all images, perfect detachment of will.

Theosophists who have translated Patanjali, make great

claims for him in the hope of finding in him an ally of their syncretism. But in the mysticism of Yoga-Sutra, there is no awareness of the most remarkable feature of the monotheistic mysticism of Islam, *shath*, which, as the positive state of a dialogued mental intermittence, reveals suddenly to the abandoned soul, the supernatural visitation. Patanjali's mysticism is an asceticism of consciousness which he has admirably pursued. The Sufis have agreed with Patanjali's method with regard to (unifying) concentration on God.

It is true that Biruni had some claim to talk of Patanjali; he had made an integral translation of Yoga-Sutra from Sanskrit into Arabic with the title, *Kitab Patanjal al Hindi fil khalas min al amthal*. He also reproduced long passages from his own work on Indian studies.

The Close Similarity of Vedanta and Sufism

Vedantik mysticism has its roots in the *Upanishads*. The *Upanishads* are made up of the utterances of dedicated men and women who were engaged in the pursuit of the highest truth. Wisdom for them involved not merely the intellect but the entire soul. It was not with the theories that they were concerned; their entire conduct of life was at stake and success depended on understanding the meaning and destiny of man and the universe. The verses of the *Upanishads* are charged with exalted emotion. They use words in which the high tension of the spirit finds relief. The sage Svetasvatara said that the *Upanishad* was revealed to him through the power of his penance and the grace of God. They were deliverances of seers in a state of God-intoxication.[22]

The *Upanishads* make it quite clear that they embody a philosophy which goes beyond Vedic thought. In many passages Vedic knowledge is held in secondary importance, if not valueless, for the attainment of the highest aims of life.

The *Upanishads* distinguish between two kinds of knowledge. One is called para (the higher), the other *apara* (inferior). *Apara* knowledge is empirical; it is the knowledge of plurality, of becoming, of the world of phenomena. In the picturesque language of the *katha*, the Creator pierces holes outwards in reality and hence, men look outwards to find the real. The world of forms is the expression of the empirical attributes of the Supreme Being. Our sense organs and their experiences, the intellect and its logic, are the means of acquiring this knowledge. Its basis is the duality of the knowing subject and the known object.

Para or the higher knowledge is the knowledge of the Absolute, of the truly Real. The end of the *Vedas* is long life and happiness on earth, dwelling in paradise after death. The reward of sacrifice is well-being and success on earth and the company of gods hereafter. The aim of the *Upanishads* is deliverance from bondage of the temporal and the phenomenal. So long as man chooses to remain under the imperious yoke of the sense, he is estranged from his imperishable and eternal centre of being.

The *Upanishads* discuss the means by which higher knowledge can be achieved. The end of this endeavour is to know the Brahman or the *atman*. It is, therefore, named the Brahma-Vidya or the Atma-Vidya. Now the *atman* is, 'The immortal veiled by the (empirical) reality'. It becomes wrapped in name and form.

The instruments of inferior knowledge (*apara vidya*) are the senses, intellect, the discursive reason. Higher knowledge (*para vidya*) is the reverse of empirical knowledge; the method of its acquisition is the reverse of that of the other, namely, the suppression of the activity of senses and the cessation of empirical thinking.

This requires the fulfilment of certain preparatory conditions and a discipline. A preparatory condition is compliance with the law of Dharma—study, worship, almsgiving, penance. But this is dispensable. Other conditions are discipleship of a teacher who knows the ways and cultivation of certain qualities. Within man is seated the *atman* which is pure bliss; it is known by tranquillity, self-restraint, self-denial, patience, collectedness and purity of body and mind.

The discipline consists of complete mastery over one's mind, and concentration. By yoga, one gains complete mastery over one's mind, and realises the unity of the Self and Absolute. The *Svetasvatara Upanishad* describes the practice and explains its philosophy. The practice consists of two parts. The first part prescribes a physiological discipline—the control of breath (*pranayama*), and the control of the senses by the mind (*pratyahara*); and the second part lays down the system of psychological discipline, namely collection of the mind and its abstraction from external activity (*dharana*), and meditation to understand the Real (*dhyana*). These steps lead to the absorption of thought into Reality, of subject into object, to the realisation of the oneness of the individual soul and the universal soul (*samadhi*).

The *Upanishads* teach that by knowing the *atman* the universe is known, for indeed, there is no universe outside the *atman*. Hence the famous phrases, 'That thou art' (*Tat tvamasi*), 'I am Brahma' (*Aham Brahmasmi*), which is exactly equivalent to the Sufistic aphorism *Anal Haq* (I am the Reality).

The great theme of the *Upanishads* is to call man to his high destiny. Man may be involved in the universe of time, space and causality, but man is not merely that, for he is the bearer of a Self which transcends nature and the categories of the transient, changing world. Each individual is therefore compelled by his very constitution, to endeavour to find himself, to realise through his limitations the eternal and the immortal self which he really and truly is. The *Upanishads* do not merely propound a philosophy, they lay down a practical course of life and indicate the goal to be attained.

The *Upanishads* seek truth and pursue it by reason. They do not exclude anyone from this search because of creed or caste or colour. In fact this is not a privilege which may be granted to some and denied to others. Knowledge of the self and of truth is the right of every human being; none can be deprived of it.

According to the *Upanishads*, life is a pilgrimage, man is a pilgrim. The pilgrim's point of departure is his natural state. A firm conviction and an unfaltering faith are the prerequisites of the journey, for only those who are stout of heart and do not tire, have the chance to reach the top, and to attain the prize of unsurpassing value, beyond the dreams of desire.

Dara Shikoh's version has a historical value; but more

than that, it has inherent merits. He produced his version with the help of the most learned pundits of the time, and his rending of the ancient texts has a great deal of value in disentangling difficulties and unravelling the meaning of obscure passage.

Thus a powerful religious impulse, which drew its inspiration from Hindu as well as Muslim sources, spread all over India and sought to bring together the masses into a faith which transcended social, intellectual and communal barriers. This stirring in the Hindu society had its parallel in the Muslim community. We have seen that Sufism, even before its arrival in India, had absorbed the main features of *Vedanta*, for instance the philosophy of absolute monism. The Indian *Advaita* had become the Muslim *Wahadat-al-Wujud*.

Ibn-i-Arabi, the great master of Islamic mysticism, affirms that God is one and the universe is His reflection. Creation is a process of emanation of which the three steps are: (i) the stage of absolute unity (*ahdiat*), (ii) the stage of latent or potential multiplicity (*wahdat*), (iii) the stage of apparent or actual multiplicity (*wahidiat*). The multiplicity expresses itself in souls (*ruh*), forms (*mithal*) and bodies (*jism*).

For both Vedanta and Sufism, there is a common discipline. It includes purification of self, mastering of passions and desires, filling of the mind exclusively with the thought of God, obtaining control over bodily functions and mental processes till the objective world ceases to distract consciousness, till man passes away (*fana, nirvana*) from phenomenal existence and attains union with the divine. The soul stands self-enlightened and unperturbed by temptations and apprehensions.

The Sufis were held in high esteem among the masses who followed their simple teachings with eagerness and understanding. They laid stress upon the dignity of man, for they thought that every individual should reach the highest goal of human life by his own effort. They rejected the claim to special sanctity of priests, of books (scriptures of Hindus and Muslims), of temples and pilgrimages, of rites and ceremonies, and encouraged the establishment of direct relationship between man and God. The movement arose in the fifteenth century and continued until the end of the seventeenth.

The leaders of this group hailed from all parts of India, but their teachings reflect the distinct influence of Islam. In the Hindi-speaking regions, the most notable reformer was Kabir, who was a powerful exponent of devotional faith centred on an impersonal, transcendental God. He was a fearless denouncer of hypocritical and superstitious practices, Hindu or Muslim. Love of God and man was his religion and he accepted whatever he thought true in Hinduism and Islam. There were several other teachers whose point of view was similar to that of Kabir's, and who founded their orders in different parts of the country.

In Maharashtra, Namdeo, Eknath, Tukaram and Ramdas were noted saints who were hostile to idol worship, indifferent towards external acts of religion such as vows, fasts, austerities, pilgrimages, etc. They worshipped Vitthal, the one God who conferred tranquillity. They prayed for release from the snares of the illusory world and condemned caste distinctions, while seeking to reconcile Hindu and Muslim faiths.

Bengal produced Chaitanya, who was a devotee of Krishna but at the same time opposed the Brahmanical system of ritualism and caste. Among his disciples was Thakur Haridas, a Muslim. Sects in Bengal went far beyond Chaitanya in their criticism of Hindu orthodoxy, for example the Kartabhajas.

The Virasaivas of Lingayats of the Kannada region were a sect which came into existence in the twelfth century, and rapidly spread in Mysore and the neighbouring districts. Their belief in one God who cannot be represented by images or propitiated by sacrifices, as well as their rejection of caste, show their independence from the conservative religious ways. They did not approve of sacrifices, fasts, feasts and pilgrimages, nor did they recognise distinctions based on birth. A pariah and a Brahman were equal members of the sect. In the deep South, the Tamil Siddhars rejected the theory of transmigration and the authority of the shastras. They held that God and love are the same and desired mankind to live in peace recognising love as God.

Ample and convincing evidence exists to show that all

the higher thinkers and religious reformers among the Hindus, from the earliest times had proclaimed the unity of God, declared the equality of all devotees and placed the true faith above all religious rituals and ceremonies. The works of the Adiyars (the Saiva Saints) and the Alvars (the Vaishnava saints) of South India during the period between the eighth and the twelfth centuries may be mentioned as cases in point. It was during this period that the Saiva and Vaishnava saints of South India endeavoured to wean the people from their allegiance to Buddhism and Jainism to Siva and Vishnu worship. The devotees of Siva and Vishnu developed the Bhakti cult. The preachers of the Bhakti God, a unique, supreme, and merciful God, 'Surrender to whom and living in whose grace is the one way of attaining the life divine'.

Many sects arose out of the conflict of Islam and Hinduism and tried to harmonise the two and to provide a common meeting ground for the devout men of both creeds in which their differences of rituals, dogmas and external marks of faith were ignored. According to Havell, the advent of Kabir, Nanak, Chaitanya and Dadu was the result of such a development. These reformers won converts from Hindus and Muslims freely, and rejected the rigidities of the Brahmans and the *mullahs* alike. The Kabir-Panth (sect of Kabir) provided a connecting link between Hindu and Muslim mysticism. Kabir was against narrow communalism and the externals of the creeds. A Muslim by birth, Kabir was fundamentally monotheistic. He was first a Sufi and then an ardent disciple of Ramananda. Kabir's teaching touched the thinking souls of Hindus and Muslims, although, at the same time, it brought upon him the wrath of the orthodox pundits and *mullahs*.

Guru Nanak's first convert was a Muslim. Like Kabir, Nanak also decried idol worship, caste prejudices and polytheism. This attitude brought him nearer Islam. He was influenced by Sufism, and the *Adi Granth* proves that the basis of his creed was essentially Indian. His mission was the unification of Hinduism and Islam.

The cultural influence of the six centuries of Muslim rule

was undoubtedly widespread. This influence was direct and vivid in literature, art, architecture, customs, manners, and in the general fashions of the age. Nowhere did the Hindus and Muslims come as close to each other and nowhere did they identify themselves with each other's culture so intimately as in Bengal. This resulted in the growth of a new culture popularly called Bengali culture which was different in many respects from the general pattern of the Indo-Muslim culture of the other parts of the country.

In Bengal, Shri Chaitanya initiated the Krishna Bhakti movement. The Sufi movement in Bengal flourished through Jalaluddin Tabrezi. Shri Chaitanya had many Muslim followers who were Vaishnoi and had abundant poetic works to their credit. The close interaction of Sufism and Chaitanyaism gave rise to Baul songs (1625–1675). They were a creation of Hindu-Muslim unity. This was a movement against all externalism whether of Hindus or of Muslims. It aimed to break all external restraints.

Long before Europe had learnt to study religion with a scientific and detached spirit, many Muslim learned men had compiled books of comparative religion in which they displayed an amazingly free and rationalistic attitude of mind. Among them was the most eminent scholar Abu Rehan Al Biruni, who compiled a comprehensive treatise on Hindu religion and philosophy as early as the eleventh century.

Throughout the Middle Ages, the Muslims took enormous pains to acquaint themselves with the religious literature of the Hindus. They translated almost all important texts into Persian—the *Vedas*, the *Upanishads*, the *Mahabharata*, the *Ramayana*, the *Dharma Shastra*, *Puranas*, the *Yoga Vasistha*, the *Yogashastra*, *Vedanta shastra*, etc.

Among later writers was Mazhar Jan-i-Jahan (b. 1699). Mazhar wrote about the Hindu worship of idols : 'The process is similar to the Dhikr, contemplative ritual, which is prescribed for Muslim Sufis'.

Muhmud Shabistari (A.D. 1317), the well-known writer of *Gulshan-i-Raz*, writing on the theme of idol worship, explains the differences and similarity between it and Islam : 'The idol is the expression of love and unity in this world, and to wear the sacred thread is to take the resolve of service. As both faith and unfaith are founded in existence, unity of God is the essence of idol worship. As things are the expression of existence, one out of them must at least be the idol. If the Muslim knew what the idol is, then he would understand that religion consists in idolatry. And if the idol worshipper understood the idol, he would not go astray in his faith. The latter did not see in the idol anything but external creation, and for this reason he became kafir in the eye of the law. If thou too would not see that reality is hidden in the idol thou wilt also be not known as a Muslim according to the law'.

REFERENCES AND NOTES

1. Tarachand, Dr. *Influence of Islam on Indian Culture*. p.51.
2. Ibid., p.55.
3. Ibid., p.63.
4. Rizvi, Dr. S.A. Abbas. "Sufism in India". In *Muslim Revivalist Movement in Northern India*, p.1.
5. Habeeb, Prof. Mohammad. "Chisti Mystic Records of the Sultanate Period". *Medieval India Quarterly*, 1, no. 2 : 15–37.
6. Husain, Dr. Yusuf. *Glimpses of Medieval Indian Culture*. Bombay, 1959: p.37.
7. Nizami, Dr. K.A. *Some Aspects of Religion and Politics in India during the Thirteenth Century*. Aligarh, 1961: p.184.
8. Rizvi, Dr. S.A. Abbas. "Sufism in India". In *Muslim Revivalist Movement in Northern India*, p.29.
9. Ibid., p.30.
10. Ibid., p.34.
11. Ibid., p.46.
12. Bilgrami, Mir Abdul Wahid. *Haqai-i-Hindi*. Nagari Prachiri in Sabha, Varanasi, p.27.
13. Descriptive Catalogue of the Arabic Persian and Urdu MSS in the Library of the University of Bombay, 1935.
14. *Persian Hindu Writings, their Scope and Relevance*, p.91.
15. Husain, Yusuf. "The Arabic Version of Amratkund." In *On becoming an Indian Muslim*. p.62.
16. (*i*) *Islamic Syncretic Tradition in Bengal*, Asim Roy, Princeton University.
    (*ii*) In search of Equivalence : Conceiving the Muslim Hindu Encounter Through Translation Theory, Tony K. Stewart, in

India's Islamic Traditions (711-1750), pp. 365-371.
17. Bose, Atindranath. In *Cultural Heritage of India*, Vol. 111 pp. 460–462.
18. *History of Medieval Deccan*, Vol. II, p.195.
19. *The Struggle for Empire, History and Culture of the Indian People*, pp.467, 461, 473.
20. Tarachand, Dr. *Influence of Islam on Indian Culture*, p.249.
21. Majumdar, R.C. *The Delhi Sultanate*, p. 547.
22. Pande, Dr. Bishivambarnath. *The Vedant and Sufism, A Comparative Study*, pp.1–7.

4

Sufi Ideals, Sufi Institutions and the Impact of Sufis on Indian Society and Culture

Sufism and Sufi Ideals

In the popular sense, Sufism is known as mysticism in the West, but it is not on a par with the conception which the word 'Sufism' actually carries in Islamic parlance. One of the advantages of this cult is that its followers speedily discover all the mysteries of Nature for the benefit of mankind. Its greatest gospel is to 'Live and let live' and to bestow indiscriminating affection upon all mankind. It caters for the real peace and spiritual need of the people who are generally sick of the material world and seek a spiritual asylum. To be brief, unless one is God's chosen man, endowed with the inherent natural spark of Divine love, piety and religious devotion, and is also fit for the necessary hard *mujahedas* (probations and strivings), one cannot become a perfect Sufi.

The origin of the term 'Sufi' is rather complex, but in general it signifies one who wears the garments of 'soof', i.e. wool. In the beginning, it was a mark of personal penitence. In the second century of Islam, a particular group of ascetics of Kufa were generally called al-Sufiya, on account of their dress.[1] But by the tenth century A.D., wearing of woollen garments became the recognised badge of the Sufis of Iraq and hence the term was commonly applied to all Muslim mystics. In the same century, groups of these ascetics used to assemble to recite aloud the Holy Quran and other religious pieces, which practice gradually took on a liturgical character called *dhikr* evolving into spiritual concerts named *sama*.

Gradually a change was coming over the general character of Sufism. Its basis was 'fear of God and His wrath to come' with the mystical element of love and adoration. According to the woman saint Rabia al-Adawiya (died A.D. 801) the mainspring of mysticism is Love. She said: 'Love of God hath so absorbed me that neither love nor hate for any other thing remains in my heart.'[2]

A simple definition of Sufism (*tasawwuf*) is that it is the form which mysticism has taken in Islam. The term Sufism embraces the philosophy and practices in Islam which aim at direct communion between God and man.

According to Hazrat Khwaja Muinuddin Chishti, *Tasawwuf* or Sufism means scrupulously maintained moral character and religious discipline, which one must necessarily cultivate and observe towards all the creatures of God in the interests of peace and happiness of mankind'.

It is a Divine Knowledge and only a selected few get the credit of attaining it by renouncing the material world and devoting themselves exclusively to the worship of God. It is a gift from God bestowed upon those who can retain it and bring into play only those courses which are permissible for the uplift and happiness of mankind. In short, Sufism is the pinnacle of an all-round spiritual development in Islam.

Sufis are a specialised class of spiritual teachers in Islam who decipher and interpret the Divine code not commonly understood by ordinary human beings because the teachings of the Holy *Quran* are classified into two important categories, viz. (i) *mohakmats* and (ii) *mutashabehats*. *Mohakmats* mean clear-cut instructions or orders governing the code of man's life and conduct as ordained by the *Quran* and are easily understandable by every Muslim, while *Mutashabehats* mean that secret code of spiritual teaching which is reserved only for those who have an aptitude for this special branch of the Divine Knowledge and which can only be attained by very hard practice involving strict adherence to the principles of self-mortification, renunciation, penitence and detachment from all worldly temptations in order to make one fit for the highest spiritual attainment.

Sufism does not go by inheritance but, as stated above, is a gift from God to the deserving who have the faith, the zeal and the thirst for this Divine Knowledge. The Holy *Quran* confirms this fact by the following verse: 'We taught him (Our chosen servant) knowledge from Ourself' (Surah XVIII, V. 65).

Sufism, in spite of its loftiness in religious ideals, has been less fastidious and more ready to accept alien practices and ideas provided they produced good results. Blended with Sufism, the orthodox church was undoubtedly refreshed and strengthened and, in fact, acquired a more popular character and attraction in Islam. Large multitudes were won over to Islam by Sufism in Western Asia, North Africa, Central Asia, India and Indonesia. In the wake of Sufism, Shia'ism also suffured an eclipse and lost much of its original influence. On the whole, Sufism has made a meritorious and invaluable contribution to the promotion and prosperity of Islam in the world.

After the death of the Prophet, the over-powering influence of his religion and sacred traditions dominated the lives of his succeeding descendants and the Caliphs. During this early period of Islam, there was no necessity of any new cult like Sufism but, as time passed on, a revival of the Islamic influence was deemed necessary and it was taken up by Sufism in right earnest. The term 'Sufism' denotes nothing but a direct interpretation of the cardinal principles of Islam and certain spiritual practices to be observed in this process. Its originator, Abu Ishaq Shami was the first Sufi who preached this cult which was in conformity with all the basic principles of Islam.

According to Islamic conception, a Sufi is one who is fired with Divine love and who, as a true devotee of God is constantly impatient to seek nearness to Him. The quest of a Sufi centres round the exploration or probe into the mysteries of the Nature. He is wholeheartedly engrossed in seeking the myriad 'truths' of the Truth and concentrates on the hard task of reconciling his actions to his thoughts. This is an extremely difficult process. He has, first of all, to suppress or subdue his worldly desires inherent in the soul of man, called *nafs,* in order to attain purity and steadfastness in his character. After attaining this stage, he enters the second phase of building up his 'external' and 'internal' character through mental exercises as the result of which the knowledge of the 'hidden' mysteries of Nature or God is revealed unto him. To summarise the whole process of Sufism, the true path of a Sufi's salvation lies through the thorny wilderness of renunciation, self-mortification and annihilation of the *nafs* by incessant devotion to God. Thus a Sufi aspirant has to undergo a rigid test in morals and, by acquiring a perfect knowledge of the *Quran* and Islamic theology as well as strict adherence to the Muslim law of jurisprudence called *Fiqah* and *Hadith* which deal with the moral, social, economic and political aspects of Muslim life, he reaches his goal ultimately.

To be more precise, according to Islamic terminology, Sufism implies *Iqtida,* i.e. to adhere strictly to the laws of the *Shariat.* Briefly, it means a highly pious and enlightened way of life which may be expressed in conformity with thought and action as explained herewith.

(a) *Qualan,* i.e. expression through *Shariat* or the Divine Law (ordained for the harmonious conduct of man in this world with promise of his salvation in the next life).
(b) *Failan* or *Tariqat,* i.e. expression through human activity and discipline under the said Divine Law or *Shariat* and,
(c) *Haalan* or *Haqiqat,* i.e. the 'state' acquired by acting upon and passing through the (a) and (b) stages, as explained above, reaching the zenith of the spiritual perfection.

While the (a) and (b) stages can be analysed or expressed through the human faculties, the expression of (c) i.e. of *Haalan, Haqiqat* or Reality is beyond the scope of all human conception and is, therefore, inexpressible and indescribable because human intellect or faculties are restricted to a 'limit' and transcend no more. This is the highest and final stage of Sufism in which the aspirant is face to face with the 'Divine Light' and ultimately merges his identity with God Supreme. It is, therefore, a state of which the secrets have never been divulged to the humanity at large without spiritual development and the hard striving and probation which Sufism entails.

There are certain regulations of Sufism which are called *Adraak* and *Ehsas* in Sufi parlance. They are also known as *Arkaane-Tasawwuf* or *Arkaan-e-Baatani*, i.e. the rules and discipline for the acquirement of the hidden wisdom or knowledge. They are divided into three categories, namely:

(*i*) Knowledge, i.e. the 'divine knowledge' attainable through the rigid discipline. of *Shariat*,

(*ii*) *Amal*, i.e. action under the above discipline with unflinching faith and devotion, and

(*iii*) *Haal*, i.e. the resulting reaction from *amal* or the action.

A Sufi aspirant's first important step to act upon the above course is to seek a religious preceptor or *murshid* who should be a practical master of the Divine knowledge and its training experiences.

The most mysterious part of Sufism is the delicate subject of *Ilm-e-Ludanni* or the knowledge of *Haqiqat* or Reality which, as stated above, is beyond all human conception and intellect. It actually means that hidden knowledge which directly emanates from the Almighty God and none else. No human being has ever achieved it without His will and grace, and those who did achieve it had to relinquish the world and its passing show. They are the God's chosen few and humanity on the right path of 'Truth and Love' whenever it goes astray.

A perfect Sufi is in constant communion with God through *Ilm-e-Ludanni* and has unlimited powers to prevail upon the whole creation of his beloved God's universe.

Thus the life of a Sufi is the 'life of the spirit' regulated strictly in accordance with Islamic theology and traditions. To attain this, his first lesson is unshakeable belief in the existence of God and unconditional surrender to His will. This entails a strenuous life attended by rigid austerity and self-denial. He has to undergo a course of training in regular prayers and meditation to attain the Divine knowledge and realisation of Truth. This particular knowledge is passed on 'in secret' by one Sufi to another having the requisite qualification, i.e. one who does not think evil, does not see evil, does not hear evil and does not speak evil. Without this Divine knowledge, one cannot fathom the 'hidden mysteries' of Nature of the soul. To sum up, the whole object of Sufism is to attain the highest spiritual perfection.

A Sufi will be distinguishable from others on account of his detachment from his parents children, wealth, power, position and comforts. His ignorance vanishes in the effulgence of the 'Divine Light' of the Most High, the Lord of all the Universe. In such an ecstatical devotion, there is neither pain nor sorrow for him, as he is overwhelmingly dedicated to the will of Almighty God. Thus a Sufi saint is the spiritual king, far above all temporal kings, disguised in the patched robes of an humble dervish.

The Sufi who sets out to seek God calls himself a traveller (*salik*). He advances by slow stages (*maqamat*) along a path (*tariqa*) towards union with Reality *(Fana fil Haqq)*. This path, according to al-Sarraj (d.988), author of *Kitab al-Luma'fi 'I Tasawwuf,* the oldest comprehensive treatise on Sufi teaching, consists of the following seven 'stages':[4]

1. Repentance *(tawaban)*
2. Fear of the Lord *(wara)*
3. Renunciation *(zubd)*
4. Poverty *(faqr)*
5. Patience or endurance *(sabr)*
6. Trust in God *(tawakkul)*
7. Satisfaction/contentment *(rida).*

By strictly adhering to the aforementioned seven stages, the *salik* is blessed with ten states *(sing. hal*, pl. *ahwal*) meditation *(muraqaba),* nearness *(qurb)* love *(mababba),* fear *(khawt),* hope *(rija),* longing *(shauq),* intimacy *(uns),* tranquillity *(itminan),* contemplation *(musbabada),* and certainty *(yaqin),* all with God as the referent (object). While the stages themselves can be arrived at and achieved through one's own effort, under the guidance of a mentor, the 'states' are spiritual feelings and dispositions over which a man has no control and are a gift from God. Also, as 'states' are divine gifts they can take many forms and colours and are often beyond description.

Sufism really denotes the attitude of mind, that is to say, a Sufi, while accepting all that orthodox Islam has to ofter, finds lacking in it an emotive principle. He is repelled by the idea of a straightforward religion containing primarily a command to do certain things and abstain from others. The Sufis, having imbibed many traditions of Christian asceticism, Arab piety and oriental esoteric cults, and having been influenced by the traditions of the Shiates, Iranians, Greeks and Indians, have developed certain tendencies both in the matter of belief as well as organisation. At first there was a great divergence between orthodox Islam and mysticism as but as a result of the efforts of Al-hujwari, Al-Qushari, Al-ghazali, Hazrat Abdul Qadir Gilani and Hazrat Shahabuddin Suhrawardi, a workable synthesis had been found between Sufism and orthodoxy. A distinctive Sufi theology was evolved, which developed its own terminology characteristic of practices and instructions which the Sufis in India fully accepted.[5]

The basis of the teachings of the early Sufis was a clear distinction between the 'real' and the 'apparent', between the 'external' and the 'internal', between the 'formal' and the "spiritual". The codes of beliefs and behaviour prescribed in the two were the *Shariat,* which they called 'external science' and the *Tariqat* (the path or way) or the 'internal or spiritual science'. The starting point of the spiritual progress, they argued, was the *Shariat* but their distinctive contribution to the religious life of the Muslims was the emphasis which they laid on *Tariqat*. They bypassed the abstract and colourless scholastic discussions of faith and ritual, and supplemented the inspiring orthodox attitude of commands and prohibitions with an 'emotive principle and a living religious experience'. Sufis sought to restore the religious balance and brought Islam into geater harmony with the prevailing Indian traditions.

The Sufis emphasised that ultimate Reality could be grasped only intuitively (*maarifat* or gnosis). It was veiled from the human eye and intellect, and constituted a mystery which could be apprehended by none but the advanced spirits. Although they described in vivid detail how *maarifat* could be achieved, they never concerned themselves with the nature of the Reality. There are clear traces of immanentist belief, of pantheism and of monism, although, in general, they believed in a transcendental omnipotent God as the Creator of the universe.

The next important feature of Sufi belief was divine love. From the time of Rabia Al-Adawiya (died A.D. 801), it had become the mainstream of Sufism, while in India it had become the dominant feature of the popular Bhakti movement.

Love, according to Sufis was the emotive force of life, in fact, its raison d'etre. This powerful emotion dominated every thought or sentiment, contemplative life, theology, ritual, thought of heaven and hell and all else. 'The heart of a mystic is a blazing furnace of love which burns and destroys everything that comes into it because no fire is stronger than the fire of love' says Khwaja Muinuddin Chishti.

The mystic belief in gnosis and love is usually accompanied by characteristic ethics. The Sufis had fully followed and systematised certain ethical concepts before Islam came to India. The Indian Sufism merely reiterated these beliefs although there was difference in the degree of emphasis. The basis of the Sufi attitude is that the Veil, which hides Reality from mankind is that of *Bashariyat* (creature-hood). The nature of man consists of sensual, intellectual and spirtual features. Intellects, according to them, performed a restricted function. The central pivot of spiritual life was the *qalb* (heart) or the *rooh* (soul). They were regarded as ethereal in nature and hence capable of communion with God. This function, however, could never be performed until the heart was purified of the dirt of sensual or lower self called in Sufi terminology the *nafs* (appetitive soul). The struggle against *nafs* regarded as wholly evil, therefore, became one of the main concerns of the Sufis. This implied an outlook of renunciation, penitence, asceticism, poverty, self-mortification and quietism, in short, other worldliness.

Sufism, the form which mysticism has taken in Islam, is not so much a set of doctrines as a mode of thinking and feeling within a specific religious domain. It represents in a way, a reaction against the intellectualism, cold formalism and ritualism of Muslim orthodoxy.

It might be said that spiritual practice is the core of Sufism and Sufi writers have certainly elaborated upon theories and metaphysical points of view, but it is in meditation, prayer, fasting, and day-to-day practices that we find the life of the mystical path. A great many Sufi writings in fact treat these kinds of practices in great detail.

Dhikr is regarded as the most important element of Sufi meditation. For the Sufis, *dhikr* is a method of spiritual concentration consisting of an invocation of the Divine Name or repetition of a sacred formula under the direction of a spiritual master belonging to a legitimate mystical order with an authentic chain of transmission (*silsila*). The spiritual master or shaikh gives the practitioner the necessary permission to perform *dhikr*.

The performance of *dhikr* is essentially a spiritual exercise through which Sufis are able to experience God's presence in every fibre of their very being. It is through *dhikr* that they achieve *fana* or 'annihilation' and subside in God for ever (*baqa*). Junaid says: 'Whosoever repeats the Name of the Lord merges into the Name and the Name merges into the Lord'. Another Sufi says: 'The first stage of *dhikr* is to forget self, and the last stage is the effacement of the worshipper in the act of worship, and total absorption in the object of worship'.

Dhikr was followed by meditation to allow the individual thoughts of Sufis to emerge and envelop them. Generally, a dervish meditated on some particular verse of the *Quran* and at the same time the image of the *pir* was recalled to mind. *Muraqaba*, the Arabic word for meditation, literally means 'vigilance' on awareness.

Thus meditation means forgetting all else besides God and is an intense remembrance of Him. Those who have undergone rigorous training under the guidance of a spiritual mentor may achieve this even when not in their teacher's presence. But though all these practices set Sufis apart from the body of the community, they were always very much an integral part of it and played a major role in shaping the popular face of Islam.[7]

They tend to put more stress on looking inward than outward, on contemplation over action, spiritual exercise and development of the self over dry legalism, and cultivation of the soul over social, worldly interaction with people. The aim of meditation in Sufism is to activate spirituality. As the Sufis believe that the heart is the centre of spirituality, therefore it is the heart that needs to be activated by turning to practice of meditation. Once the heart is activated a Sufi can reach his goal.

The Sufi Silsilas

The various Sufi Silsilas (Sufi schools of thought or Sufi *sampradaya*) played an important role in propagating Sufi ideology in general. There were some differences in their ideologies and practices. For an understanding of the ideologies and practices of Sufi Silsilas, are the following details.[8]

Although Abul-Fazl in *Ain-i-Akbari* mentions 14 Sufi Silsilas as active in India by the sixteenth century, the fact remains that in terms of their following and better organisation, only six Silsilas should be recognised as active and influential. Of these the Chistiyah, founded in India by Khwaja Ajmeri (though begun by Khwaja Abdul Chisti (d. A.D. 966) in Iran attracted the largest number of devotees, both Muslims and Hindus, and also made a profound impact on the course of the new Bhakti movement among the Hindus that gained momentum in the fourteenth century, and spread out to many parts of the country in the next 300 years. The only other *silsila* active in the Sultanate period (A.D. 1206–1526) was Suhrawardia, with its headquarters in Multan, and later extending to Sindh, which was established in India by Shaikh Bahauddin Zakaria (d. A.D. 1192). Then came the Firdausi Silsila, mainly restricted to Bihar, which was founded by Shaikh Badruddin Samarkhandi and was spread by the prolific writer of mystic literature, Shaikh Sharfuddin Yahya Muniri around the thirteenth century, followed by the Qadiriyah and the Shuttariyah Silsila in the middle of the fifteenth century. The Qadiriyah was established in India by Shah Naymatullah Qadiri, and the Shuttariyah by Shah Abdullah Shuttari (d. A.D. 1458); the former has spread in Uttar Pradesh (UP) and the Deccan, while the latter is seen mainly in the Madhya Pradesh and Gujarat regions.

It must however be noted that the Sufi *silsilas* are not sects. They grew because people went to Shaikhs or *murshids* (religious masters) for spiritual guidance and training, who invested those of their disciples whom they regarded as spiritually fit to cater for the spiritual and moral needs of others. Traditions, no doubt, envolved differently in different *silsilas*. What is common between the various Sufi *silsila* is the Sufi outlook. The characteristic feature of a particular *silsila* is confined to a few spiritual practices, like *auraad* (verses from the *Quran*), *sama* (audition), certain festivals, institutions like veneration of the shrines, the etiquette of visiting them and the devotion to certain leading personalities of the order.

The Chishti Sisila

This spiritual order flourished in Iran until Khwaja Moinuddin Chishti came to India and settled in Ajmer. Khwaja Moinuddin Chishti founded and popularised the Chishtiya Order in India. In India, the success of the Chishtiya Order was due to the fact that it knew how to adapt itself to the conditions and customs of the country. The early leaders of the Chishti Order were very learned. They found out the spiritual value of music and introduced it into their circle. A blending of Islamic and Hindu music began. The spiritual musical performances gave rise to *Qawwali* and *urs* began to be celebrated. The Chishti Sufis, though admired by the kings, did not interfere in state affairs. They criticised any deviation from the high ideals set by the Prophet. The Chishti Sufis were on friendly terms with Sufis belonging to other brotherhoods, and a spirit of extreme tolerance prevailed among different mystic orders. They were liberal in their outlook towards the non-Muslims. They never condemned them on the basis of their religion. They tried to attract them with their moral and spiritual qualities. Their doors were open for all. The system of running a free kitchen for the needy without distinction of caste, creed or colour was a typical Chishti practice. Whatever they received in the way of money and other things, they never kept for themselves but spent in feeding the poor and meeting their needs.

Among the Chishti Sufis, Khwaja Moinuddin was the greatest lover of humanity and had profound sympathy for all men. He could not see anyone in pain. He told his disciples to help the helpless, to fulfil the needs of the needy and feed the hungry. The Khwaja's simple and ascetic life was an inspiration to both Hindus and Muslims. They found in him a sincere spiritual guide. In those days Hindu society was shackled by a rigid caste system. Humanity was categorised according to lower and higher birth. Justice was not done to the lower classes as they were regarded as inferior by birth. When these people saw that the Khwaja treated all human beings alike, without the slightest discrimination, nothing could stop them from coming closer to him. He looked after these poor and needy people like his own brothers and sisters. Not only did he fulfull their physical needs, he also took full care of their spiritual needs. However, the Khwaja never attempted to convert them to Islam. It was the Islamic concept of the equality of all human beings that played a great role in bringing them into the fold of Islam. They themselves found a religion which treated everyone on an equal footing irresistible. Even to this day, both Hindus and Muslims throng his shrine in Ajmer. He was popularly known as Khwaja Gharib Nawaz.

After Khwaja Moinuddin, his great disciples and Caliphs spread the teachings of the order. Chishti Sufis were believers in Monism; the concept of unity of existence played a great role in infusing the sense of unity of humanity, which can be said to be a great cause of Hindu–Muslim unity in the past. Chishti Sufis guided people of all strata through their actions, words and writings.

Chishti Sufis were spokesmen of the public and through them the voice of the public reached the ears of their rulers. Due to Sufis, the Muslim society was morally and spiritually consolidated. The love of humanity is another Chishti characteristic. Ethical ideas were inculcated in the minds of the disciples. Missionary work was peaceful, based on the example, precept and spread of spiritual education. They were exponents of the doctrine of inner light and theology of the heart. For them, the value of a human being was higher than his religion or position in the society. The rich and the poor sat side by side and the message of equality and brotherhood was practised and followed.

Chishti Sufis did not lead a life of asceticism, and never lost touch with the realities of life. They never forgot the socio-moral aspects of life in the interest of spiritual exaltation and ecstasy. They had wives, children and household responsibilities, which they never shirked. In their monasteries the needy were satisfied, the hungry fed, and spiritually dejected comforted. They never visited the rulers or accepted high posts from them. Keeping away from the court and the king was a typical Chishti tradition. Thus Hindu–Muslim contact developed a new language, Urdu. The Chishti Sufis used Urdu in its earliest form while preaching before the general public. They did not write much because, considering themselves torch-bearers of principles of equality and justice, they proved these principles through their lives and personal example.

Khwaja Muinuddin had two highly able and talented disciples—Shaikh Hamiduddin of Nagaur and Shaikh Qutbuddin Bakhityar Kaki. Shaikh Hamiduddin was of a highly spiritual disposition, and lived a very simple and austere life. Although the Chishti saints were allowed to receive cash gifts, he preferred to work for his living. He had a small plot of land in a village called Suwali near Nagaur. He made his living solely from the income from this land. He did not accept any offerings.

He was so sensitive that he did not allow any harm to be done to any form of life. That is why he asked his followers to have only vegetarian food. This also shows his sensitivity to those of his fellowmen who were vegetarians.

These Sufis were, in fact, humanitarians par excellence. They did not love Muslims alone, but rather loved all human beings for the simple reason that they were God's creatures. And one who loves God in the true sense can never despise His creatures. These noble human values, cherished by the Sufis, were in fact so contagious that Islam spread among the masses like wildfire.

Shaikh Hamiduddin, being a religious scholar, had a good grasp of Islamic sciences. In fact, he believed that ignorance was the greatest curse for man. He believed that the *Shariah* and *Tariqa* were interrelated, just as the body and soul are. Treading the path of God and the Prophet to him meant severing all relations from everything which was not God, and persevering in the pursuit of God alone.

A number of Shaikh Hamiduddin's descendants continued his mission and Nagaur gradually developed into a strong centre of Sufism. This to a great extent was due to Khwaja Husain Nagaur, a descendant of Shaikh Hamid Khwaja Husain who, following in the footsteps of Shaikh Hamiduddin, lived a very simple life. The Chishti order became established in Ajmer and Nagaur, thanks to the efforts of Khwaja Muinudin Chishti and Hamiduddin Nagauri respectively. They were succeeded by worthy disciples who worked hard to spread the teachings of the order. The other able and important disciple of Khwaja Muinuddin Chishti, Qutb-ud-din Bakhityar Kaki left Ajmer and arrived in Delhi as he was needed more in Delhi than in Ajmer.

The immense popularity of Khwaja Qutbuddin among the masses as well as the elite was testified to by the large number of people who visited him daily for guidance. He was, like most of the Sufis, a humanitarian in the real sense of the word, always advising his disciples to help the poor and the needy to the extent that they were able. When offered the post of Shaikhul Islam by the Sultan, he did not accept it. The Khwaja regarded *sama* (audition) as a means of inducing a mystical state of ecstasy. He was opposed by the Ulama on this account.

Khwaja Qutbuddin had a number of disciples, two of whom are well known—Shaikh Badruddin of Ghazna and Shaikh Farid ud-Din Masud Ganj i-Shakar of Punjab. Badruddin loved to take part in *sama* and danced in ecstatic states.

Shaikh Fariduddin's ancestors came to Punjab from Kabul in the twelfth century. Khwajah Qutbuddin willed Baba Farid to be his successor. Baba Farid settled at Ajodhan, where he remained until his death. He lived a very simple and austere life, in a small house built of mud. In his house there was a separate cell for meditation. He slept on the floor and his visitors did likewise. The shrine, or *jamaat khana,* was run by his disciples, many of whom came from far-off places. The offerings received were either used by those of his disciples staying in the *jamaat khana* or were distributed among the poor and the needy. Nothing was kept for the following day.

Baba Farid, being a scholar, composed poems in Arabic, Persian and the local dialect known as Hindavi. He was very humble. He held the ulama in high regard but felt that they were not humble enough, in the way that the Sufis were, to give proper guidance to the people. Shaikh Farid took great pains in the training of his chief disciples, for it was they who would shoulder the responsibility for communicating the message to the people.[11]

Baba Farid had seven very distinguished Khalifas, Shaikh Nizam-ud-din Auliya being the most prominent. Shaikh Nizam-ud-din Auliya, the celebrated Khalifa of Baba Farid, was the most popular mystic personality of the fourteenth century in India. He did not discriminate between Hindus and Muslims. They were all God's creatures, equally worthy of respect and deserving of help whenever it was needed. Shaikh Nizam-ud-din's *langar* (free food) was served to both Hindus and Muslims. There was not the slightest trace of the communal in his thinking. He was the epitome of tolerance, broadmindedness and lack of bias.

Amir Khusrau, the famous Persian poet, was the Shaikh's most beloved disciple, who in return loved the Shaikh more than anyone else. Besides being a prolific writer, he also invented several musical instruments, including the sitar, and composed a number of melodies based on a mixture of Persian and Indian themes. These were used in *sama* rituals, in which he also participated. Thus the Chishti order has a very long continuous history and has become the most popular among the Sufi orders.

The Qadiri Silsila

The Qadir Silsila named after Shaikh 'Abd al-Qadir Jilani (1077–1166), figures prominently in Islamic spiritual history. Shaikh Abd Al-Qadir was born (1077–78) in the village of Nif in the district of Gilan in northern Iran. He was descended from Imam Hasan, the Prophet's grandson. Although from the organisational standpoint, it took almost half a century after the death of the saint for it to come to the fore, its reachings strongly influenced the thinking and conduct of a considerable number of Muslims during his lifetime.

Shaikh Abd al-Qadir had a highly persuasive way of encouraging people to distance themselves from obsessions with material things, and to turn instead to matters of the spirit. Having awakened the spiritual side of their nature, he dedicated himself to instilling in them a profound reverence for moral and spiritual values. His religiosity and earnestness made a great impression on his fellowmen, who flocked to his side.

Shaikh Abd al-Qadir's movement for spiritual uplift was so effective that a number of Sufis adopted Qadiri mystic ideals and began to disseminate them. This led to the formation of *silsila*, whose aim was a large-scale regeneration of the spiritual culture of society.

One of his greatest achievements was the thorough revitalisation of Muslim spiritual culture. Some of the founders of mystic orders, like Khwajah Moinuddin Chishti and Shaikh Najibuddin 'Abdul Qahir Suhrawardi, deriving great benefit from directly associating with him, came under the influence of his mystic ideas.

In India, the Qadiri Silsila emerged into prominence under the stewardship of Miyan Mir Qadiri (1550–1636), with his *khanqah* at Lahore. Under him the *silsila* not only became popular among the masses, but also found favour with the imperial court.

Miyan Mir belonged to that category of old saints who believed in the ideal of *fana-fillah* (annihilation in God). Hence he did not lay emphasis on the propagation of the *Shariat* as on prayer, penances and meditation, and adopted the doctrine of *wahdat-ul wujud.* He is said to have engaged himself in the study of the *Futuhat-i Makkiyya* of Ibn-ul Arabi and learnt by heart every page of the commentary on *Fusus-ul Hikam* of Ibn-ul Arabi, written by Maulana Abdur Rahman Jami. Shah Jahan was much inclined towards him and met him twice.

The followers of the *Shariat* believed that after reciting the *kalima*, a *kafir* (infidel) became a momin, but the followers of the path of *haqiqat* are alleged to have believed that nothing could remedy the state of oblivion caused by complete absorption in God. The saints of the Qadiri Silisila thus made no discrimination between a *momin* and a *kafir*. The Qadiris laid emphasis on the life of renunciation and celibacy and did not associate themselves with worldly affairs.

Miyan Mir looked with contempt on association with the people. The disciples of Miyan Mir withdrew themselves and separately engaged themselves in spiritual exercises under different trees. At the time of prayer they assembled together and performed the prayer in congregation. He justified his retirement into the garden saying that he followed the Prophet in this regard, as the latter too had retired to solitary places.

Riyazat-i shaqqa (hard penances) formed one of the most important practices of the Qadiri *silsila*. The Naqshbandis did not approve of it and claimed to follow the Prophet in this regard. Instilling the *tasuwwar-i shaikh* (contemplation on the Image of the Shaikh) was one of the means of training disciples in the early stages. During the *muraqaba* the seeker concentrated on the Image of his spiritual guide.

Mulla Shah Qadiri Badakhshi used to teach his disciples the method by which they could perform *hajj* in imagination without going to Mecca. Regarding the controversial issue of the *ru'yat* (Vision of God), Miyan Mir once quoted a *hadis* on this matter and said that the 'Vision of God' was possible with the physical as well as spiritual eyes in this world and the world to come.

The Qadiri saints, it seems, were not very particular in matter of dress. Miyan Mir argued that one should wear a garment which should not serve as the mark of identification of being a *fakir*. He condemned the traditional garments of the mystics. Moreover, the Qadiris regarded dress worn by them to depend on their means. If God provided them *'aba* and *qaba,* they wore them; and if He gave them nothing, they would remain naked.

The *sama* and dance in ecstasy had for centuries been the symbol of mystics' spiritual attainment. Miyan Mir understood Indian music and was keenly interested in it. However, he did not fall into the state *of wajd* (ecstasy) or go into *ruqs* (dance).

Most of Miyan Mir's disciples, such as Shaikh Muhammad of Lahore, Mulla Khwaja Bihari, and Miyan Abul Ma'ali, adhered to the doctrine of *wahdat-ul wujud.* About Miyan Abul Ma'ali, Dara Shikoh writes that he was an exception in that he neglected obligatory prayers and turned to be *bi-qaid* (unfettered) from the bonds of the *Shariat.* Shaikh Ahmad of Delhi imparted instruction on Ibn-ul Arabi's *Fusus-ul Hikam* and *Futuhat-i Makkiyya.* Dara Shikoh himself studied some portions of the *Fusus* under his guidance. He used to say that a Sufi was one who saw Real God in whatever thing he imagined.

Mulla Shah Qadiri Badakhsi was the most famous amongst the followers of Miyan Mir. Dara Shikoh considered him as the chief of the Unitarians. Mulla Shah treated Hindus and Muslims alike, and harboured no hatred for the people of other faiths.

In a state of excessive spiritual delight and in intoxication of love of God, Mulla Shah crossed all conventional limits. Dara Shikoh was initiated into the Qadiri Silsila by Mulla Shah, and it was from him he had learnt the essence of the doctrine of *wahdat-ul wujud.* Thus Dara Shikoh believed in *kul-ul-maujudat wahidun* (All things are One). Dara Shikoh accordingly tried to find out the ideological and cultural unity between Islam and other religions, particularly Hinduism, with single-minded devotion and sincerity.

The Suhrawardi Silsila

The Suhrawardi Silsila was founded by Shaikh Abu al Najib Suhrawardi (1097–1168), the uncle and spiritual guide of Shaikh Shihabuddin Suhrawardi, a contemporary of Abdul Qadir Jilani. This *silsila* was established in India in by Shaikh Bahauddin.

One important feature of this religious order was that it was not against possessing wealth earned by lawful means. Shaikh Bahauddin was criticised for his relations with the rulers. But he had good relations only with good rulers. Sultan Iltutmish was an honest and capable monarch, so the Shaikh supported him. When he came to Delhi, he had already earned a reputation and that is why he was appointed Shaikhul Islam by Iltutmish.

Qazi Hamiduddin was the most famous Khalifah of Shaikh Shahabuddin Suhrawardi. Qazi Hamiduddin was a writer. He has a number of works to his credit. *Lawaih* (Flashes of Light) was a very important Sufi textbook, which is no longer available. Even Baba Farid used to teach these books to his disciples. Qazi Hamiduddin explains that they appear to be two separate identities, but in fact they are identical. What a Sufi has to do is annihilate his ego.

Shaikh Bahauddin disapproved of the Sufis seeking guidance from a number of different peers. He wanted them to surrender to one rather than many. He attached great importance to supererogatory prayers and *dhikr*. He did not fast continuously. He died in 1262 in Multan. His tomb became a centre of pilgrimage.

He was succeeded by his son, Shaikh Sadruddin Arif. He was Shaikh Bahauddin's disciple and son-in-law. Shaikh Sadruddin Arif's son and successor, Shaikh Ruknuddin Abul Fath, earned great renown. Shaikh Ruknuddin was a great admirer of Shaikh Nizam-ud-din Auliya. His fame spread far and wide.

One of the most important disciples of Shaikh Shahabuddin Suhrawardi was Shaikh Jalaluddin Tabrezi. He established himself in Bengal where he was responsible for spreading Islam. He built his *khanqah* at Deva Mahal in northern Bengal. Large numbers of Hindus and Buddhists converted to Islam under his influence. His disciples were possessed of a missionary zeal and in Bengal, where the lower classes were being persecuted by the zamindars. they converted to Islam to find the equality and human brotherhood they had been denied for centuries.

Shaikh Sadruddin Arif, Baha ud-Din Zakariya's son, had a scholar disciple, Amir Husain. He wrote a number of works on Sufism. Nuzhatul Arwah describes the spiritual faith of pilgrimage. It was written in mixed prose and verse. It became very popular as a Sufi text. It deals with knowledge, truth *(maarifah)*, Sufism in general and the stages of the path of the *salik*. Amir Husain took great interest in *sama*.

Shaikh Sadruddin's son, Shaikh Ruknuddin, succeeded him. The ideological difference between Chishtis and Suhrawardis was mainly over the issue of the possession of money. The Suharwardis said that if they did not have money, how could they fulfill the needs of the poor and the deprived? But the Chishti Sufis said that money was not necessary. Only knowledge was necessary.

The Suhrawardi and Chishti traditions were not opposed to one another, one main reason being that the book, *Awariful Maarif,* was the only textbook used by all the Sufis. Although the early Chishti Sufis were scholars, they did not write a book which might have served as a Sufi textbook. Another Suharawardi Sufi, Qazi Hamuddin Nagauri, also wrote a number of books, which were read with interest by the Sufis of different orders.

The *jamaat khana,* or hostel accommodation for the dervish was an important part of the shrine. The *jamaat khana* also had an assembly hall, as it was essential for conducting meditation and other spiritual exercises. The Suharwardis built *khanqahs,* with the help of grants they accepted from rulers, and merchants. Thus they had no dearth of money and had abundant food in the *khanqah.* The culture in the Chishti *jamaat khana* was somewhat different from that of the Suhrawardi. Here, everyone was welcome. It was open for all.

The concept of *wabdatul wajud* had not taken root in the early Chishti or Suharwardi Sufis. In the fourteenth century, these ideas of Ibn Arabi were introduced into India by Iraqi, the Suhrawardi Sufi. *Awaraful Maarif,* which served as a Sufi classic also dealt with the theme of *waadatul wajud*—the oneness of existence. This experience, which the Sufis claimed to have had, was based on the notion that the 'lover, love and beloved were all one' that life with God rested entirely on love.

To induce ecstasy the music of *sama* was essential. The Suharwardis attached great importance to *salat* (prayer) and *dhikr* (remembrance of God) so far as the purification of the soul was concerned. They believed that fasting in the month of Ramazan was sufficient for this purpose.

But the Chishtis believed in rigorous ascetic exercise. They laid great emphasis on fasting to achieve the goal of spiritual purification. They had learnt different techniques, particularly of exhalation and inhalation from the yogis. They employed all these yoga techniques to achieve concentration, which was essential to the enhancement of mystical sensitivity. *Sama* formed an indispensable part of the Chishti rituals. The Suhrawardis did not attach such importance to *sama* but they too indulged in it on occasion.

The Suhrawardi order was closer to the spirit of Islam. These Sufis were more orthodox and played an important part in the preservation of the classical Sufi doctrine than to the philosophy of wabdatul *wajud*, propagated by Ibn Arabi.

The Naqshbandi Silsila

The founder of the Naqshbandi order, Khwaja Bahauddin Naqshband (1317–1389) was born at Kushk-i-Hinduwan, a village near Bukhara. It was Khwaja Bahauddin who popularised this spiritual order in central Asia, attracting people to it from all walks of life.

The Khwaja lived a very simple life. He took great interest in the training and education of his disciples in spirituality. Often the disciples were converts from other faiths, so they needed greater attention, having no knowledge of the Islamic faith. He spared no effort in training them thoroughly in order that they might communicate the message to the uninitiated.

This order is also known as the Khwajagan order, for a number of important personalities like Khwaja Yusuf Hamadani (d. 1140), his successor Khwaja Abdullah Barqi, Khwaja Hasan Andaqi, Khwaja Ahmad Yisiwi, and Khwaja Abd al Khaliq Ghujdawani were associated with it. They played a very great role in its popularisation. Khwaja Alauddin and Khwaja Muhammad Parsa were the most noteworthy disciples of Khwaja Naqshband. Khwaja Attar took a very active part in training the new converts to the order. His method of spiritual instruction was very appealing. Along with Khwaja Parsa, he made a concerted effort to put the Naqshbandi doctrine into practice. Their main emphasis was on making lawful earnings, cultivation being preferable to trade. They attached the utmost importance to the tradition of personal labour being the best way of earning, a livelihood in the eyes of God. Although Khwaja was not against married life per se, he felt that it was preferable for mystics to remain single, for married life was a great distraction.

By the sixteenth century the activities of the Naqshbandi order began spreading across the Indian subcontinent, where people seemed very receptive to its ideas. The order was brought to India by Khwaja Baqi Billah, who was seventh in the line of succession from Khwaja Bahauddin Naqshband, its founder. Baqi was born in Kabul. Khwaja Baqi Billah had received full training in the principles of the order under different Shaikhs and proved himself to be a great organiser. It is amazing that, within a short span of four to five years, he managed to establish this order on so firm a footing that since then it has gone on spreading without any break.

Khwaja Baqi Billah had a pleasing personality and people flocked to him, for they found in him their sincere well-wisher. They found peace and spirituality in his company. Khwaja, like other Sufis, ran a big *khanqah*, where the trainees were allowed to stay. There they received not only food but also a stipend for the needy. Khwaja Baqi believed in the doctrine of *wahdat al-wajud*, oneness of being, as propounded by Ibn Arabi. However, Shaikh Ahmad Sirhindi, the most famous *khalif-Billah* (representative) of the Khwaja, did not accept this theory.

Khwaja Baqi Billah laid the greatest of emphasis on purity of character. For him *tasawwuf* consisted of a high standard of character. That is why he exerted his utmost for the purification of the soul. His speech and conservations were so eloquent that people were moved by his words and, within a period of just three to four years, a large number of them entered his fold.

Khwaja Baqi Billiah appointed Shaikh Ahmad his viceregent *(Khalifa)* and sent him to Sirhind. Shaikh Ahmad Sirhindi earned more renown than any of the other disciples so far as the propagation and establishment of the Naqshbandi order in India was concerned. He was, moreover, a religious scholar, and taught his students not only the *Quran*, *hadith* and *fiqh*, but also books of *tasawwuf*. He followed the teachings of the Prophet to the letter. That is why he developed an interest in the Naqshbandi order, for they strictly adhered to the teachings of the *Quran* and *Sunnah.*

Soon after the death of Khwaja Baqi Billah, Shaikh Ahmad was acknowledged by the Khwaja's followers as the head of the Naqshbandi order. People in general regarded him as a *mujaddid*, a reformer of Islam. That is why this order came to be known as the Naqshbandiya – *Mujaddadiya*. Shaikh Ahmad had become very popular among all classes of people.

Shaikh Ahmad is called *mujaddid*, because his mission was to purify Islam of all those anti-Islamic practices which, on account of indigenous influences, had become prevalent among Indian Muslims. One great contribution he made to *tasawwuf* lay in the field of its theology. His goal was to bring *tasawwuf* more in line with the teachings of the *Quran* and *Hadith*, for in his times it had come closer to yogic practices and the Vedanta philosophy. He therefore admonished people to observe the tenets of Islam as enshrined in the *Quran* and *Hadith*. He also strove to harmonise Sufi teachings with the Shariah and his efforts were certainly rewarded.

What is regarded as his most important contribution to *tasawwuf* is his concept of *wahdatush shahood* (unity of consciousness). Shaikh Ahmad Sirhindi criticised the theory of *wahdatal wajud*. To Ibn Arabi, God and the world were identical. The Shaikh believed that the world was not one with God, but proceeded from God; that the existence of God was real, while the existence of the world was unreal and imaginary; that the universe was not God, but the Shadow of God. This concept, the Shaikh felt, was entirely in consonance with the unity of God.

He explains his concept by a simile : 'The presence of the world is like the presence of the image of an object in a mirror. Thus the presence of the image is not the existence of the object. The object is real, but the image is unreal. The existence of the image is a shadow existence *(wujud zilli)* totally separate from the real existence *(wujud asli)* of the object. In this way the existence of the world is a shadow existence, separate from the real existence of God'. *Wahdatush shahud* also means unity of vision, that is to say, the experience of union or oneness is related to vision rather than reality.

The Naqshbandi Silsila as represented by Shaikh Ahmad Sirhindi and his disciples, called *mujaddadiya*, differed considerably from other contemporary *silsilas*. It laid much emphasis on the adherence to the *Shariat* and all the visible austerities that did not conform to the *Shariat* were rejected. Such practices were ascribed to the jogis, Brahmans, and Greek philosophers. However, in this *silsila*, too, the Shaikh (guide) occupied a very important position. The disciples were enjoined to do nothing, except the obligatory prayers, without the explicit permission of the Shaikh.

Against the emphasis of the Qadiris on solitude, the Naqshbandis believed in corporate life and a common *muraqaba* attended by all the disciples. An exercise peculiar to both the Qadiris and the Naqshbandis was the practice of *habs-i dam* (retention of breath). Miyan Mir and his successors were adept at this exercise.

The Naqshbandis tenaciously adhered to the *Shariat* and invariably followed the practices of the Prophet in every aspect of life. Therefore, they were opposed to the practices of other *silsilas*. For instance, they differed from the Qadiris on the question of *ruyat*. Shaikh Ahmad Sirhindi argued that it was nothing but an illusion of the Sufis, who, in a state of ecstasy, thought that they were seeing God. All orthodox scholars, he said, were unanimous in their opposition to this concept.

In the same way Shaikh Abdul Haqq Muhaddis Dehlavi, despite his affiliation with the Qadiri Silsila, rejected its concept of the Vision of God. He said that the Vision of God could be possible only with the eyes of heart and not with the outward eyes. Mystics in intoxication of the love of God only felt the illusion of witnessing God.

In the same way the Naqshbandi disapproved of *sama* and Shaikh Ahmad Sirhindi believed that it was an un-Islamic practice, and a perverse form of real mysticism which once laid emphasis on the revival of the *sunna*, purification of passion and enlightenment of the inner soul. It was on this point that the Naqshbandi Silsila split up into two branches. The sons of Khwaja Baqi Billah approved of the *sama* while Shaikh Ahmad Sirhindi dissociated himself from them on this score and founded a branch of the *silsila* in which the *sama* was rejected.

In contrast to the Qadiri Silsila, the Naqshbandis undertook the task of purging the Muslim community of non-orthodox practices and made strenuous efforts to eradicate *bidat* (heresies and un-Islamic practices) and bring the Muslims back to the path of the *Shariat*. Since none of the contemporary *silsilas* strictly followed the *Shariat*, the Naqshbandi saints did not permit their disciples to acquire spiritual training from mystics of any other *silsila*. Besides, the Naqshbandi silsila emphasised the performance of the five prayers in congregation, keeping the fasts of Ramazan, reading of the *Quran*, giving of *zakat*, and performance of *hajj*, the main recognised pillars of Islam.

Among the successors of Sirhindi, Shah Waliullah made it his mission to work for the moral and spiritual regeneration of Muslim society and succeeded in bringing about an intellectual renaissance. Like Shaikh Ahmad Sirhindi, Shah Wahiullah considered Islam to be a complete code of life, offering guidance at both individual and social levels.

In the history of Naqshbandi, Shah Waliullah, being an authority on *Hadith* and *tafsir*, made the greatest academic contribution. Shah Waliullah also translated the *Quran* into Persian. This was a very great service on his part. In India, Persian was a language of educated Muslims and non-Muslims alike and they benefited greatly from this translation.

The Firdausi Silsila

The Firdausi Silsila originated with Saifuddin Bakharzi, who was Najmuddin Kubra's disciple. Najmuddin Kubra was a disciple of Abu Najib. He was called by his *pir* 'the Shaikh of Paradise'. Hence he came to be known as Firdawsi (Paradise).

Shaikh Sharfuddin Ahmad Yahya Muniri was the best-known disciple of this order. He came from Bihar, his ancestors having settled there in the thirteenth century. The Shaikh was originally from Bukhara where he had received a proper religious education. Leaving Bukhara, he had gone on to Delhi.

Then Ahmed passed through Munyar on his way to Sunargaon in Bengal. And very soon Sunargaon became a centre of Islamic learning. Ahmad went back to Munyar, then after staying there for some time, he went to Delhi to visit Shaikh Nizam-ud-din Auliya.

People started thronging to his side. One of his devotees, Maulana Nizam Madni, built a *khanqah* for him in Munyar. Subsequently, Sultan Mohammad-bin-Tughlaq had a great *khanqah* built for the Shaikh and assigned him some land to provide for its needs. This *khanqah* became a meeting place for the common man as well as for religious scholars and Sufis. A great scholar, he made a profound study of theological and mystical subjects and was very capable of discussing theological as well as spiritual issues. He also wrote books which are regarded as great contributions to Sufism.

Shaikh Sharfuddin held the view that a Sufi must be merciful and generous to others. He should feed others, even if he had to go hungry himself. He could make do with the minimum of clothes in order to clothe others and he should patiently suffer any cruelty or injustice meted out to him. And he should never retaliate when provoked. He should rather return blessings for abuses. He held that a true Sufi must be sympathetic to everyone, just as the sun shines on enemies and friends alike.

He taught his followers to assist their fellowmen wholeheartedly. He said that acts of kindness and assistance given to the needy were meritorious in nature than even prayers and fasting. Shaikh Sharfuddin believed in ascetic exercises for the development of the spiritual self. He said that the performance of these exercises endowed devotees with supernatural powers, which enabled them to receive divine inspiration.

He believed that the observance of the *Shariat* was essential for the spiritual life of a *Salik*, for the teachings enshrined in the Shariah were based on divine revelation. First, one had to believe in divine unity and, second, in obedience to God.

The Shaikh believed that the spiritual path was beset with thorns, therefore a Teacher/Guide was required to traverse it. The Master imposes a three-fold discipline on the *Salik*. This discipline consists of: (*i*) Service of the world for a year (*ii*) Service of God for a year (*iii*) Watching the heart for a year.

The Perfect Guide is supposed to have four qualifications:

1. Complete devotion to God

2. The capacity to receive truths direct from God without any intermediary.
3. Nearness to God.
4. Acquisition of knowledge from God without any intermediary.

This stage can be attained by someone whose heart is fully purified from all kinds of worldly desires.[12]

The disciple can receive divine blessing only when he is able to fully detach himself from the world. He has to practise absorption. A disciple has to lose himself in the Teacher. He has to cast off all his desires and follow the Teacher in true submission. It is by fully submitting to his Teacher that he submits fully to his Lord.

He felt that the *Shariat* and *tariqa* were complementary to one another. He believed that it was religion which guided the spiritual journey from this material world to the celestial world. To him, the *Shariat* and *haqiqa* were essential concomitants of the spiritual life: the *Shariat* was the body and the *tariqa* was the soul.

He condemned those misguided Sufis who believed that, having been attentive to God, there was no need to say their prayers once they had reached the goal they had set their hearts on.

The Shaikh held it very important that the disciples opt for a perfect guide to help them along their spiritual path, for the absence of a guide would leave them directionless and they would go astray. The spiritual journey could not be undertaken without the guidance of an experienced teacher. It took a true guide to lead them along the right path towards God realisation.

Inspired by the ideas of Maulana Jalaluddin Rumi, Iraqi and Fariduddin Attar, Shaikh Sharfuddin believed in *wahdatal wajud.* He said that the *tawhid* of the *tariqa* was the highest step of the pursuit of the truth. To him *tawhid* or *wahdatul wajud* was the final stage in the Sufi journey to the world of Unity, where he became the recipient of the divine light.

The Shaikh had a great following of disciples numbering more than a lakh. Qazi Shamshuddin was another important disciple of Shaikh Sharfuddin. He had a large number of disciples. A number of *khanqahs* was built in Bengal. The spiritual teachings embodied in his letters spread almost all over the subcontinent within a short period of time.

Impact of Ibn-Arabi's Mystical Thought on the Sufis of India

Shaikh Muhiyuddin Ibn-Arabi (1165–1240) occupies a very special position in the annals of Islamic mysticism, i.e. *tasawwuf* or Sufism. Both his followers and others called him Shaikh-i Akbar (the greatest of the Sufi shaikhs) on account of his spiritual excellence as well as the significance of his metaphysical thought. His pantheistic mystical philosophy *wahadat al-wujud* or *tawhid-i wujudi*—the 'Unity of Being'—has been the cornerstone of Muslim spiritual thought. It has deeply influenced the Sufis of the different *silsilas* and even ulema and intellectuals all over the Muslim world.[13]

It is said that the pivotal point of Muslim religious thought during the medieval period was the pantheistic philosophy of Ibn 'Arabi. The shaikh's works, particularly the *Fusus al-Hiham* and the *Futuhat-i Makkiya,* which are the best sources of his mystical doctrine, have been accepted in the Muslim mystic circles as the guide books, especially for those who set out on a journey of the uncharted ocean of spiritual experience. Like the Sufis of other Islamic countries, the Sufis of India also appear to have been influenced by Ibn-Arabi's mystical writings, at least since the fourteenth century A.D. The medieval Sufi literature produced in India, supplies valuable information of many Indo–Muslim saints who played a serious and important role in developing and disseminating this mystical doctrine.

By the beginning of the sixteenth century, the doctrine of the 'Unity of Being' seems to have completely dominated the Sufi circles in the whole subcontinent. Its impact is clearly discernible in Indo–Muslim religious thought throughout the sixteenth century. Shaikh Abdul Quddus of Gangohi, Shaikh Amanullah of Panipat, their spiritual followers and many others are reported in different works to have evinced profound interest in Ibn-Arabi and *wahadat al-wujud.* They actively worked for the popularity and development of this Sufi spiritual philosophy and its propounder in India during the sixteenth century.

Before dealing with them, we must bear in mind the doctrine of *wahadat al-wujud*, the 'Unity of Being', as propounded by Shaikh-i Akbar so as to clearly understand the contribution and interpretations of the saints of India in the field of theosophy. We can say that Ibn Arabi's conception of *wahadat al-wujud* is an extension of the Islamic doctrine of *Tawhid*, the Oneness of God. From the concept that 'there exists but one God', he takes us to the profession that 'there is nothing in existence except God'. According to him, Being is One – it is that which exists. This being is God. Everything else is his manifestation. Hence the world is identical with God. The identity of the world and God is conceived on the basis of the identity of His existence and essence or the substance and attributes, the world being only a manifestation of His attributes.

For Ibn-Arabi, 'Being' is identical with attributes, and attributes express themselves in manifestations or modes which are the world and its objects. He holds that relation between the world and God is one of identity.

Again, according to Ibn-Arabi, God is the Reality and the world is his adumbration. But adumbration is the appearance of Reality. It is Reality appearing, manifesting itself. Hence the world is identical with God.

As to the relation between man and God, Ibn 'Arabi maintains that the relation between God and man is that of identity, of immanence, of nearness. Really, nearness means nothing other than the fact that God Himself is the very essence of the limbs and parts of man. The shaikh again argues that man is said to be created after the image of God as revealed from the verse: God created man after His own Image.

That means that man possesses all the attributes of God. In fact it is His attributes that are manifested in man. They are bodily there in man. That is why it is said that one who is cognizant of his own self comes to be cognizant of his God.

It may be remembered, the spiritual scenario of the Indian subcontinent was covered with the clouds of the pantheistic philosophical views at the beginning of the sixteenth century. Almost all the Sufis of the period were sunk in the ocean of *wahadat al-wujud*. Shaikh Abdul Quddus Gangohi, who held a significant place amongst his contemporaries, was the pioneering personality among the exponents and interpreters of this doctrine in those days.

Shaikh Abdul Quddus, in some of his Hindi verses, says that steam rising from a river is called vapour. When it rests in the atmosphere, it is called a cloud. If water from the cloud falls into a vessel, it is known as water of whatever receptacle it finds itself in. If it falls in form of rain, it is known as rain water. In all cases, there remains water. Similarly, according to him, duality is a false concept and the idea of anything besides God is misguided. People should, therefore, believe only in the 'Unity of Being'.

Shaikh Abdul Quddus started open discussions about the pantheistic philosophy. Shaikh Abdul Ahmad Faruqi Sirhindi, another famous follower of Shaikh Abdul Quddus, also earned great fame and popularity as an exponent and interpreter of Ibn-Arabi's thought.

The other important exponent of Ibn Arabi's thought, during the sixteenth century, was the famous Qadiri saint, Shaikh Amanullah of Panipat. He developed his interest in the *Fusus al-Hikam* and other famous works on the concept of *wahadat al-wujud* in the company of his teacher, Shaikh Muhammed Mawdud Lari who, becoming filled with ecstasy, used to deliver extempore lectures on the 'Unity of Being'.

Another saint of the same period is Mir Saiyid Abdul Awwal bin Alauddin Husain (d.968/1561) who had the spiritual authority in the Chishtiya and Qadiriya orders. He was a scholar of high repute. He wrote a commentary on the *Futuhat-i Makkiya* of Ibn-Arabi by simplifying the great author's complex theories.

As regards the Sufis of the Shattari Silsila, Shaikh Muhammad Ghouse of Gwalior is known as a great champion of the philosophy of *wahadat al-wujud*. Throughout his life, he was devoted to this mystic doctrine. However, he seems to have completely reinterpreted it in accordance with the need of the time.

Thus we see that Ibn 'Arabi's mystical concept of *wahadat al-wujud*, the 'Unity of Being', which entered the Sufi circles of the Indian subcontinent in the first half of the fourteenth century, had reached the pinnacle of its popularity and permeated the spiritual and intellectual life of the Muslims throughout the country during the sixteenth century. In Akbar's time it had become the dominant mystical theosophy of Muslim India. Most of the eminent Sufis and *mashaikh* of different spiritual orders had drunk at the fountain of Ibn Arabi's thought.

Activities of Dargahs or Khanqahs

Before going into role played by Sufi saints for communal harmony, one should have a fair knowledge about their organisational network. In this context one should know about the functioning of *khanqahs* or *dargahs,* which formed centres for activities, such as social contacts and interation between different communities.

Sufism is a very complex phenomenon. In India it took root in both the rural and urban areas. In some cases, the deep impact of Sufism and its popularity among the masses transformed rural regions, into flourishing urban centres. In the reign of Muhammed-bin-Tughluq, while in Damascus, Shihabu'd Din Ahmad al-Umari was told that in Delhi there were two thousand large *khanqahs*. But it is clear that by that time the *khanqahs* had exercised a deep social, political economic and cultural influence in India.

Sufi disciples gathered round their *murshids*, Shaikhs or *pirs* to learn the rites, rituals and rules of each order, which were designed to stabilise their emotional and intellectual faculties and to enable them to realise Reality or the direct intuitive recognition of God. Sufi disciples tended to deify their *pirs,* even though the latter were totally disinterested in turning themselves into Godheads. The reliance of Sufis on God, particularly in the material sense, attracted both people from economically deprived classes and members of the oppressed elite into orders. The *khanqahs* gave to most people a feeling of hope and a vision of a bright future, both in this world and the one to come.

From the time of the Khurasanian, Abu said, *khanqahs* were rendezvous for artisans and merchants. All *khanqahs* in India followed this Khurasanian tradition for the mutual benefit of both Sufis and their visitors. Merchants at this time were continually undertaking hazardous journeys to distant countries, while engaged in risky commercial ventures. Some *khanqahs* operated a type of spiritual insurance scheme in which financial pledges were made by merchants in return for Sufi prayers for protection during a journey, instalments being collected en route. The chain of *khanqahs* of Shaikh Abu Ishaq from Kazirun to China is one case in point. Naturally the system was one-sided and hardly compares with a modern insurance scheme. If the prayers of a great Sufi saint failed, the unfortunate merchants and travellers were killed, and there was no means by which the money advanced could be restored. Nevertheless the network of Chishtiyya, Suhrawardiyya and Firdawsiyya *khanqahs* in India and those of the Kubrawiyya and of other orders in Kashmir, offered greatly needed psychological comfort to merchants and other travellers during this period.

The *urs* ceremonies and other anniversaries celebrated in *khanqahs* developed into significant cultural institutions and were eagerly awaited by both the poor and affluent alike. Sufism gave birth to a very wide range of mystic symbolism and became an indispensable part of Persian poetry. This poetry was not only an expression of the mystic love of a thirsty soul seeking an intuitive understanding of God, but an avenue for emotions and feelings which would otherwise have never been expressed due to the fury of the orthodox, social inhibitions and political repression.

The typical tasks of the saints were to oversee their *murids'* spiritual education. In addition, they had to receive a large number of people who came to have, say, an ailment cured or a wish fulfilled. It was at this time that saints started to write *tawidhs* for this purpose.

In the beginning the Sufi-saints did not feel that they needed to settle down at a particular place in order to perform their functions, nor did they agree about the form they should give to their public life if they did settle down. But the advantages of working over a long period in a particular community were obvious. The *khanqah* or *dargah* thus became an institution among those Sufis who belonged to an order. As an institution it lasted longer than the lives of its founders and individual inmates, and was liable to develop characteristics that did not harmonise with the principles and ideals for the service of which it was founded. It must therefore be judged by itself. As the *khanqahs* developed, they experienced certain experimental forms of community living. When they eventually received more permanent forms, they started expanding as well.

It could be said generally of every *khanqah* that even in the bad days a person who waited long enough was sure to get some sort of meal and, with luck, a share of money or goods distributed as charity that would tide him over the next crisis. It was the shaikh and those dedicated to the spiritual who starved; inmates of the *khanqah* got what they wanted, sometimes less than was sufficient, sometimes in abundance. The small group that collected round *dargahs* began with courses in starvation, but gradually the physical conditions improved. The shaikh continued his practice of 'concealed' starvation to the end of his days; his chief *murids* did the same. But food and charitable gifts became an attraction of his *khanqah* as of every other. In every *khanqah,* ideals of austerity fought against satisfaction of physical needs... A feature of *khanqah* life which is by no means admirable is the opportunity it provided to large numbers of people to live on generosity of well-to-do admirers of the shaikh.

So, the *khanqahs* might be said to have served as a mediating institution between the shaikh and his saintly qualities on the one hand and the masses on the other. Through a *khanqah,* a saint could definitely reach many more persons than he could have otherwise. Other functions of the *khanqah* included the distribution of money, food and goods. The goods might have been donations made by a near-by worldly ruler and were distributed among needy pilgrims and the poor people of the neighbourhood.

Apart from spiritual guidance and distribution of food to the destitudes, a *khanqah* or *dargah* had several other functions to fulfill. Being handed over to a Khalifah after the *pir's* death, the main task of the successors is to cherish the memory of the dead saint, to observe the proper rites at his tomb and to guide pilgrims and visitors to the tomb in order to receive the saintly blessings of the dead *pir* via mediation by his celebration is an occasion for amusement of all sorts for devotees and visitors. Thousands of pilgrims are entertained by games, merry-go-rounds, music and plenty of food. Furthermore, when the social well-being of a family is endangered or disturbed, they might decide to go to a *dargah* in order to re-establish equanimity under the guidance of one of the *mujawars* (assistants), who mediates the blessings of the *pir*. The poor, the destitute, and the socially isolated people of the community might find the *dargah* a proper place to stay in, in order to adjust to their social handicap. Also, couples who are afflicted with the problem of childlessness may bring a red thread, have it blessed by the *mujawar* who is looking after them, and have it tied to the secluding wall of the tomb. Further, people in debt might seek the blessings of the pir.

Some *dargahs* maintain public kitchens which distribute free food *(langar)* to the poor and to travellers. The *langar* is also an essential feature of the annual *urs* celebration. The duration of the service and the amount of food cooked depends upon the amount of money donated by individuals of this particular purpose. For example, in the Dargah Khwaja Saheb at Ajmer there are two big *deghs* (cauldrons) in which food is cooked whenever some visitor to the *dargah* volunteers to pay the cost. Although this kind of mass cooking is mainly an affair of the pilgrims, it does have some side benefits for the local community.

Most of the *dargahs* provide their visitors with *qawwali* singing every Thursday night. A group of musicians sings of the life and death of the *pir* as also more popular songs of the Sufi tradition. The *qawwali* singers are either rewarded with food or by contributions from the audience.

Education is another function of most of the *dargahs*. Quranic schools are attached to *dargahs* where *Quran* reciting and reading and the writing of Urdu texts is taught, especially to children of the neighbourhood.

During the annual *'urs'* celebration administrators of the *dargahs* rent out land around the *dargah* to tradesmen at fixed rates. It is during this occasion that the administrators (or *mujawars*) also collect those contributions that guarantee the regular functioning of the *dargah* as well as the income of its servants. While the smaller sums (*nazar*) are deposited in front of an attending *mujawar*, the bigger donations placed directly on the tomb of the *pir*. Some *dargahs* stick to the old custom and distribute these presents immediately to the needy who are always present.

Another redistributive aspect of *dargahs* is begging on the *dargah* premises. Since the accumulation of beggars suffering from infectious diseases was prohibited in the *dargah* of Ajmer in 1958 because of the danger of infection, a Committee of Enquiry suggested : 'Begging within the dargah premises shall be strictly prohibited. Beggars suffering from any infectious disease shall be ejected from the dargah premises ... (others) shall be kept and maintained in a home specially provided for them'. A last redistributive aspect to be mentioned here is the providing of accommodation to large numbers of pilgrims. This task is partially met on the *dargah* premises itself.

Dargahs are centres of pilgrimage whose reputation spreads far beyond their local community. Though they serve as neighbourhood and regional centres in the four functions mentioned above, their main function and attraction is to meet the religious and psychic needs of pilgrims. This function of the *dargah* not only attracts simple people, but people of all social classes of both the Hindu and Muslim communities.

Pilgrims are normally looking for one or other of the following:

1. social well-being;
2. psychic well-being;
3. physical well-being;
4. guidance and counsel for social problems;
5. appeasement in cases of psychic problems; and
6. healing of psychiatrically recognised illnesses.

Pirs are known for their special powers and abilities. In accordance with their special reputation, they attract 'cases' from all over the country. Information concerning the special 'skills' of a particular saint seems to spread among pilgrims by word of mouth. As mentioned earlier, during a saint's lifetime the special power of *karamah* was attributed to him (in the case of martyrs, their special power is derived from the circumstances of their death). During the saint's lifetime people would come for blessings and for the cure of their ailments, which was done by issuing *tawidhs*. The *mujawars* of today fulfil the same needs by mediating the power of the *pir*. In this manner they meet the requirements of their clients/visitors. They guide them to the tomb, assist their offerings and prayers, issue blessings on written *tawidhs*, which the pilgrim may take home and have eventually re-issued and sent by mail by his particular *mujawar*.

Psychiatric illnesses and social and psychic troubles or diseases are taken care of by the *mujawars* who mediate the power of the *pir*. Physical illnesses, however, are transferred to a medical institution or to the Unani dispensary which is attached to most of the bigger *dargahs*. A *mujawar* might take certain steps like writing a *tawidh* against a physical disease, but he does not get involved in treatment or diagnosis. In the dispensary, Unani doctors or healers diagnose the patient according to the principles of Unani medicine. The appropriate medicine is concocted accordingly. Some Muslim healers, who are not connected to *dargahs*, write *tawidhs* and give medicine.

Pir–Murid Relation

The centrality of the *pir–murid* relationship is deeply anchored in the cosmology of Sufi discourse and can scarcely be validated outside its hermeneutic. For a believer, the hermeneutic is constituted in the habit of the heart. Therefore, the inner logic of that habit in the spiritual practice and perceptions of the believer should be looked into. The world and ways of the allegiance of *murids* to a certain *silsila* also should be taken into consideration. In its meanings and metaphors, motifs and moods, the hermeneutic alarmingly seems to be an esoteric semiotic contrivance to evoke a lost soul long enshrined in the tomb. As a sacred relationship the *pir-murid taalluq* is resolutely locked up in a cosmic confidentiality where whispers and silence are too intimate to be disclosed:[14]

So sensitive is the intimacy and so personal is the communion of the *murid* and the *pir* that any misreporting or misinterpretation is liable to deny the relationship its authenticity and richness. Therefore, any account of this intimacy should neither discredit the soul of the intimate, nor even question the veracity of the spiritual experience.

In Sufi belief the *pir–murid* relationship is eternally kindled by a discourse of divine love *(ishq-i-haqiqi)*. It is only through unqualified and unconditional love for the *pir* that a *murid* passes through various stations *(madarij)* in an undulating journey that culminates in the eventual merging with the *pir's* identity. Divine love sharply contrasts with the kind of love ordinarily practised by mortals. For the believer, mundane love is seldom sustained. As a captive of its own finitude, mundane love gradually isolates the self, thereby distracting the self from divine destiny.

In contradistinction, the love of the *murid* for the shaikh, the divine love in Sufi belief, is de-caged from the temporality of space and time. It seeks the immortal and endures. Rather than isolate the self, it restores to the self its divine destiny. Rather than destroy, divine love dissolves the self into divinity.

The love for the shaikh is an endless longing that cumulates with ever-increasing intensity. Such an undiminishing love bestows on the *murid*, as it endures the enhanced spiritual endowments.

It is such a divine love which evokes in the *murid* a spiritual experience devoid of any physicality. In that spiritual experience, *ishq* evolves through successive stages and, if one may say so, a biographical trajectory. At its initiation, *ishq* destroys the lover (in this case the *murid* as the shaikh's lover), so that the subject of *ishq* vanishes from its script. What remains is the object of love–the *mashuq* (beloved). At the second stage the beloved shaikh's initial response to the lover (*murid*) and his authentic initiation into *ishq* creates overwhelming discomfort and anxieties in the lover's selfless soul. The spiritual dissolution (*fana*) of both the lover and the beloved, the subject and the object of *ishq*, marks the next stage in the life of divine love. At this stage neither the lover nor the beloved remain. What survives is *ishq* alone.

In Sufi discourse the substance of *ishq* is both an expression and an imagination. While it passes through the subsequent biographical stages, it requires of the *murid* an intense imagination of the shaikh to realise itself. *Ishq* as imagination invokes the *pir* within the *murid's* own body. As an indisoluble imagination it resists any fragmentation of the mental image.[15]

Through the Sufi spiritual vision, the shaikh's ears not only mingle but become the *murid*'s ears, the shaikh's eyes the *murid*'s eyes, the Shaikh's nose the *murid's* nose; the Shaikh's tongue the *murid*'s tongue, and thus the intense imagination converts, according to the *murid*, the communion into a union. *Ishq* as imagination prompts all of the *murid's* actions but with the shaikh's permission. The shaikh's wish turns into a divine command guiding the *murid*'s actions.

It is not only that the *pir*'s words become the *murid*'s words, what is indeed striking is that the *murid*'s words are the *pir*'s words. Yet the *murid* strives to bring into sharper focus the shaikh's image.

It is clear from the very beginning that the Sufi experience of *taalluq* is spiritually very intense and intricate. In the Sufi community, a *murid* always feels that his/her proximity to the shaikh is next to none. And this is a spiritual trait well within the tradition of Muhammad the Prophet. The followers of the Prophet vied with one another in their claims to the closest intimacy *(qurbat)* with him.

Indeed, far from being ascriptive, the *pir–murid* relationship is based on achievements of station or height *(madarij)* through spiritual investment. Through an unconditional and unqualified respect for the *pir*, the *murid* expresses such investment through *adab*. The bondage of the *murid* to the *pir* is expressed literally by the term *ghulami* (enslavement). As an obedient servant of the *pir*, the *murid* hopes to occupy closer proximity and thereby perfect the personal *talluq*.

The practice of *adab* in the Sufi tradition surpasses mere habitual deference to one's spiritual leader. Just as *ishq* is boundless in its intensity, *adab* knows no limits in its expression. Through the discipline of *adab* and the passion of *ishq*, the self destroys itself inwardly while satisfying the outer imperatives by playing a role assigned in the mortal world. Thus the Sufi self remains staunchly stoic. An optimist, the self is without hope; a pessimist without despair, for in *ishq* it accepts the condition of total unity.

The *murid* believes that his rapport with his *pir* was always intimate and as old as his memory. Through a charged invocation of recollections, he rekindles his past to relive the relationship, to reinforce the *talluq*.

It is believed that there is a perennial rain of *inayat* (kindnesses) and *barakat* (blessings) which are constantly showered upon him by his *pir*. Even when a situation does not ostensibly seem related to the *pir*, in reality there are seldom segments in the *murid*'s life that are bereft of the *pir*'s benevolence. The *murid* proudly accepts the privileges he enjoyed by his affiliation to the spiritual lineage. It was the tradition of the *khanqah* that on writing a letter stating any problem faced by the *murid*, the problem no longer remained with the *murid* but shifted through a divine vow to the *pir*'s shoulders. The miseries were struck off from the text of the *murid*'s self as it was the *pir* who now had to dispense with these difficulties. The *murid*'s unflinching devotion guaranteed a spaceless spiritual stand-by.

The *murid* was assured of access every time he desired his *pir*. On the death of the *pir* his nominee inherited the spiritual patrimony to provide the *murid* continual access to the spiritual lineage.

The *pir* does not, however, plant suffering on the *murid*'s being for nothing. To the *murid* worldly suffering is willingly suffered not simply because it is authored by the *pir*. More important, the *murid* sees in suffering the *pir*'s desire to purify his soul. The worldly favours that the *pir* bestows on the *murid* are liable to contaminate the *murid*'s soul. The *pir*, too, suffers similarly. The principle of suffering is indispensable to divine realisation.

Mehfil-e-Sama

The Indian subcontinent has enjoyed a vitality and continuity of the *sama* tradition which has few parallels in the history of Islam. This vitality is directly linked to the deep local roots of Indian Sufism.

In India, an early Sufi, Ali al-Hujwiri (d. A.D. 1071) regarded listening to music permissible for mystics, except under some very rigid conditions; it was not to be listened to without a deep spiritual urge, only after long intervals, and only in the presence of one's spiritual preceptor. Of the four Sufi orders (Chishti, Suhrawardi, Naqshbandi and Qadiri) popular in India, the Chishtis alone sought ecstatic inspiration in music. The Suhrawardis were generally indifferent to it and recommended instead the chanting of the *Quran*; the Qadiris were opposed to music generally, and to instrumental music *(sama bil-mazamir)* in particular. The Naqshbandi attitude to music was even more hostile. Despite the religious attitudes towards music ranging from wholehearted acceptance to complete rejection, the devotional assembly of Islamic mysticism, called *qawwali* is popular throughout India, Pakistan and Bangladesh.

There has been an ongoing controversy in the Muslim community over the sanction and legitimacy of music. Regardless of the eventual outcome of this debate, or some broad consensus on it, it cannot be ignored that Islamic society has sought through social pressure, religious directives, and juridical pronouncements to control the vocal and instrumental arts in order to ensure that they contribute towards producing and sustaining a moral community. Thus the music which leads the listener to be more obedient to Allah has been encouraged; that which leads away from God and His directives has been avoided. The recitation of the *Quran*, therefore, has become the most important example of pitched sound-art in the whole of the Muslim world, and it has been used in a wide variety of religious and secular situations. Other genres of musical art have been appreciated, tolerated, or frowned upon according to their position.

The occasion of *qawwali* performance is also called *sama*, aptly defined as 'hearing chanted verse (with or without accompanying instruments) in the company of others also seeking to participate in the dynamic dialogue between a human lover and the Divine Beloved'. *Qawwali* considered as music is usually a group song performed by *qawwals*, professional musicians who perform in groups led by one or two solo singers.

Qawwals present mystical poetry in Persian, Hindi and Urdu (in that order of prestige) in a fluid style of alternating solo and group passages, characterised by repetition and improvisation. The vigorous drum accompaniment on the barrel-shaped *dholak* is reinforced by hand-clapping, while the small portable harmonium, usually in the hands of the lead singer, underscores the song melody. A *qawwali* song normally begins with an instrumental prelude on the harmonium; then an introductory verse is sung as a solo recitative without drums, leading directly into the song proper: a mystical poem set to a strophic tune and performed by the entire group of *qawwals*.

What is most conspicuous about *sama* is its spiritual vitality along with its professionalisation. Among Indian Sufis, the tradition of *sama* was established and it took on a special character. Saints occupy a central position and *sama* plays an essential role in maintaining that role. It is a fact that the primary importance accorded by Sufism to *sama* as a means of partaking in the experiential dimension of spiritual achievement.

In the Indian subcontinent, Sufism and practice of *sama* took root in the thirteenth century. Of the four main Sufi *Tariqas* introduced in India, the Chishtiya came first and spread most widely. Sufi geneology is an important part of Sufi tradition linking the devotee to his *pir,* Hazrat Ali and to the Prophet. The *sama* performer is not part of this hierarchy, but just a professional attached to a particular *dargah* or a Shaikh.

Later in the century, *sama* shifted from the intimate group singing in the *khanqah* to *Mehfil-e-Sama,* which served as a context for the Sufi's encounter with the experience of mystical love. The *sama* performer brings the entire vision to life, evoking the spiritual reality of the said saint during his life and after his death. The institutional importance of *sama* is directly related to its validating function vis-a-vis the saint and his spiritual descendant. It is partly spiritual and partly historical. *Sama* tradition operates as oral and *sama* poetry is preserved in writing.

The Chishti commitment and contribution to *sama* in India is overwhelming. At the core of the large song repertoire of *sama* is the textual and musical composition of Amir Khusrau, a disciple of Nizam-ud-din Auliya, and Sufi poet *par excellence.* He is considered the founding father of the *qawwali.* His music shows his love and reverence for his saint, and evokes the spiritual-emotional link to that Shaikh.[16]

Sufis identify *sama* poetry of two types—one which focuses on spiritual links addressing figures of Sufi hierarchy in praise and devotion, God in *Hamd,* Prophet in *Naat,* and saints in *Manqabat.* The second type focuses on spiritual emotion, or mystical love, ecstatic states and on separation and union. Some of this poetry is composed by the saints themselves, some addresses the saint, while some is associated with certain aspects of a saint's life and works, or with the ritual devotion to the saint and his shrine.

Music of *sama* is set within a metric framework, accompanied by the *dholak, tabla, sarangi, harmonium* and *sitar.* It is sung by a group of *qawwals* who are led by one or two solo singers. The music can be classical or folk. The *qawwals* of Hazrat Nizam-ud-din Auliya sing mostly Amir Khusrau's music, which is composed of North Indian music, some classical Persian, and some of his own creations.

In the performance of *sama,* music and poetry fuse together, and have a special effect on the listener. They reach a spiritual state which expresses itself in gestures—weeping, vocalising and ultimately a dance of ecstasy. An offering is made to the *qawwal* with *the* permission of the Shaikh or presiding elders.

Wherever *sama* is practised by the Chishtiyas of South Asia, what is crucial is the immediate power of the spiritual-emotional impact of the *sama* songs, the power of music serving the power of saints in *Darbar-e-Auliya.*

Important Sufi Saints and their Dargahs in India

The *dargahs* of Sufis even today attract a large number of devotees from all communities who visit these *dargahs* regularly for fulfilment of their requirements/desires. Thus, the *dargahs* promote communal harmony. Therefore, there is a need to give details of a few well-known *dargahs* in India.[17]

Since medieval times Islam has experienced a tension between 'orthodoxy' and Sufism, and over the centuries

Muslims everywhere have remained divided over the question of whether the veneration of Sufis can legitimately be considered a part of Islam. To orthodox Muslims such veneration has been a source of great embarrassment and even shame, and nothing would be dearer to their hearts than the purging of the cult of saints from Islam. But this opposition not-withstanding, *piri-muridi* has persisted all over the Islamic world.

As is well known, the development and eventual supremacy of the 'law' invested orthodox Islam with a rather extreme impersonality, and, consequently, 'It was as a reaction against this legal formulation of Islam, that the early pietistic asceticism changed definitely into what is technically known as Sufism with its proper ethos'. In contradistinction to the cold and unemotional formalism of the legalists, Sufism introduced in religious devotion a strong personal and individualised element. The intellectual and religious springboard for this 'deviation' in Islam was provided by the development of the doctrine of *tawakkul* or trust in God, which, 'directly led to the central concept of the relationship between man and God... The twin concepts of love and grace fused into one sentiment.'

It is not difficult to realise that saint-veneration came into existence and has persisted because the saints inspired confidence, particularly among the masses, who turned to them for spiritual guidance. For such Muslims the Sufis had brought Allah and the divinity within reach. Thus, while not exactly setting up a rival Islam, they came to rival the ulama. The appeal of Sufis, however, has not been confined to the masses. A mighty emperor like Akbar, as well as lesser-known Muslim kings in India, have paid homage to Sufi saints.

While emotional attachment and loyalty of faith in Sufis have mystical roots and religious overtones, the hold of the saints over their followers has not rested exclusively on these grounds; secular and mundane considerations, in sociological terms 'magical' have been equally important. As is well known, the saints have provided the hope to their followers of various this-worldly, material favours. Indeed, several Sufi orders had little pretensions of having anything to do with mysticism. Thus, in any effort to understand the phenomenon of saint and *dargah* veneration, due recognition must be given to the social and psychological factors that are integral parts of this phenomenon.

Veneration of saints was a common religio-cultural bond and served as one of the most powerful integrative mechanisms between the two communities. It was the personal and spiritual influence of the various saints that to some extent, allowed for the peaceful coexistence of the two communities for several centuries on the Indian subcontinent. One reason why communal harmony stands ruptured today is because the integrative role of the saints and their *dargahs* has been undermined by the forces of modernisation.[18]

The cults are marked by a high degree of institutionalisation, having well established, and often highly organised shrines. We have to differentiate amongst *mazar*, *dargah* and *khanqah*. The first is a notch above the common *qabr* or simple grave. The *qabr* is transformed into a *mazar* once a dead person begins to be venerated as a saint. *Dargah*, on the other hand, is a nobler term, meaning palace or royal court, and applies to more complex types of shrines, as, for example, the *dargah* to Nizam-ud-din Auliya in New Delhi. Ecologically, the *dargah* has a considerably more expansive centre and includes a number of courtyards, a pool, a *naubat khana* (music house), etc. The *khanqah* refers to a hospice and comes into existence, if the saint was also a member of a Sufi order.

Turning next to the behavioural aspects of cults, there are four common elements. The first is personal visits to the shrine. Next, there are the offerings which the worshipper has to bring in cash or kind. Third, there is the *fatiha*, which has to be recited, and, finally, the guardians of the shrine and the worshippers share the offerings which the latter have brought to the *dargah*. The annual *urs* (Arabic : wedding) may also be said to be a common element and commemorates the saint's death. This celebration has both sacred and profane characteristics and the rituals involved are both individual and collective. In the profane part, there is the same mixture of commercial activities and entertainment as is found at the shrines of Hindu deities.

As to what functions the cult of saints fulfils, these depend on who the devotees are, how they conceive of the saints and their powers, what roles the saints play in the lives of individual devotees and for the community as a whole.

Medieval thought had given great importance to saint 'worship' by 'constructing a whole intellectual scheme according to which it was the saints who governed the universe. It was, therefore, quite legitimate to address the saints directly'. This doctrine was widely accepted in the Muslim world. It is said that God has made the saints the governors of the universe. Through the blessing of their advent the rain falls from heaven and through the purity of their lives the plants spring up from the earth, and through their spiritual influence the 'Muslims gain victories over the unbelievers'.

There are some important saints who represent universal saints and are very popular all over the subcontinent. In contrast are 'local' saints whose influence is confined to a few villages, a town, or at most a region. There is the interesting case of the *panch* (five) *pirs* who are particularly venerated among the lower classes. The identity of the 'five' keeps changing from place to place. In some places these include the Prophet and his grandsons, in other places they are replaced by some other figures, while in still other places even a goddess of Hindu origin is introduced. One can perhaps only speculate that the Hindu goddess is either a concession to Hindu 'worshippers', or that in a syncretic situation Hindu deities are not alien and illegitimate entities for Muslim masses, and are therefore a part of the *panch pirs*.

There are some sort of patron saints who are associated with water. Washermen, water carriers and boot men and some like sweepers and blacksmiths, besides being linked to various saints are also linked with specific types of favours. Again, there are other specialists who take care of various illnesses and afflictions.

This 'specialisation' obviously suits the vast masses who have faith in saints and *dargahs*. Its strength lies in the fact that it allows for great choice and freedom to venerate whichever saint or saints the individual chooses. Moreover, there is also scope for social groups, professional groups and castes to latch on to saints of their choice. At the psychological level, such attachment provides for identity as well as security, both of which have been considerably important in pre-modern times in the lives of the rural and tribal communities of this subcontinent.

Some *pirs* are healers of specific physical and moral problems while the *murshid* is considered to be a spiritual guide, the giver of general, moral and spiritual exhortations; in many cases, however, the *pir* and *murshid* may be the same. 'Doubtless, the influence and power of pirs varies from region to region, from town to village and from *pir* to *pir*.'[19]

The Dargah of Khwaja Muinuddin Chishti at Ajmer

Khwaja Muinuddin Chishti settled at Ajmer before the establishment of Muslim rule in India. He preached the gospel of Islam with remarkable devotion, establishing the Chishti order under challenging circumstances. He transformed the moral standards and pattern of religious behaviour among Muslims and affected the outlook of non-Muslims with regard to basic concepts of the Islamic faith. His shrine has assumed an important position in the religious annals of the Muslims of the Indian subcontinent and emerged as a great centre of spiritual activity for all seekers after truth.

The various customs and ceremonies that developed under the patronage and control of the Mughals, Rajputs and Marathas generated an atmosphere of mutual understanding among different sections of society and gave stimulus to the growth of cultural affinity and a spirit of cordiality between Hindus and Muslims of the subcontinent.

The system of cooking food in a big cauldron (*deg*) was first introduced by Akbar. Since then a large quantity of food of different kinds has always been cooked in *degs* at night, and is distributed among the people after *fajar* (morning prayers). It is said at the time of Jahangir, that the Mughal emperor once ordered the preparation of *khichri* in the *deg* to be distributed among 5,000 people, taking out the first on a platter with his own hands.

The appointment of non-Muslims to the important posts of *mutawwalli* (custodian) and *amin* (revenue officers), etc., their participation in the ceremonies at the shrine in an official capacity, the grant of stipends and daily allowances to Hindus-including *zunnardars* (Hindu priest), *bairagis* (Hindu fakirs) and the fixation of their shares in the daily *langar* (free food) reflected the increasing presence of non-Muslims in the internal management of the *dargah*.

Undoubtedly, the *khadims*, who have been attached to the shrine since its inception, played a key role in the smooth functioning and in keeping strict discipline in the performances of these rituals and ceremonies.

Three important rites are regularly performed every day per schedule: (i) *Khidmat* (service routine) twice a day; (ii) *Roshni* (lighting ceremony); (iii) *Karka* (closing of the main doors of the shrine).

Khidmat literally means service, which is the exclusive privilege of the *khadims*. First, in the morning a little before dawn, the key keeper (*baridar*) of the day appears and unlocks the silver-plated eastern gate of the main tomb. One of the elderly *khadims* recites *azan* (call for prayer), performs *taslim* and *salam*, and, followed by some of the *khadims*, enters the shrine and re-closes the doors from inside. Some more candles are lit within the dome, and one of the pious and elderly *khadims*, obviously allowed by the *baridar*, moves closer to the inner circle of the tomb, softly removes the well-knitted floral garland called *sej* from the *mazar* (tomb), and puts it in a large basket covered with cloth (*jhab*).

This is carried by another *khadim* to the nearby tomb of Bibi Hafiz Sahib, where this *sej* is placed on her tomb after it is cleaned. Cloth sheets from all sides are put these on the stone structure over the grave (*tawidh*). Then they start sweeping flowers from both sides towards the foot-end of the grave, where some of the waiting *khadims* collect these flowers in huge *jhabs*, and carry them out into a courtyard to be assembled there. From there other *khadims* take these flowers and distribute them among pilgrims and devotees.

In the period between the two services pilgrims gather inside the tomb to pay homage to the saint, pray and recite the *fatiha*, offer flowers and cloth sheets, and invoke the blessings of the Almighty and Khwaja Sahib.

Roshni literally means light, and refers to the ceremony of illuminating the main inner chamber of the tomb at dusk with elaborate arrangements and a well-defined procedure. This is one of the oldest ceremonies; it is held daily in the evening, before the *maghrib* prayer. *Karka* is the term for the ceremony which is connected with the closing of the doors of the shrine for the night. It takes place generally between 9 and 10 p.m.

The *qawwals* and all the people within the campus at once get up, and the *qawwals* start reciting *karka* verses in Bhojpuri and a local dialect. The *qawwals* then start the audition *(sama)* by singing religious and devotional songs, mainly in praise of Khwaja Sahib, and continue till the doors of the shrine are closed for the night.

Besides these rituals, *naubat* is played twice a day, i.e. in the morning, and at sunset. *Langar* (a free meal consisting of soup of barley) is also prepared daily at the *langar-khana* and distributed twice (after the *fajar* and *asr* prayer) among the general public.

On every sixth of the lunar month the *khadims* also arrange a function called *chatti sharif*. At about 9 a.m. at the same courtyard in front of the shrine, first of all, *Quran-khwani*—recitation of the whole *Quran* by a large number of people takes place, and then one of the *khadims* starts reciting the *shajara-i Chishtiyya* (spiritual pedigree of the Chishti order) as well as other verses composed by Khwaja Sahib's ancestors.

Thus, during the whole year one kind of ceremony or the other takes place at the shrine, and religious activities and rituals are carried on in a manner which may, in one sense, tend to overshadow the true spirit which underlies the philosophy and thought of Khwaja Sahib. But, at the same time, all these activities keep the pilgrims and people busy in devotional activities and, in another sense, keep alive the Sufi spirit.

On the night which falls between 5th and 6th Rajab, the celebration attains its peak of excitement and exultation. The sacred precincts of the shrine are crowded with thousands and thousands of people, all occupied with performing rites and prayers, reciting the *Quran*, listening to *qawwalis* arranged by the *khadims* at their respective *gaddis* and *hujras* (cells) within the compound of the *dargah*. On 6th Rajab, at about 11 a.m., pilgrims and all kinds of other visitors are banned from entering the *dargah*. The *khadims*, dressed in their best clothes, approach the shrine carrying flowers, essence of flowers (*atr*) and sweets, etc. After laying *chiras* or *dastars* (small turbans) on each other's heads, they start performing the rites laid down by tradition for this special occasion.

After the recitation of *shajara-i Chishtiya* (spiritual pedigree of Chishti order) by a *khadim*, and of some other verses composed in the form of a *faryad* (petition), they announce their allegiance to Khwaja Sahib and humbly ask for the gift to repent of their sins and shortcomings. They pray for all the devotees, and for the peace and prosperity of mankind, and remain engaged in the recitation of verses of *Quran* prayers and *darud* till the arrival of the diwan from the *mahfil-khana,* normally at about 1 p.m. At the *mahfil-khana* the *mahfil-i sama* starts at about 11 a.m., and only the *qawwals* of the *dargah* are entitled to sing on that day. Then *golas* are blown and drums beaten to mark the end of *qul* and *urs*. After this the diwan, with one or two of his closest relatives for whose presence prior permission has been taken from the *khadims*, leaves for the shrine. At the *Jannati-darwaza* the *baridar* checks the diwan's companions and then allows them to enter the shrine. Soon after his entry into the shrine the *Jannati-darwaza* is closed. On his arrival in the shrine the diwan kisses the tomb and offers flowers, and then one of the *khadims*, who happens to be his *wakil*, like the other pilgrims, ties a *dastar* (turban) over his head, spreads the cloth sheet over his bowed head, prays for him, and then gives him *tabarruk*, consisting of flowers, sandal and sweets.

The early Chishti Sufi saints who flourished during the thirteenth and fourteenth centuries are among those most revered in the history of Islam in South Asia. In their lifetime as well as in death they have been looked upon by large numbers of people as exemplars of piety and spiritual excellence. Some of these saints gained greater popularity after their lifetime, with the result that their *dargahs* have emerged as centres of pilgrimage.

People of different creeds come to make offerings to these *dargahs*, and to be filled with a spirit of faith and devotion. The *dargah* thus plays an important socio-religious role, and has done since early medieval times. In certain cases the *dargah* has played a more significant role in the cultural integration of different religious communities in the Indian subcontinent than the Sufi saint laying buried there did in his own lifetime.

One of the oldest *dargahs* of Chisti Silsila is that of Shaikh Muinuddin Chisti, the founder of the Chishti Silsila in India who was popularly known as Khwaja Gharib Nawaz, (died in 1235). His *khalifa* (spiritual successor), Shaikh Qutbuddin Bakhtiyar Kaki, popularly known as Qutb Sahib, is associated with a second old *dargah*. Shaikh Qutbuddin Bakhtiyar Kaki died in Delhi in the same year as his *pir*, in 1235.

As for the two remaining thirteenth-century Chishti *dargahs*, they belong to Shaikh Hamiduddin Sufi Nagauri, whom his *pir* (religious preceptor), Shaikh Muinuddin Chishti, had posted in Nagaur, where he died in 1276; and the other to Shaikh Fariduddin Ganj-i Shakar, popularly known as Baba Farid, who died in 1265. The latter was the *khalifa* of Shaikh Bakhtiyar Kaki, and his *dargah* is located in Pakpatan in Pakistan. Both Shaikh Muinuddin Chishti and Shaikh Bakhtiyar Kaki were Sufi saints from Central Asia. Shaikh Hamiduddin Sufi of Nagaur and Baba Farid, on the other hand, were Indian-born Sufis. Their *dargahs* command immense respect among people of different religious communities in the countries of South Asia.

The popularity of a *dargah* depended upon the spiritual excellence and noble qualities deemed to have been possessed by the saint in his lifetime; upon the spiritual greatness of his immediate successors; and upon the expansion of the *silsila* and the legends that developed afterwards about the supernatural powers of the *dargah*.

The traditions recorded in the Sufi literature produced from the fourteenth century onwards about the *dargah* of Muinuddin Chishti in Ajmer reveal that his image underwent a change as the influence and popularity of his *dargah* increased with the passage of time. Different factors account for this. First, Shaikh Muinuddin Chishti's piety as well as the traditions of extreme austerity embraced by him in his lifetime inspired later generations of people. Second, the greatness of his spiritual successors, particularly Shaikh Fariduddin Ganj-i-Shakar and Shaikh Nizam-ud-din Auliya, contributed to the popularity of the *dargah* of Ajmer and that of his immediate successor, Qutb Sahib in Delhi. As the founder of the Chishti Silsila in India, devotees of the *dargahs* of his successors had also to cherish his memory and pay a visit to his dargah.

Siyar al-Arifin gives details which contain interesting information about the *dargah*'s role in the cultural integration of the two major communities—Hindus and Muslims—in India. Visitors to the *dargah* in Ajmer included both Muslims and Hindus who approached it, as they still do today, with different spiritual, psychological and economic problems, and returned in peace and filled with hope on account of their faith in the *barakat* (blessings) of the *dargah*.

Unconverted Hindus also often remained sincerely attached to the *dargah*, paid visits there, and made offerings in cash or kind. Their descendants followed this tradition. It is worth recalling that in medieval times Hindus and Muslims often vowed offerings to a patron saint or deity if their prayers were answered. Sometimes, faced with serious problems such as the illness of an only son or the desire for a male child, Hindus seem to have vowed that they would accept Islam. For Hindus, and often for new converts to Islam whose conversion was partial, the *dargah* was a substitute for the idol.

A visit paid by a mighty ruler to a *dargah* also raised its prestige in the eyes of the populace. The first sultan reported to have visited the *dargah* in Ajmer was Muhammad-bin-Tughluq (1324–51). In fact it had become an established custom for the sultan to visit the *dargah* of an eminent Sufi if he happened to be in its vicinity, and to distribute money to the servitors of the dargah. The motive behind such royal visits was no doubt political rather than religious, this being a method of enhancing regal popularity, even as it reinforced belief in the power of the *dargah*.

An important custom that seems to have become established in the fourteenth century was that the Sufis began to consider it obligatory to visit the *dargahs* of prominent Sufis of the *silsila* in the country. This seems to have influenced the elite and masses during the subsequent period, and as a result the *dargah* of Ajmer became one of the most popular by the time Akbar ascended the throne. It was the spirit and enthusiasm possessed by pilgrims to Ajmer that seems to have inspired Akbar, who also became a devotee. He began to pay visits, sometimes twice or thrice a year, and implored the shaikh's spirit to bless him with new conquests and the birth of sons, and maintained this tradition until 1580.

Akbar's successors also showed respect to the *dargah* of Ajmer. They visited it and had a number of beautiful buildings added to the complex. In 1614 Jahangir gave to the *dargah* a cauldron larger than the one his father had given. He also had food cooked in it that sufficed for more than 5,000 people. The beautiful mosques constructed in Ajmer on Shah Jahan's order and the gardens planted by him still fascinate tourists.

The *dargahs* of the spiritual successors of Shaikh Muinuddin Chishti, both his *khalifas* (immediate successors) and the chief disciples of the latter, located at different places in north India, also became important centres of pilgrimage for Muslims and Hindus. Their popularity also depended on notions about the spiritual excellence possessed by these men in their lifetime; the successful career of their *murids* (spiritual disciples); the legends that the servitors invented and spread about the miraculous powers of the *dargah*; and finally on the size and cultural importance of the city where the *dargah* was located. A careful scrutiny of the material on the *dargah* of Shaikh Bakhtiyar Kaki, chief *khalifa* of Shaikh Muinuddin Chishti, available in medieval sources, supports this impression. All these factors made the *dargah* one of the most important paces of pilgrimage in the metropolis of Delhi some time after his death in 1235. The *dargah* of Shaikh Bakhtiyar Kaki became another popular centre of pilgrimage. It was certainly unlike the *dargah* of Ajmer in this regard. The more popular it became, the greater seems to have been the flow of wealth to it. As regards the factors responsible for the popularity of the *dargah*, they were—besides putative spiritual excellence—the emergence of Delhi as one of the most important Islamic centres. Likewise, the progress of the Chishti Silsila through the missionary work of Shaikh

Fariduddin Ganj-i-Shakar and Shaikh Nizam-ud-din Auliya also contributed to its popularity in north India. Impressed by the traditions of the *dargah* the mighty ruler Sultan Iltutmish of Delhi, visited the shaikh in his *khanqah* twice a week. The shaikh would advise him to strive for the welfare of the people under his rule, and the sultan acted accordingly.

By the turn of the thirteenth century the *dargah* of Shaikh Bakhtiyar Kaki had gained immense popularity and prestige. In 1333, when Ibn Battuta arrived in Delhi, he found it one of the three most popular pilgrimage places in the metropolitan city of Delhi. The remaining two *dargahs* belonged to non-Sufi scholars of law. This is indicative of the fact that in the early period of the Delhi sultanate. Not only were the *dargahs* or graves of Sufis considered possessed of blessed powers, the graves or tombs of orthodox scholars who had lived pious and austere lives, without Sufi inclinations, were also venerated.

Popular belief in the sanctity and blessed power of this *dargah* led people belonging to different strata of Muslim society to bury their relations in the compound or in the vicinity of the *dargah*. People desired to be buried near the shrine, believing that their soul would be blessed by the spirit of the shaikh. Moreover people, both the elite and the masses, believed that the prayer offered at the *dargah* of Shaikh Bakhtiyar Kaki would bless them with success in difficult circumstances.

Besides there seems to have been a popular belief among Chishti Sufis since the fourteenth century that a stay at the *dargah* in the capacity of servitors would make them special recipients of divine grace. Many devout Sufis occupied cells and spent their time in prayer, meditation and in performing spiritual exercises. Many villagers who came to the *dargah* for blessings in time of distress got in touch with some Sufi there, and some of these villagers adopted the Islamic faith.

Hindus who belonged to rich families also seem to have made vows at the *dargah*, and sometimes converted to Islam, particularly if their prayers at the *dargah* were answered. The *dargah* of Shaikh Hamiduddin Sufi, another *khalifa* of Shaikh Muinuddin Chishti of Ajmer, also seems to have gained popularity in Nagaur and western Rajputana towards the close of the thirteenth century.

The Dargah of Baba Farid

The *dargah* of Shaikh Fariduddin Ganj-i-Shakar has also been an important shrine, being associated with selfless service, piety and extreme austerity of an orthodox character. It was really his popularity that led his sons to bury him in his *khanqah* against his will. Since Ajodhan was situated on the merchant caravan route linking Multan, the border city, with Delhi and other parts of the Delhi sultanate, the merchants, nobles and soldiers travelling from and to Delhi paid visits to the *dargah* and invoked the saint's help and blessings for success as well as safety from dacoits, illness and wild animals.

With the expansion of the Chishti Silsila's influence in the subcontinent through the missionary work of the *khalifas* of Shaikh Nizam-ud-din Auliya (d. 1325) in provinces as far as Sind in the west, Bengal in the east and Deccan in the south, the early Chishti *dargahs* began to receive votaries from far and near.

As regards the complex of the *dargah*, the nobles, merchants and other wealthy people seem to have spent money on raising structures for the comfort and benefit of the pilgrims around the tombs of the important Sufi saints from early times. The *dargah* of Baba Farid has a number of structures, raised during different times.

There are two doors to this apartment [in which the Shaikh lies buried], one to the north and one to the east. The one to the east, called the 'door of Paradise', is never opened except on the fifth day of the sacred Muharram, when numbers of pilgrims, both Hindus and Muslims, come to visit the shrine, believing that all who pass through this door way are saved from the fire of perdition. Like the *dargahs* of Shaikh Muinuddin Chishti in Ajmer and Shaikh Bakhtiyar Kaki in Delhi, that of Baba Farid also seems to have attracted non-Muslims to embrace Islam. It certainly played a rather more important part than the *dargahs* of his immediate predecessors in India. The popular legends incorporated in an early eighteenth-century work, *Jawahir-i Faridi,* mention a number of Hindu castes, high as well as low, the members of which embraced Islam en masse at the hands of Baba Farid.

The Sial Rajputs, who happened to be influential people in north-western Punjab, probably adopted the Islamic faith under the influence of the *dargah*. Unlike them, the fishermen and other low-caste people may have been converted by the shaikh himself, because certain privileges enjoyed by members of these castes at the *dargah* on the occasion of the *urs* (death anniversary), point to their early association with the Shaikh and his *dargah* later on.

As for the *dargahs* of the *khalifas* of Baba Farid, a few of them seem to have come into the limelight within a few decades of their passing away for the very reasons outlined earlier. Of them, the *dargahs* of Shaikh Jamaluddin in Hansi, Shaikh Nizam-ud-din Auliya in Delhi, and Shaikh Ala'uddin Sabir in Kaliyar are worth mentioning.

Visitors who came from faraway places also went to the *dargahs* of Shaikh Bakhtiyar Kaki and Baba Farid in Ajodhan. In fact, the fame and greatness of Shaikh Nizam-ud-din Auliya greatly contributed to the influence and popularity of the *dargahs* of his spiritual predecessors in the Chishti Silsila. The relevant evidence contained in an early seventeenth-century *tazkira* of the Sufis shows that visitors offered so much money at the *dargah* that the servitors lived in affluence.

The Nizam-ud-din Dargah in Delhi

The sacred *dargah* of Nizam-ud-din Auliya is located at a distance of six miles from Shahjahanabad [Delhi]. This is as soul-ravishing as paradise; the atmosphere inside exudes spiritual fragrance. The area around it is ablaze like the sun, owing to the blessed light from the [holy] grave. The blessed rays make the tomb shine like a chandelier. Needy people get relief while patients are cured through its blessing. The shaikh [lying buried] is not the lamp of Delhi but of the entire country. People turn up there in crowds, particularly on Sunday. In the month of Diwali the entire population of Delhi visits it and stays in tents around the spring tank for days. They take baths to obtain cures from chronic diseases. Muslims and Hindus pay visits in the same spirit. From morning till evening, people come in groups and also busy themselves in merry-making in the shade of the trees. They are provided with an occasion for great merriment, the sound of music coming from every corner. The *urs* is also celebrated with great enthusiasm.

Thousands of people from different parts of India and other countries, backgrounds, classes and even religions visit the Nizam-ud-din *dargah* regularly every year. Muslims are the largest group of visitors, Hindus coming next, followed by Sikhs, and occasionally a few Christians. Most of them come to pray at the tombs of Hazrat Nizam-ud-din (1239–1325) and his disciple, Amir Khusrau, which are a few hundred feet from each other. After paying their respects to the saints—first at the tomb of Amir Khusrau, since be is believed to serve as the gate-keeper of the *dargah*, and then at the tomb of Hazrat Nizam-ud-din—a considerable number of visitors meet their *pirs* (spiritual directors), who claim to be descendants of Hazrat Nizam-ud-din.[20]

People come to the *dargah* mainly to acquire something, be it from God through the intercession of the saint, or from the saint who is seen as God's representative, or from the *pirs*. It is true that pilgrims come to the *dargah* with all kinds of petitions and requests. Those who find it difficult to communicate verbally with the saint write out their petitions on pieces of paper which they tie to the grilled walls surrounding the shrine of Hazrat Nizam-ud-din. Others tie strings and pieces of cloth torn from their clothing to the grilled wall of the shrine to remind the saint of their requests and themselves of their commitment to feed or clothe the poor of the *dargah* as soon as their requests have been granted. Some pilgrims seek cures beyond the competence of ordinary doctors. A few pilgrims come to beseech a favourable verdict in their court cases. Some people are brought to the *dargah* by family members, well-wishers and friends to be exorcised from evil *jinns* or spirits.

Besides organising the feasts, maintaining the *dargah* and the peace within it so that people can pray, the *pirs* and *pirzade* claim to have spiritual powers of their own, if not on account of personal holiness, then because they are blood relatives of the saint and have been handed down these powers generation after generation. They guide the pilgrims and visitors as to the manner in which they should pray, trying to turn half-hearted Muslims into fervent ones, and leading those to their God who belong to other faiths.

People of all faiths are loved here. A different religion is no barrier since all people are the same in the eyes of the saint. Because there is one God, all people are one. The saint acts as God acts, treating all people equally, whatever their faith or status—all people are equal here. The *pir*'s effect cures as also miracles through *tawizes* (amulets), which are prayers, often verses from the *Quran*. The *pirs* and *pirzade* are also approached for advice on all kinds of problems, both spiritual and mundane, and for monetary help.

The visiting pilgrims say that Nizam-ud-din Auliya makes them acceptable to God: 'This holy man who is very close to God and still deeply concerned for us and for our welfare understands our plight, for he was a man like us. Therefore, he is able to take our case to God, intercede on our behalf and make us more acceptable to Him.' A few pilgrims talk of the strength that the saint has given them to follow more strictly the tenets of Islam, thus enabling them to be more pleasing to God. For them, Hazrat Nizam-ud-din Auliya is, in effect, the mediator between the pilgrims and God.

Generally, the response evoked is one of love, gratitude, reverence, often expressed also by distribution of alms. Once in the *dargah*, the pilgrims kiss the steps leading to the shrines of Amir Khusrau and Hazrat Nizam-ud-din, and the thresholds of the doorways to the shrines. On entering the shrines they spread rose petals on the tombs and, after greeting the saints, walk around the tomb, at the end of which they kiss the chaddar (the cloth covering the tomb) and the small marble fence surrounding the tomb, sometimes touching their eyes and cheeks against these.

The Dargah of Sayyid Salar Masud Ghazi in Bahraich

Bahraich is situated near the Indo–Nepal border in Uttar Pradesh. There is the famous shrine of Sayyid Salar Masud

Ghazi, popularly known as the *dargah* (or *dargah sharif*).[21] The saint-martyr lying buried here is affectionately referred to by the people as Ghazi Miyan, *Bale Badshah.*

There are numerous biographical works giving an account of his life and deeds. Ghazi Miyan was the nephew of Sultan Mahmud Ghaznavi. He was accompanied by a huge army of devotees. Ghazi Miyan began attracting large crowds and soon grew into a spiritual celebrity of the region around Bahraich. He tried to stop the practice of human sacrifice (*bali*) at the local temples, and to restrain despotic rulers from exploiting the people. All this made him a hero with the downtrodden.

The growing popularity of the Ghazi alarmed the rulers of Bahraich town and its neighbourhood and so Raja Sahar Dev, wanted him to go back to Ghazni. His plea that he had no worldly ambition and wanted to devote his life to the service of suffering humanity fell on deaf ears. He was dragged into the battlefield much against his will. After a series of wars Ghazi Miyan fell. He was killed at the age of nineteen.

Ghazi Miyan's grave was guarded by his surviving devotees. The local people began to venerate it, the Hindus being more zealous in their veneration than the Muslims. Years later a Hindu milkman, Jasu Ahir—whose barren wife was blessed with a son on praying there—re-built the grave with pure cow milk and costly lime. Soon thereafter the grave became an object of even deeper veneration.[22]

In the thirtieth year of the Ghazi's death Zahra Bibi, the congenitally blind daughter of one Sayyid Jamaluddin of Rudauli (now in District Barabanki, UP) who had regained her sight on praying to the Ghazi, became his staunch devotee and got his grave reconstructed under a magnificent tomb. On her death the Bibi was buried in a grave near the Ghazi's tomb, which she had kept ready. As time passed the fame of the shrine and its spiritual potency spread.

By the time the Tughlaqs ascended the throne of Delhi, Ghazi Miyan had become a legend and his grave the shrine of a miraculous saint. In 1341 Muhammad-bin-Tughlaq visited the grave, accompanied by the celebrated traveller Ibn Battuta, and paid his respects to the Ghazi.

This, in brief, is the ancient history of the Ghazi and of his mausoleum around which in the course of time has grown what is now called Dargah Sayyid Salar Masud Ghazi. Tributes have been paid to the Ghazi by many saints and Sufis of the past, including Shaikh Sharfuddin bin Yahya Muniri. Dargah Sayyid Salar Masud has an enormous complex of two different forts enveloping each other, Sangi Qila and the Qila-i Kalan. On the other side of the Sangi Qila are buried in two separate tombs Zahra Bibi and some of her relatives.

Most days are busy at the *dargah*, but there is an unusual rush on the two Idd days, on *Yaumi-I Ashurah in Muharram* and on *Shab-i-Baraat*. There are also three major periodical festivities—the *urs, the Basant Fair*, and the Great *Jeshth Fair.*

The groups of pilgrim-parties are still called *medni* or *barat* (marriage party). They bring *dahez* (bridal gifts) and offer these at the grave of the Ghazi and Zahra Bibi. The carrying and presentation of *nishans* or *alams* (long spear-headed sticks covered with costly cloth and other decorative materials) is the main attraction of the Great Fair. Pilgrims seeking the Ghazi's blessing for the fulfilment of their desires touch with the *nishans* brought by them the dome of Sangi Qila, taking a vow that if they achieve what they aspire for they will return to the shrine with *nishans* and further offerings.

Inside the tomb housing the Ghazi's grave on all the walls are always found hanging written 'petitions' of pilgrims, stating their problems and soliciting his blessings. Those blessing-seekers, who cannot come personally send their 'petitions' through friends, or even by post, and the *khuddam* hang them on the walls of the room. When the petition is answered—in the form of the problem being solved—it becomes obligatory for the petitioner to be present at the shrine of the next *urs*.

The most remarkable miracle of Ghazi Miyan's *dargah* is said to be the recovery of lepers from their disease. The water used for the bath of Mazar Sharif is believed to be a cure. Pilgrims collect it in small bottles from the pond near the Sandal tree and take it back home to treat with patients of leprosy and leucoderma. Lepers themselves also visit the *dargah* in large numbers.

Year after year, lepers are reputedly cured in these places; many stay with deep devotion for as long as they are not cured, or keep on periodically visiting the *dargah*, waiting to be picked by the great Ghazi for his blessings. It is believed that thousands of lepers have been cured at the shrine.

The legend of Ghazi Miyan is not confined to the city of Bahraich. In many other towns of northern India there are places related to his name. In Meerut a memorial to the Ghazi was reportedly built long ago by Qutubuddin Aibak, where Bale Miyan's Nauchandi is celebrated even now with great enthusiasm, attracting huge crowds of Hindus and Muslims from the town and the neighbourhood.

The Dargah of Sufi Shaikh Sharafuddin Muniri at Bihar Shariff

The Firdausi Sufi Silsila, a branch of the celebrated Suhrawardi *silsila*, was begun by Shaikh Badruddn Samarqandi, an emigrant from Central Asia in the Sultanate of Delhi during the early years of Iltutmish's reign (1210–36). Shaikh Ruknuddin Firdausi succeeded his master, Shaikh Badruddin Samarqandi. The spiritual successors of Shaikh Ruknuddin Firdausi called their branch of the *silsila* 'Firdausi' after the *pir*'s surname in order to perpetuate his memory.

It is also worth noting that Shaikh Badruddin Samarqandi and his disciples had fully established themselves in Delhi before the Chishtis arrived in India. Shaikh Najmuddin Sughra, an important link in the chain of Firdausi Silsila saints, had already been appointed the Shaikh ul-Islam (Minister for Religious Affairs) by Iltutmish.

The early Firdausi saints practised sobriety and considered the display by Sufi saints of miraculous power an irreligious practice, calculated to gain cheap popularity. They set traditions of austerity and emphasised its importance, so that their followers could also emulate them. Consequently, their influence remained confined to the elite in Delhi. With the emergence of Shaikh Sharafuddin Yahya Muniri as a great Firdausi saint, a new chapter opened in the history of the Firdausi Silsila in India.[23]

Shaikh Sharfuddin Yahya Muniri, who lies buried in the town of Bihar Sharif, was a leading saint with a wide reputation. The references contained in his *malfuzat* (collection of utterances) to the visitors to his *khanqah* show how his influence and popularity had spread in different parts outside Bihar.

In adopting this ascetic exercise, the Indian Sufis were not directly influenced by yogis. Long before their arrival in India, the Sufis had adopted yogic practice in Central Asia under Buddhist influence. Shaikh Sharfuddin Yahya Muniri's source of information is the *Fawaid al-Fuad*, wherein the eleventh-century Sufi saint, Shaikh Abu Said Abul Khair is reported as having performed it. In the same anecdote this tradition is linked to the Prophet of Islam. The latter is said to have performed it only once. The picture of the Shaikh that emerges from the popular works of Sufis is that of a liberal-minded and saintly man.

Sharfuddin Muniri is an illuminating example of the life, teaching and religious philosophy of the great Sufi thinker of fourteenth-century India. Shaikh ul-Islam had thrown open the door of his *khanqah* to all and sundry. All were allowed to enter the circle of his *murids*. He granted the sinners *Khirqa* (robe) and caused them to repent for their sins committed in the past and turn good. Everybody, notable or ordinary, rich or poor, officer of commoner, scholar or illiterate, urbanised or rustic, nobleman or soldier, freeborn or slave, was favoured with his discipleship.

References to Shaikh Sharfuddin Muniri show that he cherished the pious memory of Shaikh Nizam-ud-din Auliya.

Sincerely devoted to the cause of religion and aware of the importance of cosmic consciousness for man, Shaikh Sharafuddin took up as his mission the work of inculcating the divine temper in everyone who turned to him for religious guidance. He agreed to settle down in the *khanqah* built by the order of Sultan Muhammad-bin-Tughluq. Unlike the Chishtis, the Firdausi saints did not consider their contact with the sultan or the state as sinful. The shaikh's own life of dedication to God and to the service of mankind was a source of inspiration to his followers, both Hindus and Muslims.

The Dargah of Hazratbal in Srinagar

The *dargah* of Hazratbal is situated on the shores of the picturesque Dal Lake in Srinagar, a city of great antiquity. Being the repository of the sacred hair of Prophet Muhammad, the shrine attracts over a lakh of devotees from every nook and corner of the valley on the eve of two important local festivals, namely *Miladun-Nabi* (birthday of the Prophet) and *Miraj-i Alam* (the day commemorating the Prophet's heavenly journey, in which he reached the immediate presence of God).

Thousands of pilgrims flock to the shrine from all parts of the Kashmir valley, carrying with them the flags of famous saints. There is abundant evidence to show that for over the last two and a half centuries the shrine has attracted people from a wide area, and thus has gradually become an important element in the religious life of the people of Kashmir.[24]

Speaking in terms of social history, Islam manifests itself in the *dargah* of Hazratbal more as a system of cultural symbols than as a doctrinal system of the ulama.

Khwaja Nuruddin Ishbari, a rich Kashmiri merchant, is reported to have purchased the holy relic for a lakh of rupees from Sayyid Abdallah of Bijapur, who had brought it to the Deccan from Medina. Ishbari died on his way home from Bijapur in 1699, but the relic was brought to Srinagar along with his dead body, where its arrival created a state of reverential enthusiasm.

Men and even women chanting litanies and *durud* flooded the streets and bazars of Srinagar to glimpse the relic. As a mark of respect to popular sentiment, Fazil Khan, the Mughal governor of Kashmir (1698–1701), ordered that the relic be housed at a mosque in *Bagh-i Sadiqabad,* situated on the western bank of the Dal lake. The place has since come to be known as Hazratbal, the abode of Prophet Muhammad.

Since the sacred hair was kept at Bagh-i Sadiqabad, the place became the centre of pilgrimage for Kashmiri Muslims. From several folk songs and poems composed in Kashmiri in praise of the relic, it is evident that there has always been an endeavour to attribute the privilege of Medina to Hazratbal. For devotees the shrine of Hazratbal, by virtue of its being the repository of the Prophet's hair, is actually a place of interaction and communication between the spiritually alive Prophet and his followers.

The religious behaviour of the devotees at the mere sight of the relic in special gatherings held on the occasions suggests that the sacred relic has almost been personified by a people who, after embracing Islam, have not given up their ancestral practices of adoring holy relics—this is so natural to the human heart. It is to be noted that the practice of visiting Hazratbal forms a feature in the religious life of Kashmiri Muslims.

The elevation of Hazratbal to Medina *thani* (second Medina) is also worthy of examination; this must have sprung not only from the devotees' unbounded veneration of the Prophet but also from practical difficulties in performing the sacred duty of the *hajj*.

No wonder, therefore, that a devotee with a mystical love for Muhammad, at the very sight of the object (relic), feels himself to be under the influence of a divine agency or in the spiritual gathering *(darbar)* of Prophet Muhammad. While in a number of Kashmiri *nats* a visit to Hazratbal is depicted as a spiritual flight to Medina, the importance of the spiritual gatherings is repeatedly emphasised by the priests in their invocations on festive occasions. It is also interesting to note here that on such occasions a number of Kashmiri verses, in which various blessings for the Prophet are invoked, are recited in chorus by the pilgrims in order to obtain the Prophet's intercessions.

But spiritual gains were not the goal of all visitors to the shrine. Health, procreation, longevity, protection from floods, famines and other calamities were and are the fruits sought by pilgrims. In a society where the *mullah* reigned supreme, people were made to believe that a visit to the shrine would secure the object of their wishes. This is the reason why devotees, not unlike the Hindus, made (and still make) a great display of their veneration while approaching the shrine: lowly obeisances are made, hands are folded, and feet bared to the holy dust of the sacred precincts.

Thus the devotion to, reverence for and implicit trust in the shrine of Hazratbal is more important to the religious life of a great number of Kashmiri Muslims than any special veneration for the *Quran* or its teachings. For them the Prophet is venerated with but little knowledge of his teachings; it is the sacred hair which protects against disease and disaster that is all important. The saviour role attributed to the relic for protecting Kashmiris has also been versified.

Devotees are seen touching the hands, body or even the dress of the custodian exhibiting the relic in the hope of receiving a *baraka*. This reverence for the sacred hair and its custodians may be seen to have fostered what can almost be termed a patron–client relationship in a system of *piri–muridi* which marked *dargah* life in the past.

The Dargah of Sufi Saint Shahul Hameed at Nagore

The Sufi Quadria order (*silsila*) entered the Indian subcontinent in the 12th century through Mohammad Ghouse Gwalior, who happened to be the spiritual guide of saint Syed Shahul Hameed, whose famous *dargah* is situated in Nagore in Tamil Nadu.

At Nagore, the Hindus worship the Sufi saint Shahul Hameed Nagore Andavar as a presiding god. Although the existence of this Sufi saint's shrine is recorded, in the earlier Gazetteers, as Palli (mosque) in fact it actually refers to the *dargah* (shrine) of the Sufi saint.

Dargah is a common place for veneration of devotees of various religious faiths. In south India, it displays many common features in architectural style and motif, and the fusion of local rituals and customs. Though the practice of offering flowers, sweatmeats and food, the way of conducting worship, and playing of musical instruments are traditionally not allowed in Islam, yet all these practices are introduced in the Sufi shrine due to the strong influence of the local Hindu traditions. Because of the Hindu devotee's involvement and participation in the dargah activities, the Hindu customs began to be accepted in its sacred performances. Such cultural fusion is vividly seen in the Kanduri festival of Saint Shahul Hameed of Nagore-e Sharif, celebrated in commemoration of his death anniversary.[25]

It is said that the parents of the saint Syed Shahul Hameed, Syed Hassan Kuthos and Bibi Fathima, migrated from Baghdad in Iraq during the rule of Sultan Feroz Shah Tughluk of Delhi. They belonged to a small town of Manickpoor, in Pratapgargh district in Uttar Pradesh. He was a true Syed by descent, which can be proved by tracing his relationship to the prophet of Islam as a thirteenth lineal descendant and to the Sufi saint Syed Abdul Quadir Jeelani of Baghdad as a fifth lineal descendant.

Hagiological literature says that Shahul Hameed came to the material world through the divine message of Allah to his parents. He performed miracles *(karamat)* even at the embryo stage when he was in his mother's womb. The God's messenger *Khilr* named him Shahul Hameed. Shahul Hameed had his Islamic education at Gwalior, under the guidance of Hazrat Mohammad Ghouse. He left home on pilgrimage to Mecca. Later he moved back in the direction of India.

He visited the Maldives, Sri Lanka and Tamil Nadu with his spiritual team. At last he came and settled down at Nagore, a small town located in Quaide Millat district of Tamil Nadu in A.D. 1533–34. This town is situated on the banks of the river Vettar, at the confluence of the Bay of Bengal. In the early 19th century, the port of Nagore played a more prominent role in the import and export of business compared to the neighbouring port of Nagapatnam.

The authenticity of the saint's birth on 18.11.1504 A.D and the death on 9.11.1570 A.D suggests that he belonged to the early 16th century. The tradition and the historical records mention that the saint came to Nagore during the period of the Maratha king Achutappa Nayaka. It is recorded that the saint cured the illness of the king who endowed him with land as offerings for curing his treatment.

The Hindu sage Sivananda, while praising the healing powers of the saint, described Shahul Hameed as 'Nagore Andavar' (meaning 'God' in local Hindu religious parlance). The saint Shahul Hameed is therefore referred to as Nagore Andavar to emphasise the dimension of cultural fusion in the Sufi cult.

The saint Nagore Andavar led a simple and pious life. He gained popularity by performing miracles, and thus fulfilling the material desires of the people. The local people, both

Muslim as well as Hindus became his devotees and his residence soon came to be treated as a pilgrimage centre. On his death a tomb was made on the graveyard and people started venerating it.

Even after the death of the saint Nagore Andavar, his miraculous powers had not disappeared. As soon as the tomb of the saint was consecrated, prayers to the tomb in the name of the saint Nagore Andavar continued to be made and the devotees continued to get something of relief and rectification of their personal problems.

There are strong sentiments among the Muslims that pilgrimage to a sacred centre gives religious merit to them after their death. The pilgrimage to Mecca is obligatory on the part of those Muslims who can afford to make the journey to Mecca. The poor Muslims of the society developed a new kind of pilgrimage to the local tombs of the saints, thinking that their visits conveyed the same merit as a pilgrimage to Mecca would. There is a popular belief among the Muslims of north India, that: 'Seven pilgrimages to Ajmer are equal to performing a *Hajj* (pilgrimage to Mecca)'. Similarly, there is a belief among the Tamil-speaking Muslims of south India that those who cannot afford to pay a visit to Mecca, seven visits to the shrine of Nagore-e Sharif conveys the same merit of *Hajj*.

The Kanduri festival of Nagore Andavar is the annual fair which is celebrated in conjunction with observance of the Saint's death anniversary at the *dargah* of Nagore-e-Sharif. Hence, the death anniversary of the saint Nagore Andavar is better known as the Kanduri festival. Pilgrims visit the *dargah* of Nagore-e-Sharif to participate in the rituals and witness the rites of the saint's death anniversary.

The observance of such a death anniversary of the Sufi saint is generally called *urs* and this *urs* observance is termed 'Kanduri' in South India and Sri Lanka by the Tamil-speaking Muslims. It may be stated that the word 'Kanduri' is dervied from the Persian word for 'table covering'. In Indonesia, the same word denotes a feast or a commemorative meal.

The saint Shahul Hameed Nagore Andavar is also called Meera Saheb. In some places, the fairs are referred to as *Jhande* (flag) festival. Saint Shahul Hameed's death anniversary is called *Quadir Walike Jhande* (flag) festival. The main attraction of his death anniversary is the hoisting and the carrying out of these *jhande* (flags) in a procession to honour Nagore Andavar. This festival demonstrates the fusion of Hindu as well as Islamic rituals. The Islamic rites include the recitation of Quranic verses, and observance of the *Fatiha* ritual is a common feature of this fair. The Hindu participation is another important feature of this festival.

The Kanduri festival of Nagore Andavar is performed for fourteen days. Just before the commencement of the Kanduri festival, the flag poles are erected on the five minarets of the shrine (Nagore-e-Sharif). Later the flags are displayed in the Mera *Palli* (mosque) at Nagapatnam. These flags contain the emblem of Zulfhikar which represents one shield and two swords of Ali (the Prophet's son-in-law), who fought and died for the sake of Allah.

The special attraction of Saint Nagore Andavar's Kanduri is the presence of *Fakhir Jamas* (mendicant priests), and the followers (disciples) of the saint who witness the festival. Since the inception of his tomb, the saint's followers have been visiting the fair and paying homage to their spiritual master, Shahul Hameed Nagore Andavar.

On the 9th day of Jamathul Akhir month, at 10 p.m., one disciple from the Malang *Fakhir Jama* is chosen for spiritual exercise. This disciple is known as *pir* in the local parlance. Hence, the ritual is referred to as installation of *pir*. It is performed at the place where the saint's body was offered the funeral prayer *Janaze ke namaz*. It is rendered by the Malang *Fakhir Jama*. The *pir* during this period observes meditation, *dhikr*, reciting the names of God. While doing so, the *pir* throws lemons at the crowd. There is a popular belief that the lemon thrown by the *pir* has miraculous powers. The pilgrims believe that the one who gets the lemon is lucky and that his/her desires are going to be fulfilled by Nagore Andavar. The women believe that if a barren woman gets the lemon, it means that she will be blessed with an offspring. So, people of different faiths continuously stand before him day and night, expecting to get a lemon. Their motive remains to get the blessings of Nagore Andavar in the shape of the lemon.

In the past the shawl of Nagore Andavar's *Rowla Sharif* (sanctum sanctorum) used to be presented by the then Maratha king of Tanjore. Later, one Hindu devotee, Palaniandi Pillai, requested the Maratha king to allow him to present the shawl to the saint. Since then, the tradition has continued and even today the descendants of Palaniandi Pillai are privileged to offer the chadar.

The shawl is displayed in the centre hall of the house of the devotee for the view of the visitors. After performing the *Fatiha*, the shawl is carried back on the back of the elephant of the *dargah*. Later on, the shawl is spread on the saint's *Rowla Sharif*, after anointing sandal paste over the tomb of the saint. This tradition is yet another example of Hindu–Muslim intermingling and communal amity witnessed in this part of India.

In the evening of the ninth day of Jamathul Akhir month, the *tabooth* chariot containing sandal paste is pulled by the pilgrims and the devotees of the Nagore Andavar. No models of the devotees are taken by them during the procession, but the procession includes a variety of musical instruments like drum *(Tappu)*, a troupe of horns *(Kombu)*, and the double reed musical instrument, Nadaswaram, which is generally played in Hindu temples.

The *tabooth*, while being pulled stops at different intervals. Wherever the chariot stops, the devotees including the Hindus offer prayer, by inviting the Muslims to their houses. The procession first moves from Nagapatnam town to Nagore to bestow the blessings of Andavar on the people of the area. Finally the *tabooth* reaches the south gate of the *dargah*.

The sandal paste is received by the saint's descendants. The two pots of sandal paste earmarked for the ritual are taken inside the sanctum sanctorum of the *dargah*. The sandal paste is anointed on the *Rowla Sharif* of the saint by the spiritual successor (*Khalifa*) of the *dargah* after performing the *Fathiha* and reciting the genealogy, *silsila*, of the saint. Then the shawl contributed by the Hindu descendant of Palaniandi Pillai is spread over the tomb of the saint. After the anointing ritual, the gates of the *dargah* are opened to the pilgrims and public.

Though this annual festival is of great importance, the daily and weekly rituals are also held at the *dargah* with great dedication and active participation of both the Hindus and Muslims. The daily rituals such as cleaning the tomb and adorning it with flowers, lighting the lamps and offering *Fatiha* are performed by the sacred specialist *Mujawar* of the Dargah. Thus, the daily and weekly rituals too have great importance in the life of the common people, both Hindus and Muslims.

People, both Hindus and Muslims, visit the *dargah* of Shahul Hameed all over India, with various kinds of motivations, including cessation of their pains such as sickness and insanity. There are also others with frustration in life, persons having high ambitions seeking success in examination, job, civil or criminal courts and barren women with the hope of offspring. All aims and expectations are placed before the saint of the *dargah* for his blessings. The *dargah* of Nagore Andavar is an essential resort especially for the insane. The poorer people strongly believe that insanity is the evil act of an evil spirit, *Jin*. They do not treat it as a psychological affliction. The sufferers visit the tomb to seek cure. Thus the poor people (Muslims and Hindus) who cannot afford better treatment depend upon the supernatural treatment of the saint.

The high praise for the saintly mystic powers and venerations by way of offering flags and lighting lamps of ghee at saint Nagore Andavar's tomb by the local people particularly the Hindus and their corroboration by the Muslims shows the importance of this *dargah* as a great synthesising shrine.

The Sufi Saint Nathervali Dargah in Trichy

The famous Hazrat Thable Alam Badusha Natharvali Dargah located in the heart of the city of Tiruchirapalli in Tamil Nadu is a major pilgrim centre for the Muslims. For, it was here that the great Sufi saint Nathervali was interned in a tomb about 1000 years ago.

He was the first Sufi saint to visit this part of the country with a mission to propagate the greatness of Islam and Prophet

Mohammed. Much like Buddha and some other great spiritual leaders, Nather (known as Hazrat Thable Alam Badusha) was also a king who ruled over part of the Roman empire comprising Asia Minor with Bahinsa as the capital (Syria and Turkey region).

Saint Nather was born in A.D. 927 in the town of Suharwardy near Samarkand. He was named Sultan Muthaharudeen and crowned at the age of seven after his father Sultan Ahamed Kabir died. The saint is believed to have performed many miracles even when he was a child. He renounced regal life at the age of 25 and handed over the empire to his younger brother and started a journey with his few friends in search of a spiritual *pir*. After a few years, he reached Mecca and there in a dream he got a Holy message from Prophet Mohammed, directing him to leave for India to serve humanity.

Accordingly, the Hazrat left for India, in a small boat with 900 disciples and landed in Bhatkal on the western coast of India. The boat *(kishti)* was only the size of a rice bowl and it was indeed a miracle that it accommodated so many persons. The Holy boat is still preserved by the descendants of the saint. The Hazrat reached Tiruchi at the age of 33 and was the first Muslim missionary to live in this part of the world. He toured many parts of the country preaching Islam. It was only after the arrival of the Hazrat that people started embracing Islam in a big way in the South.

The Hazrat lit the lamps of the Islamic zeal for righteousness and love of God in the 'dark recesses' of South India. He spearheaded a religious and spiritual renaissance in this part of the country and held tremendous sway over the hearts of his disciples. It was stated that the Hazrat lived at the Rockfort for some time and once the Chola king of the period Maharaya Harihar Thirubhavanam Devakarikala Chola, who was a great devotee of the saint, askd him to select a place and make it his home. The Hazrat is said to have thrown an amulet he was wearing, from the Rockfort, which fell at the place where the *dargah* stands today. Hazrat Thable Alam Badusha passed away at the age of 70 and his body was interned in the *dargah*, which was originally a small place of worship. It was Chandha Sahib, the Muslim King, who built a beautiful 70-foot tall dome over the *dargah*.

Notable among the other great disciples of the Hazrat were Hazrat Samaspeeran, Hazrat Sams Manzoor, Hazrat Hyder, Hazrat Baba Fakrudeen, all of them were great preachers of Islam. Among the venerable saints who did peaceful work of conversion in South India, he is the most famous of all. Thousands of Muslims and Hindus throng Tiruchi during the *urs* days to pay their respects to the great saint. The great saint was also a staunch advocate of communal harmony.

The Impact of Sufis on Indian Society and Culture

The beginning of the thirteenth century or probably a century earlier, saw the establishment in India of the mystic *silsilas* and the expansion worked a social and cultural revolution. The Sufis found a fruitful soil to thrive in India. The Muslims, in their thirst for knowledge had already translated a large number of Hindu works, literary or scientific, and it is probable that they had become acquainted with the mystic philosophy and mystic discipline of the Hindus.

At any rate one can easily detect many points which were in common between the Hindu system and the Muslim mysticism as it developed in India. In both, the elements of intellectuality went hand in hand with that of devotion, and in both ritualism and ceremonialism were not as important as the search of and love for One Supreme Reality.

Love and liberalism were the keynotes of the mystic movements in Islam and Hinduism. Mystic discipline in both were canalised towards the moral advancement of the individuals and society by making them rise above the barriers of colour and creed, wealth, power and position.

The mystic saints made many contributions in their own way to the social and cultural life of medieval India.[26] They were a group of latitudinarians, men of wide sympathies, broad minded, liberal and tolerant. They played an important part in moulding the attitude and activities of the people. They were free from lust and pride.

Thousands of people were put on the road to righteousness and started devotional prayers. They were engrossed in religious talks and works. Prayer became part and parcel of their life. Love and greed of the world, which leads man astray from the path of rectitude and righteousness had no attraction for them. All vices had to be shunned and despised, but there were certain acts which had to be condemned because of their baneful impact on society. Indulgence in blackmarketing and hoarding was the expression of a morbid desire to take advantage of human misery. Sufi mystics went to the extent of suggesting social boycott of all those guilty of these social crimes. Mystic efforts to improve the moral tone of society did not fail to have their effect. In fact, the *khanqahs* acted as a counterweight in maintaining the moral equilibrium of mediaeval society.

The charge that the Sufis took little or no notice of what was going on around them is only partially true. There are evidences to show that they did not remain indifferent to the actual conditions of the time. They had their own view about rulers and statecraft. They were guided in their attitude by the Quranic injunctions : 'Obey God and the Prophet and those who are in command over you'.

They were not responsible for the policy of the medieval states and shunned the use of force, conflict and the civil war. Unlike the Chishtis, the Suhrawardys were not averse to contacts with rulers and later associated themselves with government for giving correct guidance and securing the good of the people. They would not countenance disobedience and disrespect to the rulers but they would not hesitate to expressing their disapprobation of some their practices. Even the Chishti saints, despite their studied aloofness, made silent protests. The Sufi saints generally kept themselves aloof from kings and aristocrats. But they did not abstain from expressing their views. Some Sufis incurred the wrath of the Sultans for speaking out the truth. The gratuitious advice of the Sufi saints to rulers, officials and nobles lead us to another aspect of their lives. They served as a medium of contact between the rulers and the masses. The Sufis were expected to call upon the king only when they realised the necessity of securing some thing for others.

Sufism was not to be made a means of livelihood. They stressed the importance of earning. Religious literature tells us about many saintly people who earned their livelihood by their professional pursuits and recognised the dignity of labour. Some saints chose to beg in order to crush their ego. It gave them peace of mind, which helped them to concentrate on God. It also made them realise that everything belonged to God and the people were the custodians.

The Sufis did not encourage celibacy and complete renunciation of the world for attainment of spiritual personality. Their moral precepts and ideals of love of God did not mean complete abandonment of family life. Excepting a few outstanding saints the Sufis were all married, and did not shun the life of householder. The typical materialistic approach was discouraged, but the necessities of life had to be worked for.

The Sufi saints, unlike the worldly ulama, never cared to please and gratify men in power. Poverty and starvation was much better than the disgrace and indignities which were heaped upon those ulama who had established some relations with the rulers and the nobles.

The saints of the Chishti order regarded money as carrion. They subsisted on *futuh* and *nazur* (unasked for money and presents). Very often they had to starve. Once when the wife of Baba Farid reported that her son was about to die on account of starvation, he replied that he was helpless. God had so decreed and he was dying. Baba Farid wore worn-out and patched garments. When he died there was nothing in his house for the purchase of his shroud, and the door of his house was demolished to provide unbaked bricks for his grave.[27]

Shaikh Qutb-ud-din Bakhityar Kaki did not use any bedding. Baba Farid had only one blanket on which he sat during the day time and that blanket was spread on the cot during the night. It did not even cover the whole body.

The religious literature of the period tells us that in spite of their leading a life of starvation they were not allured by the grant of royal *jagir* and emoluments. During the time of Sultan Nasir-ud-din, Ulugh Khan (later known as Ghiyas-ud-din Balban) went to Baba Farid in order to pay his respects. He placed before the saint the royal gifts which consisted of some cash and grant of four villages. The cash was for the dervish of the *khanqah* and the land for his maintenance. The saint accepted the money and distributed it among the dervishes but refused to accept the grant of four villages. Even if the Chishti saint accepted anything, they immediately distributed that among the need and indigent persons. The saints of the Suhrawardy and Shuttari Silsila were not so rigid in their attitude and some of them even accepted land and gifts from kings and nobles not only for the poor and the needy but also for themselves. Despite the close contact of the Suhrawardy saints with the kings and nobles, some of them were critical of the court manners and customs. The Firdausi saints received grant of lands and villages not for themselves but for their *khanqah*. Of course, they received gifts and presents from the disciples. These were largely spent on the poor and the needy, visitors and the way-farers.

A mind which failed to see any wisdom or truth in any way of life or thought except its own was the greatest obstacle to the growth of social amity, and the Sufis of medieval India fought against this exclusivism and prejudice. But their toleration was not born of any timely purpose, expediency or weakness. It had its roots in the spiritual and moral strength of their convictions. True toleration is of that spiritually powerful man who, while guarding the frontiers of his own faith, can appreciate all forms of faith other than his own. Khusrau's verse,

> 'O you who sneer at the idolatry of the Hindu,
> Learn also from him how worship is done'

is an expression of this toleration of a spiritually powerful man. When Shaikh Nizam-ud-din Auliya remarked on seeing the Hindu worshipping idols

> 'Every people have got their path, their religion and their house of worship',

he not only gave to his followers a lesson in religious toleration but illustrated for all time an ideal of religious co-existence and amity that Indian society had to cherish and strive for.

The Sufis were usually broad-minded enough to recognise the truths in other faiths, and emphasised love and devotion to, and union with God. Shaikh Nizam-ud-din Auliya once observed : 'Every nation has its own way, its own faith, its own *qibla* (place turned to when at prayer)'.

In extending their help to others the Sufis made no distinction of creed or colour. Once, on the occasion of the annual *urs* (death anniversary), a Hindu sought the blessings of Hazrat Husain Balki. When the Hindu had gone away, the saint observed, 'Infidelity and faith, orthodoxy and heresy are all technical terms of differentiation, for, after all, there is no such thing as an absolute opposition or antagonism ; these are relative terms. All are God's creatures.'

It is not surprising that the Sufis commanded universal respect. The mystic saints exhibited a spirit of accomodation and compromise. They believed in peaceful persuasion and scrupulously acted on the Quranic injunction : 'There is no compulsion in religion'.

Islam is a proselytising religion and the Sufi mystics who said that there are many paths and different ways of reaching God, believed that the path they followed was the shortest and the easiest. It is by their example and by their teaching and good deeds that they won the hearts of the native population.

After throwing open the realm of spirit to all without any distinction of religion and race, the Sufi saints emphasised the basic unity and openness of human society. This was the cornerstone of their social thought. Deriving their inspiration from a Tradition of the Prophet which runs :

'All God's creatures are His family : and he is the most beloved of God

who does most good to His creatures',

they treated all human beings as 'children of God on earth'; and strove to bring their hearts closer and inspired them with a deep and abiding feeling of human love and sympathy. With these revolutionary concepts of God, man and religion, the Muslim mystics entered the Indian social scene and preached 'Unity of God' and 'Brotherhood of Man', from which emanated the entire structure of their thought and the patterns of their behaviour.

They emphasised the dignity of man, as by rejecting all caste taboos, men opened the doors of religious education for all and sundry, and brought spiritual salvation within the reach of all human beings. Thus they paved the way for a common ground of religious and moral effort for all social and cultural groups of India. Viewed in its proper perspective, the elan of Sufi activity was towards creating a feeling of spiritual affinity and oneness by emphasising that the 'way to God' did not pass through the lanes and by-lanes of caste, colour or creed. The world of spirit knew no artificial distinction between one man and another.

The Sufis thus carried the concept of oneness of human society still further and propounded 'unity of human origin'. The concept of 'high' and 'low', *sharif* and *razil* or 'master' and 'slave', which formed the basis of many medieval societies, was gall and wormwood to the mystics. They believed that there was only one basis of superiority of one man over another and that was piety (*taqwa*).

The workers and artisans—known as Hadis, Domas, Chandalas and Badhatus—and the non-descript mass of humanity known as Antyajas who had to live outside the cities, were deprived of all amenities of civil life. The Muslim mystics did not approve of this classification of society. They built their hospices outside the caste-cities in the midst of the non-caste people. A statistical analysis of earliest Indian entrants to the mystic fold would reveal that many of them belonged to the Antyaja group—makers of baskets, sellers of curd, rope-makers, etc.

The Sufi saints showed interest in the teaching of yogis and felt no scruples in appreciating the good things in others. Hindu yogis and *siddhas* frequently visited the *khanqahs* of the Sufi saints. Once, when Shaikh Nizam-ud-din Auliya met a yogi in the *Jamaat Khana* of Baba Farid, he asked him the secrets of his discipline. The yogi replied : 'Our science says that there are two words *(alam)*—*alam-i-ulwi* and *alam-i-sifli.* From head to navel it is *alam-i-ulwi* and from navel to feet it is *alam-i-sifli.* In the *alam-i-ulwi* there is all sincerity, purity, good disposition and good dealings. In *alam-i-sifli* there is purity (holiness) and chastity'. This exposition by the yogi was liked by him.

The saint observed that they were capable of it because of their severe austere practices, and in this a believer and infidel were on equal footing. These instances clearly demonstrate the attitude of understanding and appreciation by the mystic saints towards the members of other cults and creeds. The primary aim of the Sufis in discussing such topics in their *majlis* was to enjoin upon their disciples to learn the good points of the Hindus.

It was due to their magnetic personality, exemplary character, principles of equality and brotherhood, their linguistic attainments and their magical charms and incantation that the mystic saints won the hearts of the people. These factors caused the peaceful penetration of Islam.

While social contact paved the way for communication of ideas, and the development of a common vehicle of expression brought the people closer, the Sufis turned their attention towards ideological and emotional integration. Ideological integration was a long-drawn and slow process and remained confined to a segment of society comprising the higher intellectual class. But emotional integration which could be brought about through mystic songs (*qawwali*), community living in the *jamaat khanas* (big hall in a hospice where all lived and slept on the ground), and spiritual practices common to Sufis, *jogis* and *rishis* (concentration, control of breath, meditation, etc.) was easier and more fruitful.

The most important ideological support to the Muslim mystic movement came from the concept of *wahdat al wujud*. Most of the Sufi saints drew their ideological and spiritual strength from the pantheistic doctrines and constructed on its basis ideological bridges between Islam and Hinduism.

If the social milieu of the times is kept in view, it would appear that the Sufi *khanqahs* were the only place in medieval India where people professing different religions, enjoying different social status and belonging to different backgrounds met and rubbed shoulders. Their free distribution of food *(langar)* to all; community living in the *jamaat khanas* where all lived and slept on the ground; their nonchalant attitude towards the kings; their practice of distributing among the needy and the poor whatever came to them as gifts *(futuh)*; instruction to sweep and clean the stores every day so that nothing of the worldly goods remained to distract their attention and, above all, their readiness to listen sympathetically to the problem of every visitor, made them centres of love and affection for the Indian people.

To the Chishti *khanqahs*, for instance, came the Hindus and Muslims, the *jogis* and *qalandars*, old and young, villagers and townfolk, men and women. In the *khanqah* of Shaikh Farid of Ajodhan, Sayyid Mohammad Gesu Daraz of Gulbarga, Shaikh Ahmad Khattu of Ahmadabad, Rishi Nuruddin of Kashmir and others, views were exchanged between the Sufis and the yogis in an atmosphere of goodwill and understanding.

No social contact could be of any avail if there was no identification with the milieu. When the people found that the mystics had identified themselves with their life-conditions, the impact of their teachings became stronger and deeper.

The practice of spiritual preceptorship known as *piri muridi* was prevalent in the Sufis. Those who entered into a particular fraternity of Sufi saints were called *murids* (disciples). The *murid* had to pledge absolute submission and devotion to his spiritual guide called *pir*. The *murshid* was under obligation to examine the state of his disciple, and judge and assess what points he had ultimately reached. From the *malfuzat* and *maktubat* of the Sufi saints of the period, we get a true picture of the relation that existed between *pir* and *murid*. The *pir* must be a man of insight and spiritual attainment and should possess vast knowledge of the mysteries of God. The *murid* was expected to undergo a course of discipline under the guidance of his *murshid*. The *pir* was to prepare and qualify his *murids* so that they might get nearness to God.

Generally speaking, two types of persons entered the fraternity of a particular order—one for the attainment of the ultimate goal and the other for the development of spiritual personality.

The rules and methods of devotion inculcated by the *pir* and followed by the disciples constituted the *tariqah* (way) of the Sufi. He had to fight against the temptations of the flesh and practise abstinence from all worldly pleasures and enjoyment. Repentance *(tauba)*, firm faith *(yaqeen)*, trust in God *(tawakkul)*, contentment *(qanaat)*, control of ego *(inkesar-i-nafs)*, fear and hope *(khauf-o-reja)*, concealment of poverty *(sirr-i-faqr)*, patience, fortitude and humility *(tahann-ul-o-tawazu)*, civility to creatures *(madarat-i-khalq)*, charity *(sadaqua)*, resignation and satisfaction, intimacy *(uns)*, and decent manners *(adat)* are the virtues he had to cultivate. It was only through the cultivation of these virtues that a disciple could keep his heart pure.

In discussing the *pir–muridi* system, mention may be made of certain social practices prevalent during the period. Among the Chishtis the popular practice was to shave the head at the time of entering into its fold. Religious literature refers to the practice of becoming the *murid* (disciple) of a dead saint after shaving the head and wearing a cap at his grave.

The attitude of the Sufi saints towards languages was free from all prejudices. The contribution of the Sufi saints in the sphere of languages was that (a) they discouraged linguistic chauvinism, (b) developed the languages of different regions, and (c) evolved a common medium for the communication of ideas, known as Hindivi.

Wherever the mystics settled, they strove to build linguistic bridges to establish contact with the local population. Their role in the evolution of vernacular languages in different regions of the country cannot be over-emphasised. They helped in the development of the Hindivi, the Punjabi, the Bengali, the Dakhani, the Gujarati and other regional languages. Significantly enough, in the early history of these languages it is the *khanqah* which stands out prominently as the main nursery where the languages of the elite and the language of the common man come together and paved the way for the emergence of new languages intelligible to both.

The Islamic mystic saints played a very important part towards the evolution of a common language, known as Khariboli or Hindustani. We get genuine specimens and authentic evidence of the linguistic assimilation in the religious literature of medieval India.

The *Malfuzat* and *Maktubat* of the Sufi saints contain not only conversational Hindi sentences but also Hindi *dohas*. The language of those *dohas* is largely Apabhramshaic, and therefore, difficult to understand for one with an average knowledge of Hindi. Some of these *dohas* are very difficult to understand, but parts thereof are clear enough to get at their meaning. It is the Sufi saints who were the real progenitors of the Khariboli or Hindustani, and their acquaintance with both Persian and Hindavi of the time was a factor which helped the rise and growth of a common language.

The Sufis, despite their strict adherence to the laws of the *Shariat* and practices of orthodoxy, instead of criticising the religion, mythology and folklore of the Hindus, were broad-minded enough to study them in their Hindavi verses. Some went to the extent of quoting verses from Hindi poems while delivering religious sermons from the pulpits. Sufi saints used to quote from the words of Sufi priests like Mulla Daud, Qutban, Manjan and Jaisi.

It is significant that all earliest extant copies of *prem kathas* of Muslim poets are found in Persian scripts and belong to Sufi *khanqahs*. Another thing worth attention about them is the introductory pieces containing the praises of God, the Prophet of Islam, the spiritual ancestors of the author, and of the reigning king. The themes of all the personalities mentioned, and the scenes and objects are all Indian and one finds scrupulous avoidance of Persian words and expressions in the main text. The Nath cult figures prominently in the books. The Muslim authors wrote in the language in which they spoke. The fact that they composed their works in Hindi, but wrote them in Persian script shows that they were meant for the Muslims. The Sufis were real pioneers of the movement of national integration.

Majlis-i-Sama which the Sufis sanctioned was totally different from the *Majlis-i-Tarab* or that for the musical entertainment. To the Sufis music was a means to an end. *Sama* exhilarated their spiritual spirit and lifted the veil between them and God, and helped them in attaining the supreme stage of ecstatic swoom which at times proved fatal. It is said that Hazrat Bhaktiar Kaki used to fall unconscious after listening to *qawwals*.

The mystic saints of the Chishti order patronised *Sama*. Qazi Hamid-ud-din Nagauri of the Suhrawardy order introduced *Sama* in Delhi. The saints of the Shuttari order did not allow it.

References are found to the assemblies of *Sama* held in Bihar. The mystic literature of the period gives us the name of some eminent musicians who participated in the audition parties of the Sufi saints. Often musicians went from one *khanqah* to another and sang ecstatic songs.

Throughout the medieval period there was some dispute among the ulama as to the lawfulness of *Sama*. Some ulama of the time declared the audition assembly as illegal. They objected to the hearing of song or hymn and in their opposition displayed the utmost zeal.

Shaikh Nizam-ud-din Auliya grades *Sama* into four categories—*halal* (lawful), *haram* (unlawful), *mobah* (permissible), and *makrooh* (undesirable). If one is inclined towards Divine love, *Sama* is permissible, if he is absorbed in ecstasy during the audition and if he is not acting under the sexual impulse, it is lawful ; but if it is full of mundane objects, it is detestable. He prescribed rules of audition, firstly, the singer should be a perfect man. Shaikh Nizam-ud-din Auliya emphasised that participants of *Sama* should be free from anxieties. The place where *Sama* is held should be beautiful and exhilarating. The participants of *Sama* should be lovers of *Sama*. The auditors of *Sama* should sit after applying scent. They should wear neat and clean clothes.

The rules prescribed for the audition assembly were sometimes not rigidly followed. *Majlis-i-Sama* kindled the flame of Divine love in their hearts. The Sufi saints gained spiritual advantages from audition. According to Al-Ghazali, the saints, by means of *Sama*, stir up in themselves greater love towards God, and by means of music, often obtain spiritual vision and ecstasies. Their hearts become in this condition as clean as silver in the flames of a furnace, and attaining a degree of purity which could never be attained by any amount of mere outward austerities. The Sufi then becomes so keenly aware of his relationship to the spiritual world that he loses all consciousness of this world and falls down senseless.

The mystic saints were conscious of nothing except the Divine love. *Sama* delighted the ear. It reminded them of God. It was the spiritual interpretation of a line of poetry that made them ecstatic. The listeners of *Sama* were more in perfect state than the musicians or the recitors of poetry. The musician might sing with or without true feelings, whereas the listeners felt truly, because the spiritual reality appeared before their vision.

REFERENCES AND NOTES

1. According to conventional knowledge, the term 'Sufi' is derived from four possible sources: (i) from the Arabic word, pronounced *soof* (Sufi) which literally means 'wool', referring to the material from which the simple and coarse robes of the early Muslim mystics were made, (ii) from *Ashab-e-Suffa* (companions of the platform), i.e. those pious, poor and ascetic companions of the Prophet, who congregated and lived on the platform of the 'Masjid-e-Nabwi' (the mosque of the Prophet) at Madina, in A.D. 623 and were later recognised as the first Sufis in Islam, (iii) from the Arabic word *safwa* (piety) to denote the clean, righteous and pious behaviour of true men of God, and (iv) from the Greek root, *Sophia* (divine wisdom), which was later corrupted and applied to pretenders of knowledge (the Sophists).
2. Begg, W.D. *The Holy Biography of Hazrat Khwaja Muinuddin Chishti of Ajmer*, p.25.
3. Ibid., p.28.
4. Khanam, Dr. Farida. *A Simple Guide to Sufism*, p. 162.
5. Begg, W.D. *The Holy Biography of Hazrat Khwaja Muinuddin Chishti of Ajmer*, p.31.
6. Khanam, Dr. Farida. *A Simple Guide to Sufism*, p. 166.
7. Ibid., p. 172.
8. For details of various Sufi orders, their teaching and practices, see
   (*i*) Trimingham, Spencer. *The Sufi Orders in Islam*. Oxford, 1971.
   (*ii*) Subhan, John A. *Sufism : Its Saints and Shrines*. The Lucknow Publishing House, 1960.
   (*iii*) Khanam, Dr.Farida. *A Simple Guide to Sufism*. Goodword Books, Delhi: 2006.
9. Khanam, Dr. Farida. *A Simple Guide to Sufism*. p. 34.
10. Ibid., p. 40.
11. Ibid., p. 45.
12. Ibid., p. 149.
13. Sabir, Iqbal. In "Sufis and Sufism". *Impact of Ibn-Arabi's Mystical Thought on the Sufis of India during 16th Century*. pp.129, 130. Ed. Neeru Misra.
14. *Muslim Shrines in India*. Ed. Christian W.Troll, p. 127.

15. Ibid., 130.
16. Qureshi, Regula B. "Contemporary Relevance of Sufism". In *Localising Islam : Sama in the Royal Court of Chisti Saints.* Indian Council for Cultural Relations, p. 318.
17. Syed, A.R. "Saints and Dargahs in the Indian Subcontinent". In *Muslim Shrines in India*, p. 240.
18. It is a fact to be noted that in every part of the country, in every town or small village, a *dargah* of a Sufi can be sighted. In a way this shows the spread of the Sufis in every nook and corner of the country.
19. For a detailed study of Indian *dargahs*, refer to *Muslim Shrines in India.* Ed. Christian W. Troll. New Delhi: Oxford University Press: 1989.
20. Desiderio Pinto, S.J. "The Mystery of the Nizamuddin Dargah : Accounts of Pilgrims". In *Muslim Shrines in India*. Ed. Christian W. Troll, pp. 113, 114.
21. This *dargah* is not in conformity with other Sufi *dargahs*; because of its popularity, details of this *dargah* are given here.
22. Mahmood, Tahir. "The *dargah* of Sayyed Salar Masud Ghazi in Bahraich". In *Muslim Shrines in India*, pp. 28, 29.
23. New Light on Bihar's Eminent Sufi Shaikh Sharafuddin Maneri and his times Iqtidan Husain Siddiqui, pp. 262-263 in *Muslim Shrines in India*.
24. Khan, Muhammad Ishaq. *The Significance of the Dargah of Hazratbal in the Socio-Religious and Political life of Kashmiri Muslims*. In *Muslim Shrines in India*, pp. 173, 174.
25. Saheb, S.A.A. "Sufism in South India : A Study of the Shrines of Nagore-Sharif in Tamil Nadu". In *Culture, Religion and Philosophy*. Ed. N.K. Das, pp. 265-269.
26. Rashid, A. *Society and Culture in Medieval India*, pp. 242–248.
27. Prakash, Dr. Satya. The Great Sufi Saint Baba Farid—Study in Life, Teachings and Achievements. In *Perspectives on Shaikh Farid*. Ed. Gurbachan Singh Talibi, Baba Farid Memorial Society, pp. 35–40.

5

The Bhakti and Sufi Movements

The immense, prolonged and richly variegated movements of medieval India are generally known as the Bhakti movement and the Sufi movement. The Bhakti movement originally started under compulsion of the social situation in the south from about the seventh century A.D.

It was during this period of strenuous activity that the foundations of later religious development in the south were laid. The Saiva and Vaishnava saints combined to wean the people from their allegiance to Buddhism and Jainism to Shiva and Vishnu worship. They sought to attain their aim by making an appeal to the heart, and so in affecting verse they sang of devotion and of the happiness of dwelling in the presence of God and of seeking of His grace. Their poems were all in the language of the people, and in this as in others matters they were indebted deeply to the religions which they attempted to supplant. For they took over from Buddhism its devotionalism its sense of the transitoriness of the world, its conceptions of human worthlessness, its suppression of desires and asceticism as also its ritual, the worship of idols and stupas or *lingams*, temples, pilgrimages, fasts and monastic rules and its idea of the spiritual equality of all castes; from Jainism they took its ethical tone and its respect for animal life.[1]

The assimilation of these ideas into Pauranic theology and the pervasion of the whole with warm human feeling was the achievement of the saintly hymn-makers of Tamil land, the celebrated Adiyars (the Saiva saints) and the Alvars (Vaishnava saints), who flourished between the seventh and the twelfth centuries.

The movement had two wings—one Saiva and the other Vaishnava. They were contemporary and cooperative and had many close resemblances. They have both left a precious heritage of popular hymns of high literary quality marked at times by great philosophical insight and always reflecting the spiritual exaltation experienced by the hymnists as they stood worshipping in the shrines of their favourite deities.

There came a succession of great leaders among the worshippers of Shiva and Vishnu, the former known collectively as Nayanars (leaders) and the latter as Alvars (divers, into the Divine). They evolved a new type of *bhakti*, a fervid emotional surrender of God which found in due course its supreme literary expression in the *Bhagavata purana* (tenth century), a *bhakti* very different from the calm, dignified devotion of the Bhagavatas of the early centuries. An outspoken hatred of Buddhists and Jains, which finds expression in almost every one of the hymns was among the chief characteristics of the new epoch.

Parties of devotees under the leadership of one gifted saint or another traversed the country many times over, singing, dancing and debating all the way. This great wave of devotional enthusiasm attained its peak in the seventh century and had not spent itself in the midst of the ninth. The shrines visited by the saints and celebrated by them in song were deemed particularly sacred, and princes, nobles and merchants who wished to build and endow temples generally chose them for their particular attention in subsequent times.

Later tradition has recognised the number of Mayanars or Adiyars, devotees of Shiva, as sixty-three; most of them were individuals though occasionally a group of devotees was counted under one name. The most popular Saivite Tamil saints who produced enormous devotional literature (hymns) in Tamil are Appar, Sundarar and Manicka Vasagar.

The Vaishnava wing of the orthodox movement is represented by twelve Alvars. Alvar signifies a devotee sunk in the beauty and glory of his Lord. The more popular Tamil

Vaishnava saints are Nammalvar, Kulashekhara Alvar, Perialvar and Andal. Their hymns are collectively known as *Nalayira Divya Prabhandam,* which is considered as sacred as the *Vedas.* These hymns are often recited in the Vaishnava temples in the south.

The Bhakti Movement travelled from south to north India where it strengthened Vaishnavism and led to the teachings of Bhakta Puranas, which prepared monotheistic faith based on the conception of God as free, changeless, primordial and without constituents *(nirguna). Bhagavath Gita* and *Bhagavath Purana* are the main sacred texts which influenced the North Indian Vaishnava Bhakti Movement.

When Ramanuja, following a line of Vaishanava *acharyas,* decided to give an exalted status to the *Prabhandham* of the Alvar saints, it was a marked departure from the convention that the *Vedas* alone, the monopoly of the Brahman intelligentsia, had a claim to be the 'Word of God'. Ramanuja's *bhakti* prescribed charity of the oppressed and the injured, and it was a more progressive doctrine than Shankaracharya's Advaita, which obliterated all social differences and degrees at the transcendent level only to insist on rigidly enforcing them in day-to-day life.

But Ramanuja showed a patronising attitude to the *stri* (woman) and the *sudra,* did not overturn the ritual supremacy of the Brahman, and preserved the overriding status of Sanskrit as the sacred language. However, Ramananda, a later follower of his sect, settled in Banaras (Varansi), and threw the doors of *bhakti* open to all castes and professions, including the most despised and degraded. His great disciples abandoned Sanskrit altogether to speak in *'bhasha'* or the language spoken by the people. They totally ignored the ritual purity and supremacy of the brahmin which found a place even in the *Bhagavata Purana* and allowed true spiritual authority to a genuine *bhakt* from any caste. There is here a clear transition from notions of ritual purity of those of sincerity and spiritual purity, dramatically demonstrated in many of Kabir's iconoclastic acts. The age-old caste structure was simply laid aside. The emotional fervour of *bhakti* must have acted as a solvent to rigid social taboos and prescriptive communal rules.

A later North Indian saying declared that *bhakti* first arose in the south, was then revealed by Ramananda, and finally spread broadcast by Kabir. It was the emotional leaven, with close and deep links with popular feeling, that brought *bhakti* to its influential radical stage.

Ramananda, who was the chief inspirer of the worship of Rama in the Bhakti Movement in north India towards the close of the thirteenth and beginning of the fourteenth century saw the spread of Islam through Sufi hospices under the Khiljis, and he seems to have come in contact with learned Muslims at Banaras. His followers can be grouped into two schools.

The first, strictly orthodox, accepted the authority of the *Vedas*. It is represented by Nabhadasa (the author of *Bhaktamala*) and Tulsidas, who exalted the puritanical cult of Rama as an antithesis to the other Bhakti doctrine, the erotico-mystical cult of Krishna preached by Nimbarka (twelfth century), Vallabhacarya (fifteenth century) and Chaitanya (1485–1533). This orthodox school of the followers of Ramananda is firmly situated within Hinduism, though it seems to have received some stimulus from Islam, mainly in its puritanical challenge to the orgiastic sensuality of the Shakti and Krishna cults. The second school, which is represented by Kabir and his followers is more eclectic; it is sceptical in its approach to the *Vedas* and to the Hindu religious ritual, extending in its eclecticism the same principle of scepticism and rejection of the scripture and ritual to Islam, with which it seeks to establish a spiritual modus vivendi, though based on the unswerving homage and worship as Rama of the supreme God.

From the thirteenth century onwards Sufi missionaries, who spread all over India met with considerable success among the lower castes of the Hindus, for whom conversion to Islam meant release from the humiliating disadvantages of belonging to an inferior social group. Brahmanical formalism could hardly rise to the occasion to meet this challenge of conversion of Islam in the lower strata of Hindu society. But in the sources of the Bhakti movement there was already a suggestion of the possibility of transcending the caste system. According to the *Bhagavad Gita*, 'in the sight of God all devotees are equal whether they are born in sin or not, and to whatever caste or sect they may belong.'

Historically the growth of the Bhakti Movement can be divided into two phases: the first, from its early development in South India to the thirteenth century; the second, from the thirteenth century to the seventeenth, when in north India it came in contact with Islam, was inspired by its monotheism and stimulated by its challenge, and developed against it a system of self-defence and self-preservation for Hindu spirituality by borrowing Islam's monotheistic egalitarianism.

Divergent views have always been expressed on medieval *bhakti* movements. Whereas some have considered these as an offspring of Islam or a corollary to the Islamic Bhakti Movement, popularly called Sufism, the others have denied it on the gound that the concepts of monotheism and attainment of salvation through *bhakti*, propagated by the Muslim saints, merely rekindled the latent features of Hinduism, which had once formed the core of the ancient Hindu philosophy in the form of the *Bhagavad gita*, the Upanishads and the like, simply because they are unaware with the genesis of monotheism and *bhakti* in Islam. Unable to catch hold of all the finer points of the issue, some have even gone to the extent of suggesting that the Islamic Bhakti Movement was something different from Islamic *Shariat* (law) in the sense that it vied for attaining spiritual upliftment not through the cold formalism of shariat but through the warm yearning of the mystics after God in their own peculiar way called *tariqat*.

Similarly, ignoring the one and the same end for which these were marshalled by the mystics, some other features, concepts, institutions like *khanqah* and *silsila*, and forms of the Islamic mysticism wherever tallying to some extent, with the like in non-Islamic sources, often tempt some to hold the conviction that it derived its inspiration and learning from these although the migratory saints brought all these to India in a fully ripened state with them. However, while jostling with the cobwebs of all these, one often fails to perceive that the main aim of the Muslim saints was not merely the preaching of these doctrines and concepts but something nobler and loftier concerning humanism and the upliftment of the human dignity in a land where it had been denied for centuries together.

Interaction between Hinduism and Islam led to a powerful spiritual movement all over the country. It gave rise to a liberal religious movement in the form of Bhakti, which made rapid progress and swept the entire country the fourteenth century onwards. The movement drew both the Hindu and Muslim in its fold and sought to reconstruct the Indian society by snythesising Hinduism and Islam to ensure the communal goodwill and to create an environment of tolerance and co-operation.[2]

Bhakti, like Sufism, was the religion of love and devotion. It was brought about by Hindu saints who had great respect for Islam and were impressed by its simplicity and insistence on oneness of God. Besides its ideals of human equality and universal brotherhood influenced them greatly. Their close interaction with the Sufis and their own study of Hindu scriptures convinced them that God is one and all divisions are artificial. They attempted to reform and reconstruct the Hindu society in the light of new principles. The Bhakti Movement thus had both social and religious dimensions.

The saints sought to bring the two communities spiritually closer by incorporating all that was good in both the religions and discarding all that obstructed or stood in the way of the well being of the people. They boldly criticised the ritualism, sectarianism and hypocrisy of their age and preached universal love. They explained in popular language and by means of homely simile, the great spiritual truths, which they realised and the vision of God they had experienced.[3]

The Bhakti and Sufi Movements in the North are parallel movements which succeeded in bringing about interaction between Hinduism and Islam. In some cases, the Bhakti poets cannot be differentiated from Sufi poets. While syncretic movements, mixing Hindu and Sufi elements, led by the founders of different cults flourished, the followers of the syncretic movements, enriched the modern Indian languages of the medieval period with devotional literature with their enliving poetic works.

It is a truism that the Bhakti Movement cannot be studied without reference to Islam and Sufism. On a close analysis the movement appears more complex and heterogenous than it is generally assumed, and reveals at least two distinct variants. The earlier is a linear development of the Indian devotional tradition, anteceding the spread of Sufic influence in India. This refers to the devotional impulses in the Alvar Vaishnava movement in South India, continued and developed further in the works of Ramanuja, Madhava Nimbarka and Ramanda (the fourteenth century A.D.).

The other variant of the Bhakti Movement was rather different from this in that it originated later and was, in essence, syncretistic, cosmopolitan, and more populist. The latter drew as much upon Sufic as on indigenous devotional mysticism. Its raison d'etre was to stress the unity of the godhead, transcending the artificial barrier of religious pluralism, and to provide a common ground for people of all religious and social affiliations to meet and unite. Unlike the other clearly Hindu *bhakti* tradition, the protagonists of syncretistic devotionalism, like Kabir (fifteenth century A.D.), Nanak (A.D. 1469–1539) and Dadu (A.D. 1544–1603) were not concerned with the revitalisation of Hinduism or, for that matter, of any particular religion.

The study of the contribution of the Bhakti and Sufi poets is a vast subject in itself. Only a glimpse of this vast area of the contribution of these poets can be given here.

The Bhakti Movement in Maharashtra

About the end of the thirteenth century the Muslims began the conquest of the Deccan. The Bahmani rulers of the Deccan fostered the growth of the literature and art of the people whom they governed. The Marathi language was used in the offices of the Adil Shahi and Qutb Shahi kingdoms, and Marathas were employed as revenue officers and even as commandants. Qutb Shah was a patron of culture and himself a poet of considerable power, and wrote extensively in the Dakhni language, which was a mixture of Hindi and Persian. The interaction of Hindus and Muslims produced the same cultural phenomena in Maharashtra as it had done in Bengal. The Marathi saints and hymn-singers effected the same kind of synthesis of the two faiths. The severity of the monotheistic creed of the Muslims was distinctly impressed upon the minds of these poets. The worshippers of Dattatraya or the incarnation of the Hindu Trinity, often clothed their God in the garb of a Muslim *fakir*. This same influence was at work with greater effect on the popular mind in Maharashtra, where preachers, both Brahmans and non-Brahmans, were calling the people to identify Rama with Rahim and ensure their freedom from the bonds of formal ritualism and caste distinctions, and unite in common love of man and faith in God.[4]

The history of religious upheaval in Maharashtra goes back to time of Jnanesvar who completed his Marathi commentary of the *Bhagavad Gita* in A.D. 1290. Jnanesvar had a tremendous influence on the language and thought of Maharashtra, but the first of the saintly array of men who changed the faith of this region and turned the minds of men from the priest-ridden ceremonial of a narrow creed of freedom and love was Namdev. He is remembered by every saint of Maharashtra, Rajputana and the Punjab as the great historic name in the long list of *bhaktas*. He belonged to the 14th century.

In Maharashtra the Bhakti cult of Rama developed in the tradition of Ramanada; its first exponent was Namdev (fourteenth century) whose eclecticism has interesting parallels with that of Kabir, like whom he repudiates ritual in Hinduism as well as in Islam: 'Hindu is blind, Muslim is one-eyed. He who understand is wiser than both. Hindus pray in temples, Muslims in mosques. He (Namdev) serves the Name which has no temple and no mosque.' The favourite name of Namdev's personal God is Vithoba. Like Kabir, he rejects caste system and idolatry. Unlike Kabir, he shows traces of pantheism. 'He is the idol. He is the temple and He is worshipping Himself'. His disciples also included some Muslim reconverts to Hinduism. The Maharashtrian Bhakti Movement centred around the shrine of Vithoba of Pandharpur. It encouraged the growth of Marathi literature, loosened the rigidity of caste, subordinated ritual to devotion in worship and brought about a certain measure of reconciliation with the presence of Islam in India. The most influential among Maratha saints was Tukaram, whose conception of God was very much like that of Kabir and who occasionally used Sufi terms in his hymns.

Bhakti in Maharashtra centred round the shrine of Vithoba at Pandharpur on the banks of the river Bhima. But although associated with a particular temple and a particular image, it was really not idolatrous in its character. Vithoba was a symbol and a convention, but not an idol. Thus the characteristics of the Krisnaite religion of devotion in Maharashtra were hardly distinguishable from those of the radical reformers of the north. Its results were the development of the vernacular literature, the modification of caste exclusiveness, the sanctification of family life, the elevation of the status of women, the spread of humaneness and toleration, the partial reconciliation with Islam, the subordination of rites and ceremonies, pilgrimages and fasts.

Namdev was a disciple of Khechar who was definitely hostile to idol worship; he received the following instructions from his Guru :

'A stone-god never speaks. What possibility then of his removing the disease of mundane existence? A stone image is regarded as God, but the true God is wholly different. If a stone god fulfils desires, how is it he breaks when struck? Those who adore a god made of stone lose everything through their folly. Those who say and hear that a god of stone speaks to his devotees, are both of them fools. Those who extol the greatness of such a God and call themselves his devotees, should be regarded as worthless persons, and their words should not be heard by the ear. In the village of Dvadasi (Barsi) instruction was given that there is no place which is devoid of God. That God was shown to Nama in his heart, and thus Khechar conferred a blessing on him'.[5]

This is how Namdev exposes the inefficiency of the external acts of religion :

'Vows, fasts and austerities are not all necessary; nor is it necessary for you to go on a pilgrimage. Be you watchful in your hearts and always sing the name of Hari. It is not necessary to give up eating food or drinking water; fix your mind on the feet of Hari. Yoga or sacrificial ceremonies or giving up objects of desire is not wanted. Realise a fondness for the feet of Hari.'

Namdev was the leader of a goodly host, which carried forward the traditions which he handed over to them. Among these saints a few were women, a few were Muslim converts to Hinduism, nearly half of them were Brahmans, while the remaining ones were drawn from all the other castes.

Tukaram, who after Namdev was the greatest of Maratha saints, and who wields the widest influence in Maharashtra, was equally eclectic. He was a contemporary of Shivaji and one of the inspirers of the spirit which welded the Marathas into a people united in common aims and aspirations. Tukaram became intensely disgusted with worldly life, gave up all business and devoted himself completely to contemplation and devotion. His life of piety and service made him popular with the people all round.

Tukaram's teachings are embodied in his numerous *Abhangas* which number between five and eight thousand. They deal with all aspects and every problem of religion as it presented itself to the peoples of India in that period, namely, the nature of God, His relation with the world and man, His grace, the destiny of man, the method of realization, the standard of virtue, the path of devotion, the obstacles, sufferings and triumphs of the devotee, the emotions accompanying various stages of religious life, the snares of the world and of sense, the character of saints, the need of the preceptor, the uselessness of externalia, the iniquity of social distinctions and so on.[6]

Tukaram's conception of God was almost identical with that of Kabir, He says :

'He has neither form nor name, nor place of abode; He is present wherever we go, Vitthal our mother and sister. He knows neither form nor change of form. He pervades the moving and immovable world. He is neither with nor without attributes.' In a number of *Abhangas,* he indicates the nature of true worship, and rejects ceremonies, offering Vedic sacrifices, visiting holy places, worshipping stones, putting on saints' guise, fasts, and austerities. Tukaram's attempt at reconciling Hindu and Muslim faiths is evidenced in the hymns translated below :

'What Allah wishes that is accomplished, O! my friend (Baba), the Maker is the sovereign of all.

My mind dewells, O! friend, on my Lord (Sahib) who is the Maker.

'First among the great names is Allah, never forget to repeat it.

Allah is verily one, the Prophet (*nabi*) is verily one.

There Thou art one, there Thou art one, there Thou art one, O! friend.

There is neither I nor thou.'

The Varkari Panth

The Varkari Panth, with its vast following in Maharashtra overflowing into Karnataka, Andhra and Gujarat is a phenomenon about 1000 years old. Arising from within mainline Hinduism, it is an inspiring example of a collective protest against religious communalism that marginalised vast masses of the Maharashtrian society in spiritual, cultural, social and economic spheres. This Maharashtrian version of Indian Vaishnavism acted as a catalyst that set in motion a long-lasting process of integration and unification in a fragmented and disintegrating society.

This trend-setting movement affirmed the primacy of *bhakti* (devotion) over *jnana* (knowledge) and *karma* (action). It affirmed the fundamental equality of all, ignoring the differences of caste and sex as was being done in the traditional Hindu society. Women were admitted into the religious fellowship. Religious literature was until then available only in Sanskrit. Chakradhar and his followers, departing from tradition, employed the local language of the people, namely Marathi, for their religious discourses and commentaries.

The Varkari Panth came into existence just when the Mahanubhav Panth was gaining ground. Many perspectives and ideas are common to the two sects which are a striking departure from the established traditional course. Even so the Varkari Panth, in the course of time, displaced the once popular cult and itself developed into the most collective expression of the people's hopes and aspirations. This was achieved precisely by steering clear of the excesses committed by the Mahanubhav adherents.[7]

The very concept of God in this spirituality is remarkable for its conciliatory perspective. It unites the two distinct modes of the divine, i.e. the *nirguna* (the one without attributes) and the *saguna* (the one with attributes). The *nirguna* is the ultimate reality of God in its transcendent, absolute, quality-less state, beyond all manifestations. The *saguna* is the same ultimate reality in its manifest, phenomenal, relational form.

Philosophers tend to think that the *nirguna* Brahman is higher than the *saguna* Brahman. For the Varkaris, the two modes are equal. In the 16th century Eknath translated some other Sanskrit religious texts into Marathi. He wrote a voluminous commentary on the eleventh book of the Sanskrit *Bhagavat Purana*. The Varkari leaders made no secret of their vigorous opposition to the oppressive domination of Sanskrit.

The Varkari's revolutionary use of Marathi opened the flood-gates of spiritual knowledge to the general public. The use of the so-called language of the gods, Sanskrit led to esotericism, elitism and exploitation. With Marathi, on the other hand, the Varkari leaders established a dialogue with and within the entire community of the local people. Through their religious discourse in Marathi, the Varkaris affirmed the sanctity of this popular language on a par with Sanskrit.

An outstanding feature of the Varkari Panth is that it has set aside the ancient iniquitous caste system in the contest of *bhakti*. It proclaims God's universal love for all without discrimination. All need to be liberated and therefore people of all castes, high and low have the right and the privilege of enjoying blissful communion.

Traditional Hinduism had discriminated against women too. The Varkari movement opened spiritual treasures to women on terms of equality. Women were allowed and encouraged to be Varkaris. A number of them was also recognised as leaders, spokespersons and saints. The *abhangas* of Muktabai, Janabai and Bahinabai who are revered as saints are read, recited and sung with reverence and devotion. The Varkari's consistent reference to God in terms of mother has helped in integration of sexes.

Namdev, Eknath and Tukaram composed hymns in Hindi. Probably they intended to address the Muslims as partners in dialogue. They employed Islamic terms like *khudayee* (concerning God), Allah (God), Mundha (spiritual leader), *malang* (*fakir*), dervish (mendicant). Eknath's Hindu-Turk dialogue is a classic example of reconciliation, tolerance and acceptance. Initially they distrust and argue with each other. But as their dialogue proceeds, both get enlightened and admit, 'Oh brother, Hindu-Muslim are both created by God'.

Shaikh Mohammed was an admirer of Tukaram, by whom he was deeply influenced. The Varkari composers let themselves be influenced by the soul-stirring mystical utterances of the Muslim Sufis and vice versa. The followers of Shaikh Mohamed who became *bhakts* observe both Ramzan and the Ekadasi fast and make pilgrimages both to Mecca and to Pandharpur. The leadership tradition (guru parampara) inherited by Eknath was associated with the Sufi sect. The biography of Eknath's guru Janardanswami reveals close ties between the Hindu and Muslim communities.

The Hindus make common cause with the Muslims in their great festivals, and this feeling is reciprocated by the Muslims. Some Muslims *fakirs* have been ranked with the Hindu saints in general veneration and there are some saints who are venerated by both communities alike. These features of tolerance and moderation have been developed in the course of centuries and they constitute some of the most stable elements of the national character.

The Varkaris can certainly be regarded to have contributed in big measure towards this happy interaction between the two Hindu and Muslim faiths. The Varkari leaders affirmed the primacy of the *bhaktimarga* over the *jnanamarga* and *karmamarga*.

The *bhaktimarga* taught a religion of the heart. This way of love and surrender towards God was available to all. It steers clear of the rigours of the *jnanamarga* and the cumbersome complexities of the *karmamarga*.

These are four methods:

The Namasmaran : This is a prayerful, loving devotional recitation or chanting of the divine name.

The Bhajan : It consists of the chanting of the divine names and the singing of hymns, to the accompaniment of musical instruments.

The Kirtan : It is service of devotion conducted under the guidance of a leader who has around him a team of fellow devotees playing different musical instruments.

The Vari : The Varkari Panth is characteristically the spirituality of pilgrimage. In the name Varkari, the word 'vari' means the practice of proceeding regularly or recurring monthly or annual periods on pilgrimage to any sacred place.

The exponents of the spirituality rendered yeoman service to the cause of social unification and integration by their courageous use of Marathi for spiritual literature.

Bhakti Movements in Gujarat

The genesis and development of the Bhakti Movement in Gujarat and Rajastan cannot be dissociated from similar developments in other parts of India. The movement launched in north India by Ramananda, Kabir, Rabidasa, etc. has sent waves in Gujarat and Rajasthan as well. The southern Bhakti Movements, based on the theistic interpretations of Vedanta, were also able to exert influence on Gujarat. The Marathi Bhakti Movements launched by the Mahanubbavis and Virakari-panthis also had contributions to the development of Bhakti Movement in Gujarat.

The Gujarati Bhakti movement was centred on a renovated concept of Krishna-Vishnu as a personal deity who could be easily approached by simple love and devotion. The Krishna legends were very popular in Gujarat, especially because the city of Dvaraka was his seat. In Jain tradition Krishna was also acknowledged as a divine entity. In north India, Bhakti Movements, the central figure was Krishna or Vishnu, who had also been equated with Rama. The Chaitanya movement of Bengal was Krishna-oriented. The same held good in the case of the southern Bhakti Movements. The Mahanubhava-panthis of Maharashtra were worshippers of Krishna.

In Gujarat and Rajasthan, Vaishnavite Bhakti Movements came in two waves. The pan-north Indian wave was due to the influence of Ramananda and his followers while the second wave was from the south led by the Vallabha movement. A follower of Ramananda, Bhalan (A.D. 1494–1554) led the foundation of an elaborate Bhakti Movement through his literary pursuits in Gujarati language. A translator of Bana's classic *Kadambari*, he was well versed in the epics and *Puranas* from which he churned various *akhyanas* or episodes dealing with various aspects of the bhakti *akhyanas*. These *akhyanas* were so popular that they became a typical medium of literary expression.[8]

Bhalan was also influenced by Jayadeva's *Gitagovinda*, Bopadeva's *Harililamrta* and his own *Saptasati*. He gave a new dimension to the folk-songs relating to the love sports of Krishna. Bhalan also wrote in Braja-bhasa which testifies his special attraction towards the *madhuria-rasa* of Vaishnavism. The *akhyanas* of Bhalan became so popular that there developed a class of professional bards called *gagariabhats* who used to sing them in public. Among other poets of the *bhakti* tradition, Kesava Hrdayarama (c. A.D. 1536) and Nakar (c. A.D. 1550) composed similar *akhyanas* from the Puranic tradition under the shadow of Bhalan's influence.

Mirabai (A.D. 1498–1546) and Narasimha Mehta (A.D. 1500-80), the two greatest exponents of the Bhakti Movement of Gujarat, appear to have been influenced by the Vrindavana school founded under the inspiration of Sri Chaitanya. Numerous devotional songs of Mira are sung all over India even today.

According to the tradition, Mira was the daughter of Raja Ratan Singh and the daughter in-law of Maharana Sanga of Mewar. She was devoted to Krishna whom she used to call *Giridharilala* from her childhood. She is said to have been initiated into the doctrine of pure *bhakti* by the saint Ravidasa who was one of the twelve principal followers of Ramananda. Her earlier songs addressed to *Giridharilala* were written in pure homely Rajasthani, the parent of modern Gujarati, Mewari and Marwari, whereas her later songs have the impress of Braja-bhasa. Mira regarded herself as a *gopi* of Krishna in Vrindavana, having the pleasure of hearing time and again the sweet strains of Krishna's magic flute and the ecstatic glimpses of his eternal *rasalila* or the love-sport.

The central figure of the medieval Bhakti Movement in Gujarat was Narasimha Mehta (1500–1580). An erudite student of Advaita Vedanta and gifted poet of the first order, Narasimha had made a conscious attempt to bring a spiritual renaissance in Gujarat. His approach was based both on *jnana* (knowledge) and *bhakti* (devotion). He appears to have been influenced both by the saints and poets of north India and by those of Maharashtra and Karnataka, especially by Jaanadeva and Namdeva. The similarity of his views with those of Sri Chaitanya probably is due to his association with the Chaitanyite Vaishnava saints of Vrindavana.

It is also to be remembered that Sri Chaitanya himself visited Gujarat and it was not improbable that he had some followers there, with whom Narasimha came in touch. His poems on the love of Krishna and the *gopis* recall the Chaitanyite approach to the Divine. Though a Brahman by birth, Narasimha did not believe in caste-distinction and untouchability. He mixed freely with the untouchables, whom he used to call *Harijan* or the men of God. The term *Harijan* was his coinage which was later adopted by Mahatma Gandhi. The liberal teachings of Narasimha Mehta had a great impact not only on the religious life of the masses, but also on the intellectuals of his time and after. About his well-known song, *'vaisnava jana to tine kahiye'* Gandhiji wrote: 'That one song is enough to sustain me, even if I were to forget the *Bhagavad Gita*'.

For centuries together the *padas* and *bhajans* of Narasimha have been handed down orally. They include *Hara mala Shamalshano Vivaha, Govinda gamana, Surata sangrama, Sudama carita, Rasa Sahasrapadi,* etc. Several poems of Narasimha Mehta relate to the episodes in Lord Krishna's life as described in the canto X of the *Bhagavata Purana, Sri Krishnajanma* deals with the miraculous birth of the God.

Narasinmha Mehta, apart from an ideal *bhakta* and mystic was a genuine subjective poet. There is an unmistakable ring of sincerity in his poetry. His poetry is not only devotional and philosophical in content but is lyrical and melodious in character, like the *Gita-govinda* of Jayadeva.

Another exponent of the Bhakti Movement in Gujarat was Akho or Akha Bhagat. Like Narasimha, he made a synthesis of *jnana* (knowledge) and *bhakti* (devotion). He had his own interpretation of the *Vedanta* which he had simplified for masses in a poetical language that they can easily be understood and that is why he was popularly called *Vedantakavisiromani*. His *Akhegita* is a classic in Gujarati.

Dadu, the most celebrated disciple of Kabir was born at Ahmedabad in Gujarat in 1544 and died in 1603 in the village of Narana in Rajasthan where his followers have now their chief centre. There were twelve branches of the followers have now their chief centre. There were twelve branches of the followers of Kabir in Kathiawar and Gujarat.

Among the exponents of medieval Bhakti Movements, Dadu stands next to Kabir, who actually thought of a religious syncretism. He was one of those who laid greatest emphasis on the unity of religion between the Hindus and the Muslims. The tradition of Kabir was continued by him. He is regarded as a great poet and his works show an admixture of Braja-bhasa and Khari-boli as in the case of Kabir. Dadu founded the *Parabrahma Sampradaya* with a view to uniting different faiths in one bond of love and comradeship. He admitted both Hindus and Muslims as his disciples. Two of the eminent disciples were Sundaradasa and Rajjab. At his order his disciples made a collection of the devotional writings which included many hymns even of the Muslim saints like Kazi Kadam Shaikh Farid, Kazi Mohammad, Shaikh Bahawad, Bakhna and others. The second of this kind is probably the *Granth Sahib*. He inculcated devotion to Rama and meditation on him.

In Gujarat and Rajasthan the sect of Vallabhacarya (A.D. 1473–1531) had the largest number of followers among the rich trading and cultivator classes.

The Vallabha sect had a remarkable influence in northern India on account of the activities of its followers like Hita Harivamsa, Haridasa Swami, Sribhatta and, above all, Tulsidas. The ideas of Vallabha were given a new tone and coulour by his son Vitthalanatha (A.D. 1516–76), who insisted more on the Radha cult. He engaged Kumbhandasa, Surdasa, Paramanandadasa and Krishnadasa.

The influence of the Vallabha sect was to a great extent responsible for the spread of the Bhakti Movement in Gujarat and Rajastan. Vallabha believed in the principles of equality and liberalism and as such the Vallabhite movement had a great possibility of reaching to the masses.

The Sufi Movement

North India witnessed revolutionary changes in the political, social and religious fields during the medieval period. The life-style of the people was greatly influenced by the religion, culture and civilisation of the Muslim rulers and Sufi saints. There was a cultural fusion between the Hindus and Muslims. The Muslims adopted Hindu ideologies partly and the Hindus also were influenced by the Muslim concepts.

Those great souls of the Muslim community, who had taken the initiative in adopting Indian thoughts were called Sufis and those Hindus who similarly tried to adopt Muslim thoughts were called saints. Both were held in high esteem by all concerned. The ancient Sufism, which was influenced by Vedantism and other Indian thought emerged in a new form and shape when it reached India, during the above-cited period. The aspect of love was given the same importance as devotion by the Sufi saints. Sufi saints have to pass through the same stage to reach the Almighty as a lover has to pass through stages to reach his sweetheart in worldly love affairs.

Islam and Hinduism found a meeting-ground in the masses of new converts to Islam, people who belonged to the lowest and most despised castes and were subject to grim exploitation and oppression. Another meeting-ground was found in the minds of travelling peddlers and small traders, whose livelihood tended to free them from local prejudices and customary inhibitions.

The new converts could hardly have been deeply immersed in Islamic traditions. They had embraced Islam, moved by the piety and loving humanity of the Sufi saints, but the entire hinterland of their mind was still under the spell of age-old Hindu concepts and attitudes. They had every reason to resent Brahmanical tyranny and humiliation, but both the language and ideas of Islam were only partly assimilated by them. That is why the mission of the *bhaktas* which made use of ideas familiar to them and yet transcended the narrowness of orthodoxy had such an impact on them. Many of them must have drifted towards various forms of *bhakti*, along with other castes that had not changed their religion.

In the medieval period the Sufis taught people disinterested virtue, purification of the soul and divine love and thus, raised the standard of life from the spiritual point of view. They laid more emphasis on the inward rather than on the outward aspects of life. It was due to this fact that they had a greater hold on the people than the scholastic theologians or formal jurists, and their mode of training was more effective. Their motto was service to humanity at large, irrespective of caste or creed. They always showed unity of thought despite professing different religions.

'It was through Sufism that Islam really found a point of contact with Hinduism and effective entrance to Hindu heart'.[9] Really, with the emergence of Sufi movement in India, the trend of assimilation between the two major religious communities began. Islam with its clear, definite and simple creed, which stood in contrast to the indigenous vagaries of the imagination and speculation about God, appealed to many Hindus as a satisfying solution of the vexed problems of theology. To others its social democracy granted a welcome release from the bondage of caste. On the other side, 'owing to the ancient guru-chela practice existing among the Hindus and the universal belief in the worship of local gods and goddesses, which was the heritage of the majority of the Muslims of India through their Hindu religion, it became all the more easy for saint worship to become part of Muslim religious life. The process of sharing of each other's merits and demerits continued for a few centuries till a composite culture and philosophy started developing in India which flowered in the form of Bhakti Movement. In the 15th century practically all parts of India witnessed the emergence of groups of saints, poets and reformers who represented a new synthesis. They vehemently attacked religious rituals, priestcraft, social inequalities and hypocrisy. Their approach was simple, devotional and popular.

During the medieval *bhakti* period of Hindi literature, many top-ranking love stories were written by the Sufi saints. It writing the first Hindavi verse romance, the *Chandayan,* Maulana Daud adapted the Ahir folk-epic of Lorik and Chanda into a distinctive Sufi story in 1379. He developed a narrative formula for representing the play of desire between God, the Sufi, and the world as an erotic relationship between man and two women.

It has been reported by Mulla Abdul Qadir Badayuni that *Chandayan* (of Mulla Daud) was most popular amongst the contemporaries because of its latent layers of meaning and it was duly recited from the pulpits of mosques at Delhi. Its importance, then,was parallel to the works by Rumi (1207–1273), Attar (1136–1230) and Sheikh Saadi (1184–1292). Because of its competence for elaborate expressionism of the symbolic, semiotic and the mystical, Hindi, along with its dialects, was extremely popular with the Sufis. The urban citizenry and the rural folks were usually familiar with these conventions. The *khanqahas,* abode of Sufi dervishes, were the centres for propagating social awareness and the spiritual culture by them.

An environment of equality and fraternity pervaded, where thousands of rich and the poor, oppressed and the untouchables would assemble. Those centres maintained a sort of ethical balance in the rigid medieval society. They left their imprint over the renaissance of *bhakti* (14–15C A.D.). That influence is clearly perceptible especially in Kabir, Guru Nanak (1469-1539) and Namdeva. The teachings and the norms of *khanqahas* as institutions, had their immense reformist impact upon the caste conflicts, class-conflicts, political upheavals and multifarious immoralities of contemporary society. The Bhakti Movement owes its deep debts to such Sufi ethos also for its humanistic goals of human love and the equality of all men before God.

They were all Sufi saints of high standing. Those poets used to reflect the element of spiritual love through the medium of worldly love, as the way to realise God. It is noteworthy that these Sufi saints did not resort to the style of criticism and condemnation like Nathpanthis and other saints. The attitude of these saints was not only emotional, but also committed to the realities of life. In other words, they were not saints of words, on the other hand they were saints of deeds also. The uppermost desire in their minds was to establish love and affection among Indians by presenting an idealistic life-style, full of good conduct and an attitude of well-being. Their poems contain heart-touching expressions, as far as the love-element is concerned.[11]

One of the major genres of pre-modern north Indian poetry is the Awadhi or eastern Hindavi *prema-kahani* (literally love-story) composed by Muslim Sufi poets, members of the Persian-speaking courtly elite of the Delhi Sultanate, from the fourteenth century onwards. These narrative poems, called Sufi romances by modem critics, are commonly assumed to put forward the equation of human love and love for a divine being. Written and performed in Delhi, Jaunpur, and the eastern province of Bihar, they mark the inauguration of a new literary culture in a local language, an Indian Islamic literary tradition.

The Chishti Sufis, the first known composers, of the Hindavi mystical romances, describe the ascetic quest of the hero towards the revelatory beauty of a heroine (or God) by linking mortification, fasting, and prayer with a female object of desire. Drawing on the local language of ascetic practice, they make their hero into a yogi, while the heroine is a beautiful Indian woman. While eroticism and asceticism have frequently been linked together in Indian religious traditions and in Sufi mysticism, the Hindavi romances are distinctive because in them the hero attains his divine heroine after an arduous ascetic quest and brings her to live with a hostile wife who represents the world.

This Indian Islamic literary tradition marks the full indigenisation and assimilation of Islam into an Indian cultural landscape. Indigenisation accounts for the Indian elements in Indian Islamic culture as the result of conscious and purposeful adaptations made to the local environment by agents who remained Muslim in their religious orientation, in contrast to the widespread explanation of a haphazard syncretism or accretion of disparate elements.

These poems are distinct both from Persian and the older classical traditions of India, an Indian Islamic creation which emphasises its double distance from these older canons even while borrowing important ideas and conventions from them. The poets of the genre used Hindavi, a spoken local language that they elevated into a literary medium, and the earliest manuscripts of their poems are written in Persian script. Their romances express a Sufi message through a poetics derived in part from Persian, in part from Sanskrit and in part from regional literary conventions, an indication that these poets had arrived on the cultural scene and that they were fully indigenised as Muslims.

The Indian Sufis were fully steeped in the conventions and symbolism of the various genres of Persian poetry both lyric (*ghazal*) and narrative (*mathnawi*). At the same time, they were fascinated by the poetics and alluring imagery of Indian poetry as they encountered it in musical and dance performances and in poetic recitation.

The cultural history of Sultanate India is in part the history of the enthusiastic participation of Sufis and other Muslims in the formation of the canons of Indian poetry, art, and music. The genre of the Hindavi Sufi romance should be read against this larger background of cultural appropriations, comminglings, and creative formulations. The Hindavi Sufi poets used Sanskrit *rasa* theory and the conventions of Persian poetry to create a mystical romantic genre centred around the various meanings of *prema-rasa,* the juice or essence of love. The Hindavi romantic ideal of desire and its transformation into Sufi love is set in a fantasy world of marvels and exotic locales, of supernatural helpers and agencies who aid the hero along his way.

Malik Mohammed Jayasi is the most popular of all Sufi poets. His *Padmavat* is considered to be the best love-epic of Hindi Sufi poetry. This is the first ever *maha kavya* (epic) of the Avadhi language (dialect). In this work, he is at his height in depicting romance, union of lovers, separation of lovers and realistic description of the changing seasons.

Padmavat has to be accepted as a supreme achievement of medieval Hindi poetry in the Sufi branch of the *nirguna* school. There is systemic mobility from the rural to urban; folk to classical, signs to symbols, metaphors to metamorphosis etc and this dynamism of binary oppositions generates brilliance of the best of Hindu and Muslim ethos in its composite unity, harmonious cultural identity and Indianness of the literary tradition.

Jayasi has described the romance of Ratnasen, the king of Chittor and the princess Padmavati of Sri Lanka. The first part of the book is imaginary and the second part is historical. According to the poet himself, the characters Ratnasen, Padmavati, Nagamathi and Alauddin are symbols.

Through *Padmavat*, Jayasi opens the eyes of all those who advocate separation between the followers of the two religions. He says that 'Viyog', of Ratnasen for Padmawati was the same as that of Allauddin for her. It evokes emotions and feelings irrespective of caste, colour or religion. There is unity of emotion among all human beings. The total aim and objective of *Padmawat* is the extension of broad and liberal human values and refinement of human sentiments and feelings. During the course of this interaction the bonds of caste, religion and nationality break down automatically and there emerges a perfect being whose heart becomes tender, liberal, permissive and powerful. Jayasi appealed to the entire personality of man—the heart as well as mind, reason as well as emotion, moral as well as spiritual. This is the all-pervasive input of his philosophy. In short, Jayasi, by his creative writings played a vital role in removing the feelings of differences from the hearts and minds of Hindus and Muslims.

Poet Noor Mohamed was the last link in the unbroken chain of Sufi poets. It is noteworthy that Muslims alone became Sufi poets. Noor Mohamed was compelled to state repeatedly that he was a staunch follower of Islam, answering queries of orthodox Muslims. The only exception was a Punjabi Hindu poet named Surdas who wrote *Naldamayanti Katha* in the Sufi style.

Prominent Muslim Sant Poets

Apart from Muslim Sufi poets, there were some prominent poets who could not be called Sufi. They are called Muslim sant poets though they were influenced by Sufi ideology. The prominent among them are Kabirdas, Dhariya Saheb and Dadu Dayal.

The great Kabirdas is considered (A.D. 1368–1448) to be the very best and representative poet of the Nirgun Sant poetry of the Bhakti period of Hindi literature. Kabir fought with his mighty pen to put an end to the monopoly of the upper-class society and thereafter bring them closer to the common man. That is why Kabir is called a revolutionary and visionary poet. It is noteworthy that though Kabir was illiterate, he could influence the common man better than the so-called scholar-poets. Kabir is considered next to Tulsidas, as far as popularity is considered.

The impact of Hindu culture on a par with the Muslim culture is evident in his words and deeds. That is why we see a harmonious blending of both the cultures. Kabir, having been influenced by the emotional mysticism of the Sufis, ritualistic mysticism of the yogis and non-violence and *prapathi* of the Vaishnavites along with the Indian Brahmanical rites, popularised his own cult.

Though Kabir was illiterate, he had the benefit of the good company of saints and *sanyasis* during his wanderings. He used to sing songs, giving good advice and criticising and condemning the evils. The work of Kabir is known by the name *Kabir Bijak*. It consists of three parts called *Sabad, Ramaini* and *Sakhi*. This 'Bijak' is considered by his followers as a religious text. Some people are of the opinion that Kabir had composed more than 57 books containing 17,000 stanzas, collectively called *Kabir Granthavali*.

The society at the time of Kabir was riddled with many religious beliefs as well as a plethora of thoughts. Kabir absorbed the quintessence of these different thoughts by virtue of his *satsang* with the saints. The greatness of Kabir lies in the fact that he could absorb the good aspects and discard the unsavoury ones. The credit goes to Kabir for having propagated a new sect consisting of the virtues of all the schools of thought and discarding what was not palatable to society.

Kabir was a free thinker. He criticised the external paraphernalia of all religions. He abused the bad practices of the *pandas, pujaris, sadhus* and equally the *takirs* and *mullas*. Kabir used to make fun of the high-caste Brahmans and advise them to cultivate humanism. He tried his best to bring the Hindu and Muslim communities closer and closer, so as to enable them to live in amity. He used to condemn the petty religious quarrels. He advised the Hindus to get rid of idol-worship by making a sarcastic remark that it was better to worship the grinder-stone at home than the temple-idol, as the former one was at least useful for grinding food items. Similarly he criticised the Muslims by saying that they observed fasting throughout the day and then killed the cow at night.

Kabir used to worship the formless God (*Nirgun*). He called his God 'Ram'. This concept was entirely different from Raja Dasharath's son Ram. This Ram is *nirgun, nirakar* (formless) and a symbol of Brahma. The mysticism of Kabir was a blended form of the Advaita of the Hindus and the romantic love of the Sufis. His mysticism is full of spiritualism. No one can deny the established fact that Kabirdas is supreme in the Muslim saint poets who was a very prominent figure in the medieval Bhakti Movement.

Dariya Saheb was known as the Kabir of Bihar on account of his area of activities. He had more than 36 disciples and Daldas was the most prominent among them. His disciples are scattered in Bihar, Gorakhpur and Cuttack. His followers are indifferent to the religious customs of the Muslims and they are vegetarians and their area of operation is Bihar and Uttar Pradesh. He had authored more than 20 works, including *Dariya sagar, Daria nama, Ganesh ghosti, Kalcharitra* and *Amarsar*. His poems are filled to the brim with love for the God he believed in. There are many similarities in the words of Daria Saheb and that of Kabir. He upheld morality and good conduct in his poems. The poetic and musical elements speak volumes about the poetical eminence of Daria Saheb.

Dadu Dayal is considered to be a Muslim cotton-comber. His followers are found scattered all over Rajasthan, Rohtak, Bhatinda, Hissar, Patiala and Delhi. They used to carry *Sumarini* and greet with the word *Satyaram*. Because of his liberal and tender behaviour, Dadu used to be called 'Dadu Dayal'. He was honoured by Emperor Akbar in recognition of his literary achievements. His poems are comparable to that of Kabir.

In Sufism, supreme love is of utmost importance, but at the same time, it is very difficult to practise. It is meaningless in the context to go on a prilgrimage, sport a beard, put sacred ashes on the body, and search for an audience. In fact, this can be achieved by the grace of a guru (teacher). The Sufi saints are always desirous of having glimpses of the beloved lover every moment. Further, he is impatient to tell his story. His heart throbs with love for the Almighty. He may feel helpless, like a fish out of water.

The Sufi saint has to implement many a precept to become eligible for obtaining union with his beloved. Consequent upon the difficult meditation (*sadhana*), the Sufi saint attains union with the Almighty. Afterwards there comes the separation and the imaginary pangs of separation are intolerable for him. The Sufi saints have totally adopted the Indian thinking and the beauty of Indian culture. Thus the Vedanta and tasawuff came so close that the philosophers were compelled to unequivocally declare the unfailing influence of tasawuff on the Vedanta. Exactly like this, the tasawuff was also greatly influenced by the Vedanta. As a result of the influence of Sufi thought, new areas of description were thrown open and along with that love got mixed with worldly spiritual love for the first time. The Indian folk-songs and folk-stories got a new appearance by being moulded in the Masnavi style. Needless to say, these poets of the masses were capable of recognising the contemporary activities and composing poems full of contemporary ideas. That is why their literary creations were free from communal colour.

Muslim Krishnite Poets

Raskhan was the best Krishnite poet of the Bhakti period of Hindi literature. Though a Muslim, he was a devotee of Krishna and used to compose poems in Brijbhasha. His poems are reverberating with genuine feelings of a heart full of devotion to the deity. The poet, Bharathendu Harischandra has aptly remarked that all the Hindus should salute this Muslim Hindi poet. The literary importance of Raskhan is unquestionable. The natural and strong feelings described by Raskhan hold the readers spellbound.

It is said that Raskhan happened to read the Persian translation of *Srimad Bhagavad* and subsequently got merged into the Krishna cult. Consequently he left Delhi for Govardan Dham and lived there till the end.

Raskhan was equally good at Arabic and Persian. He was also attached to Hindi poetry. As a result of his stay in Brindavan, he became an expert in Brijbhasha and composed all his works in that language. Two of his works are available at present, namely: *Premvatika* and *Sujan Raskhan.* The theme of both the books is love. He was very popular among the people for his free verses on Lord Krishna. He worshipped Krishna in the *madhuriya* form. There is no doubt that he was greatly influenced by the Sufi emotion of love. His devotion and love are entirely different from that of the other Krishnite poets. Raskhan's concept of Krishna is unique in the sense that Lord Krishna sometimes transforms himself into the lover Krishna and he is made to dance according to the tunes of the *gopikas*. The entire lot of *gopikas* surrenders at the feet of this attractive Krishna of Brindavan.

Raskhan is notable for his effective description of love, both in unison and separation. Truly this description of *unison love* is par excellence. There are some stanzas depicting *vatsaliya Sringar* also, which are indeed marvellous. In short, Raskhan's poetry is filled with joy and sweetness upto the brim for ever. All these stanzas are touching and indelible to the core. The poet himself writes in one of his stanzas that if at all he will have another birth, it should be in Brindavan. Of course, no other poet has expressed this ardent wish, not even a Hindu poet. The last but not least point is that the poems of Raskhan can be read, appreciated and enjoyed by the common man without command over the language, for the simple reason that the language of the poetry of Raskhan is sweet, simple and marvellous.

Abdul Rahim Khankhana

The poems of Abdul Rahim Khankhana are full of *sringar*, *bhakti*, *neeti* and love. In other words, his poems are a spontaneous outflow of powerful feelings and emotions. Though his poems are simple, interesting and appealing, they are very moving. He was popular among common men. He commanded more respect from the lower strata of society than scholars. In conclusion, he was indeed a darling poet of the people.

Rahim was famous as a philanthropist. He was kind and considerate towards the needy. He used to donate all his wealth to the needy and the poor. He was a renowned scholar and linguist. His poems are compiled in a book name *Diwane Parsi.* Rahim has composed poems in Brijbhasha, Eastern Avadhi and Khariboli. But mainly he was a poet of Brijbhasha. He was very particular about the sweetness of his language. His choice of words and syntax are very commendable. His greatness lies in the fact that he was an expert in expressing very deep ideas in simple language.

Shah Barkatullah 'Premi' (1668–1729)

His surname was *Ishki* in Persian and *Premi* in Hindi. *Premprakash* is his most famous book. His *dohas* reflect the changing seasons and complete description of a beautiful damsel. He is ever remembered among the Krishnite poets for this book *Premprakash.* It is written in Persian–Hindi mixed language. He has dealt with Krishna and his *gopikas* in detail. He is greatly influenced by the *Srimad Bhagavad Gita,* hence was philosophical in nature. No doubt, Hindi was his mother-tongue, which is why he wrote *Premprakash* in Hindi, though its script was originally Persian. Moreover, the Muslims did respect the Radhakrishna cult just like the Hindus.

Tansen

Tansen was the most famous musician in the court of Akbar. He was not only a musician, but also a poet of name and fame.

Songs composed by him on various *Raga -Raganis* are proof of his ability as a singer and composer. It is acknowledged that Tansen was the son of Makrand Pande, a *goud* Brahman and disciple of Swami Haridas. Afterwards he learnt music from Shaikh Mohamed Ghouse, a native of Gwalior. It is also said that the teacher touched the tongue of Tansen with his own tongue and this blessing transformed Tansen into a melody king. It is also believed that Tansen got converted into Islam consequent upon this incident. There is hearsay that Tansen got married to Mehrunnisa, daughter of Akbar and this also added to the glory of his story.

Tansen had a close relation with the devotional poet Surdas. Being influenced by Surdas, he composed poems on Lord Ganesha, Mahadev and Saraswathi. Besides, he had written poems on religious festivals like Holi, Dussehara, Eid, etc. His poems are also full of descriptions of the childhood activies of Krishna, and Radha-Krishna love-plays.

Krishnite Muslim Poetesses

1. Poetess Taj

The poetess Taj has proved beyond doubt her devotion to Lord Krishna by dedicating herself at his feet by breaking the barriers of caste and religion. She has violated the narrow religious boundaries of medieval India in the course of her spontaneous emotional expressions. Some glimpses of her life and poetic work along with ample quotations are included in the famous books *Muslim writers of Hindi* and *Services of Muslims to the cause of Hindi*. Taj was an ardent Vaishnavite devotee, though she was a Muslim by birth. She metamorphosed herself into a Hindu for the sake of Lord Krishna.

Her poems make an indelible impression on the minds of the readers on account of their beauty and sweetness. They depict incidents of Lord Krishna's life. The poetess has given more importance to the physical side of the life of her Lord.

It is crystal clear that this famous Muslim poetess was an ardent Krishna devotee. On many an occasion her concept of Lord Krishna degenerates to the level of duplicate Krishna, dancing in the company of *gopikas* in *Rasamandali*. Due to the predominance of the physical beauty of Lord Krishna depicted in her poems, the emotional side has become weak. But this does not minimise her devotion and faith in any way. Her concept of Krishna is a combination of Krishna, the warrior of *Mahabharata*, preacher of *Bhagavad Gita* and *Kanhayya* of the Brijbhoomi. Her devotion to Lord Krishna is unique in nature, inspite of all the variations. She had ample faith in the real *darshan* of the Lord. She has deprecated the exhibitive methods of the Hindu religion in plain words. There is not even an iota of satire or irony in her criticism of the exhibitionism of he Hindu religion.

Taj, though a Muslim, was an expert on Hinduism, as is evident from her poems, dealing with the various aspects of Hindu philosophy. The readers are surprised at the expertise of the poetess in describing the memorable incidents, incorporated in the mythological stories of the Hindu religion. She derived satisfaction in the concept of universal God of Islam. After many experimental attempts in the spiritual realm, consequent upon her distraction with worldly love, she devoted herself to the sweet personality and feelings of Krishna.

Poetess Shaikh Rangaregin

Shaikh Rangaregin was born in a Muslim family belonging to dyer caste. Consequent on her love for the poet Alam, great devotional feelings surged in her life. Her famous book is *Alamkeli,* which contains *Sringar Kavya.* Her poems bear ample testimony to the fact that she was harbouring the idea of sweet Krishna along with devotion. Though her characters were worldly heroes and heroines, the poetess has fulfilled the tradition of describing the worldly love of the common man through the symbolic characters of Radha and Krishna. In short, poetess Shaikh Rangaregin adorns the highest position among the Muslim Hindi poetesses.

Apart from the above Muslim poetesses, Babari Sahiba, Jebunnisa and Rani Roopmati Begum have also contributed to the enrichment of Hindi Krishnite poetry.

Mir Abdul-Wahid Bilgrami

The popularity of Vaishnavite themes used in Sufi *sama* rituals of Hindi-speaking regions was a remarkable development. The Sufis regarded them as welcome additions to their devotional poetry to induce ecstasy. Mir Abdul-Wahid Bilgrami (1509–1608) compiled a Persian dictionary of Hindi songs entitled *Haqa-iq-i-Hindi* in 1566. This work is divided into three sections. The first section gives a mystic explanation of Hindi words used in *Dhrupad* songs. The second section allegorically explains the words used in Vaishnavite songs in Brajbhasha, the dialect of Mathura region. Mir justifies the popularity of the names of *kafirs* used in Sufi *sama* on the grounds that *Quran* itself uses the names of both *kafirs* and enemies. The third section gives the Sufi explanation of the words used in Hindi Sufi poetry. The explanations given by Mir Abdul Wahid in *Haqa-iq-i-Hindi* about Krishna theme and symbols are as follows :

Krishna : Sometimes Krishna and his other names in Hindavi (Hindi) indicate Prophet Muhammed and sometimes the (perfect) man. Often it indicates the reality of the creation of man which is related to the Unity of Being.

Gopi and Gujari (milkmaid) : Sometimes the words represent angels : sometimes they indicate the reality of mankind in relation to the Unity of Being. If wise men perceive in them a different meaning the source of difference is the intellect itself. The symbols themselves do not warrant any difference.

Uddhava : (A companion and relation of Krishna) It indicates followers of Prophet Muhammed who are intermediaries between him and God.

Braj and *Gokul* : (regions of Mathura associated with Krishna's life). These words stand for the three ontological dominations of the *Jabarut*, representing the highest point in the spiritual world; the *Nasut* or physical world and the *Malakut*, or intermediary psychic world.

Mathura : This indicates the temporary station in the *Ma'rifat* which are related to *Nasut*. The permanent station are *Malakut* or *Jabarut*. Starting from the temporary stations, the Sufi journey leads to permanent stations.

Dwaraka : This is the permanent station of Sufis. The knowledge and ascetic exercises of Sufis carry them to permanent stations.

Thus the attempt made by Mir Abdul-Wahid Bilgrami was to find equivalence between Vaishnavism and Sufism. It is said that at Akbar's invitation, he visited the Emperor's court and received a huge grant from him for his living expenses. Mir Abdul-Wahid's Persian work *Saba'-i Sanabil* is a very famous treatise on sufi doctrines and ethics. The Mir also wrote another short treatise on Sufism entitled *Kalimat-i-Chand.* Much better understood and more widely known than the above work by Mir Abdul Wahid is the Hindi poetry modelled on the Persian *masnavis*.

The Muslim Sufi Poets of Dakhini

The south has played a prominent role to give a wide basis for the Hindi language. It is a well-known fact that the preliminary development of Hindi, in the from of Dakhini Hindi had taken place in the Southern States of India. The truth is that the Southerners had taken the initiative to shape the Dakhini Hindi for qualifying itself to be a literary language.

It may not be possible for us to give detailed descriptions about all the Muslim Sufi points of Dakhini and their works, though they were all alert, awakened and alive to the composite culture. Undoubtedly their works rank not in the religious literature, but they are full of literary values with a message of cultural coordination.

Poets Nizami Shah Burhanuddin Janam, Mulla Wajahi and Gawasi were the most popular Dakhini Sufi poets who aimed at cultural synthesis through their poetical works. The credit for writing the first descriptive poetry in Dakhini Hindi goes to the great poet Nizami. His work is known as Masnavi *Kadam Rao-Padam Rao*.

The pioneering efforts that the great poet Nizami has taken are relevant not only at that time, but even today. This poetic work can be taken as the first and best example of Hindu–Muslim cultural coordination. Though when compared to North Indian situations the South was comparatively free from such conflict and confusion, it was also suffocated with stupid superstitions. It is but natural that the poet is influenced by the social life around him. Consequently social reform was the main aim of the poetic work.

The great poet Nizami is irrevocably committed to the cause of safeguarding Indian composite culture. Shah Burhanuddin Janam is also one of those Sufi poets who had contributed a lot to the cause of cultural synthesis. Seeds of Sufism sown by the Sufi saint Bande Nawaz and Meeraji sprouted and grew in the poetic woks of this poet Janam. *Irshad nama* is the most famous work by poet Janam. All through his life he tried his best to eradicate Hindu–Muslim enmity and establish amity between these two communities.

Mulla Wahahi is one of the top-ranking poets of Dakhini Hindi literature. *Kutub-Musthari* and *Sabaras* are two of his prominent works. *Kutub-Musthari* depicts the love story of Bhagmathi and the emperor. Though the theme is a love story, it bears a spiritual overtone. The reason is that the Sufi saints express spiritual love through worldly love.

Gawazi's *Saiful Mulk-Badiayuzzamal* is a romantic poem based on love between the Egyptian prince Saiful Mulk and Badiyuzzamal, the princess of Ajana.

Sindhi Sufi Poets

Sufism arose as a movement of revolt in the middle period of our history against religious fanaticism and ritualism, communal hatred and hypocracy. It has played a very significant role in social integration and communal harmony, especially through the Sufi and Saint poets of the Indo–Pak subcontinent. During that period both Sufi and Bhakti movements had a great impact on people.

Sufism had a very great impact on Sindhi life and literature, with its humanist outlook and harmonious approach, especially through the secular poetry of the great Sufi and Saint poets like Qazi Qadan, Abdul Karim, Shah Inayat, Shah Latif, Sachal Sarmast, Sami, Roohal, Bedil, Bekas, Dalpat, etc.

Shah Abdul Latif and Sachal Sarmast were the late participators in the Bhakti movement which had a major impact in Sindh through the spread of Guru Nanak's (1469–1539) teachings. Qazi Qadan, Shah Abdul Karim, Shah Inayat, Shah Abdul Latif and Sachal Sarmast formed part of the Bhakti Movement in Sindh. But it was Shah Abdul Latif who stood in it as its representative figure for in him Indian Sufism, which was tempered with the thought of Vedanta and the emotion of *bhakti,* found an embodiment. In fact, Sufism envisaged devotional surrender to God with the ultimate goal of merger in Him. Like the Bhakti Movement, Sufism too protested against all forms of dogma and priestly authority. *Bhakti* is a blanket term for many kinds of religious experiences existing simultaneously in one poet or in different poets of one period.

The *nirguna* poetry, as of the Sindhi poets including Shah Abdul Latif, has intertwined in it one strand, monism of both *Advaita* and *tasawwuf*. Then the term *bhakti*, which literally means devotion, humility and seeking grace from God, also makes room for the metaphysical quest or rational endeavour to know oneself beside the Supreme Self and to get merged ultimately in Him.

The Bhakti Movement, curious as it is, represents both devotion and knowledge in a mutually inclusive way. It not only gives expression to the *dasya bhava* or emotion of voluntary servitude (as in Ravidasa) the *sakhya bhava* or emotion of friendliness (as in Surdasa), the *madhurya bhava* or emotion pertaining to husband and wife (as in Mira, Kabir and the Sindhi Sufi poets, including Shah Abdul Latif), but also to the *suprabhakta ekatva bhava* or feeling of Oneness. The *ekatva bhava* may come through the stages of the above *bhavas* (sentiments). Out of these *bhavas*, one *bhava* may be prominent in one poet, and the other in another one, as the *madhurya bhava* is conspicuous in the Sindhi Sufi poets, but they all, more or less, prevail in every poet and lead him, one by one, to the consciousness where the *dvaita* or duality between *dasa* (servant) and *swami* (master), between two *sakhas* (friends), and between wife and husband simply does not exist.

The Bhakti Movement espoused the view that the Ultimate Reality is One, without *guna* or *rupa*, that is, without attributes or forms. Even if the Sufi poets invoked the name of Rama it was not strictly in an anthropomorphic sense; it was as a synonym of God. The Bhakti Movement inspired, among other things, a new confidence in the subjects. Sufi poets stood for sartorial freedom, and also used languages of the masses. They gave expression to the native legends and folk-stories. The works of the Sindhi Sufi poets are prominently marked by the features of this movement. It is because of this synthesis of Sufism and Vedantism that Hindus–Muslims lived a peaceful life.

The Sindhi Sufi poets helped generate love and friendship between the two religious communities with all their sects and castes. The Hindus, who would previously avoid taking the name of Allah or mouthing some such words for fear of being forcibly initiated into Islam by the fanatic Muslims, felt so confident in the new body-social of Sindh that they would not hesitate to recite quotations from the *Quran* and the *Hadith* in their baits for those quotations revealed, along with the unfolding of Vedantic thought therein, their composite view. Shah Abdul Latif could see that if someone tried to establish Islam in exclusion of all other religions, that fanatic might as well endeavour to establish one particular sect of Muslims in exclusion of other sects. He was a spiritual teacher of both the sects as also of the Hindus. He used to say that he was neither a Shia nor Sunni, nor a Hindu, but was all in one. Though the Sindhi Sufi poets were born in the religious group of Muslims, they were not bound by any creed.

It is Shah Lateef (A.D. 1690–1750) and Sachal (A.D. 1739–1829) who had the mass influence and are household names for both Sindhi Muslims and Hindus till today in not only in Sindh but also in India. Sami (A.D. 1743–1850) a saint poet of Vedantism is known to the literary class of Muslims only but has a mass influence among Hindus till today. The rest of the other poets had followed in the footsteps of this *trimurti* of Shah-Sachal-Sami.

Lateef, like a true secular poet emphasised communal harmony which was disturbed due to fanaticism of the *mullas* who were openly and vehemently condemned by him in his poetry. More than half of Lateef's poetry deals with Sindhi life which is influenced by Hindu customs and conventions. The other greatest Sufi poet and preacher of communal harmony and religious tolerance of Sind, Sachal (A.D. 1739–1829) was Sindhi. He openly said, 'I am Mansur-al-Hallaj', 'God', etc. The third great poet of *trimurti* Saint poets, Sami has also expressed the same sentiments and views as Shah Latif and Sachal, by giving instances from Hindu philosophy of *Vedanta* and way of life. At the same time he has cited Sufi ideas, phrasology and Persian poetic, symbols in good number of his poems, emphasising the unity and equality of all religions and communal harmony.

Sami says : 'Whether you speak *an-al-Haq* or Rama-Rama, it is same thing ..... There is same essence in Quran and Puran ..... Persian and Hindu Saints speak with same voice ......' He has also condemned the fanaticism and ritualism, formalism and hypocracy of Pandits and Brahmans, Kazis and Mullas also. Real love for God should be that of Laila and Majnu'.

The Bhakti Movement in Bengal : The Muslim 'Vaishnava' Lyrical Literature

The syncretistic spirit of Bengali Muslim mysticism assumed a characteristic form in a large corpus of lyrical compositions written by them in the popular middle-Bengali *pada* (short song) style of Vaishnava origin. Ranging from the sixteenth down to the early years of the present century, these Muslim *pada* compositions have been gradually recovered and published in relatively old and recent compilations of Bengali padas.[13]

The nature of these Muslim *pada* compositions is not easy to determine. Broadly speaking, the Hindu commentators had not only regarded these compositions as direct Muslim contributions to the tradition of Vaishnavism, but also accepted their authors as Vaishnava themselves. Undeniably, the entire atmosphere of this literature is saturated with characters, places, objects, images, symbols, and nuances, characteristic of Vaishnava tradition and of Vaishnava lyrical literature as well: the love dalliances of Radha and Krishna; the *gopinis* (the milkmaids); Lalita and Bisakha, the two closest companions of

Radha; the standing annoyance of Radha in her *nanadini* (the sister-in-law); the bemusing flute of Krishna; places like Mathura, Vrindavan, Gokul, and Braja; the river Yamuna or Kalindi or Kaliya; the *kadamba* tree under which Radha and Krishna frequently engaged in amorous sports; and, finally, the festival of *phagu*, *phag*, or *holi* in which Radha, Krishna, are all there in the Muslim *pada* compositions.

A critical analysis of the literature reveals that a fair proportion of the Muslim poets merely used Vaishnava symbolism to express their own mystical urges and concerns. Even where the writers fully adopt a pure Vaishnava tradition as a literary theme,we cannot establish a necessary co-relation between their personal faith and their literary interests and objectives. Some of the greatest Hindu *pada* writers themselves were not adherents of the Vaishnava faith. Vidyapati of Mithila was not a follower of Vishnu, but a *smarta-panchopasak*, who composed verses on Shiva and Gauri as well as on Krishna and Radha.

Certain Bengali Muslim writers chose other Hindu traditions without becoming necessary coverts to the particular cults. Shaikh Chanda, dominant mediator-writer on mysticism, wrote also on the tradition of Shiva and *shakti*. Besides, some writers chose more than one Hindu tradition as literary themes. Shaikh Faiz Allah, for example, is credited with literary pursuits of nathism as well as Vaishnavism.

The Muslim critics of this literature, on the other hand, are generally predisposed to attaching nothing more than allegorical and symbolic meanings to these mystical compositions couched in Vaishnava terms and forms. Famous literary critic E. Haq not only does not view the Muslim *pada* as essentially Sufic in spirit; he goes to the extent of characterising the totality of the Bengali literature on Gaudiya (Bengali) Vaishnavism as 'fully impregnated with the spirit of Sufi literature under 'a Hinduistic veneer'. Radha and Krishna of the Bengali Vaishnava literature are, in his opinion, imbued with the 'form and essence' of the Sufic concepts of *ashiq* (lover) and *mashuq* (beloved), of *saqi* (the cup-bearer) and *bat* (wine), or of *shama* (lamp) and *parwana* (moth). Haq also notes close resemblance between Vaishnava lyrics and Sufi *ghazal* in respect of their 'content and style', between the Vaishnava concepts of *viraha* (separation) and *milan* (union), on one hand, and the Sufic notions of *hijran* and *bishal*, on the other. Haq's views on the Vaishnava literature stem from his general opinion that Bengal Vaishnavism, as enunciated by Chaitanya (A.D. 1486–1534) and his immediate followers, owed most of its basic features to Sufism.

It is claimed that the strong monistic attitude in Bengal Vaishnavism, 'the legacy of Islam', that its anti-caste tendency is the result of 'the influence of Islam', and that the Vaishnava concept of *prem* (divine love) indicates the influence of the Sufi concept of *ishq*. He also asserts that the Sufi practice of *halqa*, referring to 'an assembly of persons met together for the purpose of devotional exercises through the medium of *dhikr*, accompanied by *sama* or musical performance', 'perfectly resembles' the Vaishnava practice of *nam-samkirtan* or *kirtan*, involving congregation, singing God's name (*nam*), with the help of music and dance, leading to an ecstatic condition called *dasa* in Vaishnavism and *hal* in sufism.

The Bengal Vaishnavism of Chaitanya clearly belonged to the main stream of Hindu *bhakti* tradition. Its fundamental tenets grew from 'the general course of development of the Vaishnava faith in India'.[14] The two most fundamental elements forming 'the texture of Bengal Vaishnavism' are derived more or less from Vaishnavism in general, the first and foremost being the general doctrine of *bhakti*, or emotional service of love and devotion as a means of spiritual realisation. The other, no less important, is the Krishna cult, intimately connected with it, as forming the ground of this devotional attitude. In addition, the Vaishnava theology, in its attitude to the godhead and in its concept of divine love, follows very closely in the tradition of Ramanuj-Nimbark rather than of the dominant *wujudi* concept of Sufic thought in India, as we shall see more fully below. The Islamic context of Bengal Vaishnavism is indubitable, but then one cannot attribute this multi-faceted religious phenomenon to this particular factor alone.

As we turn to the question of Islamic impact on Bengal Vaishnavism, we need not jump to any conclusion regarding the problem of origin. We are only concerned about the similarities found in them. An apparent similarity between Hindu and Islamic practices or beliefs may, in effect, conceal a basic conceptual difference.

The most dominant feature of the *pada* literature of both Hindu and Muslim authorship is the element of love binding the devotee and the deity. The divergent mystical attitudes to the deity, as reflected in the whole range of the *pada* literature of Hindu or Muslim authorship, cut across the religious affiliations of the lyricists. A significant number of compositions adopting the Vaishnava approach to the deity can be traced to Muslim lyricists, just as there are a number of Hindu *pada* written in the monistic spirit of the Sufi mystics.

The Sufic symbolism in a particular type of *pada* compositions is, therefore, unquestionable. Significantly enough, the Bengali Muslim poets of this category chose to adopt the locally popular Radha-Krishna motif of Bengal Vaishnavism. Unlike the Muslim mystic poets elsewhere in India and outside, their Bengali counterparts were conspicuous by their indifference to the popular Islamic motifs such as *Yusuf-Zulaikha, Laila Majnun, Shiri-Farhad, Saif al-Muluk-Badi al-Jamal, Gul-i-Bakawali* and so on. Bengali Muslim writers no doubt made use of almost all those themes, but with a crucial difference. They stripped these stories of their mystical content and presented them in the forms of a secular romantic narrative poem—a literary genre which Bengali Muslims had the distinction of introducing into the corpus of Bengali literature.

Nasin Mahmud, a famous Bengali poet took up the theme of pastoral pursuits of young Krishna. Mir Faiz Allah depicts the amorous play of Krishna and the milkmaids. Nasir's was the theme of 'separation'. This piece is of some importance to illustrate the point that the attitude of the poet to the Radha-Krishna *lila* is the determining factor in a Vaishnava composition. Alawal, a very gifted Bengali Muslim poet, adopts a pure Vaishnava theme for a lyric. He writes on Radha's secret meeting with Krishna, going out early in the morning and returning at nightfall.

REFERENCES AND NOTES

1. Tarachand, Dr. *Influence of Islam on Indian Culture*. p. 69.
2. Jawed, Dr. Ajeet. *Heritage of Harmony*, p. 27.
3. Ibid., p.28.
4. Ranade. *Rise of the Maratha Power*, pp. 50–51.
5. Bhandarkar, Dr. R.G. *Vaisnavism, Shaivism and other Minor Religious Cults*. p. 90.
6. Tarachand, Dr. *Influence of Islam on Indian Culture*, p. 181.
7. Engineer, Dr. Asghar Ali. *Sufism and Communal Harmony*, pp. 161, 162.
8. Bhattcharya, Manjula. *Medieval Bhakti Movement in Gujarat*. In *Medieval Bhakti Movements in India*. Ed. N.N. Bhattacharya, pp. 99, 101.
9. Titus, Murray T. *Islam in India and Pakistan*, p. 36.
10. Mohamed, Dr. Malik. *The Culture of Hindi*, p. 109.
11. Ibid., p. 110.
12. *The Great Integrators : The Sindhi Sufi Poets*, Motilal Jotwani, pp. 42-46.
13. Malik, R.M. (*i*) *Musalman Vaisnav Kavi*. Calcutta, 1895.
    (*ii*) Sanyal, V.N. *Musalman Vaisnav Kavi*, 4 vols. Rajashahi, 1906.
    (*iii*) Shastri, R.K. *Krishna-Bhakta Muslman*. *Prahbha Patrika*, 1921.
14. De, S.K. *Early History of the Vaishnava Faith and Movement in Bengal*, p.2.

6

The Efforts of Muslim Rulers for Unity and Harmony

Religious liberalism and magnanimity of the Muslim rulers

Muslim rule in India began with the advent of the Delhi Sultanate in the beginning of the tenth century. Muslim rulers were aliens and belonged to a different religion. After conquering the land, their main aim was to maintain and consolidate their rule. This political compulsion forced them to be tolerant and to refrain from antagonising the Indian masses by interfering in their socio-religious matters. With the passage of time, they cut off their foreign roots and made India their homeland. For the continuity and stability of their rule, it became imperative for them to win over the natives and to wipe out any notion that they were aliens. They refused to pay any heed to the orthodox ulema, who expected them to act as protector and promoter of Muslim Faith. Instead, they sought the guidance, support and blessings of the native saints and tried to identify themselves with the people of the land. In running the affairs of the state the Sultans were motivated by political interest and the principle of religious tolerance.[1]

Before the establishment of the Sultanate, Sind came under the rule of Mohammad-bin-Qasim in A.D. 712. The invasion of Sind by Mohammad-bin-Qasim was not motivated by any religious consideration. The cause of Arab invasion was that Raja Dhar of Sind had looted Arab's ships anchored at Vibal now known as Karachi, Qasim the commander of the Arab forces, then attacked and conquered Sind. During his rule which lasted for a brief period, Qasim practised toleration towards the religions of this land and thus won the hearts of the people of Sind. When he attacked Multan, he saw there a famous shrine revered highly by the Hindus of the land. Qasim did not pull it down. On the other hand, with the permission of the priest, he paid a formal visit to it. The Arabs ruled in Sind for nearly two hundred years. All religious customs and ceremonies of the Hindus continued to the performed throughout the Arab rule. During the rule of these Arabs which was confined to Sind, Hindus were neither persecuted nor was a single temple destroyed.[2]

Sultan Iltutmish, who is regarded as the first ruler of the Delhi Sultanate, gave it an independent status by severing all relations with Ghazni and Ghaur. He shifted his capital from Lahore to Delhi and ruled as he pleased, ignoring the dictates of the ulema. When approached by some ulema with the request that Hindus should be forced to accept Islam, Iltutmish refused to do so. He never implemented ulema's schemes in the political field.

Iltutmish's daughter Raziya abolished the *jaziya*, or the poll tax on the non-Muslims despite stiff opposition from the orthodox. During her reign, orthodox did not have any say in the state matters. Raziya gave full protection to her Hindu subjects. She was a fair and just ruler.

In the matter of punishment and exercise of punishment and exercise of royal authority Balban acted without fear of God and whatever he regarded to be in the interest of government, irrespective of whether it was in accord with the *Shariat* or not, he carried it into action. He was a strong ruler and defied the Ulama by declaring himself as the 'vice-regent of God'. This was an affront to Islam. He made no distinction between his Hindu and Muslim subjects.

Sher Shah, through a devout Muslim showed respect to Hindu saints and did not discriminate among his subjects on the basis of religion. So much so that he was described as 'externally Muslim but Hindu internally'.

In fact the Sultans never intended to spread Islam by the sword, besides, they did not pay any heed to the counsels of the ulema if it did not promote their political interests. Instead, in order to win over the hearts of the people, they followed the traditions of the land while making state policies and were not guided by the *Shariat*. This attitude initiated the process of liberalism of the Muslim rulers and laid the foundation of religious tolerance. With the passage of time, their initial policy of toleration had changed to respect for all religions, which became the cardinal principle of the state policy during the Mughal rule.

Sultan Alauddin has his own theory of Government, which he observed throughout his rule. Barani writes : 'When Alauddin became king, he came to the conclusion that the policy and government are one thing and the rules and the decrees of the Sharia another. Royal command belongs to the king and Sharia's decrees to the ulema. Sultanate is not bound by the Sharia'.

Despite the ulema's displeasure new public temples were built and old temples continually repaired during his reign. Jain sources enable us to know that Alauddin held religious discourses with Acharya Mahasena who was brought from Karnataka for the purpose. It is also reported that the Digambara Jain Purna Chandra of Delhi and Swetambara ascetic Ramchandra Suri were in the favour of the Sultan. Because of his catholicity and impartiality, Alauddin was showered with praises and tributes by his non-Muslims subjects.

The Jain monks were invited to the royal court and Jain laity occupied special positions in the state services. Samar Singh Jain was made commissioner by Qutbuddin Mubarak Shah. Sultan Ghiyasuddin Tughlaq regarded him as his own son and sent him to Telingana where he built many temples.

Like his father, Muhammad-bin-Tughlaq has great respect for Jain monks. The Sultan had the courage to rise above the rank of bigotry of his age and without succumbing to a blind superstitious reverence for everything that passed in the name of religion, allowed himself to be guided by a rational spirit. His regime rested on the principle of religious tolerance. The Sultan hated the orthodox and kept them at a distance. He regarded the narrow-minded ulama as degenerate bigots steeped in ignorance and vanity. He never consulted them in state matters.

Firoz Shah was obliged to the ulema for the throne. Consequently, in his reign the influence and interference of ulema was evident. However, Firoz's orthodox posture was merely for demonstration, as he did not allow the ulema to have an upper hand in the governance of the state. During his rule, which lasted for almost four decades, his subjects enjoyed freedom in their religious and social affairs. New temples were erected and old ones renovated.

Though all the Sultans used to have a group of theologians and often consulted them, the entire history of the Sultanate shows that the Sultans followed them only when it suited them. Even Sikandar Lodi, who is characterised as an orthodox Sultan who maintained a select group of theologians who were in constant personal attendance, never allowed them to eat in his presence though they were served food along with the Sultan. In fact, Sikandar was neither fanatical nor strictly orthodox but was quite prepared to make pretense of one or the other in order to realise his ambitions and to further his themes of conquest and consolidation.

During the Lodi period, the tendency to have religious discourses with the Hindu yogis developed further. Some of the Muslim nobles are said to have changed their faith under their influence. Among them were Ahamad Khan, son of Mubark Khan Lodi, the governor of Lakhnoti and Nasir Khan, Muslim controller of Kalpi, who renounced Islam and adopted Hinduism.

Thus, the rulers were Muslims but the state was not theocratic. It was not ruled according to the *Shariat* but with the clear-cut motive of retaining power and expanding the empire. Most of the Sultans sought the support of the ulema by giving them honours, favours and deference but did not allow them to interfere with the statecraft. Ironically, the ulema had high praises for those Sultans and held them as Ghazi.

The early Sultans did not hesitate to adopt Hindu symbols on their coins, though it was a violation of the popular sentiment among their co-religionists. They stamped on their coins such Hindu symbols as lotus, trident, *swastika*, the letter *sree* and portrait of Goddess Lakshmi. On the coins of Sultan Muhmud of Ghazni is found the portraits of the Hindu bull, Shiva's emblem; and the *Kalima* is in Sanskrit. *Tankas* were issued with humped bull or Rajput horseman and the sovereign's name in Sanskrit till 1280. Sultana Raziya's coin bears the portrait of the Rajput horseman with Nagari script around as *Sri-Hamirah*. Even Balban used Nagari script on his coins. Mohammad bin Tughlaq struck gold coins in imitation to the Hindu kings of Kanouj with the portrait of Goddess Lakshmi on the obverse.

In smaller Muslim states, which had made themselves independent of the Sultanate, like Bengal and the Bahmani kingdom of Deccan, or which did not fall under the sway of Delhi, i.e. Kashmir, a much more equitable policy had been followed by the rulers which endeared them to the masses.

In the Deccan the religious liberalism was more profound than in the north. Alauddin Hassan (1347–58), the founder of the Bahmani kingdom, was a servant of a Hindu astrologer named Gangu Bahman. Later Hasan became the sultan of Daulatabad. After being crowned, Hasan called Gangu to his court, appointed him incharge of the finance department and called him Gangu Bahmani and his regime as the Bahmani kingdom.

Shahabuddin Ahmad I (1422-36) was a disciple of the Sufi saint Gesuderaz. He believed in universal brotherhood and had a high regard for Hindu saints. He was loved and respected by both communities. He was called Hazrat Ahmad Shah Wali by the Muslims and Allama Prabhu by the Hindus. Even today, on his death anniversary hordes of Hindu and Muslim men and women assemble at his grave and beg him to intercede with the Almighty on their behalf. Every day, during the *urs*, the *jangamor*, the religious leader of the Lingayats, used to enter the sepulchre in the garb of a Muslim dervish, accompanied by a group of musicians and makes offerings of flowers which shows what strong influence the sovereign had on his people during his life time.

Shahabuddin's son and successor, Alauddin Ahmad II (1436–1458) is praised by the writer of *Guru-charitra* as a raja who is a devotee of the Brahmans and gracious to his subjects without distinction of caste or creed. He used to have discussions with the pundits on religion and sought their counsel. Saint Narasimha Saraswati comforted him in his last illness.

Similarly, the Adil Shahis of Bijapur (1490–1686) and the Nizamshahis of Ahamad Nagar (1490–1637) held liberal attitudes and adopted liberal policies. Ali Adil Shah (1558–1580) took delight in being called Adil Shah Sufi; held discussions with Brahmans and did not allow the ulema to interfere with the state policies. They tried to dissuade the king from praising the gods of the Hindus as it was unbecoming for a Muslim.

Ibrahim Adil Shah II had two pundit advisors named Anter and Lakhu. He worshipped the Hindu goddess Sarswati. Signs of his reverence to this deity spilled over into the revenue bureaucracy as many of his official government documents, written in the Perso-Marathi language began with an invocation to her—*aj puja shrine Saraswati.* He used to join the Hindu musicians in their worship at the Saraswati temple in Bijapur. It is also said that he had an image of Saraswati installed in the royal palace of his personal worship.

In Bengal, Husain Shah was a liberal ruler. He gave equal respect and honour to all the religions and himself instituted the common worship of new god, Satyapir. During his reign the Bhakti Movement, led by Chaitanya flourished and even two of his ministers got converted to Vaishnavism.

Sultan Muzaffar Shah II, who ruled Gujarat in the 16th century revered Goddess Saraswati and respected the Brahmans. In Kashmir the kings followed the path shown by the Sufi saints. The Muslim kings performed the *Homa* ceremony at the time of coronation, a *tika* (Hindu mark) was applied on their forehead and offerings of gold and silver were made. The kings also performed *yagna* (a religious Hindu ceremony) to avert the famine.

Shihabuddin continued to scribe the figure of Goddess Lakshmi on his gold coins, a fact which indicates the extent to which religious liberalism existed. After Shihabuddin's death, his brother Qutbuddin became the Sultan. He, too, like his brother was liberal in religious matters. There was a temple, which was visited every morning by the Sultan and his Muslim subjects. To avert famine Qutbuddin once performed the *yagna* and distributed large gifts to Brahmans and, in contravention of Islamic teachings, he had two wives who were sisters.

In Kashmir, religious tolerance was at its zenith during the reign of Zainual Abidin. He issued a decree that in his dominions there should be no discrimination between one another on the basis of religion. The Sultan, on the advice of Sriyabhatta, reduced *jaziya* to the nominal. That he did not entirely abolish the *jaziya* was due to his respect for the opinion and sentiments of the ulema. In actual practice, however, it was as good as abolished, for it was never collected. He banned cow-slaughter, revived Hindu pilgrimage and constructed buildings for the accommodation of pilgrims. He repaired old temples and built new ones. He frequently visited the famous Hindu shrines of Amarnath and Sharda Devi temples and had built rest-houses there to provide comfort to the pilgrims. He performed *havans*, studied the *Nilamatapurana*, *Vasishta*, *Gita Gobind* and practised yoga. He restored grant of stipends to leaned Brahmans and took an agreement from them that they would not act in contravention to what was written in their books. Zain knew many languages including Sanskrit Tibetan, Persian and Kashmiri. He held the Sufis, Brahmans and pundits in great respect and granted them lands.

The Mughal emperors, except Aurangzeb believed in harmonious co-existence. They did not mix religion with politics and theirs was a liberal state. Religious liberty during their rule was not confined to believing in one's own religion but ushered a new atmosphere in which new religions like Sikhism and many syncretic cults emerged and freely flourished.

Babar, the founder of the Mughal empire in India, after the victory over Ibrahim, halted on the Jamuna bank opposite Delhi, in order to pay respect to the tombs of the Sufi saints. During the invasion of Syedpur, the inhabitants were made prisoners on the order of Babur. Among them were Baba Nanak and

Mardana. Hearing Baba Nanak's hymns and Mardana's spiritual music on the rebeck, Babar approached Nanak and asked for forgiveness. On Nanak's advice Babar released not only all the prisoners but also ordered that all the prisoners should be clothed with robes of honour. It is also said that Baba Nanak went to Babar again for getting the release of prisoners of other villages. He stayed with him for three days. Babar released all the prisoners.

Babar followed Nanak's advice throughout his life. In his short reign orthodoxy and fanaticism had no place. Babar gave the same advice to his son and successor Humayun. He instructed him to be just and kind towards his subjects and to respect all religions. In his secret Will Babar advised his son thus : 'O my son! The empire of Hindustan consists of various religions, domination and sovereignty whereof has been bestowed on you by the grace of Almighty. It is incumbent that religious bigotry should be wiped off the tablet of the heart and justice meted out to each religion according to its tenets. Specially abstain from sacrifice of cows, as this would tend to win the hearts of the people of Hindustan. And the populace of the country would be adherent to royal favours'. Babar's counsel was followed by Humayan. When he was fleeing from Hindustan after his defeat, he went to Guru Angad, the spiritual successor of Baba Nanak, at Lahore to seek his blessings and guidance. The Guru blessed him.

Emperor Akbar, like his grandfather and father respected all the religions and religious saints. He visited the saints to get their blessings and guidance. In his reign complete religious freedom prevailed. Sikhism flourished and the *Guru Granth Sahib,* the Holy book of the Sikhs was compiled. The Sikh Gurus too prayed for the prosperity and stability of his empire. Guru Amar Das (A.D. 1479–1574) advised Emperor Akbar that he should establish a common and conciliating rule in India with the active assistance of Hindu kings and nobles to maintain a balance against Afghans from whom the Mughals had wrested the empire of Hindustan in A.D. 1526.

Akbar was blessed by the fifth Guru Arjan Dev (A.D. 1563–606). The emperor called himself the slave of the Guru and sought his instructions for happiness and peace for the soul. The Guru said: 'The welfare and happiness of the monarch depend upon cherishing their subjects and doing justice. The monarchs whose subjects are happy shall himself be happy in this life and in the next obtain praise, glory and honour'. Akbar followed the advice and won a place in Indian history, which no other monarch has ever occupied. He was the most popular, highly respected and deeply loved emperor by his people. Akbar's fifty-year rule is regarded as the hallmark of religious liberalism, which cemented the relation between Hindus and Muslims as never before.

Even Emperor Jahangir, as Prince Salim is said to have called himself, made a grant of land in Kartarpur to Guru Arjan Dev in admiration and veneration. The Guru was held in high esteem by the emperor and even used to be invited by the ladies of the royal family for consultation. Jahangir also visited Guru Hargobind at Amritsar, on his way to Kashmir.

Emperor Bahadur Shah, Aurangzeb's son and successor had high regard for Guru Gobind Singh. In the war of succession between Bahadur Shah and his brothers, Guru Gobind Singh sent his army to fight for Bahadur Shah, which helped him to win. After the success the two became good friends. The Nizam of Hyderabad made an endowment for the upkeep of Guru Gobind Singh's mausoleum at Nanded by the grant of five villages in addition to the salary of the *granthi*.

This spirit of religious liberalism was not confined to Mughals only. In fact it was the norm of the day. The Nizam of Hyderabad made an endowment for the upkeep of Guru Gobind Singh's mausoleum at Nanded by the grant of five villages in addition to the salary of the *granthi*. A well-known gurdwara, *Akal Bhoonga* was built there.

In the quest for realising the Almighty, not only the masses but the rulers also sought the guidance from the saints belonging to different religions. Akbar used to hold discussions with saints in order to ascertain the religious truth. Akbar acquired the knowledge of Hinduism and he listened to the *Vedas* and respected the Hindu saints. Dadu was one of them. It is said that he wished to attend Dadu's Brahm society and accept its teachings. In 1586 Akbar met Dadu and talked to him for forty days. Akbar was deeply impressed by his devotion and even took his women-folk to receive the saint's blessing. Akbar along with Tansen visited Mirabai. He paid homage to her and she accepted from him a necklace as an offering to be made at the lotus feet of her Lord Krishna. The emperor also went to see Saint Surdas along with Tansen. It is said that Akbar's relations with saint Jadrup initiated him into the doctrines of Vaishnavism. Akbar held the saint in a high esteem and whenever he passed Ujjain, he paid a visit to Jadrup in his cave. He used to have religious discourses with the saint, who satisfied his spiritual quest.

All religions flourished during Akbar's reign, as he being the sovereign paid respect to all alike. He gave generous endowment to temples and himself raised a temple in Kashmir. On the order of the emperor a small temple was built within the fort of Fatehpur Sikri. As was the emperor so were his ministers. Abul Fazl too had a high opinion of Hinduism and held the Kashmiri Brahmans in high esteem. He even rationalised and justified idol worship. Thus the gods of other religions were no strangers and were equally respected and revered by the believers of other religions. Akbar, like a Hindu devotee, presented a golden umbrella to the shrine of the fire goddess of Jwalamukhi in the modern district of Kangra in Punjab.

Abul Fazl writes in *Ain-i-Akbari* that on the emperor's command the epics of other religions were read to him. Akbar also issued two gold and one silver coins, known as Sia-Ram coins (one gold coin is kept in the British Museum and another in France.) His reverence for Hindu gods won him the highest regard from the Brahmans who regarded him as Ram-Krishna's incarnation. Akbar wanted all faiths to flower and their followers to live in peace and with equal dignity.

Akbar also promulgated a decree, which declared that no person was to be interfered with on account of his religion. Strict action was taken against those who tried to impose their religious convictions upon others. Under one of his regulations, Hindus who had become Muslims under pressure were allowed to return to the faith of their forefathers. His ministers were vigilant to ensure that the state should be secular and stood for justice. When a Mughal official converted a Hindu temple into a Muslim school, he was severely punished by Todarmal.

The Hindus were made to feel that the emperor considered himself as much their protector as of anyone else. In deference to the Hindus' sentiments, he prohibited the slaughter of the cow. It was a crime punished by amputation. In 1563 he abolished the tax on Hindu pilgrims at Mathura and other Holy places and in 1564 *jaziya* was done away with throughout his dominions. In such a cordial environment, diversity in spiritual matters led to the development of all faiths much to the annoyance of orthodox who were denied any special privileges and interference in the running of the state administration.[4]

Jahangir, the son and successor of Akbar followed the path shown by his father. He respected Hinduism, held religious discourses with the Hindu saints, sought their guidance and visited the Hindu shrines. Jahangir was deeply influenced by Saint Jadrup whom he met with his father who had taken the prince to the saint for his blessings. When Jahangir became Emperor, he visited the saint many a time and revered him like a true devotee.

The Muslim nobles were not slow in following the footsteps of their masters. Many Muslim nobles visited the saint Jadrup and sought his blessings. Abdur Rahim Khan-i-Khanan used to offer *sijda* to Jadrup. He revered Saint Surdas and Tulsidas and is said to have visited Swami Tulsidas to get his blessings.[5] Both the saints wrote their immortal works during his reign. Had the state been theocratic or hostile to other religions, these works could not have been written.

Like his father, Jahangir too used to offer salutations to the sun as it rose in sight. Jahangir continued Akbar's practice of inviting Hindu scholars and divines to the court and held discussions with them. He was very keen to meet the *jogis* and visited for the purpose the Gorkhkhatri near Peshawar which was an important centre of the *jogis*. The emperor visited the temple of Goddess Durga at Kangra. When he visited the Jwalamukhi temple, he gave orders that the adjoining buildings should also be repaired and added to the temple. He visited several other important Hindu religious centres.

At Kangra, he visited the famous Bhawani Temple located inside the fort (Punjab). Magnificent temples were made during his reign at Brindaban, Banaras and Mathura and were visited by a large number of Muslim pilgrims besides Hindus. The emperor gave rich grants to the temples and the pundits. He issued a *farman* and provided land in Mauza Pushkar to Hindu religious leaders who were responsible for looking after the ceremonies of the Hindu pilgrims. Jahangir maintained the secular approach of the state.[6]

Akbar's policies continued during Jahangir's reign. Jahangir's son and successor Shah Jahan and Prince Dara, Shah Jahan's son had a liberal outlook in religious matters. Shah Jahan honoured Pandit Jagannath with the title 'Panditraja'. The emperor reserved the right of giving final decision in religious matters and was daily blessed by Pandit Jagannath with address as *Dillishwara-ba Jagdishwara* (The Lord of Delhi is the Lord of Universe). Orissa peacocks, regarded as sacred animals were not allowed to be killed during Shah Jahan's region. Dara was a disciple of Baba Lal and patronised a number of Banaras Brahmans. Goswami Narsimha Saraswati and Pundit Jagannath enojoyed his special favour. The great dream of Dara's life, which was shattered by his untimely death was the brotherhood of all faiths and unity of mankind. For long years he studied Sanskrit and along with his sister Jahanara studied Hindu epics and the *Vedas* with great avidity. At his command, fifty of the *Vedas* were translated into Persian. He gave full liberty to Jai Singh, Raja of Jaipur to appoint the presiding priest at the temple of Brindaban built by Man Singh.

Dara's study of Hinduism and Islam had convinced him that there was no difference between the two. Besides, Dara wrote an interesting introduction to the Persian translation of a compendium of the *Joga Vishshta Ramayana* made under his supervision with the title *Tarjuma-Joga Vashishta in 1656.* Dara's approach towards Hinduism like his great grandfather Akbar was that of a seeker of truth, in whose heart was burning passion for knowledge. In this quest for unity of God, he came to know that Monotheists had given a clear exposition of the same. Dara wrote in his work *Risala-i-Haqnuma* : *'ba-zer-i-but imanist pinhan'*, i.e. Faith lies hidden beneath the idol. He translated the *Upanishads* because he regarded them as Divine secrets.[7]

Dara's *Majma-ul-Baharin* (meeting of the two oceans) in which he made a comparative study of fundamentals of Islam and Hinduism, again annoyed the fundamentalists. However, Dara convinced of his viewpoint never cared of their opposition. He and his wife, like Akbar and Jahangir, made their obeisance to the sun every morning and when the lamps were lit in the evening, every member of their household stood up in reverence to the Goddess of Fire.[8]

Even the orthodox emperor Aurangzeb, who is known for demolition of temples held Hindu saints in respect and conferred *jagirs* on the temples and the pundits, *maths* and yogis, while camping at the fort of Mandsaur, on his way to Deccan. About four hundred years have passed since the death of Aurangzeb, yet up to this day the priests of many Hindu temples in India have in their possession copies of royal *farmans* according to which *jagirs* were bestowed upon those temples under orders of Aurangzeb. The Hindu priests of the temple of Someshwarnath in Arail, near Allahabad and of the Jangamwari Shiva Temple in Banaras still have copies of Aurangzeb's *farman* in their possession.[9] From 1659 to 1685 he issued *farmans* in favour of Jangum Badali Shiva temple and the great temples of Mahakateshwara Ujjain, Balaji temple Chitrakut, Umanand temple Gauhati and the Jain temple of Shtrunjal and Abu. He gave land endowments to Hindu temples at Maheswar Nath, Benars, Mahshpur Multan and to the *maths* in the state of Marwar. Besides, he continued all through the fifty years of his reign strict enforcement of the prohibition against cow-slaughter throughout his empire.

Besides, Sikhism, Hinduism, Jainism, Zorastrianism too developed and received favours from the Mughal rulers. Jain Gurus were held in high esteem and Jain institutions were given liberal grants. Vijayasena Suri, Bhanuchandra Upadhayaya made a profound impression upon Akbar and influenced his mode of life. In obedience to their teachings, Akbar almost wholly abstained from eating flesh, renounced his beloved sport of hunting, prohibited slaughter of animals, earmarked days on which consumption of meat in any form was totally prohibited and ordered the release of the caged birds.

Emperor Jahangir had many Jain monks in his court. One of them, Siddhi Chandra was honoured by him with the title of *Nadir-i-Seamen* and *Khushfahm*. During his reign many Jain images were consecrated and in the inscriptions of some of them the name of Padshah Jahangir were also engraved. In the middle of 1618, the emperor, in accordance with the tenets of Jainism took a vow not to injure any living creature. Shah Jahan and Dara Shikoh also respected Jain monks and their religious institutions.

Zorastrianism too had an impact on the life and thinking of the Mughal rulers. Its influence reflected in the reverence of fire by Akbar. He adopted the Persian names for the months and days and celebrated the fourteen Persian festivals. He bestowed on the Parsee priest Dastur Maharajji Rana of Gujarat two hundred *bighas* of land as a free grant in perpetuity and in 1595 added further grant of a hundred *bighas* of land to his son Kaikubad.[10]

Christianity was also given equal respect. The Mughals, from Akbar to Dara Shikoh were cordial towards Christian fathers. Akbar received the Gospel with reverence and sometimes took off his turban to show respect to the Christian's sacred book and relics. Akbar used to visit the Chapel and prostrated before the pictures of Jesus and Mary.[11]

Akbar's broader outlook led him to entrust the education of his son Murad to the care of Fathers. He charged Abul Fazl with translating the Gospel and to distribute among the ulema. He often subscribed his letters with the sign of cross and as a symbol of appreciation of Christianity, he wore round his neck a cross and a locket containing the portraits of Jesus and Mary. Jahangir too had great regard for the Jesuit and bestowed several gifts upon them and their Churches. He also provided them a large sum to erect their religious places. The emperor also wore round his neck a locket-containing portraits of the Saviour and Virgin, marked his letters with the Christian symbols.[12]

The non-sectarian and 'peace with all' approach on the part of the rulers was not confined to north. It was a principle followed by the rulers all over the country. The Mahabhan Math of Otur (Poona) which was established by Chaitanya received land grant from the Nizamshahi rulers and confirmed by the subsequent rulers.

The rulers of Hyderabad respected Hinduism, the Hindu saints and their institutions. The Nizam made a grant to the Temple of Sitaram in the town of Hyderabad. Contributions on marriages and other occasions continued. Later, in A.D. 1813. Chandulal, a prime minister of Nizam addressed a letter to Swami Narsimah Bharti expressing his pleasure at the swami's proposed visit to Hyderabad and submitting an order from the government of the Nizam to the effect that no one should disobey the authority of the swami in the matter of religion.

In Mysore, Haider Ali and his son Tipu Sultan were the patron of the Hindu saints. Colonel Wilks described Haider as 'half a Hindu' because he had ordered 'the Jebbum to be performed in the Hindu temples'.[13] The Sultan used to seek the blessings of both Hindu and Muslim saints before embarking on any military campaign.' The letters of the Sultans make evident the nature and depth of their respectful attitude towards the Hindu Shrine of Sringeri.

The Sri Ranganathan temple was venerated by Haider as well as by his son Tipu. Tipu Sultan was no less a devotee of the Sringeri *math*. He sought the help of its Guru like a real Hindu when he was hemmed in with danger and often prayed for his blessings. Several of Tipu's letters are in Kannad and bear the 'Sun' seal of Tipu along with his signature in Persian.[14]

In one such letter Tipu requested the Swami to feed one thousand of Brahmans every day and to perform the ceremony according to the prescribed rites, making money gifts to the Brahmans engaged. Tipu sent orders to forward a palanquin for Goddess Sarda and another for Swamiji's personal use. Thus Tipu had great reverence for the Swami. Tipu did not confine his patronage to Sringeri temple; he extended it to other temples of the kingdom as well. More than hundred and fifty six temples received lands and grants annually from Tipu. In one instance he even ordered the construction of a temple. When Tipu visited Kanjeevaram during the third Anglo-Mysore war, he made a grant towards the construction of the temple and during his stay there he participated in the celebrations of the chariot festival and bore the cost of the fireworks on the occasion. As was customary with the rulers of Mysore, he daily visited the temple of Lord Ranganatha located inside the fort of Seringapatnam before taking his breakfast.

The last Mughal emperor, Bahadur Shah used to visit the Hindu temples with a hallowed mark on his forehead and was welcomed by the Hindu priests who took him for a Brahman. (With formal sandal mark on his forehead, Zafar wears round his neck the Brahmanic thread. Verily Bahadur Shah Zafar has become a Brahman out of his love for the Idol).[15]

Thus the Muslim rulers, though devoted to their own religion, had deep respect for all the religions of the land. They revered not only Allah but also Rama, Krishna, Nanak and Christ. They prayed not only in mosques but also visited temples and gurudwaras and sought the blessings of all the gods and goddesses The observance of counsels of saints belonging to different religions liberalised the outlook of rulers.

Inter-religious marriages

The inter-religious marriages by the Muslim rulers too contributed the spirit of assimilation and harmony and did much to soften the acrimonious differences between the two communities and intensified the process of liberalisation of the Muslim rulers. The Mughals were not the pioneers of this policy. The practice had begun as early as the Arab conquest of the Sind. According to *Chach-Nama,* Muhammad-bin-Qasim had married a Hindu woman named Ladi.[16] Ala ud-Din married Kamla Devi of Gujarat and princess Jhitai, daughter of Ram Deo of Deogger. Prince Khizar Khan was publicly married to Dawal Rani, a Rajput Princess in 1315. Amir Khusrau's mother was a Rawal Rajput lady. Sultan Tughlaq's brother Rajab was married to Bibi Naila, the daughter of Rana Mall Bhatti of Abhor. She was held in high esteem and her son Firoz became the king in spite of other claimant to the throne. Sultan Firoz Shah was married to a Hindu Gujar girl. Sultan Bahlol Lodi had married a Hindu wife and nominated her son Sikandar as successor to the throne to the exclusion of his sons and grandson of purer Afghan lineage.[17] The daughter of Rana Udai Singh of Mewar was married to Ghias Shah. Bhawani Das, a relative of Rana Rai Mal gave her daughter's hand to Abdul Muzaffar Nasiruddin Shah in 1504. She was given the title of Rani of Chittori. Sultan Kutbuddin of Gujarat was married to Rani Rup Manjari. His successor, Sultan Mahmud Bigarha was also married to a Hindu. Sultan Muzaffar Shah II too married three Rajput princesses—Rajbai, the daughter of Rana Mahipat, Laxmibai, daughter of Gohal Rajput and Bibi Rani. In Bengal, Sultan Shamsuddin Nika married a Hindu widow, Fulmati who exercised great influence in state matters. Husain Shah's two daughters were married to the highly respectable Brahman Raja of Sakotia.[18]

In Deccan the Bahmani Sultan Firoz married the daughter of Devaraya, king of Vijayanagar in 1407. It was an arranged marriage and the Sultan along with his baraat went to Vijaynagar where the marriage took place with great pomp and show.[19] The Sultan, Ibrahim Qutub Shah married a Hindu lady named Bhagirati. Sultan Mohammad Quli was born from her. Prince Mohammed Quli too was married to his beloved a Hindu girl called Bhagmati. It was an arranged marriage and it is also said that she was not converted after the marriage.

Yusuf Adil Shah, the first king of Bijapur married the sister of Mukand Rao, a Brahman and she became his chief queen. In Rajputana, Muhammad Shah of Gujarat married the daughter of the Raja of Idar in 1485.

In Kashmir Sultan Shihabuddin married Lakshmi and Shoba. He founded a town named after his wife Lakshmi. Sultan Qutbuddin was married to Sura Rani, a Hindu. Their eldest son Sikandar, who ascended the throne after his father, married Mira, the daughter of the Raja of Ohind. Sultan Zain-ul-Abidin married a Hindu girl Sunder Devi, daughter of Sunder Sena Raja of Rajauri. She was called Sundermaji with affection.

In Punjab, Maharaja Ranjit Singh had two Muslim wives—Gul Bahar and Moran. He had arranged marriages with both of them and consulted them in state matters. Moran was Ranjit's favourite wife. She did not wear a veil and used to appear unveiled in public with Ranjit Singh. She was the only one in whose name Ranjit Singh issued a coin *Moran Shahi.* The coin bore a figure of a peacock in keeping with the queen's name. There is a mosque named after her near the Moti Chowk in Lahore.

Emperor Akbar married Jodhabai, a Rajput princess who exercised a great influence upon him. Akbar's marriages with the Hindu princesses were not forced upon Rajputs. These were the willing alliances as matrimonial alliance was not treated as a test of loyalty and submission.[20] Akbar's son Salim (Jahangir) was married with Manbai, daughter of Bhagwant. She was given the title of Shah Begum. Jahangir's another son Khurram (Shah Jahan) was born of Jagat Gosain. Shah Jahan was married to Bai Lilawati, a grand daughter of Raja Gaj Singh. Aurangzeb also had two Hindu wives. Nawab Bai was the daughter of the Rajput Raja of Rajouri in Kashmir state. Sulaiman Shikoh, the eldest son of Dara Shikoh was married to the daughter of Amar Singh. Emperor Farukh Siyar had a Hindu wife named Inder Kunwar. Emperor Muhammad Shah was married to Udham Bai. The mother of the last emperor Bahadur Shah Zafar was also a Hindu named Lal Bai.

The inter-religious marriages worked in a big way in the process of Indianising the Muslim rulers, secularising the Indian State and harmonising the Indian society. Ghiyasuddin Tughlaq, Sultan Firoz Shah, Sikandar Lodi, Mohammad Quli of Golkonda, Muzzafar Shah, Sultan Sikandar and Sultan Ali Shah of Kashmir, Emperor Jahangir, Shah Jahan, Ahmad Shah and Bahadur Shah Zafar were born of Hindu mothers. They thus were as much Muslim as Hindu. Both mother and father shaped their ideas, ideals and outlook. They not only respected but also adopted the traditions, customs and ways of life of both the communities despite the ire of the orthodox of both the religions.

The Hindu customs and conventions influenced the Muslim kings. Ibn Battuta witnessed the ancient Hindu custom of carrying away the bride by real or pretended capture during the marriage of Sultan Muhammad Tughlaq's sister with

Bedouin Sayyid. Akbar followed many Hindu customs and ceremonies both in his private and public life. He did not circumcise his son Jahangir. His wife Jodahabai stuck steadfast to some orthodox practices of her birth by retaining the Ganges water, sacrificial fire, tulsi plant and a Brahman cook. Besides, he performed Jahangir's wedding with a Rajput Princess in Hindu fashion. The ceremonies observed were both Hindu and Muslim. Akbar personally participated in the marriage ceremonies. First of all Nikah took place in the presence of a Qazi. After this the customary Hindu ceremonies of walking arround the fire were observed. The couple went round the fire to the chanting of Vedic mantra by pundits. Akbar, like a Hindu scattered jewels and coins over the bride and the bridegroom from the Raja's residence to his own place of encampment.

Prince Azam, son of Aurangzeb was married to the daughter of Kirat Singh, son of Raja Jai Singh. The princess was not converted to Islam. Emperor Farukh Siyar was married to the daughter of Ajit Singh. On this occasion both Hindu and Muslim ceremonies were observed.

Ibn Battuta, Mohammad-bin-Tughlaq's contemporary, writes that the Sultan, like a Hindu used to kiss his mother's feet in public. Sultan Firoz performed tonsure like a Hindu during the period of mourning on the death of his son Fateh Khan. On his mother's death Akbar shaved his head, beard and moustaches. He participated in the traditional *yagya* ceremonies to bring solace to the soul of the deceased. Emperor Jahangir observed his father's *shraadha* in the mausoleum at Sikandra.

Hindu teachers were engaged by the rulers to teach the young princes about Hindu mythology and philosophy. Emperors including Aurangzeb observed Hindu ceremony of *Tula Dan* (weighing himself against different commodities and giving them away to ward off evil.) The rulers also followed the custom of making the tika sign on the forehead of their Hindu Rajas when they ascended the throne.

Native names were adopted by the Muslim rulers as early as the establishment of the Sultanate. Balban's nephew and other nobles had Hindu nicknames like Chajju and Kachchan. Mohammad-bin-Tughlaq named his temporary capital on the

Ganga as Swargdwari. However, with Akbar Indian names of places and different products became common practice.

All the Mughal rulers consulted Hindu astrologers before embarking on any campaign or taking any action. Humayun, on the advice of a sadhu, had avoided seeing his newborn son for thirty days. As an enthusias adept at astrology, Humayun fitted up seven houses of audience named after the seven planets. He himself wore clothes of the colour of the planet of the day and he recommended the same practice to his entourage. Humayun would invariably lead with the right foot and if anyone entered his residence with the left foot he would require him to go back and return in the correct fashion. Gobind Ray was an astrologer of Akbar and Jagannath was that of Shah Jahan. Hindu Pundits prepared the horoscopes for Akbar, Salim, Murad and Daniyal. Jotik Roy, the court astrologer of Jahangir was once weighed against gold and silver for reward. Aurangzeb sat on the throne on the day suggested as auspicious by his astrologers.

Emperor Muhammad Shah got the Delhi Jantar Mantar built in 1710. The observatory was used for naked eye sighting, continuously monitoring the position of the sun, moon and planet in relation to background stars in the belt of the Zodiac. Tipu Sultan had a firm faith in astrology. He himself wrote a book on astrology, named *Zabarzad*.[21] He used to consult astrologers daily about his stars. He daily fed the Brahmans and sought their advice. Various Hindu and Muslim festivals were celebrated by the rulers with great enthusiasm and impartial splendour. Sultan Zain-ul-Abidin, the ruler of Kashmir, used to participate in the feast and festivals of his non-Muslim subjects. He used to see the display of lamps on both sides of the river on the occasion of the worship held to celebrate the birth of Jhelum.

Many Hindu festivals were officially recognised by the Mughals, like Diwali, Shivratri, Dussehra, Baisakhi and Ramnavami. Akbar included the festivals of different communities within the list of the holidays of the Empire. Special ceremonies were connected with each of them and the state treasury make grants specified for the purpose. They sent soldiers to accompany *tazias* on Muharram and to follow the immersion of Hindu idols. On Dussehra, the imperial horses and elephants were arrayed in a decorated canopy and paraded for inspection. On the occasion of the Sankrati festival of Hindus, Emperor Jahangir used to give alms of one thousand *tolas* of gold and silver and several thousands of rupees.

At the time of Diwali, a puja Darbar was held and two decorated cows with garlands of cowries placed round their necks used to be brought in to the royal garden by the Brahmans. All the Mughal emperors including Aurangzeb observed the custom of giving banquet on the occasion of Dussehra. Aurangzeb used to distribute robes of honour among his Hindu nobles on that day. Diwali was celebrated with gaiety. Lamps were lighted and palace decorated.

Govardhan puja followed Diwali. It was observed as cows' day when cattle were washed, ornamented, fed and worshipped. Akbar also took part in the celebrations and several adorned cows were brought before him. Shivratri was observed and both Akbar and Jahangir used to meet and eat with the principal *jogis* on the night of the festival. On the Rakshabandhan day, the Hindu nobles fastened strings (auspicious threads) on the emperor's wrist. Mughals played Holi and allowed their Hindu wives to perform *havan puja* and to visit their holy places to offer prayers. Even during the reign of Aurangzeb, the festival of Holi was celebrated with great enthusiasm. Muslim nobles too joined freely with their Hindu brothers in this festival.

In Bengal the Muslim Nawabs like Murshid Quli Khan Alivardi, Sirajuddaula and Mir Jafar too celebrated Holi and other Hindu festivals with great enthusiasm. The Nawabs of Oudh adopted such Hindu symbols as fish, sun and cow on their standards. They regularly observed different festivals and feast of Basant Panchami along with their Hindu subjects. No less enthusiasm was displayed in the southern states. Dussehra was celebrated with great pomp and show in Mysore. Both Haider and Tipu participated in the festival and blessed their subject. Tipu not only attended the Chariot Festival of certain Hindu gods at Kanchi, but he himself walked in the festive procession. He used to ignite the fireworks to heighten the festive spirit of the occasion.

This proximity was reflected in the social relations also. A Hindu did not mind greeting his Muslim friend with *Salam* and the Muslim with *Ram-Ram*. Raja Ram Singh, as a token of respect, touched the feet of the older Shaista Khan who embraced the Raja and kissed his head. The Muslim rulers shared the happiness and the sufferings of their Hindu relatives like their own kith and kin. When Bahadur Shah invaded Chittorgarh, Rani Karnawati, the youngest wife of the deceased Sangram Simha sent a *rakhi* (bracelet) to Humayun, calling for his aid. Humayun was so pleased with the trust, engaged as he was in the conquest in Bengal, that he responded to the call of chivalry. He went and expelled the foe from the Chittorgarh and restored Rajput supremacy.

Religion did not stand as a barrier between the Muslim rulers and their Hindu relatives. Akbar displayed complete confidence in the Rajputs. His relation with them was based on trust, respect and affection. He appointed Jodhabai's brother Bhagwant Singh and nephew Man Singh in high posts.

Shah Jahan, who was more a Hindu than Muslim, (his father Jahangir was born of a Hindu mother and mother Jagat Gosain was the daughter of Moti Raja) trusted the Rajputs. Prince Dara had very warm relations with Rajputs and his son Prince Sulaiman Shikoh was married to Jai Singh's daughter. He used to call Jai Singh 'Dada Bhai'.

The attitude of Muslim Kings towards their subjects

Medieval India witnessed kings belonging to different creeds, enjoying love, affection and an unflinching loyalty of their subjects. They completely identified themselves with the interests of their subjects and worked for their well-being. To maintain their rule and to run the administration, they needed the support and cooperation of the natives. They could not afford to antagonise the people by being intolerant and oppressive, as they themselves were not only outsiders but also few in number. This compulsion made them make such policies as could win them the confidence of the people. Mohammad-bin-Qasim, the conqueror of Sind who ruled over the Sind region was very popular with the Sindhis on account of his liberal attitude and tolerant administration.

Even King Mahmud tried to prove himself a just ruler. In Punjab where he had set up his rule, he did not make discrimination between the Hindus and Muslims. Qutbuddin Aibak, the first Sultan of Delhi, was an efficient general and generous ruler. Throughout Asia, he was known for his generosity and had earned the sobriquet of *Lakh Baksh* (the giver of charity). The roads, during his reign were free from robbers and Hindus both high and low were treated with royal benignity. Aibak left a 'permanent reputation' as a competent and efficient ruler and his kingdom was governed by best laws.

Iltutmish was a just ruler. He took prompt action against crimes. He started the practice of hanging a chain of justice outside his palace and of going about incognito in order to see if justice was administered satisfactorily. Iltutmish did not consider his sons worthy to sit on the throne, hence he nominated his daughter Raziya as his successor. She had proved herself a good administrator when she was entrusted to manage the state affairs in the absence of Iltutmish, wh`en the latter went on military campaigns. Iltutmish was so much impressed by Raziya that her name was included along with that of the king in a series of coins. She was an enlightened ruler, progressive in outlook, dynamic in action, an able warrior and politician. She advocated social and emotional integration of Hindus and Muslims and stood for placing the former at high posts but was opposed by the powerful nobles of her Court. Despite her short span of rule, she opened schools, academies, research centres and public libraries where the books of great philosophers were studied. The Hindu treatises on sciences, philosophy, astronomy and literature were also given special recognition and were included in various courses in schools and colleges. Her non-discriminatory and pro-people approach won her the love of all her subjects. It reflected when, in her hour of need her subjects, especially the Hindu Rajas and the Hindu people rallied round her in their thousands and took up arms to uphold her right to the throne of Delhi after she was dethroned by her courtiers.

In 1246, Nasir-ud-din, a grandson of Iltutmish, became the Sultan. He was just, efficient and generous. He used to support himself by copying books and never took a single pie from the treasury for his personal use. He appointed Ghiasuddin Balban as his minister. He ruled for twenty years and after him his *wazir*, Balban occupied the throne. Like his master, Balban was impartial with his subjects.

Jalaluddin Khilji is said to have humanised politics and Indianised the system of government. His genuine piety treated all living beings with kingly impartiality. Sultan Alauddin believed that the interest of the state was the only norm which the ruler should adopt. He used to say that he issued such orders as he conceived to be for the good of the state and for the benefit of the people. The Sultan was generous and richly rewarded those who were found sincere, honest and hard working. Among his personal bodyguards were two Rajput brothers of the Tanwar clan, named Parmal Dev and Adhar Dev. Battuta found the memory of the Sultan enshrined in the hearts of his subjects as a paternal ruler.

Mohammad-bin-Tughlaq was a very popular Sultan and had endeared himself to his subjects because of his non-discriminatory attitude and policies. The Hindus were happy in his regime and never rose in revolt against him. The Sultan also gave impetus for the spread of education in the country; and in the province of Delhi alone there were about one thousand schools. He was the forerunner of Akbar both in his restriction on *sati* and his employment of Hindus in high military and civil posts. Ibn Battuta informs us that both Hindus and Muslims lived on good terms.

Sultan Firoz Tughlaq was a 'father' of his people. He was loved but not feared. He was the first Muslim king of India who believed in the principle that the duties of the Sovereign are not limited only to the protection of the person and property of his subjects but that the state must also adopt measures which contribute to their happiness and general welfare. He provided jobs to the weak and indigent and freely fed the blind and the helpless.

In fact, during the Sultanate both Hindus and Muslims

closely cooperated and contributed together in taking India ahead of other countries in the world. The Sultan was believed to be the richest person in the country as there was no distinction between his privy purse and the state treasury but none of the Sultans seems to have built up a fund of personal wealth. Their entire revenue was spent on building cities, palaces, dams gardens, etc.

In the kingdom of Kashmir most of the Sultans commanded respect from their entire subjects for their non-discriminatory approach and policies. The Sultans took into service persons known for their ability and integrity. Udayasari and Kota Bhatta were two ministers in whom Sultan Shihabuddin placed great confidence. Sultan Zainul-Abidin had forbidden the acceptance of gifts by revenue collecting officers. He also enforced the joint responsibility of villagers for thefts and robberies committed within the borders of the village. Whenever a theft or robbery was committed, the village headman was fined and this system is said to have prevented crime. He established non-sectarian residential educational institutions where students were provided with teachers, books, clothing, and food free of charge. The Sultan had a high sense of justice. He did not favour the infliction of capital punishment, which he reserved for the serious crimes. Zain's officers were loyal and competent and worked with their Sultan for the extension of the boundaries of the state. Zain extended his sway over the Punjab, from Peshawar to Sarhind, which was regarded as the southeastern frontier of the state.

Bahlol Lodi was a just and virtuous Sultan and treated the Hindu and Muslims nobles and ministers with equal regard. He appointed Pratap Rai as the Governor of Manipuri and Bhongaon and awarded great honours to Narsing Rai. During his reign of thirty-nine years, he did not sit on the throne and worked for the welfare of the country. Sultan Sikandar Lodi, Bahlol's successor was benevolent; and courageous. His equity beheld the weak and the strong with the same eye and always tried to make his subjects happy.

Sher Shah Suri was another king who was deeply loved and respected by his subjects. His real name was Farid. The well-being of his subjects was his aim for which he worked relentlessly throughout his life. Though he was a ruler, he worked like a common man. The efficiency of government was at its best under Sher Shah. His maxims were: 'it behoves the great to be always working' and 'a king should not have corrupt vakils or Vazirs'. He was like a father-figure to his subjects. Under Sher Shah's rule, the soldiers had to watch that no damage was done to fields or crops. No one slept hungry during his rule as the private kitchen of Sher Shah was very extensive and several thousand people were fed there every day. He provided justice to everyone and regarded it as the most excellent religious duty. In the exercise of this duty he did not spare even members his family. He did not discriminate between his subjects on the basis of religion. The Hindus of his kingdom loved Sher Shah.

Babar, the founder of the Mughal empire in India, from the very beginning of his rule treated Indians as his subjects and not as his prey and severely punished marauders among his own soldiers. He was kind and humane. No part of his character is more admirable than his uniform humanity and kindness of disposition. The good of the people always guided his policies.

Humayun, Babar's son and successor followed his father's footsteps. He was just, kind and generous towards his subjects. Akbar, the most secular and beloved emperor of India, imbibed in himself all that was good in Zainul Abidin, Mohammad-bin-Tughlaq and Sher Shah. He was the first emperor who won over the hearts of all his people Hindus, Muslims, Sikhs, Christians and Parsis alike. The result was that the people of Hindustan united together along with their emperor in building a new India based on the principles of equality, freedom, and fraternity. The boundaries of the country were extended, economy flourished, amity prevailed, and orthodoxy declined and rational outlook had its heyday. It was, in fact, the golden period of Medieval India.

Akbar was the greatest ruler of his time. He took his duties as sovereign seriously. He enjoyed immense popularity because he interacted and intermingled with his subjects as one of them. Akbar treated all his subjects equally and recruited the best of talents irrespective of their race, religion, or caste to run the administration of the country. His ministers served him with total loyalty, ability, and devotion. He treated them as his kith and kin and shared their sorrows and happiness by paying personal visits to their houses. More than half of his army consisted of Hindus and the commander-in-chief of the army was Man Singh, upon whom he conferred the title of *Farzand* (son) and *Mirza.* Raja Man Singh, throughout his life, fought and won many battles for his master. He subdued all those who stood against Akbar or refused to submit, even if they were Rajputs.

Raja Todarmal, a devout Hindu, was Akbar's Prime Minister. He was the son of a poor peasant, had first served under Sher Shah and was later employed by Akbar in the revenue department. Both Hindus and Muslims held him in high esteem. His unflinching loyalty towards Muslim rulers like Sher Shah or Akbar did not mean that he was anti-Hindu or anti-Hinduism. In fact, Hindu pandits depicted him as the first incarnation of Vishnu. Akbar too respected Todarmal's religious feelings.

Raja Todarmal, like Man Singh did not join *Din-e-Ilahi* yet remained very close to the emperor and enjoyed his confidence. Birbal, an orphan Brahman, was the hot favourite of Akbar. He became Raja Birbal because of his poetic talent, ready wit, humour and sagacity in political affairs. Akbar conferred upon him the title of Raja and the *jagir* of Nagarkot. Akbar twice saved Birbal's life. Akbar's nine jewels not only adorned his Court, but also cooperated with him in making India a land of plenty, prosperity and happiness. The all-round progress during his reign was the outcome of his non-discriminatory and humanistic approach.

Guided by reason and humanistic approach, Akbar sought to reform the entire social structure. In the words of Dr. P. Saran: 'In the comprehensiveness of his reforms—religious, social, political, educational, cultural, eugenic—history can hardly show a parallel to Akbar among the crowned heads of any age or country.' To enlighten the people and to change their outlook he laid emphasis on rational and scientific education. In *Ain-i-*

Akbari, there is a directive of Akbar, stating that education of people of heterogeneous elements, diverse creeds and conflicting religions, should be state controlled and absolutely secular in form and spirit. Accordingly, religion was not part of education and the pupils were not required to learn either the elements of Hindu religion or Islam. He passed many regulations to rescue Indian women, both Hindu and Muslim from all kinds of exploitation.

He was against the custom of sati. He took strong exception to a woman being forcibly made sati. However, he had very high regard for the Hindu women's sacrificing spirit. Akbar also ensured that none was deprived of justice and culprits were punished adequately. People fearlessly placed their cases before the emperor, as they knew that he was just and belonged to everyone. The emperor showed himself at the window (*jharokha darshan*) at least twice a day and listened to everyone who wished to speak to him.

Akbar advised his sons to protect the feeble from the strong and to work for the progress of the country. He remained a symbol of patriotism, humanism and secularism. He was not only a great emperor but also a great man. Viewed in relation to the age in which he flourished, he may justly be regarded as one of the finest characters in all history.

After Akbar, Jahangir became the emperor and, like his illustrious father, he wanted to see his countrymen flourishing and happy. The regulations made by Akbar continued during Jahangir's reign also. No woman, who was the mother of children, was allowed to be sati. He was just, generous and kind and people used to pray for his long life. Jahangir was a lover of justice. After becoming the emperor, he made it known to all his nobles that as all mankind, both high and low, were equal in his contemplation, his love of justice did not permit him to overlook an act of oppression in any man. He also stated that if there occurred the slightest proof of oppression or injustice, the punishment would be exemplary. He maintained the administration of justice as part of the *jharokha darshan*. His audience was given to anyone bringing a written petition.

Nurjahan, the empress was the chief advisor of Jahangir. She used to appear before the public and had her name struck along with that of Jahangir on the coins as well as on the imperial seal. Jahangir was so enamoured of her that he allowed her to conduct all affairs of the state.

Shah Jahan, the successor of Emperor Jahangir, reigned not so much as a king over his subjects but rather as a father over his family and children. Like his father and grandfather, Shah Jahan used to show himself at *jharokha* to his subjects at 6.45 a.m. and listen to their complaints. He used to sleep only for six hours and devoted all his time working for the well-being of his people. During Shah Jahan's reign the splendour of the court was formed throughout the world. Extensive workshops were maintained, not only at the capital but in the chief industrial centres of the empire. None was deprived of justice as the most important duty of the state. The emperor himself used to see that it was delivered without any bias. Shah Jahan made all efforts to ensure justice to everyone including the foreigners living in the country. There was religious freedom as voluntary conversions took place and new cults were formed. When Guru Hargobind captured Kiratpur, the entire village was converted to Sikhism. When the Mugahls recaptured it, there is no reference that the converts were brought back to Islam. Hindu teachers taught the Muslim disciples and the Muslim teachers had Hindu disciples. The harmonious co-existence and the consequent peace and progress of the country under Shah Jahan's rule was highly praised by all the poets of his time.

Aurangzeb had other sides to his character too. In his normal dealings with his people he was quite humane and considerate. He formally banned the practice of sati. During his rule it was a penal offence. He banned the drinking of wine. The cultivation of hemp (*bhang*) was forbidden. He also projected himself as impartial in delivering justice. Even in his old age, he personally accepted petitions from his subjects and issued orders on them with his own hands. He took strong action even against his own sons for their complacency in matters of justice. In letters written to his sons, Aurangzeb advised them to devote themselves to the task of protecting the poor and chastising the oppressors, promoting ministers and noble of sound judgement. He led a simple life and earned his livelihood by making skull caps. However, he was not loved by all his subjects. The killing of his brothers, imprisonment of his father and destruction of Hindu temples had completely alienated him from the Hindus and the liberal elements of the Muslim community.

People disliked Aurangzeb but the harmony at the social level continued. The imposition of *jaziya* was not resented by the Hindus alone, the unorthodox, minded Muslims-both commoners and nobles, criticised Aurangzeb. The successors of Aurangzeb did not follow his religious policies. They adopted the path of religious liberalism and tried to conciliate the annoyed sections of the Indian society.

Many of the Muslims kings were progressive and ahead of their times. No wonder, in such harmonious co-existence, the social relations were governed not by religions but by mutual friendly interest and understanding. History cites numerous instances when a Hindu willingly sacrificed his life for the sake of his Muslim friend and a Muslim did not betray his Hindu friend.

In fact, religion did not stand as a barrier between the rulers and the ruled. A generous ruler, whether Muslim, Hindu or Sikh was loved by his subjects. One such ruler was Maharaja Ranjit Singh of Punjab. Not only did the prominent Hindus, Muslims and Sikhs play an important role in placing him on the throne of Punjab, they all joined him in making the state a land of peace and prosperity.

Mysore also witnessed benevolent, efficient and impartial monarchs in Haider Ali and Tipu Sultan. In the words of Upendranath Ball, 'It was Hyder Ali who realised that India was in danger of losing her freedom in the hands of English and tried to organise the Indian powers in league against them.' The inhabitants of the territories conquered by him were happy under his rule. He was a born soldier, bold in the execution of his plans and skillful in tactics. He was farsighted as a statesman. He was a genius and a man of remarkable abilities. Tipu also respected the old traditions of Mysore and allowed his Hindu subjects to be governed by their own laws. Tipu was particularly friendly to the rural population. Forced labour in villages was totally abolished and oppressive methods of collecting rents or revenue were strictly banned. 'Tipu made the cultivator happy and protected the Indian merchant'. During his reign prosperity flourished. He connected all the parts of his kingdom by making a chain of roads. He looked after his people like a father. Tipu was extremely popular with his subjects. Tipu exhibited his valour even at the last moment of his life. He fell fighting. When the English found him, he was almost dead.

Thus religion did not stand as a barrier between the king and his subjects as all religions existed amicably on the Indian soil.

Hindu Elements in the Muslim Administration

After the occupation of Sind, the policy of the Arabs there was to retain as many features of the local forms of administration as were compatible with their administrative outlook. In Sind, Muhammad-bin-Qasim was its first Muslim governor who allowed the broad features of Hindu administrative system to continue to operate; and the civil and revenue administration remained either in the hands of the Hindus or converts from Hinduism. His boldest innovation was the appointment of Siskar, the former minister of his vanquished adversary Raja Dahir, as his adviser after Siskar had accepted Islam.[22]

In the context of the less liberal Turco-Persian conquest of north-west India, it has to be remembered that Mahmud's iconoclasm was aimed against images and not men. He regarded administration of the state as a practical proposition not necessarily related to religion. While he sacked Hindu temples, he also mobilised three Hindu divisions in his forces and at least three Hindu generals, Sundar, Nath and Tilak rose to position of high responsibility in the Ghaznawid army. Sundar was the commander of Hindu troops under Masud (1030–40). Tilak, the son of a low-caste barber, who would have had had no opportunities to distinguish himself in the caste-ridden Brahmanical society, took up service in Mahmud of Ghazna's court, and by his eloquence in Hindi as well as in Persian, his ability as an interpreter, his alertness of mind, and his capacity of securing the loyalty of the scattered Hindu military communities in the Ghaznawid Kingdom, he rose to a position of trust and power.

Under Muhammad-bin-Sam Ghuri the whole of north India came under Muslim dominance, everywhere the Hindu framework of administration was accepted and retained. In the army, if not the Hindu generals, at least those who had been converted to Islam had considerable share in stabilising the Delhi Sultanate and in extending its frontiers. Most distinguished of them was Malik Anbar, who extended the Khilji empire deep into the Deccan. Ibn Battuta testifies to the employment of Hindus in Muhammad-bin-Tughluq's administration, one of whom rose to be governor of Sindh. Despite Firoz Tughluq's theocratic policies, the finance and revenue departments of his state continued to be run by Hindu petty officials, though they hardly ever rose to positions of high responsibility. His policy was one of leniency to the Hindu chiefs unless they showed hostility.

At the time of Babur's conquest, the revenue system of the country and its trade was still run mainly by the Hindus. Despite the Persianisation of the administration by Sikandar Lodi and later by Todar Mal, there is reason to believe that revenue records were kept in the Indian languages, except at the headquarters. This implied the appointment of a large number of Hindus some of whom were paid by the state, others by the cultivators.[23] Akbar's great administrative achievement was the enlisting of Rajput chiefs , who from Prithvi Raj to Rana Sanga had offered stiff resistance to the consolidation of Muslim power in India, to the service and stabilisation of that very power by the simple process of integration and liberalisation. To that extent his eclecticism was motivated by political considerations. Within one generation the redoubtable Hindu warrior caste of the Rajputs was completely won over, and still remained loyal to Aurangzeb.

To achieve this Akbar had to take some revolutionary steps such as intermarriage with the Rajputs, the appointment of a Rajput to the highest rank among the *mansabdars* before a Muslim was raised to that rank : a Hindu, Raja Todar Mal, was given the highest revenue appointment in the state. Perhaps no medieval administrator, Hindu or Muslim, did more to revolutionise the revenue administration than Todar Mal.

More tolerant Rajput chiefs like Bhagwan Das, who built a mosque at Lahore, and his son Man Singh, who took a tolerant interest in Islam, were actually responding to Akbar's eclectic liberalism. Under Jahangir, Hindu generals continued to serve and extend the frontiers of the Mughal Empire; for instance, Udaji Ram played a considerable part in the Mughal campaigns in the Deccan. Shah Jahan reversed Akbar's policy to some extent, giving Muslims preference in service, but on the whole no dislodgement of Hindus from public services seems to have taken place during his reign. Shah Jahan's personal bodyguard and his most trusted servant was a Hindu, Mahesh Das, who stood behind the throne where the emperor's weapons were kept, and followed him wherever he rode out.

The consolidation of Aurangzeb's power and his success against his brother was due partly to the loyalty of his Rajput general Jai Singh, who also led the first Mughal expedition against Shivaji and secured his submission for a short period. More fluctuating were the loyalties of Jaswant Singh, who finally crossed over to Aurangzeb's side in 1659, was raised to the highest rank among the *mansabdars* and was twice appointed governor of Gujarat.

Aurangzeb's fanaticism, like that of Mahmud of Ghazna, was directed primarily at the 'false gods' and had its counterpart in his continuation of Akbar's enlightened administrative policy. Despite all the theoretical decisions taken by Aurangzeb against the employment of Hindus to higher revenue offices, in actual practice he appointed more competent Hindus as higher *mansabdars*, in the interest of sound administration, than any of his predecessors, including Akbar. The number of lower *mansabdars* under Aurangzeb exceeded several times those under Akbar.

The policies of the Deccan kingdoms in regard to the appointment of Hindus to high offices of the state were even more liberal. For a time, in Bijapur Hindi and Marathi were used as official languages along with Persian. This liberal tradition was continued by the Nizams of Hyderabad, whose first noble, the *peshkar*, used to be a Hindu and was often also the chief minister of the state.

Cultural Eclecticism of the Hindu Administrative Communities

Some Hindu communities like the Kayasthas, the Khatris, the Pundits of Kashmir, and the Amils of Sind adopted the Muslim culture, cultivated Muslim languages and literature, participated in Muslim administration effectively, and even moulded their domestic life to the Muslim way of living, a social development not unlike the Westernisation of the elite of other civilizations today. Apart from their religion, the members of these communities were hardly distinguishable from the Muslims, whereas in some Muslim cultural strongholds they went to the extent of adopting some secondary Muslim religio-social practices, such as writing elegies (*marsiyas*) on the martyrdom of Husain.[24] Some of them adopted part-Muslim names like Firuz Chand, Mahbub Karan or Jawaharlal. In their self-identification with Muslims some, though not all of them, went to the extreme of partly seceding from their own culture.

The most remarkable of these communities is that of the Kayasthas. From the eleventh century individuals of their caste began to rise to high administrative positions. There are many theories relating to their origin. In some parts Brahmans regard them as equal to Kshatriyas, though generally they are considered a mixed caste like the Shudras. The chief festival of the Kayasthas is the celebration of the day sacred to Saraswati, the Hindu goddess of knowledge and eloquence, when they worship the inkstand *(dawat-puja)*. Writing is taboo among them on that festival day, and the next day they begin the use of new pen and ink. Kayasthas were probably the first among Hindus to take up the study of Persian introduced in schools in the reign of Sikandar Lodi, and then under the Suris. Of all the Hindu castes they came into closest contact with the Muslims. Compared to other Hindu communities, they were less observant of the orthodox ritual, and under Muslim and Bhakti influence less conscious of caste distinctions. By the time of

Akbar, they mastered Persian and from the seventeenth to early nineteenth century, they enriched the Persian literature written in India with Hindu sensitivity embedded in Muslim tradition, while in certain fields such as diplomatic and official letter-writing *(insha)* they became specialists. In the eighteenth century in the reign of Muhammad Shah they came to monopolize nearly all the clerical posts.

The Khatris (Kshatriyas of Uttar Pradesh and the Punjab) seem to have adopted Muslim culture as Mughal mansabdars, in the milieu of Muslim civil and revenue co-administrators and military comrades-in-arms. Some Rajput chiefs, even at the end of the nineteenth century, continued to retain Muslim cultural orientation by employing Muslim tutors for their children, having their food prepared according to Muslim custom and participating superficially in Muslim festival and prayer.

In Kashmir, during the rule of Sultan Zayn al-Abidin, the Kashmiri pundits, especially the Sapru clan took up the study of Persian. Because of their sharp intelligence, and as the only group of Brahmans who took to the Muslim culture, they soon distinguished themselves in their own land and, after Akbar's annexation of Kashmir, in the Mughal court and administration in which they rose to become an influential element. Steeped in Persian intellectualism, some of them adopted the externals of the Muslim way of life, while others combined it with erudition in Sanskrit and the study of their own religion. From among the Kashmiri pandits rose in the twentieth century men like Tej Bahadur Sapru, who remained a champion of Urdu in the darkest days of Urdu-Hindi controversy and communal strife.

The Amils of Sind are a hereditary caste of government servants, though recently they have spread all over the world as petty merchants. It is possible that they obtained their first veneer of Islamic culture soon after the Arab occupation. In any case, after the incorporation of Sind in the Delhi Sultanate, they turned to the study of Persian and soon became indispensable to the lower as well as higher administration of Sind.[25]

Muslim Patronage of Sanskrit and Hindu Religious Literature

Before the medieval period, the main stream of Hindu religious and intellectual consciousness continued to flow through Sanskrit literature, which almost ignored the Muslim presence. It was written for the most part in the Hindu states of south India and in Orissa under the patronage of Rajput rajas. It continued to develop traditions and genres which were purely Hindu in religious and secular writing alike. Its orientation was conservative and Brahmanical with a concentration on the commentaries on the *Puranas*, and the *dharmasastras*, though including such works of philosophical speculation as those of Madhava. Non-religious writing continued to cover such fields as medicine, astronomy, linguistics, lexicography, poetics, music and erotica.

To this essentially Hindu creative activity, Muslim contribution in the way of participation was nil, and in the way of patronage insignificant. But some patronage there was, though until we come to the age of Akbar, it was sporadic. It is said to have begun with Mahmud of Ghazna, who is credited with having bestowed several forts and a robe of honour on the defeated Chandella raja of Kalinjar for composing 'Hindi' verses in his honour. The Hindu bard Kedar (A.D. 1150) is said to have attended the court of Ala al-din Jahansuz, the destroyer of Ghazna.[26] Jala al-din Khalji (1209-6) is probably the first Muslim sultan of Delhi who showed some intellectual curiosity for Hindu learning and Sanskrit studies.

Muhammad-bin-Tughluq's intellectual curiosity in Hindu learning forms a landmark. He enjoyed the society of Hindu *yogis* and extended his patronage to Jain divines. Ziya al-din Nakshabi's adaptation of fifty-two short stories from Sanskrit into Persian in 1330 under the title *Tuti Nama* (Book of the Parrot) is by far the most outstanding achievement of Muhammad bin Tughluq's reign in this field.

Despite Firoz Tughluq's theocratic policies, the official patronage of Sanskrit learning continued. He commissioned translations of medical works from Sanskrit. A treatise on Hindu astronomy and astrology was translated into Persian under the title *Dala il-i Firuz-Shahi,* while other translations from Sanskrit during his reign include works on music and wrestling.

Genuine Muslim effort towards an understanding, patronage and participation in Sanskrit learning begins with Sultan Zayn al-Abidin of Kashmir (1420-70) patron of Jonaraja, who continued the great Sanskrit historical work *Rajatarangini* and a number of Hindu scholars including the physician Sri Bhat. He also commissioned the translations of *Mahabharata* and *Rajatarangini* into Kashmiri, the first indication of Muslim interest in the pre-Muslim Hindu history of India.

Muslim participation in and patronage of Sanskrit learning reached its highest watermark in the court of Akbar. Some of the Hindu nobles in his court wrote in Sanskrit as well as Persian, like Raja Manohardas[27] or Todar Mal (1523–89) who translated *Bhagvata Purana* into Persian. Among Akbar's Muslim nobles, Abdul Rahim Khan-i-Khanan, Abul Fazl and Faizi knew some Sanskrit and translated from it, while other intellectuals and writers, including Badauni, translated Sanskrit works into Persian with the help of Hindu pandits. Abul Fazl's account of Hindu religion and sciences, of Hindu institutions, of Hindu cosmogony and geography, of the learning of the Hindus, the Jains and other sects marked the re-establishment, after an interval of nearly 500 years of the Muslim tradition of Hindu studies.

Essentially, the programme of translations from Sanskrit into Persian under Akbar was not an isolated or specific development. It was a part of the intensive project for the improvement of his mind which also included translations from Arabic, Turkish, and Kasmiri. Among the Hindu scholars employed to help Muslim translators like Faizi, Abul Fazl, Haji Ibrahim Sirhindi, Badauni, Naqib Khan, Mulla Shah, and Muhammad Sultan Thanesari were Kishnjoshii, Gangadhar, Mahesh Mahanand, Devi Misra, Satavadhava, Madhusudana-Misra, Chaturbhuja, and Bhavan.[28] This joint enterprise rendered from Sanskrit into Persian epic classics like *Mahabharata*, Valmiki's *Ramayana* and several religious and metaphysical works including parts of the *Puranas*. Faizi paraphrased the first two *parvas of Mahabharata* into Persian verse.

Jain literature associated with the court of Akbar included *Hira Saubhagyam* by Devavimala describing the visit of Jain monks to the court of Akbar and a biography of Khem Chand, who introduced Jains into Akbar's court, by Jayasoma.[29]

Akbar's court developed complementary but separate intellectual traditions, the Muslim and the Hindu, which co-existed in mutual tolerance, but did not merge. The Hindu intellectual enclave received equality of patronage with the Muslim. But the great Persian literature written in this period, with the exception of some of the writings of Faizi and Abul Fazl remained almost totally uninfluenced by and indifferent to Sanskrit.

The net achievement of Akbar's patronage of Hindu studies was the relative familiarity with fragments of Hindu religion and epical literature of the Muslim elite under the Mughals, compared to its predecessor under the Sultanate.

This partial intellectual familiarity with Hinduism is reflected in Jahangir's accounts of the sociological basis of the four ashramas of the Brahmans, the four Hindu castes, the psychological motives of sati, and his equation of Vedanta with Sufism. He continued the patronage of translations from Sanskrit into Persian as well as of Hindu scholars who wrote on Hindu law, sciences and lexicography written during his reign.

Outstanding in the Hindu scholarship of the reign of Shah Jahan were works on Hindu law; of which the *Nirnaya Sindhu* of Kamalakara Bhatta and writings of Nilakantha Bhatta have been recognised as authoritative works on Hindu law in modern times by the High Courts of Bombay (now Mumbai) and Calcutta (now Kolkata). Popularisation of Hindu religion seems to have been the keynote of the Hindu literature written under Shah Jahan, which probably received patronage from Dara Shikoh.

Among Shah Jahan's proteges were the famous court poets Sundardas and Chintamani as well as Kavindracarya who wrote a commentary on the *Rigveda*. Jagannath Misra, the most distinguished of Shah Jahan's Hindu court-poets, wrote Sanskrit panegyrics in the honour of Dara Shikoh as well as tracts in praise of the Ganges, the Jamuna and the sun. Hindu savants and poets associated with Dara Shikoh, himself a scholar of Sanskrit, were Kavi Hari Ram, Pancraj of Benares, and Phatan Misra. The learned Kavindracarya seems to have wielded some influence in the court of Shah Jahan, possibly through the support of Dara Shikoh, for he successfully led a deputation of pandits requesting the emperor to abolish the pilgrimage tax on Hindus in Benares and Allahabad.[30]

Despite Aurangzeb's negative attitude to Hindu culture, his court included Hindu scholars or poets like Indrajit Tripathi and Samant, while one of his Muslim courtiers, Fazil Ali Khan was a patron of the Hindu poets Jai Dev and Nathand, and of the prosodist Sukhdas Misra. Outside the Hindu stream, the most remarkable work interpretative of Hindu good-living ever written in Persian, was the *Tuhfat al-Hind* of Mirza Muhammad, commissioned by Kokaltash Khan for the instruction of Aurangzeb's son Jahandar Shah. The book deals with the orthography and sound laws of Indian languages, especially Hindi, comparing the rules of Sanskrit prosody with those of Arabic, and with Hindu arts of love and of music. It is followed by three chapters on the Hindu science of sexual knowledge, physiognomy and lexicography.

At least in one respect the contact with and patronage of Muslims awakened a new feeling in Sanskrit and other Hindu literatures—a feeling for history. After latter parts of *Rajatarangini*, another Sanskrit work written partly as a direct result of Muslim patronage, covering a Muslim historical theme is the *Sarvadesavrittanta Samgraha*, a history of the Mughals up to the reign of Akbar. Mughal historiography rather than the ancient Rajput epic seems to have been the inspiration of the Jaipur and Udaipur Khyats and Kaviyas, chronicles of the Rajput dynasties composed in the Mughal period.

Of the languages and literatures that have descended from Sanskrit, next to Hindi and Urdu, Bengali has been the most susceptible to composite influences. From the beginning of the thirteenth century, with the establishment of Muslim rule in Bengal, Arabic and Persian loan-words, chiefly the vocabulary of administration, luxury and good-living, made deep inroads into the Bengali language, displacing the older vocabulary of Sanskritic origin.[31] On the popular level one comes across Muslim influence in Bengali folk-tales such as the introduction of fairies in the story of Madhumala. The *Mahabharata* was translated from Sanskrit into Bengali by order of Ala al-din Husain Shah (1493–1518) and his son Nasir al-din Nusrat Shah (1518–33), Sultans of Gaur. Another patron of Hindu learning in Bengal was the Muslim general Chutti Khan. Muslim Bengali poets sometimes wrote on Hindu themes. Alaol wrote poems on the familiar Hindu love theme of Radha and Krishna, and showed considerable first hand familiarity with Hindu religious ceremonies, ritual and customs, with Sanskrit classification of feminine emotions, and with Sanskrit prosody. Still, the Muslim Bengali literature retained a distinct personality and identity of its own, which accepted without any inhibition the Arabic and Persian heritage of Muslim culture.[32]

The Hindu Contribution to Persian Literature

Sikandar Lodi's (1489–1517) Persianisation of the administration yielded literary results almost immediately, and there is no doubt that even under the Lodis individual Hindus came to attain a high degree of proficiency in Persian, and a Hindu poet 'Brahman' composed commendable verses in it. In the succeeding generations among Hindu poets of Persian, there was Mirza Manohar Tausani, a devoted retainer of Akbar. In the reign of Jahangir, Kayasthas achieved a high degree of proficiency in *insha* (epistolography) and the work of Munshi Harkaran came to be considered later of a standard high enough to be prescribed as a textbook in schools.

The first Hindu to achieve literary distinction in Persian prose and verse was Chandra Bhan 'Brahman', the son of the imperial scribe, and a disciple of the Muslim divine 'Abdul Hakim Siyalkoti', in whose company he might have acquired some of that eclectic spiritual understanding, which placed him in the right atmosphere in the service of Dara Shikoh. His prose chronicle, *Chahar Chaman* and his *Diwan* of Persian verse is delightful reading. One of his contemporaries was Jaswant Rai Munshi, who also composed a *Diwan* in Persian.

Bhopat Rai, better known as Begham Vairagi (d. 1719) a Khatri of Jammu was the disciple of a preceptor of his own sect Narayan Vairagi, as well as of a Muslim Sufi Muhammad Sadiq. In his famous Persian *masnawi*, Vedantic and Sufi elements interfuse into a unified ecstatic experience, which shows remarkably enough some influence of Jalal al-din Rumi. Among the eighteenth century Hindu poets in Persian are Anand Ram 'Mukhlis' a disciple of 'Bedil'; Lala Amanat Rai who chose devotional themes from the *Ramayana, Bhagavad Gita* and Vedantic literature for his poems; Lala Hukum Chand who translated the *Bhagavad Gita* into Persian verse; Shri Gopal 'Tamiz' author among other works of a *masnawi* in praise of Mathura; and Basawanlal 'Bedar', disciple of the eclectic Naqshbandi saint-poet Mazhar Jan-i Janan. The remarkable feature of the Persian poetry written by Hindu poets in the eighteenth century is its choice of Hindu religious themes.

Official correspondence (*insha*), a great and courtly art in Persian, became the speciality of the Kayasthas in the eighteenth century, as the immigration of Persian *munshis* ceased. The tradition of Kayastha Persian epistolography which had begun with Harkaran and continued through Chandra Bhan had already achieved classical status in the *Insha* of Madhu Ram during the reign of Aurangzeb. Hindu contribution to some branches of Persian writing had already overtaken and in some cases surpassed contemporary Indian Muslim achievement. For instance, in the field of lexicography Tek Chand Bahar's encyclopaedic *Bahar-i Ajam* and Siyalkoti Mal's *Mustalihat-i Warusta,* a dictionary of idioms based on the linguistic authority of the usage of solely the Persian poets of Iran, came to be recognised as authoritative works.

The development of Hindu historiography, for which Persian served as the main vehicle during the eighteenth and nineteenth centuries is an interesting field of study. In the absence of a classical Hindu tradition it identified itself entirely with the Muslim style. It began in the seventeenth century with works like Chandra Bhan Brahman's *Chahar Chaman,* which is modelled to some extent on Abu'l Fazl's *Ain-i Akbari,* though with a much more conscious concentration on style, and the

Shah Jahan Nama of Bhagwant Das. Banwali Das Wali, who was attached to the entourage of Dara Shikoh, made use of the Hindu epic and legend in writing of the ancient rulers of Hindu India, though the technique and framework of his history remained that of a Muslim historiography. Aurangzeb also found a Hindu historian to celebrate his victories; he was Ishwardas Nagar, the author of *Futuhah-i Alamgiri.*

Munshi Sujan Rai's *Khulasat al-tawarikh,* written in 1695, is perhaps the most interesting work of history written by a Hindu in Persian. Written in the age of Aurangzeb, it deplores intolerance and takes an eclectic view of religion, regarding the establishment of Muslim rule in India as an act of Divine will. Sujan Lal is idyllicly sensitive to the beauty of Indian landscape and seasons, to the fragrance and the teaming life in its cities. Like Banwali Das, he also draws upon the *Ramayana* and *Mahabharata*, but his account seems to be based on their Persian renderings undertaken in the Mughal court. His other sources are the translations of later Hindu histories, like Madhu Ram's Persian version of the Hindi *Rajavali* as well as Imad al-din's translation of *Rajatarangini*.

An interesting work which confounds history with myth but forms a landmark between Abul Fazl's *Ain-i Akbari* and the modern *Gazetteer* is Ramlal's *Tuhfat al-Hind.* Its syncretism keeps the two components quite distinct. Thus, the Muslim accounts of the creation of the universe, and the accounts of the Hindu avatars precede the legends of Moses and Solomon.

The most striking feature of this work is the author's complete self-identification with the Muslim viewpoint. This leads to an apologetic approach to Hindu religion; tracing the origin of idol-worship in sun-worship, which is supposed to have been followed by Brahmanical ancestor-worship.

REFERENCES AND NOTES

1. Jawed, Dr. Ajeet. "Little Known Dimensions of Muslim Rule". In *Heritage of Harmony*, p. 81.
2. Alvi, Azra. *Socio-Religious Outlook of Abul Fazl,* p.36.
3. *Indian Historical Quarterly*, Vol. XIII, 1937: p.312.
4. Jawed, Dr. Ajeet. *Heritage of Harmony*, p. 84.
5. Ibid., p. 86.

6. Prasad, Beni. *History of Jahangir*, p. 407.
7. K.R. Qanungo. *Dara Shikoh*, Vol. 1., p.401.
8. Lal, Muni. *Shah Jehan*, p. 289.
9. Dr. B.N. Pande gives an elaborate list of the *farmans* issued by Aurangzeb in his book *Historical Distortions*.
10. Srivastava, A.L. *Akbar the Great*, p.239.
11. Ibid., pp. 255, 256.
12. Buke, S.M. *Akbar the Greatest*, p. 119.
13. Sen, Surendranath. *Studies in Indian History*, p. 166.
14. Rao, V. Raghavendra. *Indo-Muslim Culture*, p. 59.
    Dr. B.N. Pande gives elaborate details of Tipu's grants to Hindu temples in his book *Historical Distortions*.
15. Husain, Mahdi. *Bahadur Shah*, p.37.
16. Husain, Mahdi. *Tughlaq Dynasty*, p. 18.
17. Dow, Alexander. *History of India*, vol. IV, p.139.
18. Kumar, Sisir. *India Vision and Fulfilment*, p. 89.
19. Sheswami, Haroon Khan. *The Brahmanis of Deccan*, p. 101.
20. Satish Chandra, *Mughals Religious Policies*, p.23.
21. Hasan, Mohibbul. *History of Tippu Sultan*, p. 378.
22. For the study of Hindu nobles serving in Muslim administration, see *Maathin al-umara*, Shah Nawaz Khan, pp. 169–358.
23. Sharma, S.R. *The Religious Policy of Mughal Emperors*, p. 27.
24. Qatie, Mirza Muhammad Hasan. *Haft Tamasha*, p. 467.
25. Thakur, U.T. *Sindhi Culture*, p. 56.
26. Grievson, G.A. *The Modern Vernacular Literature of Hindustan*, p. 2.
27. Ibid., p.37.
28. Sharma, S.R. *A Bibliography of Mughal India*, p.89.
29. Sharma, S.R. *The Religious Policy of Mughal Emperors*, p. 87.
30. Hasrat, Bikramjit. *Dara Shikoh*, pp. 112, 115.
31. Sen, D.C. *History of Bengali Language and Literature*, pp. 381-82.
32. Huq, Inam-al. *Muslim Bengali Literature*, p. 28.

7

The Syncretic Cults : Blending of Hindu–Muslim Elements

Syncretism as an important constituent of multi-cultural mainstream offers an opportunity to reinforce greater cultural amalgam and multi-confessional harmony. The vast region of south Asia in general and India in particular symbolises a remarkable confluence of cultural strands and cross-fertilisation of religious ideas and ethnic/linguistic intermingling. Here cross-fertilisation of sacred ideas and civil thoughts took place, in the midst of ethnic, linguistic and regional diversities, alongside growth of numerous religious cults and sects, in various historical phases.

The sociologists and social anthropologists have thrown much light on the variety of religious forms through their studies of belief systems, rituals, symbols and meanings all over the world but they have not paid adequate attention to the phenomenon of syncretism, which represents a blend of multiple religious beliefs, in variegated degrees. The concept of syncretism uncovers a remarkable dimension in the exploration of cultural reciprocation.[1]

Religions show enormous variety in terms of beliefs, rituals, spiritualism and symbolic imagery. Religion appears in several forms but there are some widely recognised religious forms. It ascribes sacredness to moral principle rather than to a deity. On the other hand, Christianity, Judaism, Islam and Hinduism are *theistic* religions. Believers worship one or several gods. Another type is *animism,* in which followers believe that spirits can help or harm people but can be manipulated to serve human needs.

People everywhere in their myths and rituals have attributed misfortune and suffering to certain extra-human, extra-physical power and also related the same to divinity and the sacred. The essence of a mystical experience is the search for or attainment of a sense of nearness to or unity with a transcendent power, usually God. This means an enhancement of the self, a heightened state of awareness, which seems to throw a new light upon the nature of reality for the mystic. A supernatural event or a miracle is an unexpected performance resulting from supernatural power, exercised by direct divine intervention or through the agency of a divinely inspired person, such as a saint.

As a matter of fact, the religious beliefs of the people, as developed through extensive contacts and adoptions, were hardly ever rigid or sealed. People in most cases, often follow multiple religious traditions without necessarily drawing boundaries between them, even though they may affirm their overt allegiance to one religion at a given time.

There is no doubt that significant culture changes to take place but the pre-change culture traits and religious customs indeed survive in greater or lesser degree in many societies and therefore 'acculturation' persists in such societies only as an incomplete and partial process. Thus we witness the coexistence of dual religious beliefs and traditions, often prevailing determinedly and willfully. In due course, a course of syncretism automatically sets in which gets evolved in varied degrees depending on verve and impact of new beliefs and variegated intensity of contact amidst such societies.

Syncretism, according to Brandon, is to be found in all places where there has been contact between religions. The term syncretism was originally used by Plutarch for 'fusion of religious cults' which occurred in the Graeco-Roman world, 300 BC-200 CE. 'Syncretism' has been defined as the 'attempted reconciliation or union of different or opposing principles, practices or parties, as in philosophy or religion' (*Webster's Unabridged Dictionary*).

Exchange and sharing of traits, thoughts and ethos contributed to cultural synthesis. One scholar has perceived Indian society as a 'honeycomb' in which communities are engaged in vibrant interaction, sharing space, ethos and cultural traits. Between themselves the communities look more at commonalties than differences and they easily establish rapport. The data set of *People of India* project suggests that people in the religious sphere share a high percentage of traits : Hindu-Muslim (97.7 per cent), Hindu-Buddhist (91 per cent), Hindu-Sikh (88.99 per cent) and Hindu-Jain (77.46 per cent). Other religious communities with a high percentage of sharing of religious traits are Muslim-Sikh (89.95 per cent), Muslim-Buddhist (91.18 per cent) and Jain-Buddhist (81.34 per cent).

Other forms of traditional linkages are participation in each other's religious ceremonies and festivals. Such sharing, includes performing actual roles in religious ceremonies. The proportion of such communities as Hindus, Buddhists, Sikhs and Jains visiting 'other religious shrines' vary from 80–92 per cent while 60–75 per cent of the communities following Islam. These facts explain that despite contradictions and diversities, there exists vibrant sharing of cultural and religious traits. A basic sense of harmony prevails which dissolves our animosity and ultimately contributes towards shaping our unique homogenisation.

Religious movements and a plethora of religious ideas, in varied historical phases, motivated the people and brought them closer towards numerous religious cults, sects, reform movements and diverse belief systems. The underlying assumption seems to be that people need solace and assurance about fulfilment of all their wishes ultimately; hence they solicit refuge and sanctification of their expectations through their trust on varied religious and sectarian dogmas.

Mingling of numerous exogenous religious beliefs with pre-existing religious dogmas of people may not be regarded as an aberration. It is also not a system within a system but the survival of multifaceted religious belief systems existing as a rational order. Syncretism is a matter of degree some societies have blended prominent aspects of two religious dogmas, in others only certain aspects of the original or adopted religion/sect has been internalised. Syncretism pertains to a commingled religious sequence whose ill-defined frontier shapes its fundamental collective character.

Indian society is characterised by the caste system. It is a system of social hierarchy in which social groups are arranged in a rude order of ritual purity and pollution. Hence there prevailed immense space for dissent and reform within the society. Reformist groups and sects emerged from time to time as a result. Quests for equality, salvation and often some mobility aspiration remained integral parts of reformist movements. Most of these movements that aimed at reorganising the society in India were couched in religious terms. Social pressures had often encouraged adoption of new religious denominations and formation of sectarian and dissident religious orders in India.[2]

Religious orders such as the Sikh and Vira Saiva, have emerged as deviants from the orthodox Hindu religion. Sectarian-cultist orders had occurred as challenges to established doctrinal positions. New sects proliferate when the pre-existing religions fail to satisfy the need for meaningful interpretation of life problems. A sect is a religious group that rejects the social environment in which it exists. Sects function to satisfy a society's needs.

Religious sects, in general, promote integration, homogenisation and egalitarianism by calling attention to needs unmet by established religions. New religious sects also arose to bring emotional satisfaction in the lives of marginalised and disadvantaged sections of society, sections not adequately served by established cultural institutions.

In the remote past intensive religious activity had taken place which aimed to overthrow the predominance of Buddhism and Jainism in peninsular India. In this period we witness even 'breaking of barriers of caste' inherent in the Vedic religion by admitting devotees even from 'untouchable' castes into the order of *bhaktas*, thereby sowing the seed of the Bhakti Movement. During the medieval period (thirteenth to seventeenth century) Hinduism underwent a drastic transformation. Focus was now on one god.

Centuries of contacts between the two communities (Hindu and Muslim) gradually led to the emergence and evolution of many popular cults. They were the mixtures of both Hinduism and Islam. Love, harmony and peace were the cardinal principles of these cults.

Islam and Hinduism were two different religions. However, the quest of knowing the unknown Supreme Being led the saints of the two communities to study the scriptures of the two religions. This in turn made them critically examine their own religion in the light of the newly acquired knowledge, and in this process they evolved new cults which provided them spiritual satisfaction and revealed a new path for the realisation of God. They formulated their own philosophies, beliefs and practices and kept doors of their sects open.

The atmosphere of religious toleration and amity resulted in the birth of certain Hindu sects following both Muslim and Hindu religious rituals and customs. Efforts to compromise between Hinduism and Islam by selecting certain elements from each and rejecting others. In most cases this kind of syncretism had a base in one of the two religions while it borrowed from the other. In some cases it chose a middle position outside the pale of both.[3]

The earliest syncretic beliefs were perphas quite spontaneous; they grew in Sind, the first scene of Muslim impact, out of the old cults of the worship of the river Indus. The inherent anthropomorphism of the Hindu religion at the popular level made possible the syncretisation of some Muslim saints whose identity is established in history.

In the case of Muslim syncretic sects, which are less numerous, Hindu elements are usually survivals of Hindu ritual after their conversion to Islam. Not all superstitions in Indian Islam were of Hindu origin. For instance, visits to saints' tombs, a practice which resembled Hindu temple-worship, had its origins in Sufi encouragement and was as common in the sixteenth century Ottoman empire as in Mughal India. The veneration of tombs was popular in the late nineteenth century in Syria, at a time when it was under heavy attack in India. Nor was the traffic of supersition all one way. A number of Muslim superstitious practices imported from other countries of Dar al-Islam were adopted by various Hindu sects. Much animism, much supersition is common to all humanity.

Both the Bhakti and Sufi saints had helped to recast and reorient the prevalent value system of the time. These saints propagated the fundamental equality of mankind. These saints patronized the *nirguna* theological stance, based on a notion that the divine is formless, 'without qualities'. A directness and unorthodoxy that was to give form to the priorities of new-sprung religious thought and practice typified the wave of Bhakti.

Much as Bhakti did, Sufism de-emphasised the role of the clergy and elevated the love between a devotee and his god to ecstacy. Studies have revealed that the *pir* and *darvez* in different periods played a positive role in bringing about synthesis between the Hindu and Muslim cultures. The Fakir, Darvez, Qualandar and Baul are all known wandering mendicants of India.

The Baul sect arose in Bengal with the coming of the Turks and then Islam, which was established in the thirteenth century. The Sufi movement had considerably coloured the Bengal Vaishnavism in the sixteenth and seventeenth centuries. The Islamic spirit of mystic songs had been deeply ingrained in the songs of Bauls and Marfati. The Marfati songs are significant in relation to Islamic spiritual heritage for the whole of humanity. They exemplify the syncretistic tradition in a unique manner.

The Baul songs too are associated with the sects of both the Hindus and Muslims. A Baul is a wanderer. Spiritualism is his philosophy, he dances in ecstasy and sings in joy, longing for mystical union with the divine. Among the Bauls of Bengal we also find the continuity of the Sahajiya movement, a more systematised form of which is found in the Buddhist form of Sahajiya school.

The Bhakti consciousness was more prominent in the impressive verses and songs of the saints whose *monism* found no room for Brahmanical orthodoxy or the traditional stratification of Hindu society. Vernacular poetry found a new role in expressing sentiments and theologies of Bhakti. This saint tradition is most fully represented by the great mystic poet Kabir. He dismissed the dogma and external observances of both Hinduism and Islam, insisting that the true search for god must be an inner one, accompanied by contemplation on the divine name. Kabir found an easy method of spreading his ideas. Since his audience consisted of illiterates and being illiterate himself, his message could be spread only by word of mouth. Kabir's ideas were sought to be carried forward by Raidas (b. 1415), a cobbler by profession. Following Kabir, Raidas and Nanak, all emphasised the concept of human equality. Dadu Dayal (b. 1603) similarly asserted that all human beings had the same spirit derived from god and differences of religion are meaningless just as the water of a flowing river in different pots is the same.

At the folk level, there evolved various forms of syncretistic blends of Islam with local cults, as reflected, for example, in the poetry of Sayyid Sultan of Bengal (sixteenth century). In his poem *Nabi-Bagsa*, he treated the major deities of Hindu religion such as Rama and Krishna as successive prophets of god, followed in turn by Adam, Noah, Abraham, Moses, Jesus and Mohammed. He identified and correlated the Muslim notion of prophet with the Hindu concept of avatar, an incarnation of god.

The Balmikis of Delhi are divided into several endogamous religious groups, such as Hindu Balmiki, Sikh Majhabi and Muslim Mussali. The Bazigars (Punjab) have adopted Sikhism. Earlier they venerated the *pirkhana*. They now visit the gurudwara and also celebrate Holi, Diwali, Dashahra and Lohri (1995:200). The Banjaras (Himachal Pradesh) are divided into the Hindus, Muslims and Sikhs. The Hindus and Sikhs inter-marry, hence there has been a great deal of admixture between their religious life and practices. The Beda Jangams are the Lingayats of Karnataka.[4]

The Bhangis of Gujarat consider Balmiki Muni as their god. They are also followers of Kabir, Ramananda and Nanak. The Chamars profess different religions and sects. In Himachal Pradesh, they are Ravidasis and also Nirankari Sikhs. In

Haryana, the Julaha are the followers of Kabir, though some Julahas have adopted Buddhism.

One example of the evolution of the syncretic cults in South India can be best illustrated by the Ayyappan cult, which has become an all-India phenomenon now. As the story goes, Ayyappan though a divine and princely baby who was to become heir apparent was abanded in the forest, by a jealous queen. But Ayyappan set forth and had a fracas with a Muslim trader Vaver, who was his equal and settled a treaty of friendship with him. Neverthless, Ayyappan was disgusted, he renounced the world and retreated forever into the forests of Sabarimala. Due to the earnest prayers of his devotees, he conceded to them the right to travel on pilgrimage to his seat during a period of six weeks every year, after observing strict vegetarianism, abstinence from sex, etc. The devotees take saranam in Ayyappan, an indication of the Buddist influence in Ayyappan's conversion. The friendship and tolerance with Islam is also significant. Some Muslims who claim descent from Vaver present themselves at the Sabarimala temple during the annual pilgrimage season.

It is noteworthy that the pilgrimage has always been open to all without discrimination, of religion or caste and all the devotees who are called Ayyappans are equal no caste pollution is observed. The essential rites continue to be taking vow of pilgrimage by wearing a chain in the neck, observance of abstinence for 41 days, taking refuge in Ayyappan, filling of a peculiar head-load pack in which sacrificial coconut filled with ghee and sealed with wax is kept in one compartment and provisions for the pilgrim in the other compartment, chanting 'Ayyappan Saranam' as many times as possible every day, setting out on the pilgrimage under the leadership of a veteran, and also paying homage to Vaver at the mosque in Erumeli (Pettathullal). The whole process of Ayyappan pilgrimage points to Hindu–Muslim amity.

The Husaini Brahmans are one sect of the syncretic cults. They are Hindus, but they have adopted many Muslim practices and beliefs and are special devotees of the shrine of Khwaja Moinuddin Chisti. It is said that Khwaja Moinuddin Chishti formed the Husaini sect. They believed in Adharva-Veda and narrate the story of Hazrat Imam Husain. They observe fast during the Hindu Shivratri and Muslim Ramzan. They give feasts for the Muslim Idd and the Hindu Ramnavami. The men mark their forehead with Tilak, but wear Muslim dress and the women put on the Hindu vermilion dot on their forehead.

It is a fact that Islam in various parts of India demonstrates the strong pull of original religious-cultural beliefs. There is the coexistence of pre-change religious beliefs with the adopted religious beliefs. The prevalence of the concept of 'ritual purity' (as amongst the Bohras) is an example of perfect synthesis of two counter-forces in the Indian religious scenario.[5]

History reveals that the abstract monotheism as preached by the Sufi saints and philosophers not only came to be accepted by the Hindu masses but also formed a bridge between the traditions of Hinduism and Islam. At random, we have discussed briefly the various minor syncretic sects and cults. Still there are a number of minor syncretic sects showing mixture of Hindu and Muslim religious and cultural elements, apart from some major syncretic sects or cults which we will discuss in detail later.

The Khojah Ismailis

Among the Muslim communities of South Asia, the Khojahs constitute a distinctive minority on the basis of both numbers as well as their religious history and beliefs. Believed originally to be members of the Hindu Lohana caste, the vast majority of them today identify themselves as Shi'i Muslims of the Nizari Ismaili persuasion. They regard the Aga Khan to be their religious and spiritual leader *hadir* Imam (present Imam) or Imam-i zaman ('Imam of the time').

According to their belief, the Imam, by virtue of his direct descent from the Prophet Muhammad's daughter Fatima (d. 633) and son-in-law Ali (d. 661), is endowed with special knowledge (*ilm*) to interpret the Quran and provide authoritative guidance on all matters, religious or otherwise. They are referred to by other Muslims as 'Aga Khanis'. The Khojah Ismailis, like their fellow Ismailis in other parts of the world, have been conspicious for stressing the esoteric dimension of their faith over the exoteric. Their religious vocabulary includes terms like *pir, murshid, murid, dhikr, jama at-khana, tariqa,* which resonate with Sufi tradition.

In their understanding of Islam as well as some of their religious practices, the Khojahs have also been strongly influenced by their cultural ancestry. Until recently they understood the Shii Muslim concept of the Imam through a reformist interpretation of the concept of *avatara* from Vaishnava Hinduism. Specifically, they identified the Shii Imam Ali with the long-awaited tenth avatara of the Hindu deity Vishnu, and the religion of Islam as the completion of Vaishnava Hinduism. Through such formulations, members of the community could and did consider themselves simultaneously as true Hindus and true Muslims. Not surprisingly, neither the orthodox Muslim nor Hindu would claim him as a co-religionist.[6]

Many reformist groups, such as the Faraizis and the Wahhabis, assaulted a range of practices among Muslims which they considered as borrowings from Hinduism, and therefore, in their opinion, un-Islamic. Hindu revivalist groups joined the battle on the other side, producing aggressive, propaganda aimed at re-absorbing these 'half-baked' adherents of Islam into their ancestral Hindu tradition.

Earlier, the Khojas participated in several identities simultaneously. Their religious life was 'a unique blend of Hindu and Muslim, as well as Shii and Sunni customs and beliefs'. At the same time, they clearly saw themselves and were perceived by others as a caste closely associated with trade. In fact, tradition claims that the title 'khojah', meaning 'lord, master', was bestowed on converts to Islam by the fifteenth-century preacher-saint Pir Sadr al-Din. It was a replacement for the original Hindu Lohana title 'thakur' or 'thakkar', also meaning 'lord, master', the intent being to bestow some sort of caste status on the new converts who lived in a milieu in which caste was fundamental to defining social status and societal relationships.

In many social customs, the Khojahs followed traditional Indian or Hindu norms, marriages being accompanied by a host of rituals and ceremonies dictated by local custom. Widow remarriage, as in the case of Hindu castes, was a strict taboo. In personal law, including matters of inheritance, which was limited only to males, the community was, according to one scholar, 'caught within the meshes of Hindu customary law'.

Notwithstanding the above, the Khojahs were of course Muslims; the association of trading communities with Islam was not uncommon in the history of Islamic civilisation. Their version of Islam integrated multiple and supposedly 'contradictory' strands. On the one hand, there was a Sunni *mulla* at the masjid, or mosque, at their cemetery in Bombay who conducted the funeral ceremonies, while a Sunni qazi, or judge, presided over the official *nikah* ceremony, at Khojah weddings. However, the Khojahs were clearly not Sunni, for they displayed deep reverence towards Ali, the first Shii Imam, and participated in all the traditional Shii rituals commemorating the martyrdom of Husain and other Imams in the month of Muharram.

Unlike most other Shii groups, however, the Khojahs did not believe in the hidden Imam, for they had living Imams. They venerated the Ismaili Imams in Iran as their leaders, regularly sending tributes to them. They also went to see them as part of a pilgrimage rite considered more significant than going to Mecca.

In terms of their prayers, they recited the traditional *namaz/ salat* only during the two Ids; otherwise they had their own ritual prayer in the Gujarati language, containing a sprinkling of Arabic and Persian phrases, which they recited three times a day. Other rituals practised by them resembled the prayer ritual of the Shaktipanthi Lohanas. They also recited hymn-like poems called *ginans* during religious ceremonies.

Among the literary genres associated with the Ismai'li tradition, the *ginans* of the Khojah communities of South Asia are unique. Composed in several India language and dialects, these hymn-like poems have been strongly influenced by north Indian traditions of folk poetry and piety. They thus represent a distinctive regional strand within a larger corpus of Isma'ili literature that is mostly in Arabic and Persian. Not surprisingly, the *ginans* are markedly different in their style and ethos from the more scholarly Arabic and Persian Isma'ili treatises.

The apparently 'syncretistic' manner in which the *ginans* employ Indian or Hindu mythological and theological concepts to present religious ideas has raised questions about their 'Islamic' character. The courts of colonial British India drew on evidence from these very hymns to determine that the Khojah were indeed Muslims of the Nizari Ismai'li seat.

The *ginans* are of particular interest for the prominent role they play in the religious life of Ismai'li Khojah communities in the Indian subcontinent and elsewhere. Like many genres of Indian devotional poetry, they are intended to be sung in designated *ragas* or melodies. The singing of *ginans* constitutes a prominent item during prayer meetings held every morning and evening in the *jamaat khanas* (halls of congregation).

To sing a *ginan* in the context of Khojah religious practice is to pray. The singing of *ginans* constitutes ritualised worship, a phenomenon generally characteristic of the Indian religious landscape. Participation in *ginan* singing, especially in a large congregation, can have a powerful and sensual impact on individuals, even those who may not fully understand the meanings and the significance of the words they sing. During a particularly melodious *ginan* recitation, it is not uncommon to observe individuals being moved sometimes to the point of tears.

Beyond their role in worship, *ginans* permeate communal and individual life in many ways. At a communal level, functions or meetings, be they religious or secular, frequently begin with a short Quranic recitation followed by one from the *ginans*. Verses from the *ginans* are often cited as proof-texts during sermons, religious discussions, and in religious education materials. Occasionally, for both entertainment and religious edification, special concerts or *ginan mehfils/mushaira* are organised, during which professional and amateur singers recite *ginans* to musical accompaniment.

At a personal and family level, too, *ginans* are used in many different contexts: individual verses can be quoted as proverbs; verses can be recited in homes to bring barkat, spiritual and material blessings; housewives in a usage that stresses the links between the *ginans* and the folk tradition, often recite them while working as lullabies; audio-cassettes with *ginans* sung by popular singers or recordings of *ginan mehfils* can be found in many an Isma'ili home and even in automobiles.

The fact is that the *ginans* enjoy a scriptural status in the Khojah Isma'ili community, for they are commonly perceived as being 'holy' or 'sacred'. Some members of the community declare them to be a 'divine literary corpus'. The *ginans* have been described as 'an unbounded and immeasurable sea of knowledge, a unique storehouse of wisdom, and guidelines for everyday life'. Indeed their function as vehicles for imparting religious teachings and precepts is reflected in the very name, which is derived from the Sanskrit word *jnana*, meaning 'knowledge' or 'sacred wisdom'.

In the community's traditional self-image, the *ginans* originated in medieval times, approximately around the eleventh or twelfth centuries. when they were first composed by Iranian preacher-saints called *pirs*. The *pirs* were sent to north India by Isma'ili Imams from Iran on missions to convert Hindus to Isma'ili Islam and to provide spiritual guidance for the newly created convert communities.

These preacher-saints, in order to overcome cultural and linguistic barriers facing potential converts, composed *ginans* to explain the gist of the *Quran* and Isma'ili Islam to Indian populations in their native language and idioms. According to one community publication, these poetic compositions provided the faithful with an understanding of the 'true meaning' of the *Quran* as well as the true meaning of religion. Another explains that they are living commentaries on the *Quran*, serving to penetrate its 'inner (*batin*) signification'. The *ginans* are, in effect, 'secondary' texts generated in the vernacular to transmit the teachings of 'primary' scripture—the *Quran*—to non-Arabic speaking peoples.

For those who revere them, the *ginans* are sacred since they were uttered by the *pirs*. These preachers were no ordinary missionaries and evangelists; in the community's understanding, they were spiritually enlightened individuals whose religious and spiritual authority the Ismai'li Imams had formally endorsed by bestowing on them the title of *pir*. The *ginans* extol the virtues of love and unquestioning obedience to the *pir* and his teachings, for he is the true guide (*sat guru*) who can guide the faithful on the path of salvation. Since the Imams resided in Iran, the *pirs* became tangible symbols of the Imam's authority with total control over the community and its members. Not surprisingly, the *pirs* stand out in the tradition's history as figures of dominating importance, next only to the Imam. In fact, in many contexts the *ginans* do not always distinguish between the *pir* and the Imam, both being merged in doublets such as *gur-nar* and *pir-shah*, meaning 'guide and lord'.

About the earlier Pirs, nothing much is known. Some knowledge about the later *pirs*, like Pir Shams, Sadr al-Din, and Hasan Kabir al-Din are available. A fourth figure, Imam Shah (d. 1513), about whom we possess somewhat more reliable information, was allegedly the founder of a 'schismatic' movement that resulted in the formation of the Imam-Shahi subsect. Consequently, the Isma'ili Khojah tradition only accords him the status of *sayyid*, a rank inferior to that of *pir*. To these four personalities, who reportedly lived between the twelfth and fifteenth centuries, are attributed the vast majority of *ginans*.

Khojah tradition itself, as well as scholars who have studied the *ginans*, concur that these religious poems began as oral literature and for a considerable period in their history were transmitted orally before being recorded in writings in Khojki, a script peculiar to the community.

Khojki (or Khojaki) is the name of the script used by the Nizari Isma'ilis of the Indian subcontinent to record their religious literature. Originating in Sind, the southern province of modern Pakistan, and commonly used to transcribe several languages including Sindhi, Gujarati, Hindustani, and Persian, the script was in active use within this particular Isma'ili community from at least the sixteenth century, if not earlier. The name 'Khojki' is most likely derived from the word 'khojah'. According to Ismai'li tradition, the fifteenth century *dai* (preacher, missionary), Pir Sadr al-Din, who bestowed this title on new Indian converts to Isma'ili Islam, was also responsible for inventing the Khojki script.

The eighth-century Muslim settlement in lower Sind, have uncovered a 'proto-Nagari' script with characters remarkably similar to those found in modern Khojki. This script, clearly the prototype of Khojki, has been identified as Lohanaki or Lari, the script of the Hindu Lohana community. As it happens, the Lohana community was one of the communities among whom Pir Sadr al-Din (c. 1350–1400) was most active.

Khojki and most of the scripts used for writing Sindhi belong to the Indian scripts that have been classified by Grierson under the 'Landa' or 'clipped' alphabets. They were employed especially by the Hindus of Sind and Punjab for the purpose of commerce. In fact, in Sind, Landa was called Baniyan or Waniko, indicating its use primarily as a mercantile and commercial script. According to the Khojah Isma'ili tradition, the adoption of Khojki script, a 'local' script, was the most likely part of the attempt to make religious literature more accessible by recording it in a script with which the local population had the greatest familiarity.

Salar Masud Ghazi Myan Cult

Popular saint worship appeals more to the lower Muslim castes called *Ajlaf* or common folk. At the *urs* festival and also on each *jummah-raat* (Thursday night) after sunset, *qawwali* singers with their hymns addressed to the specific saint transfer their devotees into a state approaching trance; at times one of them, particularly in the Chishti order, actually falls into a genuine trance begins to dance (*sama*).

Muslims living in the villages, however, often lack basic knowledge of the contents and practice of their religion because they have never been completely alienated from their Hindu or tribal traditions and because they have no standards on which to orientate their beliefs and conduct. Therefore, the folk religion of this social group of Indian Muslims exhibits strong degree traces of pre-Islamic influences. The Meos, who live south of Delhi are a good example of a rural Muslim community with a low degree of Islamisation. The Meos also belong to that group of Muslims that worships Salar Masud Ghazi.

The cult which has grown up around Salar Masud or Ghazi Miyan gives evidence not only of a process of Islamisation having taken place among the North Indian lower castes and of the existence of an Islamic folk religion, but also of the continuity of pre-Islamic and Hindu influences. It is certain that in the course of the Muslim conquest of Indian regions, forced conversions occurred on a some scale. But the majority of indigenous Indian Muslims was probably converted peacefully by wandering *fakirs* and Sufis. Indian temples and sacred places were taken over by Muslims who sometimes converted them into Islamic pilgrim centres. The local, not yet converted, inhabitants continued to visit these places or began to try their luck with newly founded *dargahs*, were consequently converted, or incorporated the Islamic cult into their system of beliefs by identifying the Muslim saint with one of the gods already familiar to them.[7]

The cult of Syed Salar Masud or Ghazi Miyan in Bahraich, a northeastern district in Uttar Pradesh, has been described in various sources. It is said that one Zohra Bibi, blind daughter of a rich merchant of Lucknow visited his grave on pilgrimage. She was cured and out of gratitude decided to construct a *dargah* on the former site of the sun temple in the village Parasi, outside Bahraich.

Salar Masud is worshipped by Hindus and Muslims in North India, Rajasthan, Punjab, Bihar and Bengal. However, the local ceremonies vary considerably. The central festival which draws between 50,000 and 100,000 devotees from all parts of North India takes place on the first Sunday in the month of *Jeth*. The festivities and the bazaar continue over a period of several days. The most important ceremony, the wedding, is performed and one of the more important processions originates in Rudauli, the birthplace of Zohra Bibi, the bride. The local leader of the untouchable sweeper caste has the privilege of carrying the bridal bed *(palang perhi)* to Bahraich. *Hijras* or eunuchs play the part of the parents at the wedding. Other processions bring further presents from Banaras, Jaunpur and

Mirzapur. The generally chosen form is cash for the dowry of the bride. *Charhana Mazar Sharif* is a religious offering or present from the groom to his bride and consists of cash or merchandise.

On the occasion of the *urs* festival, a *mela* or bazaar takes place in the locality where traders from neighbouring villages offer merchandise for sale. The majority of pilgrims is, however made up of those who are looking for help of some kind or the other, and who often offer all their belongings to the *dargah* hoping for relief or cure of illness. These are blind, crippled, lame or leprose, since Salar Masud is particularly known for his power of healing these very infirmities.

There is an imitation of the *dargah* of Bahraich in Banaras which is frequented by the Doms. Here the pilgrims, particularly Dhanuks, a sub-caste of the Doms, hope to be cured of sterility. The Sansiyas, on the other hand, believe Ghazi Miyan to be the king of snakes.

Another form of devotion of Salar Masud is that of the *panch pirs*. The classical *panch pirs* are Shiite, and consist of Muhammad, the Prophet, and his family members—Fatima, Ali, Hasan and Husain. These five names are depicted in Ali's hand on the Muharram standards and in Shiite shrines. The hand recurs in the local cult of *panch pirs*. Among the Hindus, the cult of the Five appears under the name of *panch devata*. In Indian popular usage, a variety of combinations of Muslim *pirs* and Hindu gods is found, each put together by local and individual preferences.

Salar Masud or Ghazi Miyan is very frequently found among the *panch pirs*. The Meos around Delhi, who maintain that they were converted to Islam by Salar Masud, erect such a standard (*nishan*) once a year and celebrate a festival.

In eastern Uttar Pradesh the worship of the *pirs* is also quite widespread, particularly among the lowest Hindu castes. In Banaras are five different versions of the *panch pirs*, but in each case Ghazi Miyan tops the list, a proof of the popularity of the Bahraich legend in the area.

The priests of the cult belong to the drummer caste of Dafali who wander around singing, beating the drum and narrating the story of Ghazi Miyan. These drummers also lead the wedding procession at Bharaich. An iron wire, an abstract from of the standard or hand, wrapped in red cloth and decorated with flowers, represents Ghazi Miyan and is carried by the drummers from house to house. The lowest castes—the Pasis and Chamars—worship Ghazi Miyan and the other four *pirs* in the form of five wooden piles set up in the yard of the house.

The cult surrounding Salar Masud and the *panch pirs* in North India clearly bears influences of Hindu and tribal traditions. It was not only practised by Muslims, but also by a large number of Hindus. Half of the pilgrims coming to Bahraich had been Hindus. Salar Musud was worshipped by Hindus, whose ancestors had suffered heavily at his hands. He explained this attraction of the Hindus of the lower castes with that ever-present fear of everything powerful and their endeavour to pacify this evil by making offerings.

The majority of Ghazi Miyan's and the *panch pirs* devotees are the lower caste Hindus (Doms, Nats, Mirasis) and those converted from the lower castes to Islam (Lal Begis, Julahas, etc.). These groups were essentially tribals who had only only just settled down and begun to take up professions such as musician (*dafali*), sweeper (*doms*), beggar, artist, etc.

Some sub-castes of the Doms identify Lal Beg with Ghazi Miyan. It could further be concluded that Ghazi Miyan (Lal Beg) was regarded by those castes that worship him as their ancestor; other caste ancestors such as Dhanuk and Sansiya, sons of Balmik, gave their names to the castes of Dhanuks and Sansiyas which are partly Muslim.

It is also possible to prove a relation between Balmik and Ghazi Miyan in the case of the mound or anthill. The mound or anthill stands out prominently in the worship of Ghazi Miyan in all the regions (Bengal, Chhota Nagpur, Madhya Pradesh, Uttar Pradesh, Punjab).

The participation of Hindus in the festivities at Bahraich can be explained by another factor. The sources frequently mention that Salar Masud was buried at the original site of a sun or Mahadev temple.

Unlike other Muslim martyrs who are known as malevolent, Salar Masud was benevolent. He possessed the same healing powers as the sun god. Thus, the cult of the sun god was transferred upon him. The fact that the temple at Bahraich was also identified with Mahadev (Shiva) is explained by the absorption of the sun cult by Shaivism. The annual wedding of Salar Masud with Zohra Bibi appears to be un-Islamic. The cult around Salar Masud represents a complex of various traditions of the lower Muslim and Hindu caste in North India which allows us to observe the sequence of its historial development.

Islam, the religion of Salar Masud, as represented by the upper-class Indian Muslims, exhibited and still exhibits a considerable factor of conflict in India, because it has to safeguard itself against such an integration. Muslim society inside Hindu society remained in the diaspora and had to resist such a fusion in order to maintain its identity. It is clear that the folk religion of Islam as represented by saint worship had been integrated into an already existing religious framework by the lower castes so that the latent conflict created by the conversion of members of these castes to Islam was neutralised. This integration prevented social groups from breaking away from the existing order.

The Mira Datar Dargah

The Mira Datar Dargah in Unava has specialised in helping people who are afflicted with madness. The *dargah* dropped—or never developed—all other functions which are usually associated with Muslim shrines. Its only function is the religious guidance of pilgrims who are seeking social and physical well-being; and the religious healing of those afflicted with some kind of psychosis or neurosis. More precisely, it has a reputation for healing those striken by a *bhut*. Already in the last century Mira Datar Dargah was listed in the District *Gazetteer* as an institution being visited by many suffering from epilepsy (India, 1883:128).

The *dargah* attracts 'mad' people from all over India, including Indians from East and South Africa and England. It has the reputation of being a powerful *bhut*-casting institution, the saint's spirit being one of the most powerful exorcists in the country. Mira Datar is a name well-known to the people of the poor quarters of cities like Mumbai, Delhi, Ahmedabad, etc. Mira Datar has a widespread reputation as healer of all kinds of undefinable diseases.[8]

There is one Mira Datar Dargah in Mumbai. The Mumbai *dargah* is more or less a walk-in place, where people cannot stay and nor are they encouraged to do so. Quite different is the *dargah* at Unava. It is a very busy place all day and all the quarters are inhabited. There is another Mira Datar Dargah in Poona (now Pune) which is related to the main *dargah* at Unava in a very interesting manner.

People who come to the *dargah* as patients must have been faced with the problem that something was wrong with them. Caught within so much psychic insecurity and dissatisfaction with courses of treatment, the patient might be taken to a *dargah* or another faith-healing institution by his relatives who act as a therapy managing group. Since the Mira Datar Dargah's special capacity for healing mental illnesses is recognised by all other *dargahs* in north-western India, the patient may be sent to Mira Datar's *dargah* by an official from some other *dargah*.

After entering the *dargah* the patient is received by the *mujawar*, who will attend on him during his stay in the shrine. For the patient he is the mediator of the healing capacity attributed to Mira Datar. The *mujawar* asks the patient first to tell him something about the nature of his disease. He places a red thread into the hand of the patient and recites one verse, appealing to the saint to curse the illness. Patients comprise Hindus and Muslims. There are two similar *dargahs*, one in Ervadi (Tamil Nadu) and another in Mempuram (Kerala) where patients go for relief of metal illness.

The Hindu cult of Ramdeo Pir

Hindus, Jains, Muslims, and Sikhs come to seek Ramdeo's favour in the same way as at the shrine of any other popular deity in India; this god is supposed to cure sterility, paralysis, and business problem. People from higher castes have no scruples now in worshipping him, because in current hagiography he has been accepted as an incarnation of the great god, Vishnu.

Like the mausoleum of a Sufi saint, Ramdeo's temple is often baptised as a *dargah,* while the deity himself is invoked as *pir* (spiritual master among Muslims). Taking into account the popular Hindu deities or saints who have shown, like Ramdeo, certain syncretic features, some writers attribute this Muslim influence to the general atmosphere of the medieval times when there was some kind of understanding between Hindu ascetics and Muslim Sufis. This hypothesis appears to be confirmed by the presence of words taken directly from the Islamic mystical tradition : *dargah, pir,* etc. Speaking generally, traces of Muslim influence on certain Hindu traditions have always been explained in terms of the impact of Sufism. But Islamic elements in the Ramdeo tradition are not limited to the vocabulary; they can be found also in the architecture of these old places of worship and in innumerable legends of which the untouchable Bhambi and the Kamad worshippers of Ramdeo are self-appointed keepers.

The large temple dedicated to Baba Ramdeo is constructed literally inside a Muslim cemetery (*kabristan*) sheltering a Hindu shrine. Also worshipped there, is a number of other tombs (*mazar*) in the court, which are enclosed by a boundary wall. The characteristic cylindric 'bump' on them would suggest they are men's tombs.

In the main shrine, the sacred image is in Ramdeo's supposed tomb, a tomb which is currently referred to as *samadhi.* Like the tombs by its side, where members of his family and some other disciples are buried, Ramdeo's tomb is covered with an ornamental sheet, resembling those which adorn the tombs of Sufi saints. No inscription is found there except a verse from the *Quran* engraved on one of these tombs.

The shape of Ramdeo's tomb does not at all resemble a *samadhi,* the funereal monument of a Hindu ascetic.

The untouchable religious chiefs, the Kamads, who were originally Bhambis, but now form a distinct caste; second, the *pirs,* most of whom are Bhambis, sometimes *malis* (gardeners), but rarely Rajputs or members of other Hindu castes.

There are principal *gaddis* and secondary *gaddis,* whose chiefs are called *pirs.* They have, under their dependence, a certain number of villages, where Ramdeo's worshippers (mostly Bhambis) are regrouped under the aegis of the Kamads (also called Kamadiya, Kamadia Pir, Kamadiya Jogi). The Kamads define themselves as householder ascetics.

This mysterious religious order, which so many Kamads and Bhambis take pains to define, could have been founded by an ambiguous person, whom they sometimes call Shams Pir, with his Muslim name, and sometimes Samas Rishi, in order to integrate him into a Hindu context.

The oral tradition of the Kamads and the Bhambis affirms that Shams Pir came to this region also and converted many people and, in his preachings, Islamic ideas were interpreted in a Hindu context. The *julahas* (Muslim weavers) and *niyariyas* (ancient godsmiths/silversmiths who were originally Hindus from Multan) of Rajasthan were converted to the Isma'ili faith much earlier and are now absorbed by the local community of or Sunnis. They claim that Shams worked many miracles in this region, converted the untouchable Bhambis, and spread his message 'up to the bank of the Ganges'.

But it is to Shams Pir of Multan and therefore to the Isma'ili Nizaris that the Bhambis and Kamads link their particular religious tradition. According to the oral sources of the untouchables, Shams should have been the guru of Ramdeo's paternal grandfather, Ransi Tanwar, who was also a *pir*, Ransi settled at Naraina.

The majority of the converts to the Isma'ili faith were untouchable, traditionally worshippers of the Goddess and of Shiva (but who could not enter the great Brahmanic temples). After conversion they developed the cult of the Divine through these symbols.

Sadr-al-din is also considered the founder of the local Isma'ili congregation, *jama*, which was conducted by two religious functionaries : the Mukhi and his assistant the Kamadiya. The latter name naturally recalls the Kamad or Kamadiya who is, in Rajasthan, the ascetic of the Bhambis and the priest of Ramdeo's cult. Kamadiya perhaps refers to the ancient Shaiva ascetics, who were later converted to the Nizari Isma'ili faith.

At the time when Ramdeo flourished (end of fourteenth, beginning of the fifteenth century), the Imam of the Nizaris lived in Persia, far from the Indian community. This state of affairs continued till the first Agha Khan came to India around 1840.

A famous Rajasthani saying goes thus, 'Ramdeo found only pariahs,' that is to say he succeeded in covering only untouchables. Traditionally, as worshippers of the goddess Hinglaj and Shiva, they practised tantric rites. It is believed that most of the untouchable *pirs* at the Nizari centres recognised Ramdeo's divinity sooner or later and snapped their ties with the Imams of Persia. Ramdeo was, thus, worshipped as a Hindu god in the main gaddis, shrines, as well as in villages where the Kamads were heads of local communities.

Ramdeo has promised that he will come at the end of our cosmic age in the form of *nikalank avatara*, the immaculate incarnation; he shall come particularly to save the pariahs, oppressed so long in Brahmanical society, install a reign of justice and peace, and reconcile Hindus and Muslims. He is, therefore, at the same time, the Mahdi of the Shi'as and the Kalki of the Hindus. We have a striking example here of the confluence of the two different religious currents.

The Madari Sufi Brotherhood

The Madaris are a group widely acknowledged to be part of a shared religious tradition in India. They are street performers who do magic tricks, or walk around with monkeys, bears, or snakes. However, the tradition of the Madaris has been traced back to Badi-ud-Din Shah Madar, who was a Syrian Sufi of the fifteenth century. According to the Sufi tradition, Shah Madar came to India after travelling for many years in the Arabian Peninsula. There, he founded the Sufi brotherhood of the Madaris and settled in Makanpur, a village 60 km north-east of Kanpur. He died around 1436. His tomb, or *dargah*, is venerated by thousands of people to this very day.[9]

They are called by the terms, *be-shar* and 'unorthodox', 'syncretic', and the Mughal prince, Dara Shikoh calls them *ajlaf*, a term that is indicative of the low class of the Madaris.

The term *be-shar,* for example, is translated as behaviour not according to the *Shariat*. Mostly, groups of wandering dervishes from the time of the Delhi Sultanate are classified as such. The opposite category is *ba-shar*—behaviour according to the *Shariat*.

It is believed that Shah Madar, as he was called, was a native of Aleppo in Syria. In his spiritual genealogy he is connected to Abu Yazid Bistami (d.874), but he is regarded as *an uwaisi* too, which indicates a direct guidance through the spirit of the prophet.

Shah Madar came to India at a time when Delhi had been ravaged by Timur and many of its inhabitants had migrated to other places. Consequently, towns east of Delhi, like Kalpi and Jaunpur, became centres of Islamic culture and learning, as independent rulers welcomed scholars, Sufis and artisans.

Shah Madar had shown a keen interest in the physiological concepts of Yogis and, as a result, he incorporated in his own rituals the practice of holding one's breath. Interestingly, the inclusion of the practices of Hindu ascetics seems to have been a widely acknowledged norm during the course of the fifteenth century.

The importance of the saint and his shrine was unquestioned. Two mosques have been built at the *dargah* and land endowments have been granted by various rulers; Aurangzeb even visited it. The mystic teachings of Shah Madar have had a wide dissemination and they have been incorporated at Sufi centres like Kakori, Laharpur and Salon.

Today, the Madaris are active in several areas of Gujarat, Rajasthan, Maharashtra, Madhya Pradesh, Uttar Pradesh, Bihar, Hyderabad and Kolkata. Makanpur in Uttar Pradesh is undoubtedly the centre of the Madari brotherhood today. Around 250 families live there, who consider themselves to be the descendants of the nephews of Shah Madar. These Madaris are *sayyids,* as they trace the genealogy of Shah Madar to the Propher Mohammed.

The system of mystical teaching, which revolves around Shah Madar, is commonly handed down orally in the *pir-i muridi* tradition, but the basic features of the saint's life and his powers are recounted even by children in Makanpur. The *dargah* in Makanpur is a major religious centre in the region and its popularity has been undiminished through the centuries. Badauni writes about a visit during the reign of Akbar.

The ritual practice at the *dargah* follows a cyclical rhythm. There are monthly *dhikr* ceremonies in commemoration of the saint and, twice a year, a major *ghusl* (washing of the tomb and changing of the *chadars*) is performed. However, the most important festival is certainly the *urs*, which is celebrated during Jumada ul-Awwal. The second major festival is celebrated during Basant Panchami. The *mela* is held for eighteen days, but during the three main days, the *dargah* attracts many Hindu pilgrims. These pilgrims perform the *mundan* ceremony, the first cutting of the hair of a child. The whole *dargah* is full of hair of little children at this time. During the night, *dhikr* ceremonies are held, which are attended by Hindus as well as Muslims.

The *dargah* offers space for rituals of the other religious community as well. However, there is no attempt to mix the two religions. It is the comprehension of the concept of the Sufi which is important here for an understanding of this phenomenon. Since one name of God is *rabb ul-alimin,* the lord of the universe and of all creations, the proper friend of God does not differentiate between human beings on the grounds of their religious creeds. Hindus, thus, are always welcomed as lay followers by Sufi *pirs* who, besides teaching, give guidance in daily matters or use their religious knowledge for healing purposes.

The Imamshahis of Gujarat

The main shrine at Pirana, a village located near Ahmedabad in Gujarat, known as Imam Shah Bawa Rauza, is one of the many Muslim sacred spots of South Asia that attracts devotees of various creeds. Muslims and Hindus belonging to different castes and religious traditions freely mix within the precincts of the *dargah,* particularly during the annual *urs* festival during Muharram. The shrine thus functions as an open, shared space transcending communal barriers, very much like the famous Ajmer *dargah* dedicated to the Sufi saint, Muinuddin Chishti.

The shrine is not only a centre of Sufi and popular piety; it is also the main seat of a particular sectarian tradition referred to as Imamshahi or Satpanth, the followers of which are said to number about nine lakh.[10]

The interest of the *Satpanthis* or ex-*Satpanthis* in the shrine is of a totally different nature from that of people seeking non-sectarian devotion. Non-sectarian devotion, which has a universal character should be clearly distinguished from the beliefs and practices of the *Satpanthis.*

The 'composite' nature of the Imamshahi tradition has been largely misunderstood. Imam Shah is portrayed as a tolerant Sufi saint of the fifteenth century who, 'fed up with Islamic rigidities', created a sect where elements drawn from various Hindu traditions were associated with Sufi Islamic beliefs and practices. In this way, he is supposed to have attracted both Muslim and Hindu followers without demanding a formal conversion from the latter. The 'official' division of the *Satpanthis* into Hindus (who make up about 85 per cent of the sect, and of whom the *Patidars* constitute 75 per cent) and Muslims has been made along these lines.

The *Satpanth* is actually an offshoot of South Asian Nizari Ismailism—itself a branch of Shiite Islam—which was also, till recently, referred to as *Satpanth* and whose members are now mainly known as *Agakhani Khojas.* Some groups of Imamshahis continue to perform the same rituals *(gat-pat)* and share the same literature *(ginans)* as the 'mainstream' Agakhani Nizaris.

It is observed that the syncretism of some south-Asian Nizari compositions 'is less an amalgam that results from a compromise reached between two different religious traditions than a conscious, clever and creative strategy to effect a smooth process of conversion'. The syncretic tradition has been the necessary concomitant of the process of Islamisation rather than its culmination.

The Imamshahi Satpanthi configuration, however, can be termed 'liminal', provided one does not forget that such a categorisation implies a particular perspective. By examining in detail the complex history and the different systems of philosophy developed by the Ismailis, one can surmise that three main factors influenced the origion of the satpanth, the 'acculturated' Indic form of Nizarism that was referred to in Arabic as *sirat-e mustaqim.*

In reality, a careful study of the old *Fatimid dawa* or mission work shows that this 'strategy' of conversion had different and also deeper implications. Eventually, religious dissimulation, referred to as *taqiyya*, a major feature of Shiism, was also responsible for the fact that the *Satpanth*, whether 'mainstream' or Imamshahi could appear, according to the context, as a Sunni Sufi movement or as a Hindu tradition similar to the numerous local sectarian movements or *panths* prevalent in medieval South Asia.

The Nizaris had to resort to *taqiyya* to protect themselves from the persecution of the Sunni rulers and of their ulema who sought to either convert or exterminate them. Those who chose to love in the guise of 'orthodox' Sufis openly interacted with the various local *tariqas*, at times even taking formal initiation into these orders, and remained so inconspicuous that to this day many people regard some famous Ismaili Pirs as 'Sufi shaikhs of Sunni Persuasion'.

Among the Imamshahi followers, the sayyids who claimed to be the descendants of Imam Shah, along with some other converted communities, were gradualy led to adopt a stricter Sunni or Shia identity.

A prominent leader of the Imamshahi mainstream community, Sayyid Ahmad Ali Khaki had himself adopted an outwardly Sunni identity, and started to publish a series of pamphlets and edited a number of Imamshahi sacred texts, among which was the ritual prayer a variant of the Nizari Khoja *du'a* to which he gave a new 'Hinduised' title : *Yagya vidhi.* The text itself, which remained largely unchanged beginning with the traditional *Bism'illah* invocation, was provided with extensive footnotes explaining the 'Hindu' meaning of Muslim terms. He was so successful in stressing the Vedic equivalents of Islamic concepts that in 1931 the Hindu Mahasabha declared that the 'Satpanth' should be cleared of any suspicion as it was undoubtedly a 'Vedic' tradition.

The Sayyids replied that their ancestor Imam Shah was a Muslim by birth and had always lived as a Muslim, performing *namaz, roza* etc., he was never a Hindu saint. His descendants are, therefore obviously Muslims and not *Satpanthis*. So why should they preach the *Satpanth*. The Sayyids argued that they were entitled to certain rights and privileges in the shrine as the Muslim descendants of Imam Shah whose sacred mausoleum it was, and not as *Satpanthis*. Actually, the Sayyids stressed their Muslim identity by listing the different dues according to the tasks usually performed by them—*fatiha, bismillah*, etc.,—rituals that, according to them, proved their Islamic identity beyond doubt. But this was questioned by the *Satpanthi Patidars* who claimed that earlier, the Sayyids performed 'puja like the Brahmans', conducting the ceremonies of *ghat-pat* which included the use of a vessel *(kalash, ghat)* and of consecrated water.

The Sayyids describe the Pirana tradition : 'Pir-Imam Shah established a religious denomination (order or school of thought) which became popular in the state of Gujarat as Satpanth (the correct path). Consequently, several religious right practices, observances and functions predominantly Muslim came to be established which have been customarily performed by Satpanthis for more than five centuries and which have become an integral part of their religion'.

While it can be proved that initially, the Imamshahi Satpanth was an offshoot of Nizari Ismailis, itself an undoubtedly Muslim tradition, it is not difficult to show that this branch of Islam took a distinctive character in the subcontinent, that gave it–from a particular perspective–a 'syncretistic' appearance, but also made it distinctive as 'heterodox' to other dominant Muslim groups.

The Imamshahi 'Hindu' *murids,* having recently declared their allegiance to the Aga Khan, have joined the Ismaili Nizari mainstream (which has itself reformed considerably to come closer to the Sunni mainstream) but continue with their earlier Gupti customs. They have been permitted by the Imam to worship in separate *jamats* and when asked about their identity, generally reply : 'We are both Hindus and Muslims—Hindus by custom and Muslims by religion.'

These Nizari Ismailis have been said to have separated owing to the fact that, from a certain period onward, they started to recognise a line of Imams that is different from the one accepted by the mainstream Agakhani Khojas.

The Muslim Bhartrhari Jogis of Gorakhpur

The Muslim Bhartrhari *jogis* of Gorakhpur lead family lives while adhering to the two apparently opposed faiths, Shaivism and Islam. As Muslims, these *jogis* observe the five basic Islamic duties, observe Muslim festivals and are buried. At the same time, as Gorakhnathi *jogis*, they are supposed to accept the authority of the local Gorakhnathi temple.

The city of Gorakhpur derives its name from the neighbouring Gorakhnath monastery, which is a centre of Shaiva Naths. This monastery is the most important Kanphata sanctuary in north India, even though the branches of the Nath sect had great influence in Punjab, Rajasthan, and Bengal. As compared to other cities of north India, Islam came to Gorakhpur quite late. The best known and the most numerous among them were weavers, *julahas*, and it is from this caste specially that the Bhartrhari *jogis* come.

The historical connection between the Nath sect and the Muslim Sufis has been noted. The Gorakhnathis believed that their saint was Prophet Muhammad's spiritual guru. This saint is also believed to have taught his disciple, Guga, the basic tenets of Islamic faith. In the Gorakhpur monastery, one of the many wall paintings is dedicated to Gorakhnath's disciple, Ratan Nath, who was honoured as a Nath in Nepal. Ratan Nath is supposed to have visited Afghanistan and Mecca. Bhartrhari *jogis*, who hold the fourth position in the hierarchy of the twelve original Nathpanths, owe their name to Bhartrhari. The Bhartrhari *jogis* are perhaps the most Islamised Gorakhpanthis and they trace their origin to Mainath, an orphan who was adopted by Meo Muslims and who later became Gorakhnath's disciple.[11]

For nine months of the year these *jogis* live in their village homes and lead ordinary lives. They are mainly weavers and cultivators; many are landless. Some of them work as domestic servants. But they have a special function in the village. As professional musicians and disciples of Gorakhnath, they are called upon to play the sarangi and to sing occasionally in honour of this god. As Muslim *fakirs*, they have a number of semi-sacred and semi-religious functions; they are keepers of village graveyards and small shrines, and they receive the bedding and the clothes of the dead. They receive gifts on Eid.

However, every year when they are no longer needed on the farms, these householders leave their homes and become itinerant renunciants. They put on the ochre dress of *jogis*, and carry with them the beggar's beg *(jholi)*, a pair of tongs *(chimta)*, the pilgrim's baton, the turban, and a blanket *(gudri)*. Their itinerary, which lasts for about two months, takes them to places sacred to Naths, to the tombs of Muslim saints, and to 'mixed' shrines like those in Chunar and Biharsharif. These 'renunciants' start with a homage to Bhartrhari's spiritual master Jalandharipa, at his shrine in Badhal Ganj. Then some of them go to the Gorakhpur monastery.

Gorakh ka Tila in Banaras is often the final halt of these *jogis*, before they return to Gorakhpur. At the shrines they sing the legends of Gorakhnath and his disciples, in Bhojpuri mixed with Hindi, Urdu, and Awadhi. These narratives have two functions: sometimes they are used for edification, and sometimes as an accompaniment to the therapy of persons in trance.

The presence of these Muslim *jogis*, who specialise in reciting Shaiva Nath texts has been noted in Punjab. Unlike the Giri sanyasis of central Nepal, these *jogis* cannot be related to the Shaiva tradition either through their initiation, or through the manner in which their bodies are disposed of. They are of course buried (not cremated) although so are Hindu renunciants.

In the villages, the Bhartrhari *jogis* are asked to sing during the grand Shaiya festival as well as during several domestic ceremonies. On Mahashivaratri day, they sing in honour of Gorakhnath, while his feet and those of Matsyendranath are being washed. During marriages, the *jogis* sing 'Shiva's marriage song'. When somebody dies, they are called to sing *nirgun* (mystical songs which recall the vanity of the world and exhort renunciation).

The Bhartrhari *jogis*, who are Muslims, have borrowed two ideas—reincarnation and purity–from the Hindu milieu of caste and sect. As a Muslim caste, the Bhartrhari *jogis* have a very ambiguous relationship with the monastic organisation of the Naths. As weavers, these *jogis* occupy a relatively higher position in the caste hierarchy of Indian Muslims. Coming after the Ashraf and the Rajput Muslims, they top the list of the service class.

The Bhartrhari *jogis* held a key position in the Middle Ages, when they easily benefited from the patronage of small Rajput and Muslim princes on account of their double affiliation and their status as itinerant singers.

The Sidi Sect

Gujarat is the state where different religious communities have settled side by side for centuries. High and low Hindu castes interacted on various levels of power and dominance with high and low Muslim *jamat* (kinship associations), Jain communities, Parsis and Christians. Rarely did these communities co-exist in a state of hermetical enclosure. Rather, religious pluralism manifested itself through the historical proliferation of context-bound practices that fostered communication across socio-religious boundaries.

The name 'Sidi' refers to people whose ancestors have immigrated from East Africa as slaves, seamen or traders. Overtime, a Sidi kinship network emerged in Gujarat which is collectively referred to as *jamat*. The social network of the *jamat* includes both ordinary Sidis and professional *fakirs*. Situated at the margins of the world of Sunni Muslims, Sidi *fakirs* administer tasks that contribute to the social regeneration of a regional social milieu at the lower end of the Muslim society. The Sidi and most of their clients belong to the class of have-nots—no money, no high status descent, and no political power.

The specific Sidi cult of Sufi saint veneration enjoys great regional popularity especially amongst the poorer sections of the population. In the Sidi world, religion is understood as an important part of social life—complementing the mundane world. In this sense, religion refers primarily to actions and interactions within established social relationships. Strategies of ritualisation are closely embedded in the overall fabric of socio-economic life.[12]

The network of the Sidi *jamat* extends from towns in south and mainland Gujarat to Saurashtra and Kutch and also includes a few villages. In almost every town in Gujarat, at least two or three Sidi houses are crammed in between the houses of craftsmen, servants, workers and other inhabitants of urban lower class quarters and shanty towns. Mirroring regional population patterns, Sidis not only live in Muslim but more often in mixed neighbourhoods composed of lower caste Hindus, adivasis, and Muslim workers. Most Sidi families are engaged in a continuous struggle for making ends meet. Their precarious economic situation is circumscribed by poverty, little education and lack of land or other means of production to secure a regular basis of income. People find employment as domestic servants or work on a contract basis for traders in local handicraft productions. Both men and women are employed by members from all the major religious communities (Hindu, Muslim, Jain, Paris). In villages, some Sidi may own small plots of land while others work as a day labourers.

In spite of their marginal presence in terms of number and economic achievement, in their immediate surroundings Sidis are quite famous. Everywhere they are called *Badshah loko* (king people) which has also became a surname of some families. Sidi Badshah are highly reputed for their ability to joke and make fun as well as for their commanding powers over the darker forces of the universe such as evil spirits and demons. It is these qualities that draw members of diverse social backgrounds to their cult and make them visit one of the shrines without which no Sidi settlement is complete. Indeed, a salient feature of the world of the Sidi is the presence of a shrine for an ancestor saint *(kuldada or kuldadi)* in every neighbourhood, however small it may be. Varying in size, Sidi shrines provide ritual arenas both for the performative affirmation of a collective Sidi identity as well as for ritualised communication between actors across social and religious boundaries.

In the first sense, shrines are conceptualised as resting places for consecrated male and female ancestors who are said to have led the Sidis from Africa to Gujarat. At the annually held saint's day rituals *(urs)* that are organised by *fakirs* and attended by the members of kinship networks of the local *jamat*, the ancestor-saints are commemorated. Their journeys, supernatural powers, and emotions are enacted and spiritual bonds between the living and the dead are reaffirmed. The climax of Sidi *urs*—rituals consists in the 'play' (*knel*)—of the ancestors with their Sidi descendants in possession dances referred to as *goma* or *dammal*.

In the second sense, Sidi shrines are places of holy Muslim men, and women imbued with beneficial powers that purify, regenerate and heal individuals afflicted with misfortune of various sorts. Smaller shrines are usually visited by people from the neighbourhood, but the larger ones may attract a regional following. This is particularly the case at the largest shrine in south Gujarat—the conceptual centre of the cult where the principal ancestor-saints are buried. This shrine represents a nodal point of a translocal network of the Sidi *jamat* and a mixed clientele of believers referred to after the name of the eldest saint as *bavagorvale*.

In the contemporary context of the cult, members of Parsi and Memon communities act as prominent patrons of Sidi ancestor-saints, while the main shrine as well as many of the smaller *dargahs* had been donated by local Rajput chiefs and kings in the past. Another mundane context of interaction consists of the urban neighbourhoods in which Sidi houses are located, Muslim or mixed, from which a large part of the less well-to-do cult followers are drawn to the regional shrine in South Gujarat. Neighbourhood shrines serve as local satellites attracting actual and potential clients for the main shrine. Thus, besides Muslims, members of pastoralist castes such as Rabaris from Kutch, low-caste Hindus and Bhils (Adivasi) from South Gujarat were also drawn to the Sidi saints. The shrines in South Gujarat were also drawn to the Sidi saints. The shrine in South Gujarat may be said to have been something like a 'cosmopolitan' centre of the lower classes.

Moreover, the shrine marks a fuzzy zone in which shifts of meanings from non-ritual to ritual take place. In contrast to their dominated position at workplaces or the marginal role of Sidi families in urban neighbourhoods, the *dargah* provides a space controlled by Sidi ritual agents or *fakirs*. Unlike most other Sufi orders, the Sidi *fakir* organisation is not restricted to men but includes women as well. The gendered universe of dead ancestor-saints is mirrored on a practical level by men and women *fakirs*. Those who are involved in the ritual organisation of a shrine are referred to as *mujavar* (caretakers of shrine). At the main *dargah* in South Gujarat, men take care of the male saint's tombs (Bava Gor, Bava Habash) whereas women look after the tomb of the equally important female saint (Mai Mishra).

The symbolic construction of the ancestor-saints contain references to and re-interpretations of the broken history of Sidi slaves and they reflect the process of acculturation of former Africans in Gujarat. In their images, multiple strata of identity merge : being descendants of Hazrat Bilal, the famous black companion of the Prophet Mohammad, the Sidi see themselves as firmly embedded in the wider religious community of Muslim believers.

The shrine in South Gujarat accommodates the principal ancestor saints of the Sidi *jamat*. Sidi saints simultaneously guard the boundaries of the social order and protect those who transgress them; they represent Islamic piety but demand for their veneration playfulness and fun instead of praying and seriousness. They simultaneously promise the fulfilment of desire, the protection of the poor and the suffering, control over spirits and demons and the power to reveal justice.

Saint's day or *urs*-rituals–held at the main shrine in South Gujarat are attended by families from all parts of Gujarat. While shrine followers from different religious communities may participate as spectators, *urs*-rituals are actually engaged with mainly by members of the Sidi *jamat*, thereby confirming their collective identity in terms of kinship relationships, habitual dispositions and ritual powers.

At the shrine, Sidi ritual agents (*mujawar*) guard the threshold that separates the sphere of power and influence of the saints from non-ritual space. Since the shrine in South Gujarat is one of the few Sidi *dargahs* that is not situated in an urban but in a rural context, the non-ritual surroundings in this case of jungle, i.e. the wilderness as the ultimate abode of spirits.

The Hindus and Bhils may find the power Sidi saints command over spirits their most attractive feature. Different conceptualisations are accompanied by different practices. Given the diversity of the cult followers' conceptualisations, tolerance according to Sidi notions consists in respecting other people's ways of doing things. The most basic difference between Hindu and Muslim followers consists in the treatment of blessed substances that are distributed to supplicants by Sidi *fakirs* stationed at the tombs. Ash from a holy fire kept in the name of the eldest brother-saint and rose petals blessed by the contact with a saintly tomb are conceived as carriers of saintly qualities Muslim followers are expected to orally consume the ash, whereas Hindus put it on their foreheads.

On the level of personal experience and motives, however, distinctions of religious backgrounds disappear. Issues of everyday life such as success in business or school, a good marriage match for son/daughter, or marital fertility are the common and most basic matters for which the protective support of Sidi saints are sought from supplicants of all communities. The same applies to existential and moral predicaments for which relief is sought at the Sidi shrine. Malevolent spirits afflict people across religious boundaries. Malevolent spirit possession, theft or adultery are occurrences located in individual actions that are seen as disturbing in any socio-religious community. Aggressive and respectless behaviour towards superiors such as it is often caused by spirits, or violations of property and marital claims are equally experienced as morally disruptive in Hindu, Muslim and other communities.

Throughout the year, Sidi families travel to an *urs* held at a regional Sayyid shrine. By singing and dancing, Sidi and other *fakirs* introduce carnevalesque elements into an *urs* celebration.

The *urs* rituals at this shrine are orchestrated by different actors. These are : Sayyid, especially the ritual head of the shrine *(sajjada nishin)* who is also the living representative of the *pir* (saint), and his relatives and their special guests; Rifai *fakirs;* Sidi *fakirs;* crowds of Muslim, Hindu and other lay followers. During the three-day-ritual which is designed to celebrate the liminality of the *pir* in his grave, each category of actors moves between the unmarked role of spectator and a marked role of a performer at different stages of the ritual process. Thus, the main performances of the ritual head of the shrine *(sajjada nishin)* consist in leading the procession of shrine followers around the shrine and culminate in purifying the tomb with sandalwood paste.

Being firmly embedded within the wider field of Sufism, the Sidi cult provides a shared space for the profession of faith based on individual choice and for making experiences that transform and comment upon the everyday world.

The version of Muslim religiosity advocated by the Sidi cult introduces different standards of piety that in addition to respecting the teachings of the *Quran* allow for the inclusion of a host of local and popular practices. Sufi-Sidi religiosity is directed primarily at subjective needs and experiences.

The Pranami Sect

Mahamati Prannath was the founder of this sect. His disciples are known as *momins* and *sunder saths*. The Holy Book, he laid down, should be considered as the spiritual body of the Guru containing his religious message and the only object of worship. The sacred text of the followers of Mahatma Prannath contains indigenous Hindu as well as Muslim elements. The only object of worship in the shrine is the sacred book, the *Qulzam Swarup.* He emphasised the importance of a householder's life and told his followers to work in order to earn their livelihood rather than to beg in the name of religion.[13]

Apart from the daily routine, with generally two main services each day, morning and evening, (at some places worship is done five times) with the recitation of some parts of the *Qulzam Swarup* and the singing of hymns, special occasions and periods of the years are kept for the uninterrupted recitation of the entire scripture (like the Sikh *akhand path*), which is referred to as *parayana*.

The anniversary of Prannath's death or of some other Pranami saint is celebrated with solemnity, like the *urs* festival of Muslim saints, and vegetarian food is cooked to feed the members of the community as well as occasional visitors regardless of their religious affiliation, caste or social status. This institution is known as *langar*—a term which is used in the Sufi and Sikh traditions to refer to the same. Pranami men and women traditionally cover their head before entering a shrine—a custom which is tending to disappear among modern devotees. Meditation is also practised and is known as *chitwani*. The followers of Prannath often bear a sacred necklace made of 108 sandalwood beads, and greet each other with the words *pranam* (salutation) from which the name of the sect is said to be derived. The followers of Prannath's religion must abstain from meat and fish, tobacco, *paan* and drugs.

Besides the celebration of some Hindu festivals, such as Holi, Diwali and Raksha Bandhan, the most important function for the Pranamis is held at Panna during Sharad Purnima (the full moon of the lunar month dedicated to ancestors) sometimes referred to as *jhilna* (a term generally used for the ceremonial washing a Muslim saint's grave) or *garba*, as this traditional dance is performed on that occasion. Like the tombs of Sufi and other Muslim saints and martyrs, Prannath's grave is then ritually washed and anointed with sandal paste. After death, some Pranamis are buried, generally according to the Islamic ritual, in the recumbent position. They call this custom 'taking *samadhi*' (the usual way of burying Hindu ascetics in the sitting position).

He is said to have discovered that the inner meaning of Islam was identical with the spiritual message of Hinduism. It is said that his travels to Arabia and Persia had enabled him to study Islam in its various aspects.

The influence of Sufism, we should add, with the aim of 'adjusting' its world view to the Hindu environment during Muslim rule, has sometimes also been perceived as a response or reaction of Hindus aimed at protecting their dharma against allegedly forced mass conversions and it is often invoked to account for the presence of Islamic elements in a number of Sant and Bhakti traditions.

Some Pranamis would emphasise the fact that Mahatma Prannath's main concern was to show the unity of Hinduism and Islam, as well as of all other religions that were represented at that time in the subcontinent and 'make peace' with the Muslim rulers, and that would be the reason why he would have given so much importance to mystical Islam.

In other Pranami sacred texts one can also find Vedantic ideas, but there is no denying that the Islamic elements, words and concepts largely prevail over the rest. More often, Hindu terms rather appear as an attempt to find the best equivalents of Islamic concepts that find no place in the Hindu philosophical heritage.

It is mentioned that the Pranamis are referred to by various names such as Dhamis Pranamis and Qayamatis. In the Pranami tradition, emphasis is constantly placed on the inner aspect of religion (as opposed to external forms of worship and the literal interpretation of the sacred texts). In the sacred book, a section of the book is entitled *mizan*. The word *tartam* (Sanskrit: *taratamya*), used to refer to the basic *mantra* which is the key to real esoteric and spiritual knowledge and is so essential in the Pranami *sampraday*, can be translated as 'sequence', 'harmony', 'gradation', 'compatibility of values', and may well be an Indic equivalent of the Arabic term *mizan*. The fact is that there is the constant use of equivalencies between Hindu/indigenous and Islamic concepts and terminology.

Prannath's Hindu title *Vijayabhinand Nishkalank Buddh Avatar* suggests very strong evidence of possible Satpanthi Nizari influence on him. Many Pranamis believe that the principal mission of the founder of their community was precisely to fight against the tyranny of communal labels, bringing people from different communities together in common worship of and service to God. Most Pranamis are to be found in Gujarat, Rajasthan, Punjab, Haryana, Uttar Pradesh and Madhya Pradesh as well as abroad. A study of the Pranami *sampraday* can help us solve a number of issues related to the history of Hindu–Muslim interaction and to the role this relationship has played in the past.

Shared Hindu–Muslim Traditions in Karnataka

Karnataka came under various Muslim dynasties, often at loggerheads with their Hindu neighbours as well as with the Muslim emperors of Delhi. These included the Bahmanis, the Adil Shahis of Bijapur, the Barid Shahis of Bidar and the Qutb Shahis of Golconda. They were later followed by the Mughals in the seventeenth century and then by the Nizams of Hyderabad in the eighteenth century.

It was principally through the agency of the Sufis that Islam spread in Karnataka. Using local motifs and idioms, the Sufis were able to exercise a powerful appeal, making numerous converts to a form of Islam heavily coloured by local influences. In addition, they attracted a large number of Hindus as well, owing principally to their charisma and the widespread belief in their powers as intermediaries with God. Consequently, the traditions that developed around the figures of many of these Sufis came to be shared by Hindus and Muslims alike.

Living together for centuries, many Hindus and Muslims in northern Karnataka inevitably came to share, to a considerable extent, a common cultural world. At the level of the political elite, a shared Indo–Persian culture emerged, to which both Hindus and Muslims made rich contributions. It was in the Deccan that Dakhini Hindi, which was to become the lingua franca of the most educated north Indians in the nineteenth and early twentieth century, first emerged. At the local level, although they maintained a sense of a separate identity, Hindus and Muslims often worshipped together at shrines of Sufi saints (*dargahs*). Many Muslims were but nominal and recent converts to Islam, and as such continued to practise several customs associated with their pre-Islamic past which they shared with their Hindu neighbours, particularly in matters of domestic rituals.[14]

The widespread veneration of Muslim holy figures among Hindus is a phenomenon that is common to almost all parts of

India. Sufi saints, seen as powerful beings capable of performing miracles, healing the ill, granting children to barren women, providing a job to the unemployed, averting the evil eye and so on, are widely propitiated as *devtas* or gods by Hindus, who see them as part of their vast pantheon of deities. The cults of the Muslim saints are particularly popular among the 'low' caste Hindus in rural areas. Even today in several places, 'untouchables' and other 'low' caste people are denied access to Hindu temples, and the shrines of Muslim saints are often the only places of worship which they could freely enter. Even today, 'low'-caste Hindus vastly outnumber Muslims at many *dargahs*.

For many Hindus, these Muslim figures are incarnations *(avatars)* of one or the other Hindu god, and hence, they are often called by Hindu names and incorporated as Hindu religious figures into the local set of deities. It appears that Muslim custodians of the shrines of these figures freely welcomed Hindus to worship therein, and some even popularised stories of their association with Hindu deities in order to win local support and even possibly as a means to preach Islam to them in an idiom and language with which they were familiar. Hence, as a result of Hindus and Muslims worshipping at common shrines and venerating common religious figures, local traditions evolved centred on what were undoubtedly Muslim figures, but who, with the passage of time, became transformed into figures with a dual identity, seen in a different way by their Hindu and Muslim followers.

The following are details of some popular, shared Hindu–Muslim shrines in Karnataka, where syncretic elements are highly visible in the observation of religious and customary practices.

Baba Buddhan Dada Hayat, Chikmagalur

The *dargah* of Baba Buddhan in Chikmagalur is one of the oldest Sufi shrines in all of South India. Baba Buddhan is also known as Dada Hayat, Mardan-e-Ghayb and Abdul Aziz Makki by Muslims and as Dattatreya by local Hindus.

The shrine was referred to as the Sri Dattatreya Swami Baba Buddhan Peetha. Baba Buddhan is said to have crusaded against powerful landlords (*palegars*), oppression of the poor, putting an end to the practice of human sacrifice, whose victims were largely from among the 'low' castes. Owing to the stories of his miraculous powers as well as his having fought for the rights of the downtrodden, he gained a large following in the area. Many people converted to Islam at his hands, it is said, while remaining Hindus, began venerating him as a powerful spiritual being, an incarnation of their own principal deity, Dattatreya.

It appears that through the centuries Hindus and Muslims freely worshipped at the shrine of Baba Buddhan, each approaching him according to their religious preference— as an incarnation of Dattatreya for the Hindus or as a 'friend' of Allah for the Muslims.[15]

It is a syncretic cult in which Hindu and Islamic practices are blended. The early Dattatreya tradition seems beyond doubt to have been an anti-Brahmanical one, part of the Avadhut tradition that upholds a formless God and sternly condemns caste and the Brahmanical sacrificial system.

There are several similarities between the figure of Dattatreya in the Deccan and some antinomian Sufis. Thus for instance, Dattatreya is revered by some Muslims in north Karnataka and southern Maharashtra as a *malang* called Shah Fakir, who is also referred to as Shah Datta Alam Prabhu. This figure was instrumental in bringing about a synthesis of devotional thought among various communities of the people of the Deccan, like the Lingayats, the Muslims, the Ananda Sampradayis and the Giri-Gosains. Sayyed Chandasahib Qadri, more popularly known as Chand Bodhale, a Muslim Sufi, who was the spiritual preceptor of Janardhan Swami, was regarded as an incarnation of Shah Datta Alam Prabhu, who, in turn, has close links with the Lingayat saint Allama Prabhu.

He has the distinction of being the first to produce the cultivation of coffee in India. He formed groups of missionaries to travel in the region as well as to nearby areas in the Nilgiris and Kerala to preach Islam, while also teaching people how to cultivate coffee.

Over the centuries, the *dargah* of Baba Buddhan has played a major role in bringing people of various castes and creeds together. Hindu rulers, such as Channamaji of Nagar and the Wodeyar kings of Mysore, as well as Muslim rulers, such as Hyder Ali and his son Tipu Sultan, endowed the shrine with lands as *jagirs* and *inams*, and would regularly visit it. It also emerged as a popular place for pilgrimage for both Hindus as well as Muslims.

Elamma, Sauditti

Elamma Dungri is the centre of the cult of the goddess Elamma. The cult is almost certainly of 'low'-caste origin. It is a blend of Mahayana and Natha Shaivite traditions, both being distinctly anti-Brahmanical. Elamma is the 'original form' of Mathamma, the patron goddess of the Madiga Dalits. What is particularly striking about Elamma are the stories of her association with a Muslim saint, Hazrat Bhaure Shah Wali.

It is said that Elamma, a poor woman who was afflicted with leprosy, came wandering into the forest and went to Bhaure Shah's *khanqah* and took refuge in its vicinity. Bhaure Shah accepted Elamma as his disciple, and, it is said, it was because of her dedication to her Sufi master that she was cured of leprosy. Many Hindu pilgrims to Elamma's temple also visit Bhaure Shah's dargah, especially during his annual *urs*.

Fakirswamy, Shirhatti

The shrine of Fakirswami is located at the town of Shirahatti. It represents a unique synthesis of Islamic and Hindu styles of architecture. In Islamic fashion, the grave is covered with a green cloth *(ghilaf)*. A silver idol purporting to be that of Fakirswami is placed on the grave. The custodians of this shrine are Lingayats, belonging to the Hiremath *Jangama* caste. Muslims, Dalits, Lingayats and Backward castes flock to this shrine in large numbers.

Besides his numerous Muslim followers, Khwaja Aminuddin is said to have had many Hindu and Lingayat devotees, one of the principal of whom was Fakirswamy. Fakirswamy was the son of a Lingayat couple.

The rituals that are followed at the shrine of Fakirswamy are a unique blend of Hindu, Lingayat and Muslim practices. The Hindu followers of Fakirswamy observe Moharram to this day. The annual fair at the shrine, held fifteen days after Kannada New Year festival of Ugadi, attracts Muslims, Dalits, Hindus and Lingayats in large numbers.

On ceremonial occasions, the swami or custodian of the shrine dresses in Muslim fashion, wearing a white *sherwani* and a green turban. Only a Hindu or Lingayat, from any caste, can become the swami, because the Muslims are considered to be in the position of their guru, just as Khwaja Aminuddin was the guru of Fakirswamy. When a new swami takes over, first the local Muslims perform various Islamic rituals and appoint him as a *fakir*. Hindus perfom their rituals after that. On the death of the swami, the local Muslims bathe the body, cover it with a shroud *(kafan)*, write the *kalima*, the Islamic creed of confession of the faith, on the head, and then offer the burial prayer *(namaz-e-janaza)* and recite the *Quran*. The local Hindus perform their rituals after this, and the body is then buried.

Hazrat Sayyed Shah Murtaza Qadri, Ilkal

The town of Ilkal in the Bagalkot district in northern Karnataka is famous for the massive *dargah* of a noted Sufi saint, Hazrat Sayyed Shah Murtaza Qadri. Hazrat Murtaza was a direct descendant of one of the most famous Sufis of all times, Hazrat Abdul Qadir Jilani of Baghdad.

He is said to have performed several miracles, including saving his followers from a deadly outbreak of cholera. Because of this, his fame spread far and wide, and scores of Hindus and Lingayats, in addition to Muslims, became his followers. A leading Lingayat priest, Shri Mahant Swamy is also said to have developed a 'deep friendship' with the Sufi.

Today, the *dargah* of the Sufi of Ilkal attracts large numbers of Hindus as well as Muslims. The remarkable inter-communal harmony that is witnessed at this shrine is, it is said, 'entirely a result of the great work of the saint who lies buried here, who drew to him people from all castes and creeds'.

Jagat Guru Abdul Qadir Ingbandh, Kowthalam

The shrine of Sri Jagat Guru Hazrat Sayyed Shah Abdul Qadir Husaini Chishti Qadri Lingbandh, a Sufi saint associated with the Qadri and Chishti orders, is located at the village of Kowthalam, in the Kurnool district of Andhra Pradesh. Just adjacent to an ancient intricately carved and sculpted Shiva temple, is the *dargah* of Hazrat Abdul Qadir. As his title of 'Sri Jadaguru' ('the World Teacher') and 'Lingbandh' ('one who ties the linga') suggest, the saint is held in great regard by Hindus and Lingayats as well as by Muslims of the area.

Koddekal Basavanna/Muhammad Sarwar, Koddekal

Located in the Gulbarga district in northern Karnataka is the village of Koddekal, centre of the cult of Muhammad Sarwar/ Koddekal Basavanna. Built like a Sufi *dargah*, the shrine is looked after by a family of hereditary Lingayat priests belonging to the 'low' caste Nekar community of weavers. The grave of Muhammad Sarwar/Koddekal Basavanna is housed in a Muslim-style domed structure with slender minarets topped with the Islamic symbol of the crescent and the star. The grave is constructed in Muslim fashion.

The ruins of medieval Muslim monuments in the vicinity suggest that Koddekal was probably a major Sufi centre at one time, particularly during the rule of the Adil Shah Sultans. There are several other Muslim-style *dargahs* in the village, which contain the graves of saints called by Hindu names by the Hindus and the Lingayats and by Muslim names by the Muslims.

From his *vachanas* it is clear that he preached an ethical monotheism and communal harmony and crusaded against caste discrimination and untouchability. This seems to have won him a large following among the 'low'-caste Nekar weavers. The syncretic nature of this cult is one of its most striking features. The followers of the Muhammad Sarwar/Koddekal Basavanna include Muslims as well as Nekar Lingayats, the latter forming the vast majority. Unlike the other Lingayats, the Nekars associated with the cult do not wear the phallic symbol *(lingam).*

The *vachanas* of the saint are preserved in an alcove inside the grave complex. Muhammad Sarwar/Koddekal Basavanna is depicted as dressed in a tiger's skin, with a wooden Hindu-style sandal *(padarakshi)* on one foot and a Muslim-style shoe *(kausi)* on the other, symbolising what is said to have been his principal mission of uniting Hindus and Muslims.

Unlike other Lingayats, the Nekar priests of the shrine and their followers do not even wear a *linga* around their necks, as God is considered by them to be beyond representation in any physical form. They are said to regard the *vachanas* of Muhammad Sarwar/Koddekal Basavanna as their *linga*.

Two festivals are held at the shrine. On these occasions, the Lingayat Jangam Swami, the head of the Mahal Mutt attached to the shrine, dresses in Muslim fashion, with a green turban and a *sherwani*, and leads a procession to the grave of the saint carrying a palanquin bearing a throne with the *vachanas* of Muhammad Sarwar/Koddekal Basavanna placed on it.

Manik Prabhu, Manik Nagar

Manik Prabhu was a nineteenth-century mystic who had a large following among both Hindus and Muslims. His shrine containing his grave is located at Manik Nagar. Manik Prabhu preached an ethical monotheism, transcending barriers of caste and creed. He was believed by some of his followers to be the fourth incarnation of Dattatreya. Some of his Muslim followers considered him to be a Sufi. He was the founder of a new *sampradaya*, the *Sakala Mata*. The *Sakala Mata* is described as a 'holistic and all-embracing school of philosophy, which basically rests on the concept of a Supreme Soul or a Universal Divinity that pervades the Universe'.

The basic teachings of Manik Prabhu are contained in a scripture known as the *Pad Mala,* which consists of mystical verses composed by him and his successors. His teachings are akin to the Vedantic Advaita or non-dualistic philosophy as well as to the Sufi tradition of *wahdat al-wujud* ('unity of existence'). Manik Prabhu preached the unity of all mankind.

Manik Prabhu was a great champion of communal harmony. The rituals associated with the Manik Prabhu cult represent a blend of Islamic and Hindu traditions. Puja is offered at the *samadhi* by Hindu devotees, while Muslim pilgrims sometimes offer *namaz* here. The main festival held at the shrine is Datta Jayanti.

Twenty-two festivals are celebrated at the shrine. Most of these are Hindu festivals, but Eid and Muharram are also observed. The death anniversary of the great Qadri Sufi of Baghdad, Hazrat Abdul Qadir Jilani, is observed here with great fanfare. On the night before, *fakirs* come here in large numbers and are given alms. A *qawwali* session is organised, which is followed by a communal meal in which Hindus, Muslims, Dalits and others all eat together.

Raja Bagh Sawar, Basavakalyan

Several small shrines dedicated to the fifteenth-century Sufi Taj Baba or Bagh Sawar, also referred to as Yamanureshwar or Yamanurappa, are located at different places in the Bijapur and Gulbarga districts of northern Karnataka. His principal shrine where he lies buried, is located at the town of Basavakalyan in Gulbarga. Basavakalyan, besides being home to several other Sufi shrines, is also famous for its association with Basava, the founder of the Lingayat religion. The sprawling *dargah* is intricately decorated inside with Arabic calligraphic symbols in the form of fierce-looking tigers.

Changadev gudi, or Rajabag Savar Dargah was a place of worship in Yamanur village considered indiscriminately as the temple *(gudi)* of a Hindu guru and the *dargah* of a Muslim saint. It is a curious shrine where an *avatar* of Vishnu and an intercessor of Allah are rolled into one in the person of an ascetic who renounced the world, was a tolerably good magician and miracle-worker, and was enrolled simultaneously under the ochre banner of Vaishnavism and the green banner of Islam. The charisma of this saint draws to his tomb followers of both the religions, as is common in popular religious practices.

What is not so common, however, is that Hindu and Muslim servants officiate side by side in this shrine. What is even rarer is the deliberate mixture of symbols associated with both religions, which allows the devotees to express their preference for either monotheism or polytheism as they worship together.

The Hindus look on the divinity as Changadev, an avatar of Vishnu, who is a key figure in their pantheon. For the Muslims, he is the 'friend of God', Rajabag Savar, an Islamic saint who intercedes with God and is the local repository of the *baraka* of the One and Only (Allah) as revealed by his Prophet, Muhammad.

The village of Yamanur in Karnataka's Hubli district, contains two shrines dedicated to Raja Bagh Sawar, one looked after by a family of hereditary Maratha priests, and the other, smaller one, by a Muslim *fakir*. According to the Maratha custodians of this shrine, Raja Bagh Sawar was not a Muslim, but a Brahman, by the name of Chang Dev. His spiritual master was not a Muslim Sufi but another Brahman, Jynandeva.

Two prayer ceremonies are held at the shrine daily, one in the morning and the other in the evening in which both Hindus as well as Muslims participate. The service starts with the beating of drums, after which the Maratha priest performs *arti* of the *alams*, brass symbols in the form of outstretched hands, each of the five fingers representing one of the five members of the 'holy family': The Prophet Muhammad, his daughter Fatima, her husband and the Prophet's cousin, Imam Ali as well as their two sons, Imam Hasan and Imam Husain. While the *arti* is being conducted, a Muslim *fakir* recites in a low voice the *fatiha*, the opening verse of the *Quran*, as well as some other Arabic chants.[16]

The *mullahs* living in Yamanur come to the shrine every day without fail. It is true that while the *pujari* performs the puja, one of them recites prayers from the *Quran*. They are the ones who sacrifice the sheep and the fowl under the huge neem tree growing in front of the temple. Once the sacrifice is over, the devotees cook the meat with rice, which they distribute no only among the *pirzade*, *mullahs* and *fakirs*, but also the Hindu *pujaris*.

Shishunala Sharif, Haveri

In Shishunala, a remote village in the Haveri district of north Karnataka, there is the shrine of the famous mystic and Kannada poet, Muhammad Sharif Nawar (1819–1889), commonly known simply as Sharif. For thousands of Hindus, he is regarded as Sharif Bhagwan, a deity whom they venerate.

Sharif is best remembered for the large number of mystical verses that he composed. He travelled across north Karnataka, singing his poems that spoke of God and the human soul, mystical love, the meaninglessness of barren ritualism, the falsity of caste and communal divisions and the oneness of all beings.

Hindus, Dalits, Lingayats and Muslims all flock to his tomb, especially on Thursdays, the special day for the Sufis, and on the night of the new moon every month, when a big festival is held, during which the devotees belonging to various castes eat together and sing Sharif's compositions. A striking feature of the *dargah* are the Lingayat and Muslim custodians who together sit at the foot of the shrine. The Lingayat does a little puja for them, while the Muslim pats their heads with a bunch of peacock feathers and smears their foreheads with ash from wood in an incense burner. Sharif's devotees call him the *triveni sangam*.

Sultan Ahmad Shah Wali, Bidar

Bidar, in northern Karnataka, is home to numerous Sufi shrines. Under the Bahmani rulers of the region, scores of Sufis from Iran, Central Asia and north India flocked to Bidar and their dargahs are till this day places of pilgrimage for Muslims, Hindus, Lingayats and Dalits alike. One of the most intriguing shrines in Bidar is the massive *dargah* of the second ruler of the Bahmani dynasty, Sultan Shihabuddin Ahmad Shah Wali (d. 1436).

The Bahmani Sultans were known for their policy of religious tolerance, which endeared them to their subjects irrespective of religion. Ahmad Shah's *dargah*, a magnificent, massive domed structure, is located at the village of Ashtur, ten kilometres from Bidar town. It is looked after by a Muslim custodian, and Hindus, Lingayats, Dalits as well as Muslims regularly visit it.

On the occasion of the annual festival or *urs* of Ahmad Shah, the Lingayat priest *(jangama)* comes walking all the way to the shrine, a journey of five days, along with a large procession of Lingayats, Hindus, Dalits and Muslims, singing songs and blowing conches. He comes dressed in a long Muslim-style *choga*, a belt with a copper buckle with Persian inscriptions on it, and a green and red stripped Muslim-style embroidered cap. He offers coconuts and flowers at the grave, and the Muslim custodian reads the *fatiha*, the opening chapter of the *Quran*, and gives the pilgrims little pieces of sugar as *tabarruk*. Kannada *bhajans* and Urdu *qawwalis* are sung.

Moinuddin/Mouneshwar, Thinthini

Located near Sirpur in the Gulbarga district of northern Karnataka is the shrine complex of the sixteenth-century saint Mouneshwar or Mounappa, also known as Moinuddin. It is said that he was a Muslim, a follower of a noted Sufi, identified variously as Hazrat Khwaja Aminuddin Ala Chishti of Bijapur or Mohammad Sarwar/Kodekkal Basavanna of Gulbarga. According to some sources, he had become a Muslim at the hands of a Muslim Sufi but retained the Hindu name of Mouneshwar in order to more closely identify with the 'low' caste Hindus among whom he lived and preached.

The Moinuddin cult is based on the worship of a formless God, an indication of a distinct Sufi influence. Mouneshwar, also known as Moinuddin, is the patron saint of the 'low'-caste Hindu Panchals or goldsmiths of Gulbarga, Bagalkot and Bijapur in northern Karnataka. His shrine at the village of Thinthini, located on the banks of the Krishna river in the Gulbarga district, is built entirely in Muslim fashion.

It is said that he was actually a Muslim, a follower of a noted Sufi identified variously as Hazrat Khwaja Aminuddin Chishti of Bijapur or Muhammad Sarwar/Koddekal Basavanna of Gulbarga. According to some sources he had become a Muslim at the hands of a Muslim Sufi but had taken on the name of Mouneshwar in order to more closely identify with the people among whom he lived and preached.

The fusion of Islamic and local traditions in the cult of Mouneshwar/Moinuddin is particularly remarkable. Dressed as a Muslim *fakir*, Mouneshwar/Moinuddin appears to unite both Hindus and Muslims. He is said to have preached an ethical monotheism and to have crusaded against caste discrimination, idol worship, ritualism and superstitions, and herein is clear evidence of his Sufi background.

The custodians of Mouneshwar/Moinuddin's shrine belong to the Hindu goldsmith *(Panchala)* caste, who regard him as their patron saint. The graves of their forefathers appear like Muslim graves, covered with a green sheet embossed with the symbol of a crescent and star. Hindus, Dalits and Muslims all visit the shrine. While Hindus perform puja, Muslims read the *fatiha*, and sometimes offer *namaz* here. Pilgrims, both Hindus and Muslims, come with flowers, fruit, incense and sweets as offerings.

The syncretic shrines of Karnataka provide an interesting example of how reified notions of community identity can be challenged at multiple levels and in striking ways. They illustrate the overlapping nature of religious identity, and point to the fact that for centuries people have sought, as many still do, to carry on with their spiritual quest and the search for Truth uninhibited by narrow boundaries imposed by religious orthodoxy.

Syncretic Movement in Kashmir : The Rishi Tradition

Kashmir is reputed to have been the abode of the *rishis* centuries before the establishment of the Muslim Sultanate in 1320. For this reason, the Valley was termed 'Rishi Vatika'. A strong folk tradition still persists, particularly in a number of villages in Kashmir, about the existence of *rishis* in ancient times. Kashmiri Muslims' devotion to the shrines of the Sufis and the *rishis* is deep-rooted in the local context rather than Islam alone.

Rishism had struck strong roots in Kashmir prior to the advent of Islam in the region, and probably one reason for its popularity was the distinct strain of protest against Brahmanical supremacy that is evident in some of the practices and teachings associated with pre-Islamic *rishis*. However, the anti-caste crusade was most forcefully articulated by founder of the Muslim *rishi* order, Hazrat Nuruddin Nurani.

Hazrat Nuruddin Nurani is regarded as the patron saint of Kashmir, not just by Kashmiri Muslims but also by many Hindus as well. Puri, writes 'If Kashmiris were to choose a symbol of their spiritual and cultural personality, they would be almost unanimity on his name by all communities'. Hazrat Nuruddin Nurani as the spiritual and cultural symbol of Kashmir'. Lawrence describes him as 'the national saint' of Kashmir, while Dar says he was 'undoubtedly, the top-most personage of the spiritual world in Kashmir'. He is regarded by the Kashmiris as not just the *Alamdar-i-Kashmir* ('the flag-bearer of Kashmir') but even as the *Shaykh-ul Alam* ('the Spiritual perceptor of the World'). He is more popularly remembered as Nund Rishi ('the Beautiful One'), or, by Kashmiri Hindus, as *Sahajananda*, because he was considered to have 'found the Truth within himself' through the mystical path of *sahaj upasana*.

From childhood itself Hazrat Nuruddin is said to have shown a marked inclination for mystical pursuits, and in this he was greatly influenced by the renowned female mystic Lal Ded. The influence of Lal Ded, also known as Lalleshwari or Lalla, on Hazrat Nuruddin was so great that no account of his spiritual evolution can be complete without a detailed reference to her life and teachings. According to some accounts, she embraced Islam at his hands and ascended the stages.

In fact, Lalla did not preach Islam, but her *Vaakh,* which was not in conflict with ontological teachings of the Sufis, served the cause of Islam in Kashmir. Lalla, indeed, propagated the mystic idea of divine unity in simple language, which had a deep and direct appeal to the common man. For her, true devotion did not imply various rituals and practices evolved by the Brahman but meant seeking God within oneself, and also in the routine of daily life. All suggest that she may actually have converted to Islam, as many Kashmiris believe.

Lal Ded's mystical poetry, known as the *Vaakh*, which is still to be heard sung in the villages of Kashmir, contains a strong element of protest against caste inequality, the oppression of the Brahmans, the worship of idols, elaborate and meaningless rituals and polytheism. Her bitter critique of the religious practices and social customs of her times clearly shows the depths to which Kashmiri Hindu society had fallen under the stranglehold of the Brahmans.

She was the first to preach in the Kashmiri language, which the Brahmans had tended to look down upon, penning all their writings in Sanskrit, which they claimed was the *'deva bhasha'* or 'the language of the gods'. Lal Ded gathered around her many followers, almost all being from the oppressed 'low' castes, who found in her movement comfort from the chains of Brahmanical orthodoxy. She was a great champion of equality and the oneness of humankind.

Lalla's approach to religion, based on mysticism, was fundamentally humanistic and individualistic. By rejecting formal and organised religion, which was based on the supreme authority of the Brahman, she helped the common man accept the Sufi ideas of equality and the brotherhood of man. She questioned the worship of idols thus: The idol is but stone, the temple is but stone.

Undoubtedly, Lalla gave a unique orientation to the evolution of a new cultural pattern in Kashmir. The influence of her *vaakh* was substantial on Nuruddin during the formative stage of his mystical career; likewise the impact of her revolt against social and religious discrimination was tremendous on the folk. She was the saviour. Lalla actually shot into prominence in an age of social ferment when Hinduism in Kashmir, as a result of its declining strength, was exposed to the radian influence of Islam through the egalitarian spirit of the Sufis. It is of great significance to remember from the viewpoint of social history the historical dimension of her elevation to *avatar* by a devout Muslim like Nuruddin Rishi.

Little wonder, therefore, that Islam (as represented by the *rishis* of Kashmir) bears the dominant influence of Lalla. The latter's poetry became a major vehicle for influencing the illiterate masses (particularly in rural society), who have had and still have an incredible retentive memory for verse. It is of some significance that it was the *rishis*, above all, who preserved the heritage of Lalla.

Through Lal Ded, the young Nuruddin came into contact with the leading Sufis of their period, with whom she established close links. Till the age of thirty, Hazrat Nuruddin led the life of a householder. However, it soon dawned on him that the path of the ancient *rishis*, of renouncing the world and subjecting oneself to harsh penance, was not the way to attain God. He realised that it was only by active involvement in the world, in attempting to reform society and combat social oppression, that God could be found.

Hence, he turned from world-renunciation *(rahbaniyat)* to work among his people, preaching the message of Islam and crusading against caste, empty ritualism and the hypocrisy of religious leaders, both Hindu as well as Muslim. In sharp contrast to the Brahmans, who looked down on manual labour as demeaning, Hazrat Nuruddin saw labour as an honourable means for the earning of one's livelihood.

Hazrat Nuruddin, while successfully reforming Kashmiri Rishism by turning it from a world-renouncing philosophy to a means for social engagement and emancipation, used it as a medium and vehicle for the spread of Islam. He made conversion to Islam, as he understood it, as an essential pre-condition for those who wanted to join the *rishi* order. Indeed, it is because of the efforts of Hazrat Nuruddin and the Muslim rishis who followed him that most of Kashmir converted to Islam. His greatest contribution is that he made 'Islam more comprehensible to common Kashmiris'. His use of rishism to spread Islam meant that the Kashmiris did not see Islam as a radical break from their traditions, for, as we have noted, rishism had been deeply rooted in the Kashmiri milieu well before the arrival of Islam there. Thus, in his poetry, Hazrat Nuruddin refers to the Prophet Muhammad as the first of the *rishis*.

This is why Hazrat Nuruddin and his disciples, who preached in the Kashmiri language through the medium of poetry and sought to spread Islam using local cultural motifs and institutions, were far more successful in their missionary endeavours than the Sayyids who came to Kashmir from west Asia and Iran. Kashmiris regard Hazrat Nuruddin's collection of poems as the *Kashor Quran,* or the *Quran* in the Kashmiri language. It is the greatest contribution to Kashmiri language and literature.

Several local features are clearly discernible in the practices of the Muslim *rishi* order inaugurated by Hazrat Nuruddin. These have both been seen as a form of 'religious syncretism', on the one hand, and as a means to make Islam more intelligible and culturally more familiar to the Kashmiris on the other. For instance, the Muslim rishis were strict vegetarians and many of them remained unmarried. Nearly all of them were known by their local Kashmiri, rather than Arabic names. Some of their ascetic practices, too, closely resemble those of pre-Islamic rishis and especially the Buddhist *shramans*.

They survive by drinking only water and eating just wild grass. Hazrat Nuruddin is said to have been initiated into the Kubrawi Sufi order by Mir Muhammad Hamadani who, recognising Nuruddin's eminent spiritual stature and the necessity to use the vehicle of Rishism to propagate Islam in Kashmir, issued him 'a letter of instruction'. Hazrat Nurani initiated several people into the rishi order and despatched them to various parts of Kashmir to spread Islam. In the manner of the Sufi, Hazrat Nuruddin spent the rest of his life travelling throughout Kashmir, preaching Islam, and the message of love, compassion and justice.

The contempt which the Brahmans held the common man in certainly touched the sensitive soul of Nuruddin. It was Muslim's commitment to an ethic of action which was valued by Nuruddin vis-a-vis the unethical egocentrism of the Brahman: Hazrat Nuruddin's sharp critique of the caste system and the inequities heaped on the victims of the Brahmanical social order struck a sympathetic chord among the down-trodden, and this was undoubtedly one of the most central importance in the popularity of the Muslim rishi movement. In fact, Hazrat Nuruddin's mystical fraternity has the distinction of being 'the only Sufi order in India to doggedly oppose Brahmanism of the basis of the ethical and social ideals of the *Quran*.

The popular perception of Nuruddin is not only that of saint but also of a champion of the commoners, including even menials like sweepers and tanners, who prominently figure in the discussions of the saint with the Brahmans. Certainly,

Nuruddin's denunciation of the caste system prompted the so-called castes and the weaker sections of Kashmiri society to break off their ties with a caste-ridden social structure. As the lower caste Hindus were attracted to Islam, though in stages, over the centuries, the *urs* celebrated at the shrines of the *rishis* somewhat solemnly in the early phase of their evolution began to assume festive colour with the passage of time.

The performances of the folk dancers have a symbolic significance for assessing the role of the rishis in drawing the peasants and farmers to their fold. The overall impact of the rishi movement was that through the performances given by the folk dancers Islam was brought to the masses in a meaningful way.

A fascinating aspect of Nuruddin's life and teachings has to do with his efforts to improve social status of women. The praise showered upon Hazrat Nuruddin's several female disciples, almost all converts to Islam points clearly to the socially emancipatory role of the Muslim rishi order.

As we have seen, it was a woman, Lal Ded, who exercised a major influence on Hazrat Nuruddin's spiritual evolution in his early years. In recongnising her as a true devotee of God, Hazrat Nuruddin opened up new spaces for women, which had been so cruelly denied to them by the Brahmanical establishment. Hazrat Nuruddin enrolled numerous females as his closest disciples. Notable among these were Shama Bibi, Bahat Bibi, Dahat Bibi, Data Bibi, Ganga Bibi and the elder and younger Sala Bibi. Sanga Bibi and Ganga Bibi, two other female rishis, are remembered for their philanthropic activities in addition of their high spiritual attainments.

Hazrat Nuruddin died in 1439 C.E at the age of sixty three. He was buried at Chrar-i-Sharif, and Sultan Zain-ul 'Abidin led the funeral prayers. The Muslim *rishi* movement inaugurated by Hazrat Nuruddin was, after his death, carried further by his disciples, who set up centres in various parts of Kashmir to spread Islam and the message of social reform. As a result of their efforts, by the sixteenth century, most Kashmiris had converted to Islam. Hazrat Nuruddin is said to have trained some 360 *rishis* in all, both men as well as women.

Other *rishis* who followed them carried on in Hazrat Nuruddin's tradition of helping the poor while spreading Islam and the teachings of the *rishi* order. In this they offered a striking contrast to both the Hindu pundits, on the one hand, and the scripturalist, court-centred Muslim ulama, on the other.

Against the background of the *rishi* movement, Islam in its historical manifestation in Kashmir emerges as a socio-religious and moral force radiating significance to life and thought of the people at the crossroads. The so-called syncretic tradition of the *rishis* was a necessary concomitant of the process of Islamisation rather than is culmination. The seeming syncretism of Islamic beliefs and local practices, in fact, concurrently marked the beginning of a movement for the realisation of the ultimate, if not immediate, objectives of Islam at both the individual and social levels. While apparently accommodating local Hindu-Buddhist practices to the Islamic framework, the *rishis* gradually paved the way for the assimilation of the people in the Islamic identity. What is, however, unique about this identity is not merely the assimilation of the Kashmiris in Islam over a period of six centuries but, more important, their urge to live with their pundit compatriots in symbiotic rather than syncretic relationship.

Kashmir is unique in the whole of South Asia in that the spread of Islam in the region owed mainly to the efforts of an indigenous Sufi order, the *Silsilah-i-Rishiyan,* The conversion of the Kashmiris to Islam, was a peaceful process set in motion by the Sufis. The Islamisation process in Kashmir is coterminous with, and in a sense, can be said to be even synonymous with a process of social reform and protest against Brahmanical tyranny. In this regard, Islam has played a revolutionary role in the evolution and emancipation of Kashmiri society. Further, the principal vehicles of Islam in the Kashmiri countryside, the rishis, also greatly contributed to spreading the message of universal love transcending narrow communal barriers.

Even now, many Kashmiri pundits continue to hold the Muslim *rishis* in high regard. It is said that pundits who hailed from Anantnag [Islamabad], but have now shifted to Jammu and Delhi, continue with the practice, held in common with their former Muslim neighbours, of abstaining from meat on the *urs* or death anniversary of Baba Harde Rishi who lies buried in Anantnag town. The average Kashmiri still remains at root deeply humane, with a sense of hospitality that is seldom matched elsewhere.

REFERENCES AND NOTES

1. Das, N.K. *Culture, Region and Philosophy, Introduction, An Outline of Syncretism*, Rawat Publications, p.11.
2. Ibid., p.17.
3. Jawed, Dr. Ajeet. *Heritage of Harmony*, p.39.
4. Das, N.K. *Culture, Region and Philosophy, Introduction*, p.24.
5. Ibid., p.25.
6. Sani, Ali S. "The Khojah Ismailis of South Asia". In *India's Islamic Traditions, 711–1750*, pp. 285–288.
7. Schwerin, Kersin Graffin V. *Saint Worship in Indian Islam : The Legend of Martyr Salar Masnd Ghazi*, 145, 154.

   "The Ghazi Miyan Cult in Western Nepal and North India". Gaboriean, Marc. In *On Becoming an Indian Muslim*. Ed. M. Waseem. pp. 244, 245.
8. Pfleiderer, Beatrix. *Mira Datar Durgah*, p. 219.
9. "The Islamic Mystic Tradition in India : The Madari Sufi Brotherhood, Ute Falasch". In *Lived Islam in South Asia*. Eds. Intiaz Ahmad and Helmut Reifeld, p. 254 .
10. "Liminality and Legality : A contemporary Debate among Imamshahis of Gujarat, Dominic Sila Khan". In *Lived Islam in South Asia*, pp. 209, 210.
11. Champion, Catharine. "Muslim Bhartrahari Jogis of Gorakhpur". In *On becoming an Indian Muslim*. Ed. M. Waseem, pp. 282, 283
12. Basu, Helena. Ritual Communication : The Case of the Sidi in Gujrat, pp. 237, 238. In *Lived Islam in South Asia*. Ed. Imtiaz Ahmad and Helmut Reifeld.
13. Although not many people might have heard of the Pranami tradition, it may be useful to recall here that such a renowned historical figure as Gandhi, following his mother and her ancestors, was associated with the Pranami religion, as he himself admits in his autobiography.

14. Sikand, Yoginder. *Lived Islam in South Asia, Shared Hindu–Muslim Shrines in Karnataka*, pp. 168, 169.
15. Sikand, Yoginder. *Hindu–Muslim Syncretic Shrines in Karnataka*, p.6.
16. Sikand, Yoginder. *Hindu–Muslim Shrines in Karnataka*, p.35.

8

Mutual Influences on Social and Religious Life

The exposure of India to Islamic influence continued unabated till the establishment of Delhi Sultanate in A.D. 1206. Thereafter, for over five hundred years, the Muslims remained politically dominant till the advent of the British in India. At the outset, it may be mentioned that the number of Muslims who came from outside India was very small. Among these migrant Muslims, only a few came with their families, and thus, the vast majority of the Muslim population of India have actually been converts from various segments of Indian population. There must have been other forces, besides the political impetus, of which we do not have adequate knowledge. Further, while conversion from Hinduism to Islamic way of life took centuries, during the long process numerous communities continued to retain Hindu influence in their social life.

A cursory glance at the customs and ideas reveals that Hindu customs and rites have far greater hold on the Muslims than Islamic customs and practices. Certain customs have been so internalised that their origin remains debatable. For example, there does exist a controversy about the origin of the purdah system, yet, there can be no doubt that Muslims have directly or indirectly enforced this practice. On the other hand, the Muslim women lost the status accorded to them in the Islamic laws by the absorption of Hindu ideas. The daughter lost her rights of inheritance as found amongst the Pangal (the Manipuri Muslims). The interplay of these two major social forces resulted in the emergence of a Muslim population of India, which presents a complete and sometimes partial conglomeration of Hindu and Islamic rites and customs. The main difference between Hindu and Islamic approach is that Hinduism was mainly a religion of a specified class, with only the Brahmans being entitled to rites, duties and privileges, acting as a mediator between common men and God, whereas, Islam was a religion of masses, where every follower was treated equally with the same law.[1]

This egalitarian essence of Islam was greatly influenced after reaching India, where the religion was confined within the ruling circle or the aristocracy who in their turn were patronised by the religious clergies like *mullah* and *Kazi*. Sufism was greatly responsible for bringing closer Islam and Hinduism, since, most of the Sufis believed in the doctrine of unity of existence being a manifestation of God. They did not distinguish between Hindus and Muslims and opened their shrines (*dargah*) for both to commemorate ceremonies such as *urs*. Thus Sufism could demolish the barriers of language and religion and Islam learnt the language of the people. The Indian Muslims represent a culturally and ethnically diversified group bound together only by their common belief in Islam. Perhaps one factor which greatly contributed to the popularity of Islam among the Hindus was that the Muslim mystics did not ask the newly converted Hindus to renounce their former customs and rituals.

Even in the religious domain, Muslims are classified into different sects and have diversified schools of legal jurisprudence. These groups form a firm basis of differentiation amongst the Indian Muslims. However, the divisions and sects among Muslims appear to be too simplistic to outsiders, more so due to the ideological overtone of egalitarianism; the actual situation reveals a most complex setup representing neither the Hindu *varna* order nor the Western class pattern, yet drawing clear boundaries through diversified ethnically and differing religious ideologies.

In practice however, it is found that some Muslim groups manifest various social and cultural differentiation which have been enhanced by restrictions on almost closed marriage circles. The Chhipa community of Rajasthan, which is predominantly found in Barmer, Jaisalmer, Pali and Kota districts, practises the age-old traditional method of dyeing by vegetable colours. Till date, the non-Muslim population of the surrounding areas utilise the services of the village Chhipa and thus, they have confined themselves to a limited area. On the other hand, the Arab community of Junagadh district of Gurajat stand out as a proof to the history when Arabs formed a part of the invading army. These families still cherish and maintain the banners which their ancestors had carried with them. These banners carry the names of the family, village and ancestors, written in Arabic. The Singis are another fast-disappearing Muslim community still found in pockets in and around the districts of Rajasthan bordering Pakistan. They derive their name from their medical apparatus made from a bull's horn (*seeng*). The Koya of Lakshadweep islands have various customs to alienate them from the neighbouring Muslim population by practising matriliny. The Bora is a trading community confined mostly to rural areas of Assam. The Ruhela or Rohilla of Uttar Pradesh are of Rajput parentage. They are confined to Bulandshahar, Saharanpur, Meerut and Muzaffarnagar districts of western Uttar Pradesh bordering Haryana and Delhi. Though numerically small, they exhibit definite customs and rites which speak of their Rajput ancestry. One of these is the avoidance of first cousin (father's brother's daughter) marriage keeping with the Hindu traditions. The neighbouring Meo and Muslim Mina (*padihar*) are examples of the Muslim rural elites who gave the converts freedom to practise and continue their pre-change religious customs.[2]

In Haryana, a large number of Muslim agriculturists was worshipping their ancestral village deities till the late part of the nineteenth century. In Rajasthan and bordering Haryana, the Mina and Meos have purely Hindu names with the suffix of Khan. They celebrate not only Diwali and Dussera but also Janmashtami. The Padihar Mina in Bharatpur, Agra and neighbouring Dhaulpur areas of Uttar Pradesh eat beef unlike the Hindu Minas living in Sawaimadhopur and Jaipur districts of Rajasthan. The presence of shrines such as Panchpira, Bhaiya or Bhairoji in the villages dominated by Meos and Minas is an example of continuance of the original faith even after conversion to Islam. The heroic and semi-divine personality Shaikh Moinuddin Chishti is venerated today by all the Indian communities. But Meo being in close proximity of Ajmer show greater reverence for the said *pir*. Yet, Meos do not marry within the *gotra*. In Ratlam and other districts of Madhya Pradesh, Kunjra, Behna and Kaji Muslim cultivators follow Hindu customs in their marriage, worship the goddess of smallpox (*shitala-mata*) and give a lot of importance to toran, the decorative paper-cloth hanging on the door, during marriage rites which is a pan-middle India phenomenon. The Mahdawi of Ahmedabad (Gujarat) are organised in a *daira* (circle) and the society does not permit any marriage beyond Mahdawi. This has resulted in the formation of a highly inbred group having minimal social interaction with other neighbouring Muslim communities such as Dawoodi Bohra, Sulemani Bohra, Khoja and Kutchi.

The Mahdawi movement during the sixteenth century had an impact on other tribes of Gujarat also such as Koli, Bhil and Siddi. Some sections of these tribes, though converted to Islam, yet, could not be weaned away from their indigenous religious practices. Likewise, a section of the Siddis of Gujarat embraced Islam. However, the survival of worship of trees and rivers among them speaks of the emergence of a new form of religious cult based on two principles, one belonging to a male fertilising element in the form of the river and other a female producing element in the nature of vegetation. The presence of the shrine of Udorelal, who is considered an incarnation of a river god reinforces their indigenous form of nature worship. The Ismaili Khoja community regarded *zaqat* to Agha Khan, who is considered the unrevealed Imam. The manual prepared by one of the *pirs* of this community, Saaduddin, is read by each Khoja and accorded the same amount of sanctity as accorded to the *Quran* by other Muslim communities. Besides Muslim Rajputs and Jats, we come across numerous smaller Muslim rural families in the Indo-Gangetic plains who believe in the miraculous powers of saints, living or dead. Even for regular daily work, they depend on miracles and magic to a great extent. This is in total contravention of Islamic tenets which believes in an omnipotent Allah. In the district of Purnea (Bihar) the dividing line between the religious beliefs and practices between lower caste Hindus and Muslims is very faint. In every village, one can find a Kalisthan-shrine dedicated to the worship of Goddess Kali, and the presence of *Khudaighar*—God's house attached to almost every Muslim house. In these shrines, the prayers are offered in which the names of Allah and Kali are used. The Bengali Muslims of Kishangunj district (Bihar) build little shrines for Baisahari (the snake goddess) which is a Hindu deity of that area. In the central districts of Madhya Pradesh such as Damoh, Saugar, Jabalpur and Mandla we find a community known as Mirdha or Patel who have Hindu names and dress exactly like the neighbouring Hindus in *dhoti* and *kurta* and revere Bhawani and other Hindu deities.

Gujarat has been a melting pot of diverse ethnic groups and beliefs. In this region, we find a diversified Islam in the form of beliefs practised by the Khoja, Bohra, Mahdawi, Siddi, Aliya, Baluch, Barot, Bora, Bhatti and others. The socio-religious practices of these communities could not be ascribed to the Islamic pattern. The presence of Husaini Brahmans in Allahabad, Ganchi, and Madari and various offshoots of Sufi sects add to the kaleidoscopic pattern of Indian Muslims.[3]

Kalpeni is one of the ten islands which constitutes the Lakshadweep islands in the south-west coast of India. The actual date and historical situations leading to entry of Islam islands are not known. However, from the accounts of Abdulla Ibn-e-Mohammad the tentative dated fixed is AH 41. It is believed that Abu Baqar's (the first *Khalifa*) grandson Ubaiduhah sailed and reached these islands, married a local woman who was the first convert. Gradually the residents of all other islands embraced Islam. Today people of Kalpeni belong to the Shafi school of Sunni division of Islam. Three distinct social divisions are found amongst them, which is contrary to the preachings of Islam. The three divisions are Koya, Mali and Melachari. All these divisions are strictly endogamous in nature. The islanders are matrilineal, the descent being traced through the mother. The traditional pattern of residence is duolocal, the husband visiting the wife every night. Thus a majority of husbands are visiting husbands. They have adopted the Malayali word *taravad*, which signifies lineage. The paternity right of the father is established by the custom of offering gifts to the wife during childbirth. The solar calendar followed by the mainland Malayali determines all the rites of intensification for the islanders, while the Islamic lunar calendar regulates their religious rites and festivals. Coconut is considered to be an auspicious fruit and is offered in the mosques. The women are in no way segregated or put behind veils. They contribute to the family and spend a considerable part of their time in rope and coir making. Blood-letting (practised by the Singis of Rajasthan) is an accepted norm of ethno-medicine amongst them and mostly people subscribe to it to keep their blood 'pure'. The rites of *nikah* (marriage) and circumcision have been adopted by the islanders which form the essential elements of Islam. However, the puberty rites similar to that of Nairs are gradually being discarded. Thus this island society presents an amalgamation of the patriarchal stance of Islam and the traditional matrilineal social structure of the mainland Malayalis of Kerala.

The liberality that was one of the salient features of Indian culture had been mainly instrumental for the gradual diffusion and acceptance of this alien religion in a land where Hindu philosophy and teaching reigned supreme for centuries. In the spread of Islam, contributions of various Islamic missionaries who, by their sheer charisma, made innumerable followers were no less important. Thus, Islam with a world view of non-hierarchy, monotheism and 'messianic historical ethos' was unlike the great Hindu tradition. Its socio-democratic attitude and non-ritualistic approach towards the common man attracted people from various segments of Indian society. Further, history reveals that abstract monotheism as preached by the Sufi saints and philosophers not only came to be accepted by the Hindu masses but also formed a bridge between the Hindu traditions and Islam. Akbar's *Din-e-Ilahi*, Dara Shikoh's synthesis of Upanishadic monotheism with Islam and Amir Khusrau's linkage of Hinduism to the Islamic sphere gave rise to many a distinctive literary works. Thus we find that the ethnographic account of the Muslim populations in various geographical zones of India clearly exhibits the retention of regional cultural characteristics and its congruence with Islamic traditions.

Hindu Influence on Muslim Social and Religious Life

Muslims and Hindus participated in each others' festivals with great elan. The Muslims adopted some of the Hindu festivals and celebrated them with much enthusiasm. The Hindus treated some days of the year as auspicious and some as inauspicious. Accordingly they celebrated their festivals on propitious days. The Muslims in imitation observed the same festivals on those days. Such occasions were popular as days of rejoicing, music and festivity.

The Muslim emperors, provincial governors and court nobles set an example for the lower strata of society by freely celebrating Hindu festivals. Amongst the later Mughals, Shah Alam II composed several poems describing Holi, which was celebrated inside the palace. Red colour was sprinkled, *gulal* was rubbed on faces, dance and music was performed by courtesans, court dancing girls and *qawwals*. The introduction of *qawwali* even gave it a Muslim colour.

Among the royal princes we find that Prince Sulaiman Shukoh (son of Shah Alam II) though a fugitive, did not lose the opportunity of celebrating Holi with great pomp and show. In the dramatic performances, exhibited on this occasion, he himself played the role of Lord Krishna, while the women attached to his haram acted as *gopis* and went in search of him. Nobles like Umdat-ul-Mulk Amir Khan Anjam (of Muhammad Shah's reign) also celebrated Holi with great zeal. Abdul Hai Taban gives a vivid description of the occasion.

The Nawabs of Awadh were very particular about celebrating Holi on the same footing as Nauroz. Shuja-ud Daula was fond of making Holi-fools, 'though he was a Musalman of highest rank.' Mir Taqi Mir gives a detailed account of the colour-throwing, the grand illumination and discharge of fireworks during the reign of Asaf-ud-Daula. Likewise, Nawab Saadat Ali Khan took keen interest in this festival.

The Nawabs and nobles of Bengal actively participated in Holi. On one occasion Nawab Shahamat Jang and Saulat Jang (nephews of Alivardi Khan) enjoyed Holi festivities for seven days in the garden of Moti Jhil at Murhidabad. Nawab Siraj-ud-Daula proceeded to Murshidabad and took part in Holi festivities in his palace of Mansurganj. Following the tradition of the ruling house of Murshidabad, Mir Jafar Khan and his son, Miran, too celebrated Holi and generally spent 5,000 rupees on it.

This festival was so popular among the Muslims that more or less every Muslim poet has composed verses in praise and description of Holi. These poems show that the Muslims arranged the Holi assemblies, arranged dance and music parties, with all their accompaniments. In that period, besides the dance of the *dominis, kanchanis, lolis, ramzanis*, the dance of handsome boys, who belonged to the Khathik caste, was also very popular. The Muslims adopted idioms from the Holi such as: '*Holi ka bharwa*' and '*Holi ka reechh*' (the bear of the Holi).

Vasant Panchami

Vasant Panchami (Basant Panchami), which falls on the fifth lunar day in the bright night of Magh (January-February) and marks the advent of the spring season, was observed by the Muslims in general and at the Mughal court. It is said that Amir Khusrau introduced this festival among the Muslims.

After the death of Aurangzeb, down to the time of Bahadur Shah Zafar, the last Mughal emperor, the festival was celebrated at the court. Shah Alam II observed rituals of this feast inside the palace with great pomp and show. Members of the royal family played with flowers. *Gurwas* (kinds of water-pot) of flowers were made and were carried on their heads by the ladies. Music and exchange felicitations formed the main items of the functions.

Following the example set by their masters, the Mughal nobles celebrated it at great expense to themselves. The ladies of the *haram* of the Nawab Saulat Jang of Bengal performed the rituals as exactly as practised by the Hindus.

The Muslims in general demonstrated great zeal and enthusiasm while celebrating this festival. Dargah Quli Khan has given us a vivid account of the manner in which the people of Delhi observed it. Following the old tradition the people assembled at the place known as 'Qadam Sharif' and stayed there from dawn to dusk. The adjoining gardens, fields and houses were over crowded with the concourse of people. In the courtyard of the shrine and in the surrounding area tents were pitched. People took eatables and spread colourful and variegated carpets. The *qawwals* assembled and sang songs. The participants sprinkled water and *itr* on each other. Similar celebrations were held for a whole week at different shrines. At the shrines of Shaikh Nizam-ud-din Auliya, Khwaja Qutb-ud-din Bakhtiyar Kaki, Shaikh Nasiruddin Chiragh Dehlavi and Hazrat Shah Hasan Rasul Numa, Muslims participated in this festival along with their family members.

Rakshabandhan

A very popular festival of the Hindus is observed on the full-moon day of Sawan (July-August). The *rakhi*, called *dasht*, by Jahangir, made of twisted linen rags, or silk cords, is tied on the right wrists of brothers by sisters. This is deemed to ward off the evil eye and misfortune. The brother henceforward was bound to protect the life and honour of his sister.

Akbar made it a court festival and had *rakhis* tied on his wrist. Thus it became the custom of the courtiers and others to adorn the emperor's wrist with beautiful strings of silk, bejewelled with rubies, pearls and jems of great value. This practice was reinstituted by Jahangir. But after some time, the festival was given up till it was revived by Shah Alam II. On one occasion, Raja Shanker Nath tied a *rakhi* on the wrists of Shah 'Alam II and the princes and sent nine *rakhis* to the Nawab Mubarak Mahal.

Dussehra

Vijaya Dashmi, popularly known as Dussehra, is observed on the tenth lunar day of Asoj (September-October), in commemoration of Lard Rama's victory over Ravana. Regarding the importance of the festival, Abul Fazl observes: 'On this day they pay particular attention to their horses and decorate them and place green sprouts of barley on their heads, and all workmen venerate their tools, and it is held as a great festival and particularly for the Kshatriyas.'

Akbar introduced this festival in the Mughal court. It continued to be observed under the later Mughals. In the reign of Jahandar Shah, who was keenly interested in the spectacular aspect of the festival, an artificial wooden effigy representing the city of Lanka, was made and burnt. Even the small orthodox section of the Muslim community, the Muslims participated in this festival without any inhibition. The festival is so entirely divested of every religious character as to be attended even by Muslims without scruples.

It was a practice both among Muslims and Hindus that the children made an earthen statue of *taisu rai* ten days before the commencement of the Dussehra festival. Every evening some children and young men used to go to the doors of their relatives and in a particular form and melodious loud voice sing a few Hindi couplets and taking one pice or more so from one door to another. Whatever amount was thus collected daily was used for purchasing sweetmeats, which they distributed amongst themselves on the day of Dussehra. The girls made an earthen pot having many holes in it and went from door to door for the same purpose. On the day of Dussehra everybody took out his particular *taisu rai* with kettle drums and flags along with the dancing 'Mughal' boys and girls. The procession went to the river and returned after throwing the *taisu rai* into the water.

Diwali or Dipawali

Diwali or Dipawali, meaning a row of lamps, is observed on the thirteenth day of the month of Kartika (October-November). Gambling is one of the chief features of the festival, which is particularly celebrated by the Hindus.

Diwali was celebrated and certain of its customs were observed by the Muslims and in the Mughal court. Under the later Mughals, the festival was celebrated with all its customary features. Shah Alam II celebrated it inside the palace and he himself has described the rites performed in his poetic style. A grand illumination was held. The ladies went to worship the goddess Saraswati, dressing themselves in finery, wearing sixteen kinds of ornaments, with marks on their foreheads and palms coloured with mahndi; they carried trays full of *puris, kachauris,* and *samosas,* accompanied by dance and music parties. Flower-garlands and felicitations were exchanged. Govardhan-puja followed the Diwali, Shah Alam II observed this too and the ladies sung a song especially meant for this occasion, known as *mangalachar*.

The Muslims not only enjoyed the festive aspect of Diwali but even performed the prescribed rituals. Mirza Qatil tells us that except a few orthodox Muslims, many Muslims participated in gambling and even those who did not take part in it, at least arranged illuminations in their houses. The ladies too observed its rituals.

Apart from this, the Muslims performed the rites of Diwali *bharna*. According to this custom, on the night of the Diwali, women purchased earthen toys in the name of their children, one for each child separately and added to them various kinds of sweets and sweet-toys. First of all, the house was illuminated, afterwards the place where sweets and toys were stored was profusely illuminated. Thenceforth the rite was performed separately for each child. If by chance they failed to perform this rite, the whole year was supposed to pass in misfortune.

Janamashtami

Janamashtami, the birth anniversary of Lord Krishna, is celebrated on the eighth of the dark fortnight of the month of Bhadaun (August–September). The Hindus observe many rituals on this day, but the most important aspect is the observance of the battle between Lord Krishna and Kans, his maternal uncle. Paper statues of Kans were made and a battle was exhibited showing the discomfiture of Kans and the victory of Lord Krishna. Some Muslims cut the paper statues of Kans and drink the honey which they had earlier filled in its stomach, considering it his blood.

The Bera of Khwaja Khizr

This custom is apparently of Hindu origin, but it was adopted and observed by the Muslims. When the Muslims adopted this festival is not clear as no account is found in this connection in the contemporary literature. It is said that Siraj-ud-Daula, Nawab of Bengal, popularised this festival among the Muslims of the Eastern Provinces but gradually it became popular throughout Northern India. The succeeding Nawabs of Bengal made it an official festival and continued to observe its rituals.

In Delhi, the Muslim water-carriers (*bhishtis*) and some other people made boats of paper and straw and let them loose in the water of Jamuna river at the ferry of Khizr. Cooked *dalia* was distributed among the poor. The Muslims of Lucknow and Awadh too observed this festival.

Puniya Festivity

Muslim rulers in Bengal had adopted the festivity to be observed on the day of Puniya. Puniya was the name of commencement of the revenue collection in Bengal, at the beginning of the financial year, which fell accordingly in Baisakh. Following the tradition of the Hindu Rajas, the Nawabs of Bengal made it a festive occasion. The day was marked with celebrations. The entire class of big zamindars and many of the officers (*ahl-i kar*) and clerks (*mutasaddi*) on that day, according to their different ranks, received khilats. On that day a grand festivity (*jashan*) and vast gathering took place.

Some Hindu Practices adopted by Muslims

Janamashtami, the birth anniversary of Lord Krishna, probably inspired the celebration of the birth or death anniversaries of some great Muslim personalities, with much pomp and show. For instance, on the 4th Sh'aban, 1212/4th December, 1797, the birth anniversary of Hazrat Imam Husain was celebrated for the first time in India at Lucknow. On that day great festivities took place. The great nobles presented *nazrs* to the Nawab of Awadh and received *khil-ats* in turn.

Likewise, the celebrations on the eleventh, the birth anniversary of Ghaus-ul Azam Shaikh Abdul Qadir Jilani and twelfth (*dawazdahum*) the birthday of the Prophet Muhammad were observed. The very fact that Amir-ul-Umara Husain Ali Khan, introduced these two festivals among the Muslims of the Deccan, makes one believe that these two festivals were not celebrated earlier, though the birth anniversary of the Prophet was observed at the Mughal court.

According to the opinion of the orthodox Muslim of the eighteenth century, the rites and customs associated with the *Shab-i Barat* are more or less similar to those of Sraddha Kanya-gata, a purely Indian festival. On this occasion the Hindus distributed alms in the name of their deceased ancestors, either in the form of money or in kind. They cooked *halwa* and *puri* for this particular offering; and this custom of theirs was adopted by the Muslims.

Though female infanticide is strictly prohibited in Islam, instances are not wanting when the Muslims got rid of their female children. Most probably, the practice was adopted by the Muslims in India through the Rajput Muslims, who even after embracing Islam, continued this old tradition of their ancestors.[4]

Mirza Mazhar Jan-i-Jahan specially laid down the condition of not killing female children, while initiating Muslim ladies as his disciples. Shah Naimullah Bahraichi remarks that this practice was followed by Muslim women, 'out of poverty', being presumably unable to arrange for dowries of daughters. Even elements of image worship penetrated among the Muslims. Among the uneducated converts and the descendants of converts of Hindu origin especially in the countryside remote from the centres of Muslim culture, many survivals of older cults continued to persist. Here a Muslim differed very little from his Hindu neighbour. He continued to worship the gods of his ancestors, particularly the village godlings, whose rites were associated with the cultivation of the soil, and the deities of diseases, especially the Sitla, etc.[5]

The second factor was that the Hindus, who had embraced Islam could not altogether give up their traditional practices and rituals with regard to the veneration of their ancestral idols. In some cases they gave them Islamic names.

During the *ashura-i-Muharram*, *taziyas* were made representing the grave of Husain. Several rites showed obvious Hindu influences. Men and women prostrated themselves before the *taziyas*, made their petitions, put edibles before them, as the Hindus did before their idols. Apart from the *taziyas*, women made stone statues and expressed their devotion to them to lead to fulfilment of their wishes. The worship of Hindu goddesses like Bhawani, Kalka or Kali was popular among the Muslim women.

The graves of famous Muslim saints attracted the devotion of all orders of Muslim society. Here one almost saw customs of idol-worship being closely copied. Such saints as Shah Madar, Sarwar Sultan, and Salar Mas'ud Ghazi were particularly venerated both by Hindus and Muslims. Sultan Sikandar Lodi made an attempt to stop the visit by women to the shrine of Salar Mas'ud Ghazi but it revived after him. Like the Hindus, the Muslims kept hair-locks on the top the head of the children, which they shaved at any one of the shrines of their choice.

The shrine of Shaikh Saddu situated at Amroha, in the Moradabad district of Uttar Pradesh offers interesting evidence of Hindu influences. The early history the saint is shrouded in darkness and seems to be mythological. However, the lower classes of Muslims and Hindus demonstrated great faith on his spiritual powers. Usually, a goat was offered to him. Meat was cooked and the food was not given to everyone, because whosoever once ate the food thus prepared, was obliged to make the offering every year, in case of a failure to do so, the spirt of the saint compelled him to submit by inflicting about physical pain on him. If he made the offering, he recovered; otherwise the illness went on increasing. On the other hand, a woman who believed in his spiritual influence, moved her head in a circular manner after having her bath and donning attractive dresses and using perfumes. Other women occupied their seats around her and sang songs in praise of the saint along with drums. This rite was known as *baithak*. Afterwards all those women moved their heads with those who played on the instrumental music. The moving of the head was a symptom that the spirit of the Shaikh Saddu had penetrated the body of the person. When she was at the height of her spiritual ecstasy, men and women both asked her about certain future events; and whatever she said was considered a revelation.

The shrine of Shah Arzani, in the city of Patna, was visited by the Hindus and Muslims alike. Every Thursday night, 100 to 500 pilgrims, Muslims and Hindus, many of them from a distance, came to intercede with the saint for his assistance, and make offerings. Similarly every Thursday, many Hindus and Muslims assembled at the shrine of Saiyid Yusuf, situated in Shaikhpura, in Bihar. Satya Pir was worshipped both by the Hindus and Muslims in Bengal.

The eclipse of the sun or moon was deemed by the Hindus to be an hour of crisis for the great luminaries. Loud cries announced the commencement of an eclipse. The Muslims too generally occupied themselves in prayers and fasting till the shadow had passed away.

In general, by the eighteenth century the differences between the Muslims and the Hindus in customs, manners, dresses, and ornaments had narrowed so much that the Muslims were to scarcely distinct from their Hindu neighbours. Almost the only difference which the convert makes is to shave his scalplock and the upper edge of his moustache, to repeat the Muhammadan creed in a mosque, and to add the Muhammadan to the Hindu marriage ceremony. As far a religion goes he worships Khuda instead of Parameshwar, keeps up his service in honour of Bhawani, and regularly makes the due oblation for the repose of the sainted dead.[6]

The Caste System

The religious influences of Hinduism were however, not as great as its social influence upon Muslims. The distinctive feature of Islamic Law is its emphasis on the equality and brotherhood in faith. Says the *Quran* : 'The most devout of the believers is the most worthy in the sight of God'. Therefore it was religious devotion and not birth which was held to determine a man's dignity. In his last message, the Prophet indicated in explicit words the basic concept of the Muslim community and Muslim social order which he envisaged to evolve.

By the eighteenth century, the dictates of Islamic Law affected only the elite in India. There were already a deep-rooted differences between the immigrant and native Muslims and between various communities within them. Above all, the caste system had penetrated the Muslims. Writing during the latter half of the seventeenth century, Bernier remarks: 'The embroiderer brings up his son as an embroiderer, the son of a goldsmith becomes a goldsmith, and a physician of the city educates his son for a physician; and this custom is observed almost as rigidly by Mahometans as by the Gentiles, to whom it is expressly enjoined by their law. Many are the beautiful girls thus doomed to live singly, girls who might marry advantageously if their parents would connect them with a family less noble than their own.'

Though all the rules and rigour of the Hindu caste system were not adopted by the Muslims, its effects and practices are to be seen in the division of the Muslims into Saijids, Mughals, Afghans and Shaikhs, and in the 'guilds' of aritsans and craftsmen.

Like the Hindus, the Muslims were very tenacious in maintaining the concept of purity of blood, which confined marriage relations to one single ethnic group.[7]

Jauhar

The Rajput custom of *jauhar* was sometimes resorted to by the Muslims as the last resort to save the honour of their family members. On one occasion Mirza Nathan, the author of *Baharistan-i Ghaibi*, gave the following instructions to Sa'adat Khan; 'You are to go and stay at the gate of the Mahal (haram). As soon as you hear that I have attained martyrdom in the field, perform the rites of Jauhar... journey to the Kingdom of heaven with eternal honour.'

This custom was partly forced on Muslim families by the political turmoil of the eighteenth century. Qudratullah Qasim informs us that: 'During the commotion which the Abdali soldiers ushered in Delhi, the respectable families generally resorted to Jauhar to save the chastity of their womanfolk and the respectable ladies in utter heplessness died by throwing themselves into wells'.

When the Sikhs of the Punjab attacked the town of Saharanpur, many a woman threw herself into wells to avoid outrages. When the Marathas invaded Moradabad and Sambhal, 'Most of the respectable (women) courted the Jauhar and killed themselves to protect their honour.' There were other cases of Muslims killing their women and children before embarking upon a desperate enterprise.

Sati

The practice of becoming a *sati* by self-immolation, upon the death of the husband, is a relatively late practice in Hinduism. Though unsanctioned by the Shastras, it predates the coming of Islam in India. Akbar officially prohibited it, but the evil could not be eradicated. At the beginning of the nineteenth century this practice was prevalent in Bihar. The Muslims of lower strata of society and most backward culturally, sometimes also resorted to the practice of *sati*. Mirza Qatil gives in detail the Muslim attitude towards the practice of *sati*. According to him there were two divergent views. Some believed that to become a *sati* was a hellish act (being on a par with suicide), but the number of the Muslims holding this view was very limited. Leaving aside the lower classes of Muslims, respectable persons considered sati as symbolic of perfect love. They shed tears for a woman who burnt herself in youth of her husband. It was a custom that before the pyre was set alight, either the governor of the place whether Hindu or Muslim, or someone on behalf of the emperor, went to her to make sure that she was becoming *sati* of her own will.[8]

Customs Regarding the Dead

The practice of taking out a dying man from his bed before he breathed his last was common among Hindus and Muslims. It was a general practice among the Muslims to inform all the kith and kin when a member of a family passed away. The bodies of the emperors, nobles and rich men were carried to the graveyard with great pomp and show, accompanied by infantry, artillery, and cavalry, and drum beating. Members of the bereaved family wore mourning dresses, and the emperors offering mourning khilats to the eldest members of the family in case he was a noble.

On the death of a member of a family, males and females remained in mourning for a long time generally, and for three days particularly. In some cases female mourners were hired. The widow did not wear red clothes, gave up application of collyrium, did not chew betels, or used scents nor wore bangles or sewn clothes, nor participated in a marriage ceremony performed in the same house or in the house of the relatives. She also did not prepare *pakwan* in the *karahi* (frying-pan) or cook meat for forty days. No one in the house slept on a cot for forty days; or prepared *sirka* for a year or *baries* or *sayweean* or vermicelli. On the death of her husband, a wife broke here bangles and took off all her ornaments as a sign of widowhood.

Rituals such as *soim (teeja), chahallum* (forteith), *shashmahi* (six-monthly) and *barsi* (anniversary) were performed in the name of the deceased, have been borrowed from the Hindus with just a change of names.[9]

During the first ten days of the month of the Moharram, the Muslims in general and the Shi'as in particular and their ladies observed the same kind of mourning as they did when some one died in their own family. They gave up wearing of bangles, use of mehndi, wearing of fine and gorgeous dresses, use of oil, scents, chewing of betels, and participation in celebration of marriages. Some superstitious practices were also observed on the occasion of death in a Muslim family.

Remarriage of Widows

Islam encourages the re-marriage of widows and Prophet Muhammad himself married a widow as his first wife; but the Muslims in the Indian environment, following the practice of the upper-caste Hindus, began to look at this practice with some disfavour. If any widow re-married or indicated a desire for re-marriage, she was chided and reviled.

Mirza Qatil says : 'The nobles of the cities and respectable persons of the towns, are similar to the Hindus in preventing their daughters from re-marriage even if they became widows at the age of sixteen or even less than this. Due to their ignorance and illiteracy they do not observe the Islamic practices. Nevertheless those who resort to this act are considered mean, low and disgraceful by them. If the (widowed) daughter of a man on her own accord establishes illicit relations with thousand men, it did not matter for him; but willingly and with his consent, he would not arrange her re-marriage.'

Rituals and Customs from Child-Birth to the Wedding

The *satwansa, naumasa, chhatti, mundan, chilla, zachcha ko tarey dekhana* (showing of the stars to the mother), *rat jaga* (vigil), and *salgirah* and the festivities on these occasions were originally Hindu customs; these were adopted by the Muslims. The wedding customs of the Muslims and the Hindus were more or less similar except for the basic marriage ritual.

The customs of *mangani, mandawa, tail charhana* (oiling of the body of the bride and bridegroom), *uptan malna, kangana bandhna, nek ghari dekhana* (consultation of auspicious time for the actual ceremony), *sehra, maqna,* for the bride, decoration of the bride and bridegroom, *sachuq, hinna bandi,* the groom party *(barat)* led with great pomp and show, accompanied by fire-works, light, music, and dancing parties, yellow and red garments of the bride and bridegroom, colouring of the palms of the bride and bridegroom, chanting of songs called *sathni,* keeping of iron weapon by the bridegroom, the bridegroom's mounting the horse-back while going to the house of the bride, *dhangana, nichawar, utarana,* distribution of the betel leaves and *sherbat*, after the *nikah, matkiyan bharna, arsi mushaf, chauthi* and *raushan chauki* and gifts showered on the lap of the bride, etc. had been borrowed by the Muslims from the Hindus. Besides, there were several minor customs which the Muslims observed on this occasion and all others seem to have been of Hindu origin. Following the traditions of the Hindus, Muslims in the countryside often married their sons and daughters in childhood. The bride did not go to live with her husband immediately after the completion of the nuptial ceremonies but continued to stay on with her parents for some years. When she attained maturity, the *gauna* ceremony was performed and she was sent to her father-in-law's house. Many rituals were performed at this time *(rukhsati)*.

On the front parts of the houses of the bride and bridegroom, some superstitious marks were painted with oil or lime. Much care was taken that the actual nuptial ceremony should be performed on a propitious days. The Muslims ladies were so superstitious that if any mishap occurred to the bridegroom, it was attributed to the bad omen, and non-compliance of certain customs. Tying of the *narah* to the *moosul* was one of the rites performed during the wedding. The *narah* is a cord of many threads dyed red and yellow. The *moosul* the heavy beam is used where rice is to be cleansed from the husks. The customs was altogether of Hindu origin.

Customs Observed on the Occasion of Child-Birth

We have discussed in detail the festivities and customs generally observed by the Muslims on this occasion elsewhere. On the sixth day, after the birth of the child, the *chhatti* rituals were performed; on the same day the newborn child and the mother were shown the stars. The maternal relatives of the child used to send *chhochak* (comprising *kurta* and *topi* (cap)), the *palna* (the cradle) and *khicheri* (rice mixed with pulse) in a procession accompanied by music and dance. On the delivery bed of the mother, an arrow and a copy of the *Quran* were placed. If a man had only one son, he performed all sorts of rituals for the safety of the child, for instance, he fed the poor and orphans and made offerings at the shrines of the saints. When delivery was expected in the royal family, the astrologers and astronomers forecast the auspicious moment for the actual birth. The announcement of actual birth was made by blowing of trumpets and alms were distributed. Like the Hindus, delivery was usually effected on the ground, the mother being made to lie on a quilt.

Male Ornaments

Men and women, both rich and poor, alike decorated themselves, and all known semi-precious stones and metals were used for this purpose. Every part of the body from head to foot had its appropriate jewellery and ornaments, made of gold, silver, pearls, gems, and precious stones. Men used to wear earrings, ear-drops, strings of beads for the neck, girdles of beads, bangles, necklaces, bracelets and rings. Hindus decorated themselves with twelve articles-gold rings in the ear, crown in the turban, finger-rings, etc.

Islamic Law prohibits the use of gold and silver ornaments for Muslim men. But due to their close contact with Hindus, all the Mughal emperors, and princes adorned themselves with all kinds of jewellery and precious stones, in their daily life and on important festive occasions.

Muslims had adopted some of the Hindu dresses and ornaments with certain modifications.

Female Ornaments

Hindu women decorated every part of their body with various kinds of ornaments—the head ornaments—*sisphul, mang, kot-biladar, sekra* (*sut-lara* or more than that) *tika* and *bindi*; neck ornaments—*gulubund, har* and *hans*; ear ornaments-*binduli, khuntila, karnphul, durbiachh, pipal-patti, champakali* (smaller than the red rose, a kind of flower), *bali, mor-bhanwar*, nose ornaments—*besar, phuli, laung* and *nath*; wrist ornaments—*kangan, gajra, jawe, churi* (bangle) and *bahu, bazu bund*, worn on the arms; *anguthi* (ring worn on the fingers); *chhudr-khantika* (golden bells) and *kati-mekhla* on the waist, *jehar, payal (khalkhal)* (small golden bells) and *ghunghru* on the ankles; *bichhwah* and *anwast* on the great toe. Besides there were other kinds of ornaments which were in use. Muslim women freely used these ornaments, some of which retained their original Hindu names, while others were given Persian names.

Women's Toilet

In addition to the ornaments, Muslim ladies imitated many of the toilet customs used by the Hindu women. For instance, staining of palms and feet with *mehndi*, betel-chewing, lining of teeth with *missi*, applying of *kajal* to the eye. The women did not leave their faces undecorated and unpainted. For this purpose they used *ghaza* (a red-coloured powder). They decorated their foreheads and eye-brows with the pieces of brocades. A kind of colour, *lali* was used for painting the lips.

Hair Dressing

Muslim ladies did like Hindu women. After the hair has undergone all the ceremonies of washing, drying and anointing with the sweet jasmine oil of India, it is drawn with great precision from the forehead to the back, where it is twisted into a queue which generally reaches below the waist; the ends are finished with strips of red silk and silver ribands entwined with the hair, and terminating with a good-sized rosette.

Ablution

Before their meals, the Hindus usually took their bath. The practice was also adopted by the Muslims.

Female Dresses

The Muslim female dresses have been discussed in detail elsewhere. The only apparel of the poor womenfolk among the Hindus was a piece of cloth wrapped round the middle part of the body, and thrown over the head, called *sari*, and an *angiya*, a small jacket worn round the chest. *Lenhga* was like the modern petticoat, worn to cover the lower portion of the body. The Muslim ladies adopted all these forms of dresses. *Kurti* was also an imitation. Most of the Muslim women in ordinary dress use the Hindu petticoat or wrapper. According to the Indian tradition, Muslim women tucked in the fold of the sari at the neck to cover up the breasts.

Superstitions

All the natives of Hindustan appear to be more or less tinctured with superstitious notions, which, in many instances, are so grafted in their nature as to resist every attempt made to root out by arguments the folly of this great weakness.

It is not possible to determine whether the Indian Muslims had developed their faith in astrology and astronomy as a result of Iranian or Hindu influences. The Mughal court employed both the Muslim and Hindu astrologers and astronomers. The Muslims in general consulted both Hindu and Muslim astrologers and astronomers, as is evident from the contemporary records.[10]

According to their traditional usage, the Mughal sovereigns of the sixteenth to eighteenth centuries maintained official court astronomers and astrologers, who enjoyed great prestige, status and influence. During the reign of Jahangir an astrologer was weighed against gold. Mubashshir Khan and Munajjim Khan were attached to the court of the Emperor Muhammad Shah. The time or the accession on the throne was fixed by astrologers. The Mughal emperors did not normally undertake an important enterprise without consulting astrologers. Ahmad Shah postponed his march against Abul Mansur Khan Safdar Jang, as the astrologer had told him that it was not an auspicious day.

The emperors and the nobles distributed large sums on the advice of the astrologers to ward off misfortune. Examples are not wanting when the time for commencing the actual battle was fixed by the court astrologers and its postponement was done on their advice. Safdar Jang marched against the Marathas when his personal astrologer, Abdur Rahim, informed him about the auspicious moment for such an enterprise.

Due to the wide influence of astrologers, which was a very lucrative profession, we find the bazars of Delhi and Agra crowded with them to whom resorted every class of people. We find references to barren women and issueless persons consulting astrologers and astronomers inquiring whether they would have any child. As a result of the general popularity of astrology and astronomy, many a Muslim took up the study of this subject. But the orthodox Muslims advised the Muslims that they should not have faith on astronomy and astrology.

Lucky and Unlucky Days and Hours

Like the Hindus, the Muslims too observed lucky and unlucky days. It is said : 'A trifling attention is shown both by the Hindu and Muslim to lucky days, and hours and minutes; and on all occasions, and even in the discharge of the most common duties of life, delay is allowed, and an enterprise may be defeated, by a clan of thunder, the calculation of chances, or the unfortunate ascendant of an unlucky sign.'

Some other Superstitions

Among the other superstitious practices were the use of the leaves of the *bed-i mushk* (a fragrant shrub) to remove the evil effects of witchcraft and sorcery. By observing the custom of *nazar utarana*, evil effects were neutralised. When Emperor Muhammad Shah entered the palace after his victory at Hasanpur, the ladies of the haram received him at the gate and trays full of money were moved around his head and distributed among the poor.

Recovery from illness, and escape from any fatal incident, were the occasions for distribution of alms and charity. There were other superstitious practices which were indulged in by Muslims. For instance, when one was laid up with fever with cold, several superstitious practices were observed; some people ate leaves of the pipal tree, some ate bugs with molasses, while others breathed in the smoke of straw. Somewhere the leaves of the pipal tree were burnt, or someone embraced the pipal tree. Some women slept covering their faces, while somewhere it was said loudly that a snake was coming out of the hole.

An interesting Hindu practice of keeping the cue was partly followed. A scalp-lock (*choti*) was kept on the crown of the head of a male child in the name of Shah Madar, or any other great saint, and shaved at the shrine after the expiry of the period of vow. *Hansuli* (neck-ring) and lion's nails were put round the neck of a male child to protect him from misfortune and ward off any evil spirit.[11]

Faith in Evil Spirits

The Muslims shared with the Hindus faith in evil spirits. The use of various protectives against the influence of malignant spirit is more among the natives of India. The ignorant sections of Muslims as well as Hindus held a superstitious belief in the occasional visitation of the evil spirits of Shaikh Saddu. On such occasions the evil spirit was to be dislodged from the affected woman either by distributing sweetmeats or sacrificing a goat in Shaikh Saddu's name.

Muslim women had a superstitious belief in the occasional visitations of the male personages, besides Shaikh Saddu, Miyan Zain, Miyan Sadr Jahan, Munney Miyan, Chahal Tan, Miyan Shah Darya, and Miyan Shah Sikandar; and there were similarly visiting female spirits like Lal Pari, Sabz Pari, Siyah Pari, Zard Pari, Asman Pari, Darya Pari and Nur Pari. These male and female personages were treated as brothers and sisters. It was also common belief that the above-mentioned females were sent by God to play with Hazrat Zuhra. They were all her servants and maidservants. Particular days were allotted for each of them and on those days the women believed that those fasts would help them in the accomplishment of their desires and held those personages responsible for it.

Sitala

Muslim women held superstitious beliefs in many deities and spirits to whom they assigned particular names. They venerated them in order to have their protection and their children at the time of calamity and misfortunes. When, for instance, small-pox broke out, Muslim women made offerings to the goddess Sitala.

Witchcraft and Incantations

There was widespread faith in the witchcraft and enchantments among Muslims. Observes Davidson : 'All natives, both Muslims and Hindus, have firm faith in magic, and dreaded its evil influence on themselves, children, cattle, and harvests, as may be seen by their amulets, and pots stuck in their fields, marked with white spots, to defend them from an evil-eye.'[12]

Grave Worship and Sacrifices at the Shrines

As already referred to, Indian Muslims did not obviously abandon all their beliefs and rites of worship immediately upon conversion; some beliefs and rites continued in changed forms and contexts. In Bengal, we find Muslims offering 'Puja' at Hindu temples. It is said that Daud Khan, the deputy governor of Zulfiqar Khan in Gujarat, worshipped a Hindu idol at Burhanpur.

But such practices were exceptional in view of the strong Muslim prejudices against direct worship of images. But the veneration of graves of saints and holding of *urs* already present in Islamic society, seems to have been particularly intensified almost to the point of grave-worship under the influence of the Indian environment.

Not only did Muslims visit the tombs of the great saints but like the Hindus, who attached miraculous powers to the rivers and the tanks (like Suraj Kund), they also attributed healing powers such as the removing of the sterility of women, to the fountains and pools attached to the tombs of the saints. For instance, the *jharna* (fountain) attached to the tomb of Shaikh Nasiruddin Chiragh Dehlavi attracted a large number of people, who had a dip in it believing that this would lead to the removal of barrenness of their wives.

Footprints of the Prophet and Hazrat Ali

The Muslims seem to have followed the Hindus in their veneration of footprints and other surviving marks of holy men. There was a stone containing the footprint of the Prophet Muhammad at Delhi. The Muslims raised a dome over it. They demonstrated great devotion to it and their faith had gone so deep that they might gain entrance to paradise. Likewise, there was a place at a distance of three miles from the Red Fort of Delhi, where the footprint of Hazrat Ali was enshrined and the Muslims visited the place on every Saturday in great number and performed the ritual of *ziyarat*.

Fairs at the Shrines

Just as fairs were held at the Hindu places of pilgrimages, the Muslims also held fairs annually at the shrines of the great Muslim saints on the occasions of their *urs*. Merchants and traders flocked there. These fairs were visited both by men and women. Writing about the fair held at the shrine of Hazrat

Makhdum Shah Jala Tabrizi at Malda in Bengal, Ghulam Husain Salim remarks : 'Every year in the month of Shab-i Barat or Zilhajh... a fair attended by a large number of people is held, so much so that lakhs of people from distances of fifteen and twenty days' journey, such as Hugli, Silhat, and Jahangirnagar, etc. come and congregate, and benefit by pilgrimage.' Even today this practice of holding fairs at the shrines is very popular in northern India.[13]

Attempts at Mutual Appreciation

The cultural synthesis led both the Hindus and the Muslims to demonstrate respect for each other's religious views and beliefs. The religious monuments (i.e. mosques and temples) were held in great esteem by both the communities. There were many Hindus of the upper strata who began to entertain cosmopolitan views, holding both Muslim mystics and the Hindu bhakts in respect.

In the literature of the eighteenth century we find scattered references in which idolatry has been appreciated by the Muslim intellectuals instead of receiving condemnation. Miyan Muhammad Raushan Joshush, a poet of Murshidabad, says, for example : 'Idolatry is God-worship'.

Mirza Mazhar Jan-i Jahan shared the liberal and cosmopolitan views of the most of the Sufis towards other religions and their followers. He deviated from the Naqshbandi teachings, as expounded by Shaikh Ahmad Sirhindi, who believed that from the religious point of view the Hindus and Muslims were two separate and antithetical entities. Mirza Mazhar Jan-i Jahan's relations with the non-Muslims were not only cordial, but so catholic that he even enrolled them as his disciples without asking them to embrace Islam first. Such disciples reposed unflinching faith in him. He spent most of his life in Delhi in the upper storey of a house owned by Kewal Ram, a *baniya* (shop-keeper), near Jami Masjid.

As a result of Mirza Mazhar Jan-i Jahan's remarkable persuavive power, a large number of the Hindus are said to have embraced Islam, after accepting his teachings. For the views of the Muslims about Hinduism, the fourteenth letter of

Mirza Mazhar Jan-i Jahan is most significant. In this letter we find the same spirit which Dara Shikoh had expressed in the introduction of Sirr-i Akbar and Majma-ul Bahrain. Mirza Mazhar Jan-i Jahan flatly refused to treat the Hindus at par with the *mushrikin* (sing. *mushrik*), infidels, of Arabia. He accepted the *Vedas* as revealed books and in this way he raised the Hindus to the status of the people of Book (ahl-i kitab). He further argued that there was very little difference between the practice of idol-worship and the *tasawwur-i Shaikh* (concentration on the image of the Shaikh).

Often the Muslims, particularly the mystics, cherished great regard for Hindu religious deities like Lord Krishna and Lord Rama. About Rama and Krishna, Mirza Mazhar Jan-i-Jahan opined: 'When the Quran and *hadis* are silent about them, the charge of *kufr* (infidelity) cannot be levied against Hindus. The Quran and *hadis* explicitly say that Prophets have been sent to every country and nation. Thus, they might have been Prophets. Lord Rama was their first Prophet whose teachings showed the way for the communion with the Supreme Being. Lord Krishna was the last one who instructed the people on mystic lines.'

Some of the Hindus were so much impressed by the teachings of Islam that they allegedly professed it secretly but never disclosed it in public. As mentioned earlier, Kunwar Anand Kishore, secretly informed Qudratullah Qasim of his being a Muslim by heart, but a Hindu in externals. On the other hand Kunwar Prem Kishore 'Firaqi', the son of Kunwar Anand Kishore and grandson of the Raja Jugal Kishore, openly declared that he professed Islam. Raja Kalliyan Singh, pen-name 'Ashiq', used to offer prayers five times every day and observed fasts during the month of Ramazan, and shared food with the Muslims. Raja Chatar Sal, was greatly devoted to Islam and its founder. He respected the *Quran* as much as the *Puranas*.

Some Hindus showed great respect for the *Quran* and had faith in it. In a poem called the *Behula Sundri*, written by Hamidullah of Chittagong, it is claimed that Brahmans, who had assembled to select an auspicious day for the hero's journey abroad, consulted the *Quran* for the purpose. The hero was the son of an orthodox Hindu merchant, but he acted upon the Quranic injunctions as if they were laid down in the *Vedas* and started on his journey praying to Allah for his safety.

The Hindus cherished great faith in the living and dead Muslim saints. Hindus used to visit the shrines of Muslim saints. Unlike the other shrines of the great Muslim saints, the *mujawars* (attendants) at the shrine of Shah Shamsuddin of Dipalpur were Hindus. Anand Ram Mukhlis had great faith in Muslim saints. He not only participated in *urs* ceremonies but whenever he faced misfortunes or adversity, he resorted to the shrines of Shaikh Nizam-ud-din Auliya and Khwaja Qutub-ud-din Bakhtiyar Kaki. He stayed at the shrines for several days. He used to participate in the *urs* fair of Shah Madar at Makhanpur. Hindus in general were not slow in participating in *urs* ceremonies and performed the rituals of circumambulation.

Celebration of the Muslim Festivals by Hindus

Many Hindus not only participated in Muslim feasts, except Eid festivals, but celebrated them as their own. There was a great concourse of the Hindu at the Imambaras of Lucknow during Muharram festival. The Hindus of Awadh in general and the Kayaisthas in particular were greatly influenced by the Muslim culture. The Hindus were employed in great numbers by the state government in different departments, and some of them held the posts of *diwans* and *wakils*. The Kaisthas kept the Muslim professional women in their houses as their wives and had no hesitation in accepting betel leaves and drinks from the hands of these women. Instead of performing the rituals prescribed in Hindu religion, some of them even offered prayers five times according to the Muslim religion and most of them tied the strings of their *qabas* and *angrakhas* on the left like the Muslim mullas. Similarly, instead of raising temples, some of the rich Hindus constructed *Imambaras* and in observance of the rituals of the *ashura-i Muharram,* they followed the rituals of the Muslims. Apart from the Kaisthas other Hindus, too, distributed *sherbet* and made earnest supplication for the health of their children like the Muslims in the name of the Martyrs of Karbala. Hindus also spent money in the observance of the rituals of *nazr-wa niyaz* (vows and options) in which the Kaisthas were again foremost.

Muslim Participation in Hindu Fairs and Festivals

Reflecting the general spirit of social and cultural harmony, the Muslims enthusiastically participated in the religious fairs organised and celebrated by the Hindus. Such instances are many. A fair known as *Athaun* was celebrated at Lucknow. Besides, there were other fairs held at Suraj Kund, and on the banks of Gomati. Mirza Qatil refers to those fairs and to the participation of the Muslims in them. A fair was held at the time of the festival of Dussehra.

A large number of Muslims every year participated in the fair at Garhmukteshwar. They pitched their tents on the bank of the Ganges, and men and women went out on boats. In Delhi many Hindu festivals and fairs were held, especially at the temple of Kalka Ji. 'Though this fair was a fair of the Hindus, yet Muslims went there for recreation. A fair used to be held on the bank of Jamuna known as the mela of *Bahta* on the side of the eastern wall of the Red Fort of Delhi. People belonging to all religious classes participated in this fair. In the same way the Muslims of the Punjab participated in local Hindu fairs.'[14]

The general amity maintained by the Hindus and Muslims towards each other was one of the noteworthy social phenomena of the eighteenth century. In the higher ranks of society, Hindus and Muslims could become intimate personal friends, unmindful orthodox injunctions to the contrary. The Kayasthas, a Hindu caste, were held in high esteem by the Muslims. At the time of marriage ceremonies and other festivities Hindus and Muslims invited each other.

In some cases not only the religious but even political differences did not disrupt social relations. The animosity between the Mughal nobles and Suraj Mal Jat is well known but even then the latter gave shelter to many Muslims who had to leave Delhi. In the days of extreme poverty, Mir Taqi 'Mir' received financial help and sympathy from Hindus. In some exceptional cases these cordial relations led even to the establishment of marital relations between the members of these two communities.

REFERENCES AND NOTES

1. Roy, Shibani and S.H.M. Rizvi. "Monotheistic Islam and Pluralistic Islamic Traditions of India". In *Culture, Religion and Philosophy*. Ed. N.K. Das, p.143.
2. Ibid., pp 144–146.
3. Ibid., p. 147.
4. Umar, Dr. Muhammed. "Hindu Influence on Muslim Social and Religious life". In *Islam in Northern India*, p.417.
5. Ibid, p. 423.
6. Crooke, W. *The Tribes and Castes of North Western India, Introduction*, p. xvii.
7. Umar, Dr. Muhammed. "Hindu Influence on Muslim Social and Religious life". In *Islam in Northern India*, p. 426.
8. Ashraf, K.M. *Life and Conditions of the People of Hindustan*, pp. 191–192.
9. Umar, Dr. Muhammed. "Hindu Influence on Muslim Social and Religious life". In *Islam in Northern India*, p. 429.
10. Ashraf, K.M. *Life and Conditions of the People of Hindustan*, p. 59.
11. For details, refer to 'A Glossary of Tribes and Castes of the Punjabi', p. 256–258.
12. Davidson. *Diary, Travels and Adventure in Upper Parts of India*, pp. 126–127.
13. Umar, Dr. Muhammed. "Hindu Influence on Muslim Social and Religious Life". In *Islam in Northern India*, pp. 435-439.
14. For details see "A Glossary of the Tribes and Castes of Punjab", pp. 241–242.

9

Glimpses of Composite Indian Culture

Etymologically, the term 'composite' was first used in the *architectural* sense (which incidentally is the only one recognised by Johnson in his famous pioneering dictionary). Later, the term 'composite' has been used in mathematics (to refer to 'composite number', which is the product of two or more factors, greater than unity); in natural history (to mean an organic aggregation of individuals, or of distinct parts).

In common terms it refers to anything made up of various parts of elements, that is, a compound. Its synonyms include words like blended, eclectic, syncretic, multiform, variegated, inter-mixed, pluralistic, etc. A thing is called composite when it is made up of various and disparate parts or elements, but existing as an organic aggregation of distinct parts.

Philosophically, a 'composite culture' would mean that peculiar brand of culture that represents the rejection of uni-cultural regimentation or mono-cultural domination and positively reaffirms the value of pluralism and syncreticism, as the valid, stable and desirable bases for cultural efflorescence in a mixed society and plural polity like India.

Composite culture is a product of borrowing, sharing and fusing through processes of interaction between two or more streams over time, in the belief that such cultural symbiosis has a propensity for greater vitality, through larger acceptability, than mono-culture, either of the dominant or the dominated ethnic segment. This would be true within a region, and much more so in the huge continental macrocosm of India.

Everywhere we get glimpses of a composite Indian culture (mixing of Hindu–Muslim elements); in the fields of arts, literature, architecture, painting, sculpture, music, dance etc. as a result of living together for one thousand years. Now, this is Indian culture and not simply Hindu culture.

Architecture

The assimilation between the two cultures led also to the birth of new styles of art, architecture, music and painting, 'in which the basic element remained the old Hindu, but the finished and outward form remained Persian and the purpose served was that of Muslim courts. The architecture of medieval India is neither purely Indian nor purely Islamic, it is a blend of the two and may be called Hindustani; and the blend is not like a mechanical mixture but like a chemical compound. Sir John Marshall observes: 'Indo-Islamic art is not merely a local variety of Islamic art nor is it merely a modified for of Hindu art'.

One of the main characteristics of Muslim architecture was its simplicity and severity and that of Hindu architecture was exuberance and decoration. Hindu and Muslim elements coalesced to form a new type of architecture. The severity of Muslim architecture was mellowed down and the plastic exuberance of Hindu architecture was controlled.

The Muslim emphasis on harmony and form blended with the Hindu emphasis on splendour and decoration. The product was exotic and elegant, exquisite and vibrant, and created marvels of architecture epitomised in the Taj Mahal, which may be regarded as the culmination of architectural synthesis of India.

Religion and art are expressions of culture in two different media. The evolution of culture may, therefore, be traced equally well in either of them, for the consciousness of a race changes organically and in all parts together. Perhaps art is a more sensitive indication of changes than even religion, which in its nature is more subjective, while art lives in objective form alone.

In estimating the influence of Islam upon Hindu art, it is essential to understand the formative influences which mould civilisations and shape their aesthetic needs and values.[1]

Muslim art, like Indian or any other art, is conditioned by certain practical needs of religion and worship. The Muslim worshipper must have a house of worship embodying his vision of reality. It must be a symbol of transcendent majesty of vast spaciousness, of sublimity and purity, and it must be a shelter for the combined prayers of an assembled congregation. Its forms must suggest to him one-pointed devotion, and the all-enveloping nature of the Reality.[2]

These feelings are realised in the mosque, whose pointed arch, aspiring dome, tall minaret, lofty portals, pillared naves and aisles, clear-cut outlines, bereft of all sculpture and possessing a minimum of mouldings, but adorned with surface decoration of conventional arabesques, interlaced geometrical patterns, and beautiful calligraphic inscriptions, whose well-proportioned and symmetrical exterior often covered with enamelled tiles or faierce, and cool, shaded and spacious interior, fulfill all the aspirations and longings of a devout Muslim's soul. The impression of these elements on the existing local schools of architecture, resulted in the growth of different styles of Muslim art in *Maghrib*, Egypt, Syria, Persia and Turkey.

On the soil of India the clash of the two divergent mentalities and their cultures resulted in the creation of a new culture whose religious aspect has already been considered. In art a similar development took place. Hindu and Muslim elements coalesced to form a new type of architecture. The buildings erected by the Musalmans for religious, civil or military purposes were not purely Muslim-Syro-Egyptian, Persian or Central Asian, nor were the Hindu buildings, temples or palaces or cenotaphs purely Hindu.

The simple severity of the Muslim architecture was toned down, and the plastic exuberance of the Hindu was restrained. The craftsmanship, ornamental richness and general design remained largely Hindu, the arcuated form, plain domes, smooth-faced walls, and spacious interiors were Muslim superimpositions.

The artistic quality of the buildings erected since the thirteenth century whether by Hindus or by Muslims is the same, although differences are introduced by considerations of purpose and use, and styles are varied according to differences of local tradition and regional peculiarities.

'In all the Indian—Muslim styles—at Delhi, Ajmer, Agra, Gaur, Malwa, Gujarat, Jaunpur and Bijapur, the form and construction of the domes of mosques and tombs and palaces, as well as the Hindu symbols which crown them; the *mihrabs* made to stimulate Hindu shrines; the arches Hinduised often in construction, in form nearly always; the symbolism which underlies the decorative and structural designs—all these tell us plainly that to the Indian builders the sect of the Prophet of Mecca was only one of the many which made up the synthesis of Hinduism; they could be good Muslims but yet remain Hindus'.[3]

The earliest Muslim constructions were two great mosques at Delhi and Ajmer built by Qutb-ud-Din Aibak about the end of the twelfth century, and from this time onwards every city which the Muslim armies occupied was adorned with mosques, palaces, tombs and other buildings belonging to the new Hindu-Muslim style of architecture.[4]

Under Akbar's enlightened rule a great impetus was given to the reconciliation of the Hindu and Muslim cultures. The buildings of Fatehpur Sikri are the expression of the same spirit as inspired the *Din-e-Ilahi.* The Panch Mahal was the translation into stone of the *Allah Upanishad*. By his encouragement a number of temples was built, which show that the Hindu builders had at last overcome the hesitance and incomplete mastery of Muslim constructional methods which they had exhibited at Gwalior. Of these temples three at Brindaban and one at Govardhan were built in the reign of Akbar and one at Brindaban in that of Jahangir.

The temple of Govind Deva at Brindaban was built by Raja Man Singh Kachwaha, the celebrated general and governor of Akbar, in the year 1590 had a truly Muslim feature. The Jami Masjid of Jaunpur, the Mosque and palaces in Mandu and Ahemadabad were a harmonising of Hindu and Muslim traditions.[5]

Tirumalai Nayak's palace at Madura, which belongs to the seventeenth century, is one of the most magnificent pillers erected in the Hindu–Muslim style. The principal hall 125 feet by 69 feet is placed at the north-west corner of the main building, and the two together correspond to the *Diwan-i-Khas* and *Diwan-i-Am* of Muslim palaces.[6]

Apparently the new Hindu–Muslim mixed style had now become universal and architecturally it was henceforward impossible to distinguish a building erected by the Hindus and the Muslims. Another effect of this cultural synthesis was the construction of tombs among the Hindus. It is impossible to fix the date of the earliest structures of this type, but the *mahasatis* and *chhatris* (cenotaphs), to commemorate the dead, begin to make their appearance about this period. As burial has never been a Hindu custom, the new departure can only be ascribed to the influence of the Musalmans.

The Hindus too, impressed by the Muslim architecture began to construct Mausoleums over their dead, i.e. *samadhis* and *chhatris*. The use of arches in buildings, vaulted roofs and the art of gardening were borrowed from Muslims. The great palaces that the Hindu princes built in their capitals imitated the Diwan-i-Khas, Diwan-i-Aam, Shish-Mahal and the Baradari and the resultant architecture differed from the earlier Hindu mansion. Qutub Minar, a masterpiece in architecture, makes evident the taste of the early Muslim rulers of the Delhi Sultanate. Firozshah Kotla, the multistoreyed citadel of capital built by Firozshah still exists in Delhi.

Sultan Sikandar Lodi built a new capital at Agra, Sikandra near Agra is named after Sikandar. In the Lodi gardens in New Delhi, the stern edifice tombs of Lodi Sultans are the last monuments of the Sultanate. Sher Shah, after defeating Humayun in 1540, built a new city called Shergah (Sher's palace), known later as Purana Qila.

The Deccan Sultans too contributed to the development of the art of architecture. Jahangir was a lover of gardens, some of them laid out in patterns like a Persian carpet. He built paradises in Srinagar (Nishat and Shalimar), Udaipur, Fatehpur, Sikri and Lahore. The Kohinoor and Peacock Throne are the symbols of the age of magnificence, 'If there is a paradise on earth, it is here, it is here, it is here!' So reads an inscription in Persian in the Diwan-i-Khas (chamber of private audience) of Shah Jahan at Delhi Red Fort. Taj Mahal, which is also known as Taj-bi-ka-Roza, depicts the crowning glory of the Mughal period. 'A dream in marble', 'Romance in stone' or 'a tear drop on the cheek of Time' still remains unrivalled in the world.[7]

Paintings

Paintings are the aesthetic expression of a culture which grew out of the synthesis of the racial experience, a synthesis which implies a balance between opposing tendencies—joy and sorrow, pleasure and pain, success and failure, worldliness and other—worldliness, attachment to life and renunciation of life, domination by sense and control of sense, ambition, activity and passion, and satisfaction, passivity and calm serenity. It is not true that the Hindu culture is more religious or less materialistic than other cultures, but the quality and content of its religious consciousness is different, the point of equilibrium between the opposing forces of life is differently situated.[8]

The meeting of the two (Hindu and Muslim) art consciousness under the fostering care of the Mughal emperors was productive of a new style. Upon the plasticity of Ajanta were imposed the new laws of symmetry, proportion and spacing from Samarqand and Herat. To the old pomp new splendours were added, and to the old free and easy naivete of life a new sense of courtly correctness and rigid etiquette. In the result a certain amount of the energy dynamism of both the Hindu and the Muslim were sacrificed; and a stiff dignity was acquired, but along with it a marvellous richness of colour and subtlety of line.

The evolution of the new style was rapid. Probably Babur introduced the models of the Timurid school to the Hindu and Muslim artists of India at Agra. Under Humayun the copying was continued, so that when the *Dastan* of Amir Hamzah was produced in twelve volumes with illustrations for no less than one thousand and four hundred passages, there was a sufficient number of trained artists to commission for the work. Among them were Persians and Qalmaqs, certainly, but not exclusively. The work was of prodigious volume and was probably finished in the early years of Akbar's rule.

Of the painters of Akbar's Court mentioned by Abul Fazl, thirteen were Hindu and four Muslim. They were entrusted with illustration of important works. The best painters illustrated the *Mahabharat, Ramayana, Nal Daman* and *Panchtantra* and a huge amount of money was spent on decorating these epics. The inventory of his library at his death had 24,000 such manuscripts.

During Akbar's reign, the art of painting not only made a great advance but was also Indianized. Indian animals appeared along with the familiar animals of Persian paintings. Indian flowers replaced Persian flowers. The mural decorations of Fatehpur Sikri are a splendid specimen of the art of paintings.[9]

Jahangir was the prince of artists and carried the art of painting of perfection. Like his father, Jahangir encouraged talents and liberally provided all facilities for their growth. Under Jahangir the Indian school completely freed itself of imitation, portrait painting acquired unusual fineness, and scenes of hunting became very popular. The reign of Shah Jahan saw the culmination of the art, the rules of perspective and foreshortening, of modelling and shading were introduced.

Shah Jahan maintained the high tradition of his father. 'Under Shah Jahan, who himself was a good painter and a past master in the art of illuminating books, miniature and portrait painting underwent a great deal of elaboration, so much so that a picture or a portrait, however, elaborate and exquisite, was considered to be wholly incomplete if it was not provided with a beautiful border of the birds and butterflies, flowers and foliage.'[10]

Eminent artists continued to be employed at the Court and by the great nobles who treated them well and appreciated their work. The houses of the nobles were decorated with the master pieces of paintings Shah Jahan had a peculiar fancy for peacock. The walls of his palace were decorated with peacock design. His peacock throne was designed in the similar way. The great

Hindu painters of his reign were Bishandas and Bichittar. His son, Prince Dara Shikoh was also great patron of painting.

Among the scenes in the early period, war and conquest received the greatest amount of attention, especially in illustrating works like *Darab Namah, Timur Namah, Razm Namah (Mahabharata);* hunting and forest scenes also abounded; later a taste for durbar, mythological, genre, domestic and fanciful (e.g. pictures of beauty) pictures developed. Through them all a mystic interest always remains in evidence; religious incidents, portraits of dervishes, scenes of princes learning divine wisdom from ascetics, of prayers in mosques, or of studying the holy book by candle light, or of assemblies of saints, are scattered through the albums and picture collections from Akbar's time onwards.

Music

In the field of music, the Muslim rulers not only patronised it but also learnt it and contributed to its development. The liberal grants made by the rulers made both the Hindus and Muslims to join together in producing fresh melodies and inventing new tunes and instruments. Not only the Court musicians but the Sufi saints and the commoners too contributed in its growth and enrichment.[11]

The patronage given to Hindustani *sangeet* or music by Mughal courts is a glorious chapter of our cultural history. The classical music was not only preserved, but was highly developed and enriched. Many new *ragas* and *raginis* were introduced and cultivated with dexterity and elegence, the beauty and melody of which stir profound thoughts and elevate the soul to ecstatic heights. In the area of dance as well, some new forms were introduced which mostly served the purposes of the court.

Music developed outside the Courts also. The Sufi saints too gave importance to music. Both the Chistiya and the Qadriya schools sanctioned Sama' musical rhythms, that enhanced the effect of the devotional poetry. They enabled the devotees to be plunged into a state of trance called *Haal*. The effectiveness of *Sama* can be gauged by the fact that many a Sufi embraced death while listening to devotional songs which intensely affected their hearts. Khwaja Bakhityar Kaki and Shah Latif were among them.[12]

Thus during the Sultanate period in the field of music, a perfect harmony of taste and sentiments between the Hindus and the Muslims had developed. The Mughals found a common musical art an accomplished fact. They further enriched it by providing liberal patronage and promoting harmonious co-existence. No wonder, the music acquired its perfection and reached its zenith in the Mughal period. Babar loved music and practised it. He also wrote a treatise on it. During Humayun's reign a large number musicians and singers was dependant wholly on the patronage of the emperor for their maintenance.

Amir Khusrau's talent in this field flourished during Alauddin Khilji's time. He wrote songs on all aspects of life and seasons in the language understood by the masses. Amir compared India to the Garden of Eden where Adam resided before his fall. He had a great genius for synthesis and was the first one to thought of combining Persian and Indian tunes and thus enriched Indian music. He invented the sitar by combining the old Indian *veena* and the Iranian *tambura*. He is said to have modified the old *mridang* and to have given to it the shape of Tabla. Besides *qawwali* mode of singing, several *ragas* like Zilaph, Sazagiri and Sarpada were introduced by him. Music being the language of the soul, the changes brought by Khusrau had far reaching social consequences in bringing together people of divergent creed. All the Mughal rulers patronised music. Famous singers like Tansen and Baiju contributed to the popularity of music.

In the Deccan, music reached its zenith during the reign of Adil Shah II. He not only provided state patronage to this art but also himself was a master of Indian music. Larger numbers of both Hindu and Muslim students learnt music from him. In Bijapur, he built the Anand Mahal, in his new capital, which he named Nauraspur the Sangeet Mahal for his dancers and musicians. He was the author of *Nauras* a work is considered a unique contribution to literature and music. In his songs collected in *Nauras* he invokes Hindu deities Saraswati and other

Hindu gods and goddesses as well as the Prophet and the Sufi saint Gesu-daraj. The tradition of patronising music survived in Deccan till the age Tipu Sultan under whom in 1785 Hasan Ali Izzat compiled his *Mufarrih-al-qulub*, intepersed with Persian and Urdu verses. In Awadh, Wajid Ali Shah was himself a musician and expert in dancing. He invented several tunes such as Jogi-Kuntur, Shah Pasand, and Johi.

Thus melodies, music and dance captivated the hearts and enthralled all its lovers Hindus, Muslims and others.

Literature and Languages

Literature produced by Muslim literary men contributed very much to the development of composite culture. In the medieval period, numerous new works were composed and translations from Sanskrit to Persian and from Persian to other language were made of the then existing literature. Hindu scholars learnt Persian and the Muslims learnt Sanskrit. The knowledge of each other's literature fascinated the literary minds and contributed greatly in breaking all sorts of barriers between the two communities and bringing them closer to each other.

A galaxy of learned men, poets and philosophers of unique ability illuminated the courts of Muslim rulers. Muslim writes wrote about Hindu gods with as much devotion as for Prophet Mohammed. These writers were not prosecuted or punished by Sultans, speaks of the liberal outlook and approach of the Muslim rulers. Muslim rulers even encouraged literary writings in dialects on account of which dialects got promoted to the status of literary languages.

In Bengal, the Muslim kings were great patrons of art and literature and it was through their encouragement that the Bengali language, which had been neglected under the Hindu kings, was elevated to a literary status. The *Ramayana* and *Mahabharata* were translated into Bengali. The first Bengali rendering of *Mahabharata* was ordered by Nasir Shah. Many works of Hindu religion were translated into Bengali because of their encouragement. For his liberal ideas and non discriminatory attitude, Husain Shah was regarded as the ideal king, comparable to Arjuna and the incarnation of Lord Krishna in the Kali age.[13]

Muslim poets and writers greatly contributed to the development of the regional literature. One Daulat Kazi wrote Sati Meenavati in Bengali. Alau'l, Syed Murtaza and Syed Sultan, wrote a large number of Vaishnavite songs. Syed Sultan also wrote books on Islamic religion like *Gyan Pradeep, Hazarat Mohammad Charit,* and *Nabi Bangash*. In *Nabi Bangash,* he counted Brahma, Vishnu, Shiva, and Shri Krishna as *nabis* and showed great respect towards them. Lal Mahmud a Vashnavite poet wrote; *"Janam niyya Musalmane, wanchit hove Shricharne'*. Sabit Khan wrote *Vidya Mandir*, Ali Raja is known for his book *Gyan Sagar* and *Dhyanmala* in which his devotion for Hindus gods is reflectsed.[14]

Muslim Sultans thus rendered great service to Bengali language and literature by granting recognition to Bengali in their Court. The practice of appointing Bengali poets in the Darbars of Hindu Rajas had its origin in what the Muslim kings had done and were doing.

Indianisation of the Muslim rulers began with the very beginning of their rule in India. Amir Khusrau (1253–1325) the *Toot-i-Hind* or Parognet of India, who still shines like a moon among the literary figures of the subcontinent, wrote his works influenced and inspired by the Indian environment.

The entire poetic work of Amir Khusrau is inspired with the noble feeling of cultural coordination. He was devoid of even an iota of communal fanaticism. On the other hand he liked and loved humanity higher than anything else. He has written a stanza, the meaning of which is : 'I am a *Kafir* of love and love alone. I do not require any label of Islam. Every nerve of mine has become a sacred thread and therefore I do not require the religious sacred thread as a show-piece.'

Kafire ishk ishkam musalmani mara darkar neeshth
Har range mun thare gastha hajthe junnar neeshth

From this it is evident that he was an embodiment of religious generosity, broad mindedness and patriotism.

The poems of Amir Khusrau are full of love and devotion to the nation. It is a rare phenomenon without comparison. His words describing his motherland (Hindustan) as the best in the whole world prove his committed patriotism for ever. He was of the opinion that patriotism is indispensable for emotional integration of the nation. That is why he has jam packed his poems with patriotism. Even today his patriotism stands apart as unique.[15]

Amir Khusrau has made a touching description of the greatness of India and Indianism in his work titled *Nooh Sipahar* (seven skies). His lines depicting the greatness of India are marvellous. He never tired of singing songs in praise of his motherland, India. Every now and then, he makes special references to the climate, trees and plants, fruits and flowers, birds and animals, skills, language and more than all these, the extraordinary scholarship of the Brahman community. These spontaneous songs directly get imprinted in the heart of the readers. This is the secret of the success of his poems. He writes in his *Nooh Sipahar,* that to those who do not agree with his tributes to India, he would like to say that the greatness of India consists of two important points—one of them is that India is his motherland and Prophet Muhammad Saheb himself has said that patriotism is an indication of one's faith.

The greatness of Amir Khusrau lies mainly in three fields. He was the first ever poet of Khariboli Hindi. He had the vision to envisage Hindi as the national language of India and he had tried his best to strengthen the national unity coupled with staunch patriotism. It is in fact a wonder that this visionary had dreamt of strengthening the national unity and composite culture through the medium of the national language Hindi which has materialised after a period of 750 years.

Prince Dara Shikoh was a great scholar. He wrote *Sirr-ul-Asrar*, a translation of fifty *Upanishads; Majmua-ul-Baharam*, a treatise on the technical terms of Hindu Vedanta with Sufi equivalents; *Dialogue with Baba Lal; Sakinat-ul-Auliya* contains lives of the Muslim saints and a Persian translation of the *Athervaveda*. His untimely death deprived the Indian literature of a literary luminary.

One of the major genres of pre-modern north Indian poetry is the Awadhi or eastern Hindavi *prema-kahani* (literally 'love-story') composed by Muslim Sufi poets, from the fourteenth century onwards. These narrative poems, called Sufi romances by modern critics, are commonly assumed to put forward 'the equation of human love and love for a divine being'. They mark the inauguration of a new literary culture in a local language, an Indian Islamic literary tradition. The Chishti Sufis, the first known composers of the Hindavi mystical romances, describe the ascetic quest of the hero towards the revelatory beauty of a heroine (or God) by linking mortification, fasting, and prayer with a female object of desire. Drawing on the local language of ascetic practice, they make their hero into a yogi, while the heroine is a beautiful Indian woman. While eroticism and asceticism have frequently been linked together in Indian religious traditions and in Sufi mysticism, the Hindavi romances are distinctive because in them the hero attains his 'divine' heroine after an arduous ascetic quest and brings her to live with a hostile wife who represents the world.

This Indian Islamic literary tradition marks the full indigenisation and assimilation of Islam into an Indian cultural landscape. Indigenisation accounts for the Indian elements in Indian Islamic culture as the result of conscious and purposeful adaptations made to the local environment by agents who remained Muslim in their religious orientation, in contrast to the widespread explanation of a haphazard 'syncretism' or 'accretion' of disparate elements. These poems are distinct both from Persian and from the older classical traditions of India, an Indian Islamic creation which emphasises its double distance from these older canons even while borrowing important ideas and conventions from them. The poets of the genre used Hindavi, a spoken local language that they elevated into a literary medium, and the earliest manuscripts of their poems are written in Persian script. Their romances express a Sufi message through a poetics derived in part from Persian, in part from Sanskrit, and in part from regional literary conventions, an indication that these poets had arrived on the cultural scene and that they were fully indigenised as Muslims.[16]

The Indian Sufis were fully steeped in the conventions and symbolism of the various genres of Persian poetry, both lyric (*ghazal*) and narrative (*mathnawi*). At the same time, they were fascinated by the poetics and alluring imagery of Indian poetry as they encountered it in musical and dance performances and in poetic recitation. The genre of the Hindavi Sufi romance should be read against this larger background of cultural appropriations, common links, and creative formulations. The Hindavi Sufi poets used Sanskrit rasa theory and the conventions of Persian poetry to create a mystical romantic genre centred around the various meaning of prema-rasa, the juice or essence of love.

Among the great Sufi poets who contributed to composite culture through literature, Malik Mohamed Jayasi is the most popular figure. His *Padmavat* is considered to be the best love-epic of Hindi Sufi poetry. This is the first *maha kavya* (epic) in Hindi. It is presumed that Goswami Tulsidas was greatly influenced by the *Doha-Chaupai* (poetic metre) style of Jayasi and he rendered the famous *Ramcharitmanas* accordingly.

Before the Mughal period, the seeds of common identity and harmony had been sown by the Muslim rulers which blossomed during the Mughal rule and caused a literary ferment which India had never experienced before.

The religious harmony prevalent in the society in the medieval period reflected in the literature also. Hindu poets wrote in praise of Prophet and the Muslims poets composed verses praising the Hindu gods. They not only had cordial relations but sought each others' help in composing verses and helping the deserved. Sanskrit was not the monopoly of the Hindus as the Muslims had acquired equal proficiency. If Rahim, a Muslim, was adept in Sanskrit then Surdas knew Persian and made use of the Persian words in Hindised form in his verses. The liberty with which Rahim sang in praise of Brahma, Rama and Krishna clearly explains that gods of both the communities were revered with equal devotion by the followers of both religions. Rahim was thus a representative of composite Indian culture.

Raskhan was the best Krishnite poet of the Bhakti period of Hindi literature. Though a Muslim, he was a devotee of Krishna and composed poems in Brijbhasha. His poems reverberate with genuine feelings of a heart full of devotion to the deity. The poet, Bharathendu Harischandra, has aptly remarked that all the Hindus should salute this Muslim Hindi poet. The literary importance of Raskhan is unquestionable. The natural and strong feelings described by Raskhan hold the readers spellbound.

It is said that Raskhan happened to read the Persian translation of *Srimad Bhagavad* and subsequently got merged into the Krishna cult. Consequently he left Delhi for Govardan Dham and lived there till the end.

Raskhan was equally good at Arabic and Persian. He was also attached to Hindi poetry. As a result of his stay in Brindavan, he became an expert about the place and composed all his works in Brijbhasha. He was very popular among the people for his free verses on Lord Krishna. He worshipped Krishna in the *madhuriya* form. No doubt he was greatly influenced by the Sufi emotion of love. His devotion and love are entirely different from that of the other Krishnite poets. Raskhan's concept of Krishna is unique in the sense that Lord Krishna sometimes transforms himself into the lover Krishna and he is made to dance according to the tunes of the *gopikas*.

Raskhan is notable for his effective description of love, both in unison and separation. Truly this description of *unison love* is par excellence. There are some stanzas depicting *vatsaliya sringar* also, which are indeed marvellous. In short, Raskhan's poetry is filled with joy and sweetness up to the brim for ever. All these stanzas are touching and indelible to the core. The poet himself writes in one of his stanzas that if at all he will have another birth, it should be in Brindavan. Of course, no other poet has expressed this ardent wish, not even a Hindu poet.

The great Kabirdas is considered to be the very best and representative poet of the Nirgun Sant poetry of the Bhakti period of Hindi literature. Kabir fought with his mighty pen to put an end to the monopoly of the upper class society and thereafter bring them closer to the common man. That is why Kabir is called a revolutionary and visionary poet. The impact of Hindu culture on a par with the Muslim culture is evident in his words and deeds. That is why we see a harmonious blending of both the cultures. Kabir, having been influenced by the emotional mysticism of the Sufis, ritualistic mysticism of the *yogis* and non-violence and prapathi of the Vaishnavites along with the Indian Brahmanical rites popularised his own cult.

The credit goes to Kabir for having propagated a new sect consisting of the virtues of all the schools of thought and discarding what was not palatable to society.

Kabir was a free thinker. He criticised external paraphernalia of all religions. He abused the bad practices of the *pandas, pujaris, sadhus* and equally the *fakirs* and *mullas.* He used to make fun of the high-caste Brahmans and advise them to cultivate humanism. He tried his best to bring the Hindu and Muslim communities closer, so as to enable them to live in amity. He used to condemn petty religious quarrels. He advised the Hindus to get rid of idol-worship by making a sarcastic remark that it is better to worship the grinder-stone at home than the temple-idol, as the former one is atleast useful for grinding food items.

The mysticism of Kabir was a blended form of the Advaita of the Hindus and the romantic love of the Sufis. His mysticism is full of spiritualism.

Baba Farid is still remembered as an embodiment of composite culture. He was the first Muslim saint of Punjab who prescribed for his disciples religious litanies and formulae in the Punjabi language. Moreover, he is regarded as the father of Punjabi poetry on account of his being the earliest known poet with Punjabi as his medium of expression.[17]

Baba Farid's impact on the Punjabi language is as wide and as profound as on Punjab's life and lifestyle. He is, in fact, the father of Punjabi literature. The contribution of Sufi poets to the language, literature and culture of Punjab is not only profound but is also vast and varied. Their mystical songs, in particular, are the pride of the whole of Punjab. They form the common and invaluable heritage of all Punjabi people. These songs are 'sweet utterances of those love-lost souls'.

Reading and listening to them, even today, the Punjabis feel elated. The lyrical effusions of those blessed men gave birth to a distinct stream of poetry called *Sufi kavya-dhara*, which inherits a long literary tradition. This important stream was started by Baba Farid during the thirteenth century, and was developed by poets like Shah Husain, Sultan Bahu, Bulle Shah, Syed Ali Haider, Fard Fakir, Hashim Shah, Maulvi Ghulam Rasool and many others.

The liberal attitude and reciprocal policy of give and take that it adopted, and the influence it exercised, proved far-reaching in the annals of the literary, cultural and religious history of Punjab. It also absorbed the essence of Vedantic and Sikh thought and influenced thought and action in due course.

The impact of this strain on the Punjabi language and literature has been considerable. These Sufi poets adopted the language of the common Punjabis for the expression of their thought and conveyed their message directly and effectively. The credit of introducing the element of popular love legends of Punjab, to Sufi verse, also goes to these poets.[18]

Punjab is justly proud of having given birth to this great moral, spiritual and literary tradition spanning a period of about nine centuries. This glorious tradition has not only initiated literary writing in Punjab, but has also developed and enriched its treasures all through this long period of history.

These mystics evolved a common and composite language which became an ideal vehicle for conveying their thought and message to Punjabis of all regions and religions. They derived the required images and similes from the everyday life of Punjab, particularly from the rural areas. The Sufi saints and poets of Punjab contributed not only to the linguistic, literary and cultural heritage of Punjab but also to composite culture.

Writing of Marsiya

Writing of *marsiya*, an Islamic/Iranian literary tradition, developed in Awadh as a genre of composite creativity. It did not remain merely a medium for invoking sorrow. As a literary genre, it represented a synthesis of multiple Indian cultural traditions and provided glimpses of the *Ganga-Jamuni tehzeeb* of north India with Lucknow as its centre. As a musical genre too, it assimilated the traits of both classical canonised forms as well as folk musical varieties then current in Awadh, and developed from *khwanandagi*, chanting, into a most sophisticated musical style. Under the patronage of the Shiite rulers of Awadh (1765–1856), the *marsiya* rose to unprecedented heights.

The term *marsiya* (elegy) is a derivative of the Arabic *risa*, which means an oration in mourning. *Marsiya*, generally speaking, is a poem recited to express sorrow on the death of a person; it is also a poem to commemorate a particular pathetic event. Amir Khusrau Dehalvi, the doyen of Persian poetry, composed two *marsiyas* in *tarkib-band* after the death of Prince Muhammad, the son of Sultan Balban (A.D. 1267–87), which can be found in the anthology entitled as *Ghurratul-Kamal*.

Gradually *marsiya* came to narrate the event of the martyrdom of Imam Husain, the grandson of Prophet Muhammad and his kinsmen at Karbala (in Iraq), during Muharram, the first month of the Islamic calendar.

The history of the evolution of *marsiya* in India is unique. It thrived on religious ritualism and in this process came to integrate ceremonies and rituals of Indian origin as well. It portrayed the ethics typical of the Indian way of life and presented a cultural canvas of northern India.

Marsiya writing in Awadh was popularised by the local poets of Faizabad—Afsurdah and Gada—and luminaries from Delhi who included Sikandar and Sauda. An indigenous style of *marsiya* writing developed in the north with Delhi as its centre, which grew due more to its popularity and cultural vitality and not royal patronage, and it drew from Indian literary and folk forms. It is important to note at this juncture that Sikandar and Sauda represented two traditions in the realm of *marsiya* writing.[19]

Sauda was one of the leading Urdu *ghazal* writers of Delhi who brought the folk form of marsiya on a par with other forms of literary expression, and it appealed to both the elite and the populace. Due to the efforts of Sauda, *marsiya*'s literary worth began to be recognised. He set new standards of *marsiya* writing and lent a literary colour to his marsiya compositions. Sauda made several innovations in the form of the *marsiya*. He enhanced the element of tragedy by emphasising bravery and chivalry as a concomitant of the narration of the actual warfare *(jung)*. He composed *marsiyas* in the memory of individual heroes and warriors and described combats, which also necessitated characterisation.

Due to the efforts of those who cared for literary excellence, the *marsiya* as a newly graded item of poetry heralded a new era in Urdu literature. It was the time when Shia rituals connected with Muharram (in the Indian context) were taking shape and a sort of social exclusiveness and sect consciousness were gaining ground among the Shias. Mourning assemblies *(majlis-i aza)* and *taziya* processions became frequent. Significantly, these processions were elaborate and provided an arena to performing artistes for a display of their skills without discrimination of caste, creed or social status.

Many new rituals were accepted in the mourning ceremonies. It attained the colourfulness of the Dussehra festival. Some of the practices such as *mehndi, jhula,* or even the elaborate processions and *ghasht* and illumination were of Indian origin. This compositeness was largely due to the fact that many Hindus also adopted *azadari*. Amongst Hindus, the Saxena and Shrivastava Kayasths and the Khatris, were *hamkasa* with Muslims, that is, they had cultural affinity with Muslims and shared their cultural practices. A highly respected class of *marsiya* writers emerged—quite different from the professional class of *marsiya-khwans*.

Anis and Dabir widened the scope to portray other sentiments also, especially Anis in whose poetry it is not very difficult to recognise the nine *ras* of Braj poetry. Dabir is one of the foremost exponents of *rubais, salams,* and *marsiyas* in a variety of styles. Many Braj and Awadhi words are woven into the fabric of Anis's *marsiyas*.

Anis's idomatic diction provide the nuances of the conversational style of the gentry that included Hindus and Muslims both. Anis makes graphic use of similes from Indian mythology. Anis deals with *rukhsat* in a manner that foregrounds the dramatic aspect of the *marsiya* and evokes emotion, intonation, and histrionics at the time of recitation. Dialogues form an important ingredient of *marsiya* literature and often bear resemblance to the *samvad* (conversation) of the Ramlila.

To sum up, it may be said that *marsiya* is representative of the compositeness and resilience of Awadh society, wherein the idioms and conversations of the other were freely adopted; a society that had faith in the strength of coexistence of diverse cultural groups. *Marsiya* took on indigenous poetic, musical, and linguistic elements and had the vibrance of Indo-Persian traditions nurtured in northern India over the centuries.[20]

In the South, the Bahmani kings greatly contributed to the development of the local literature. Their liberal patronage to the poets and writers and their non-sectarian outlook gave emergence to a revolution upsurge in the literally field. Adil Shah I (1558–1580) was a learned scholar. Sanskrit Vaman was his favourite and was incharge of his large library. As the Court language was Marathi, a lot of literature in this language was produced. Ibrahim Adil Shah II who became the ruler of Bijapur in 1580 was himself a literary figure. He had command over many languages and wrote *Nauras*, the work in which he wrote many devotional poems on Hindu gods and goddesses. Qutb Shah Dakkhini too was a Marathi poet. During his reign, a poet named Adil wrote a large number of devotional poems on Lord Krishna.

Maharashtrian poetry and music has been profoundly influenced by the Sufi *sama* (music and singing). It is a combination of *lawni* (popular Marathi singing) and Arabic music. Even subsequent Maharashtrian music and singing has been influenced by the Sufi compositions. There cannot be any doubt about it. Many of the *ragas* and *ragnis* in Maharashtra have their origin in the Sufi music. This is what Maharashtra owes to the Sufis. This debt cannot be denied. Shaikh Mohamed a great Maharashtrian Sufi considered Yoga and *tassawuf* as one and called his book on *tassawuff Yogasangrah,* used Marathi language, using Marathi and Sanskrit terms for various Sufi terms.

We find that in all regional languages Arabic and Persian words have been freely used. In Malayalam Moppila literature, Arabic and Persian words find profusely used for expressing cultural aspects.

In many regional language areas, common language cultures developed instead of Hindu–Muslim identical cultures.

For instance, in Bengal and in Tamil Nadu both Hindus and Muslims contributed to their respective languages immensely and respected more their language culture than their religious cultures.

Tamil Muslim authors have expressed their understanding of Islam through a variety of literary genres that have defined both their Islamic and their Tamil identities. Tamil Hindu authors have encountered the Islamic tradition more on the level of myth and ritual, incorporating some Muslim saints and teachers into their pantheon, making pilgrimages to their tombs, or weaving stories of Muslim devotees into the legends of Hindu gods.

For instance, Lord Ranganatha, the manifestation of Vishnu in Srirangam, has a Muslim consort, for whom there is a special shrine in the temple complex. This pattern is repeated in several other Vaishanava shrines. Performers of classical south Indian 'Carnatic' music also incorporated what were perceived to be Muslim melodies into the traditional *raga* structure of classical south Indian music, which shows significant Persian influence.

Over the centuries, Muslims in Tamil Nadu have studied both secular works and Hindu religious poetry in Tamil and skillfully utilised traditional Tamil literary conventions in their religious writings. Works on Islamic themes written by Tamil authors include several *kappiyam* (Skt: *kavya*. epic poems), of which the *Cirappuranam,* the biography of the Prophet Muhammad is the best known.

They also include descriptions of holy places like Nagore, and hundreds of devotional poems—some addressed to a goddess, others written in a mystical Sufi genre. The most famous work on Islam in Tamil is the *Cirappuranam* (Life of the Prophet) of Umaru Pulavar (Omar the Poet, d. 1703), who lived in Kilkarai, in South Tamil Nadu.

The title of Umaru Pulavar's *Cirappuranam* is indicative of the blending of languages that emerges in its text. *Cira* is the Tamil form of the Arabic *sirah,* meaning biography, specifically a biography of the Prophet. And *purana* (Tamil : *Puranam*) is a Hindu literary genre that includes pious accounts of the salvific deeds of a divine being, sometimes seen as an incarnation of the supreme diety, and containing long poetic accounts of this person's wondrous qualities.

Like the Tamil epic poet Kampan, Umaru Pulavar gives extensive descriptions of the country and the city where the Prophet is to 'descend' (*avatar*). Never having travelled to Arabia, Umaru gives a description of Tamil Nadu transposed to Arabia. Umaru does not elaborate on his analogy while describing the landscape, mountains, rivers and streams in Arabia. It is striking that he seems at home with Vedantic ideas.

He also follows the conventions of Tamil poetry in describing the city of Mecca. Umaru Pulavar uses other Tamil literary conventions with equal skill. The long chapter on the wedding of Ali to the Prophet Muhammad's daughter, Fatima *(Pattima tirumanap patalam),* contains a beautiful description of Ali's procession through the city of Medina, paralleling Kampan's description of Rama's procession through Mithila in his *Ramayanam.*

Apart from literary conventions, the poem utilises many words found in Hindu literature in Tamil. In Tamil texts the *Vedas* and the *Upanishads* were called *marai,* which means 'hidden, that which is a secret, a mystery'. And Umaru, too, uses this term, as well as the *Veda,* to refer to the *Quran.* Other theologically loaded words are found in the *Cirappuranam.* For instance, the birth of the Prophet is referred to as an *avatara* ('descent', *'Vilattattu kantam, Napi avatara patalam'),* the term used in Hindu theology to refer to the incarnations of Vishnu, who descended into this world 'to save the good and destroy evil' (*Bhagavad Gita* 4:8).

There is one Tamil Muslim scholar, and poetic genius, Shaikh Thampi Pavalar who was considered a great exponent of Shaiva philosophy. A freedom fighter and true Gandhian, he contributed numerous literary works in Tamil. Having performed the unique *Sadavadan* (performing a hundred feats at a time—answering a hundred questions on literature at a time). Mahamathi Pavalar was an embodiment of composite culture still remembered by all Tamil-loving Hindus and Muslims.

Muslim men and women have been among the most eminent scholars in interpreting the ninth-century Tamil

Ramayana composed by Kampan (known as *Ramavataram* or the *Kampa Ramayanam*). M.M. Ismail, the former Chief Justice of the Madras High Court and author of some forty books on the Tamil *Ramayana,* remarked with justifiable pride that in every generation there is at least one Muslim who is an authority on the Tamil *Ramayana.* Muslims also participate in the festival of Kampan, an annual celebration devoted to the scholarship on this poet.

Chinna Maulana Saheb, the well-known Muslim nagaswaram player, plays his instrument regularly at the Thanjavur temple. Hyder Ali, a good Muslim, is one of the leading singers in the Kathakali programmes at Kalamandalam. We have vivid memories of the late Rahimuddin Khan, the great Dhrupad singer, singing 'Saraswati vandana' in chaste Sanskrit, and the late Abdul Karim Khan singing Thyagaraja's *'Rama, nisamana mevaru?'* ('Rama, who is there to equal you?').

REFERENCES AND NOTES

1. Tarachand, Dr. *Influence of Islam on Indian Culture,* p. 184.
2. Ibid., p. 195.
3. Harvecee. *Indian Architecture,* p.101.
4. Tarachand, Dr. *Influence of Islam on Indian Culture,* p. 196.
5. Ibid., p.199, 202.
6. Jawed, Dr. Ajeet. *Heritage of Harmony,* p.289.
7. Tarachand, Dr. *Influence of Islam on Indian Culture,* p. 207, 216.
8. Pradivin, *Builders of Mughal Empire,* p. 172.
9. Jaffer, S.M. *Some Cultural Aspects of Muslim Rule in India,* p.135.
10. Jawed, Dr. Ajeet. *Heritage of Harmony,* p.276.
11. Ibid., p. 278.
12. Shustery, A.M.H. *Outline of Islamic Culture,* p.220.
13. Majumdar, R.C. *Delhi Sultanate,* p.220, 635.
14. *Khuda Baksh Library Journal,* (Patna) No. 44, 1987, p.74.
15. Mohamed, Dr. Malik. *The Culture of Hindi,* p.87.
16. *India's Islamic Traditions, 711–1750.* Ed. Richard M. Eaton, pp. 180-181.
    For further detailed study of the literary culture of the Hindavi Sufi romances, refer to *Shadows of Paradise* by Richard M. Eaton and *Madhya Kaleen Premakhianak Kavya* in Hindi by Dr. Malik Mohamed.
17. The *Guru Granth Sahib* contains 112 shlokas of Sheikh Farid.

18. Shan,Harnam Singh. "Contribution of Sufi poets to the Languages, Literature and Culture of Punjab". In *Contemporary Relevance of Sufism.* Indian Council of Cultural Relations.
19. Trivedi, Madhu. "A genre of Composite creativity : Marsiya and its performance in Awadh". In *Living Together Separately,* p.194–195.
20. Ibid., p.221.

10

Epilogue

In the preceding chapters, we had an insight into the foundations of the Indian composite culture. This culture developed gradually through the course of nearly a thousand years. In the cultural history of India, we find the advent of Islam instrumental to a second major cultural metamorphosis after the first one of Indo-Aryan fusion. The emigrant Muslims came to India to settle here down permanently.

After some time, mutual intercourse and appreciation of each other's cultural values and religious dogmas led to mutual understanding. After the first shock of conquest was over, the Hindus and Muslims prepared to find a via-media whereby they could live as neighbours. The Muslim Sufi mystics prepared the ground for this cultural synthesis. With the settlement of the Muslims in India, conciliation and concord between the various cultural groups was not only a moral and intellectual demand, but an urgent social necessity.

When the Hindu society was regimented and stratified into social classes based on religious sanction and lacked simple formulae of faith, well-defined dogmas and rituals and democratic theories of social organisation as well. 'Islam appeared upon the scene with simple formulae of faith, well defined dogmas and rites and democratic theories of social organisation.'

The Muslim rulers also brought about the best and the most harmonious relations between Hindus and Muslims. During the Sultanate as well as the Mughal period, religion was more or less a matter of personal faith and not a source of strife in society. The state was not theocratic and the ulema were not allowed to interfere in state matters. Although in the medieval period the head of State in India was a Muslim, the State was not Islamic. The State did not follow the injunctions of the holy scriptures—The *Quran*, the *Hadith*, or the laws elaborated in the four schools of Sunni jurisprudence. It is a mistake to call the medieval State in India theocratic, for it did not function under the guidance of the Muslim theologians. Almost every one of the Muslim monarchs of India from the thirteenth century onwards expressed his inability and indicated the impossibility of conducting government in accordance with the Shariat.

Prof. M. Habib says : 'It is true that Muslim kings, mostly of foreign extraction sat on Indian thrones for some six or seven centuries. But they could only do so because their enthronement was not the enthronement of the Muslim rule. Had it been otherwise they could not have lasted for a single generation'.[1]

Mutual aspirations, adjustments, admiration and understanding existed among Muslims and Hindus. The liberal religious movements in the form of Sufi, Bhakti and the numerous religious syncretistic cults, worked in a big way in creating and promoting harmonious co-existence of all faiths. The teachings of the saints, which were the combination of *Vedanta* and Islam, succeeded in convincing the masses that God was One, having two different names, Ram and Rahim. Besides, the liberal religious movements had social significance too. The saints opposed the orthodoxy, rigidity and divisions of every kind. They emphasised the principles of equality, freedom and fraternity.

The rulers not only respected and revered the saints but many of them even became their followers. The rulers because of their political compulsion or liberal outlook allowed religious freedom to their subjects. Not only had Hinduism and Islam evolved a healthy pattern of synthesis, the Sikh religion and the numerous cults founded by Hindus and Muslims, emerged and flourished during their reign.

Liberalism and not orthodoxy governed the public or private life of the rulers whether Hindu or Muslim. The Muslim rulers gave lands, *jagirs* and other presents for the construction and maintenance of temples and the Hindu and Sikh Rajas built mosques and tombs. The Muslim rulers even built small temples within the palaces and forts for their non-Muslim wives and officials. The *Quran* and *Puranas* were placed together and were read and revered alike. They respected religious feelings of their subjects and were impartial in religious matters.

The rulers considered deliverance of justice to all without any bias as their religious duty. The Hindus were treated on a par with the Muslims and were not discriminated on any ground. The Muslims rulers and the nobles not only recruited Hindus in the state services but also fully trusted them. The diverse religions, cultures and languages did not cause divisions but strengthened the harmonious co-existence and enriched the country in every field. The people lived happily, as their kings were generous, just and benevolent.[2]

All Muslims, mostly converts from the lower classes of the Indian society owed their loyalties towards this country alone. Thus medieval India was an age of enlightenment, elevation, eloquence, peace, progress, prosperity and communal harmony.

After the death of Aurangzeb in 1707 and the weakening of the Mughal Empire, the British traders who came to India as merchants of a company started meddling with Indian political affairs. By playing one ruler against another and acquiring economic and political advantages thereafter, they acquired the position of dictating their terms. They fomented all disputes; allied themselves with rulers or rebels as suited their designs; hired out troops to fight a rival and then helped the rival when the other grew strong.

The policy of pleading and pleasing the Indian rulers was given up and intrigues, conspiracies and purchase of loyalty of the nobles became the guiding principle of East India Company. Their first victory was over Nawab Siraj-ud-Daula in 1757 and the train of success continued till 1857 when their home country directly enslaved India. They dethroned Emperor Bahadur Shah, cut off the heads of the princes and presented them as *nazar* to the helpless emperor and later them hung on Delhi Gate, known as Khooni Darwaza. They mercilessly plundered India and carried its wealth to Britain. They looted not only the Indian treasury but also took away the rare manuscripts.

Tipu's huge-sized throne, which the Sultan had constructed but could not ascend was disjointed and taken to Britain. Precious Kohinoor was studded in the British Queen's crown. They injected the virus of communalism in the Indian system and worked for its rapid spread in every aspect of Indian life. No wonder that under their patronage the communalists acquired ascendancy. The age of harmony, respect and reverence for each other's god disappeared.[3]

Finding that only by dividing Hindus and Muslims on the basis of religion, could they rule this country, the British adopted the policy of 'divide and rule'. They applied many techniques to achieve their aim. They engaged their historians to rewrite Indian history and textbooks. A glimpse into official British records will show how the policy of *Divide-et-Impera* was taking shape. The Secretary of State, Wood, in a letter to Lord Elgin said :

'We have maintained our power in India by playing off one part against the other and we must continue to do so. Do all you can, therefore, to prevent all having a common feeling.'

George Francis Hamilton, Secretary of State for India, wrote to Curzon :

'I think the real danger to our rule in India not now but say 50 years hence is the gradual adoption and extension of Western ideas of agitation, and if we could break educated Indians into two sections holding widely different views, we should, by such a division, strengthen our position against the subtle and continuous attack which the spread of education must make upon our system of Government. We should so plan the educational text-books that the differences between community and community are further strengthened'. This division of religious feeling is greatly to our advantage.

Thus under a definite policy, the Indian history textbooks were so falsified and distorted as to give an impression that the medieval period of Indian history was full of atrocities committed by Muslim rulers on their Hindu subjects and the Hindus had to suffer terrible indignities under Muslim rule. And there were no common factors in social, political or economic life.

British historians have laid emphasis on difference, drawn pictures in which the relations between Hindus and Muslims bear most prominently the marks of violence, conquest, rapine and religious bigotry. They have presented the Muslims as destroyers of Hindu culture and traditions, despoilers of Hindu temples and palaces; and brutal idol-breakers who have offered to their Hindu-victims the terrible alternative of conversion or the sword.

It is hardly surprising that educated men in India drugged with such poisonous stuff from the most impressionable period of their lives grow up to suspect and distrust each other. The Hindu has been brought to believe that the Muslim period of Indian history which extends over eight hundred years and more, is a nightmare. Not only does he feel no pride in it, but when he turns back his mind to find inspiration in the past, he skips over this long interval and draws highly idealised pictures of the golden past which lies beyond.

Through their writings, the British historians wished to assert that : (i) Indian people have always been ruled by cruel dictators and capricious despots; in comparison, British rule was a rule of law by liberal rulers; (ii) British rule was not the first alien rule; Muslims, too, were foreign rulers, all that the British have done, is to replace an alien inhuman Muslim rule by a liberal rule of law; (iii) The Muslim rulers enslaved Hindus and committed awful atrocities on them; British rulers, on the other hand, rescued the Hindus from the misrule of Muslims, for which the Hindus should remain grateful to them and give them full support; and, (iv) Hindus and Muslims were always divided and at each other's throats and they can never live peacefully with each other in the absence of a third party ruling over them—the British.

This motivation is not hidden, but expressed in clear words. In his preface to the *History of India as told by its own historians*, written in 1849, H.M. Eliot, the leading British historian of the day, frankly confessed his motive in publishing his history. 'It was to make our native subjects more sensible of the immense advantages accruing to them under the mildness and equity of our rule', he declares. Referring to the emerging nationalistic leaders criticising the British rulers as 'Bombastic Babus', he advises them to see the reality of pre-British India and stop their incipient critique of British imperialism.

Other British historians did not lag behind in presenting a communal view of Indian history. James Mill, a well-known British historian divided the Indian history into three periods : Hindu, Muslim and British (not Christian or Protestant). This division of historical periods, to say the least, was totally misconceived. This periodisation is fallacious, since local and customary law had always been respected by rulers, big and small, in India throughout its history. Muslim rulers never imposed Islamic law on Hindus.

In fact, all Muslim rulers ruled through a chain of feudal intermediaries called Sardars, *Talukdars,* etc. among whom there were a large number of Hindus. They had full sway over the territories they actually governed. They were bound to their Muslim overlords only to the extent of paying tributes, i.e. a share of the revenue and providing military support during the aggressions into other territories or for suppressing rebellions. The revenue systems introduced by either Hindu or Muslim rulers were neither based on Hindu law or Muslim law, but were either more or less oppressive, depending upon the share the feudal lords were acquiring.

The communal interpretation of Indian history by British historians was not merely a wrong and misplaced academic exercise, it was a thoroughly motivated and deliberate exercise in pursuance of the imperialist policy of 'divide and rule'.

British historians and intellectuals had a very low opinion of Indians. Indians, according to them, were backward, uncultured, spiritually inclined and apathetic to material progress, cowards, listless, pessimistic—in short, incompetent to rule themselves. This, of course, was a distorted view of Indian people. However, this view spurred various reactions among Indian intellectuals. One reaction was to over-glorify ancient Indian history to assert that Indians were in no way behind the Western world in managing their political affairs. The other reaction was to reestablish the purity of original Hinduism or Islam, shorn of the 'spurious' elements that had crept in during the inevitable course of history.

British historians lead by Sir Charles Elliot, distorted Indian history by over-emphasising Hindu–Muslim difference in medieval times, and making out that the Hindus were infinitely better off under the British rule than in the previous times. Their lead was followed by many Indian historians. But this was not the only root of the communal distortion of Indian history. Many of the early 'Indologists', who did pioneering work for reconstructing the early period of Indian history, unfortunately emphasised all those aspects which were the opposite of Western industrial society, which was unfolding itself at that time. Thus, they pictured the ancient Indian society as one which was dominated by religious and spiritual values, and where vulgar materialism had little sway.

Following some British historians like Mr. Mill, Indian historians also started to divide history of India into three watertight compartments namely, the Hindu period (Ancient history), the Muslim period (medieval history) and the British period. Nothing can be more absurd, as in the first place, they should be either Hindu, Mohammadan and Christian, or ancient, medieval and modern communal division of Indian history started.

Certain schools of historiography subscribing to a communalist approach in social analysis, misread the history of the medieval period in India by injecting into the motives of armed conflicts and tussles for power, factors of religion, both in their 'crusading' and 'resisting' aspects, and viewing these as the most significant element in the making of events. This is in fact a tendentious attempt to substantiate the untenable hypothesis that the medieval period in the history of India, is a period of prolonged and bitter conflict between the two major religions, namely Hinduism and Islam. Muslim rulers and aspirants to power and dominion are portrayed as zealous 'crusaders' for the Islamisation of the country.

The communal reading of medieval Indian history is based on certain wrong hypothesis. They are : (i) political power in India and its distribution was on the basis of religion; (ii) political power meant the power of the religion of ruler; (iii) the power wielded by Muslim or Hindu ruler was, in fact, the power wielded by the people adhering to the same faith (or wielded by ruler on behalf of the people who were adherents of the same faith); (iv) all Muslim or Hindu rulers were either ruling or fighting wars for either forwarding or in defence of their faiths.

Unfortunately, this perverse historical outlook still haunts the mind of many intellectuals and a large section of common people. It is conveniently forgotten that a large majority of Muslims are the descendants of converts from the shudras, to whom Islam offered an escape from caste oppression. Indian Muslims are obstinately viewed as descendants of oppressive alien rulers, a stereotype invented by British historians.

The communal view of Hindu–Muslim relations was not limited to textbooks promoted by the British rulers. It was also spread through other media such as newspapers, magazines, story books, pamphlets and motion pictures and, above all, through speeches and private conversations.

One major distorted version of medieval Indian history adopted by the British historians (and by their hired Indian historians) was about the 'conversion' to Islam. They attempted to put forward the theory that the influence of the sword (force) and political patronage were the reason for conversion of Hindus to Islam.

It is a fact that during the colonial rule conversion took place on account of the worldwide Protestant missionary movement. Even the word 'conversion', which connotes a sudden and complete rejection of one's former religious identity in exchange for a new one has clear Protestant overtones. Comparing Christian conversion (conversion to Christianity in colonial India) to medieval Muslim conversion was an attempt by the British to turn the Hindus against Muslims.

But the projection of this Protestant model backward into medieval or early modern eras did considerable violence to the contemporary data, which seldom indicate deliberateness or intentionality of any sort much less specific motives for 'conversion' such as those just mentioned. Nothing in pre-colonial Indian source suggests that there ever occurred among whole communities a conscious or dramatic 'turning-over' of religious identity. What the original evidence rather points to is a slow, almost glacial process of religious evolution that was so gradual in pace as to go largely unnoticed by either inside or outside observers.[4]

Though communal ideology was thus built on the premises of a mischevious and sectarian interpretation of medieval history, it had cast its shadow over the interpretation of ancient Indian history as well. The Hindu communalists were out to prove that Indian society, her culture and civilisation had reached great and ideal heights in the ancient period—from which it fell into permanent and continuing decay during the medieval period because of Muslim rule.

A totally uncritical approach and cheaply romanticised presentation of ancient Indian history was adopted as a matter of national pride and patriotism. This false pride created a mind-set of racial superiority that Hindus (i.e., Brahmans, since they had the monopoly of all the so-called knowledge), or the so-called *Aryans,* (of whom they were supposedly descendants) were the repositories of all knowledge and inventions that were made subsequently, or that may be made in future.

The boosting of Aryan culture relates in direct proportion to the propagation of the Hindu interpretation of Indian history. It is quite feasible to argue that the culture represented in the Vedic literature was largely indigenous. The logical position would be to study the pre-Vedic cultures from their archaeological remains and see the extent to which Vedic culture evolved from these. This insistence on the dominant role of Aryan culture in Indian history also stems from an unanalytical use of the literary sources and the almost complete exclusion of archaeological evidence. What makes it worse is that the description of the Aryan way of life is not even accurate.

It is no doubt true that India had made great strides in the field of agriculture, architecture, craftsmanship, fine arts, science (especially mathematics and medicine), literature, etc., during the ancient period. However, one cannot lose sight of the fact that the terrible decadence of Indian society, with the process of sub-infeudations, proliferation of castes and sub-castes and acute division of society into them, the emergence of *Gavgada*, untouchability, etc. had started much earlier.

The most vexing problem in ancient Indian history is the Aryan problem. One effect of eulogising ancient Indian history is to place an undue and one-sided emphasis on the contribution of the Aryans. That the Aryan people who came to India were in many ways culturally backward, and that it took several centuries for them to attain the level of civilisation which had been reached in Mohenjodaro, Harappa, Kalibangan and Lothal before the arrival of the Aryans is well known.

However, the civilisation which subsequently developed in India is generally portrayed as an Aryan civilisation with marginal adaptation of pre-Aryan ideas and institutions, instead of being presented as an integrated civilisation of Aryans and non-Aryans. The net result of this outlook is to refuse to study the phases of the growth of society in India, and to co-relate these phases with cultural literature.

In the last fifty years a considerable amount of archaeological evidence has come to light, which forces us to look anew at the notion of Aryan culture. Other aspects of the Aryan problem have also been critically examined and now suggest a considerable reorientation towards the problem. It is extremely difficult, for example, to prove the existence of a distinct and separate Aryan race. It is equally difficult to insist on the purity of Aryan culture and its complete superimposition on the indigenous culture.

The evidence only makes sense if one assumes that Aryan applies only to a language-speaking group and not to an ethnic entity and that Vedic literature reflects the inter-mixture of Aryan and non-Aryan cultures if the two were in fact ever totally distinct entities.

On the founding of the Royal Asiatic Society, the so-called Orientalists or Indologists (British) became great enthusiasts of the culture of the Aryan-speaking peoples and studied Sanskrit. They evolved the theory of the Indo-European homeland and of the common ancestry of the Sanskritic and Greek culture.

The Aryans were seen as a racial entity, rather than a group of people who spoke related languages, and the dynamics of Aryan culture in India and Greek culture in Europe were sought to be related. There was an exaltation of the Vedic age, and the Orientalists by and large saw the ancient Indians as a people with an idyllic society.

The tensions were glossed over and the glory emphasised. This fitted in with the view of orthodox Hindus who anyway believed in the greatness of the *Vedas* and all that was associated with this literature.

Indian historians, who later picked up this train of thought, tended to ignore the motivations which had led the Orientalists to glorify ancient Indian society. The most obvious of these motivations was that many of the Orientalists were persons who were alienated from their own society and were extremely suspicious of the historical changes which Europe was undergoing, particularly as a result of industrialisation. Thus they searched for utopias elsewhere, and for many these lay in the ancient cultures of the Orient. Max Mueller, who coined for himself the Sanskritic name of 'Moksha Mula', is one example of an attempt at identification with an idealised culture of Indian antiquity.

It can be seen that the attempt by the British historians in glorifying ancient Indian history against medieval Indian history was a ploy to create divisions among the Hindus and Muslims and nothing more. Unfortunately, with this distorted historical perception of history, some Hindu communalists had to pay plaudits to *Manu Smruti* 'the most sacred, the most revered and reverable, being the great contributor to the creation of Hindu Rashtra'.[5]

In fact, any person who reads the *Manu Smruti* with open eyes, would find it to be the most inegalitarian treatise of the later phase of ancient India. It is full of invidious discrimination in the matter of treatment of different castes, the most liberal and charitable to Brahmanas and the most stringent and ruthlessly cruel to Shudras and women in all walks of day-today religious and secular life. It is the fountain of all sorts of blind faith and officially sanctions many barbarous customs not finding place in other ancient treatises.

Further, the excessive and incorrect glorification of ancient Indian history made the task of modernising present society a more onerous task, as the most negative and decadent features arising from the feudalistic order, such as *sati*, untouchability, were not only glossed over, but defended as an integral part of ancient traditions. Another effect of the false glorification of the respective separate histories of Hindus and Muslims was to paint both communities as racially and ethnically divided.

The British were bent upon implementing their policy of 'divide and rule' through many designs, so as to keep the Hindus and Muslims in separate divisions. Till the establishment of the British rule, the common language of the Hindu–Muslim communities in the North was Khariboli (Hindavi). 'Hindavi', the name given by poet Amir Khusrau in the thirteenth century became the syncretic form of the language of both Hindus and Muslims, as syncretic movements went on in the fields of religion and culture. In the language used by the Hindu writers, Persian and Arabic words were freely used. The reason for the use of Persian words in the language was that Persian was the court language for a long time.

The British linguists identified the common language commonly used by Muslims and Hindus, then known as Hindavi, by the name Hindustani. It is believed that the name Hindustani had been actually given by European scholars. When the Portugese came to India in the seventeenth century, the name of the language of this place, came to be known as 'Indostan' or Hindustani.

The dialect which was used in the royal military bazar in the neighbourhood of Delhi known as *Zaban-e-Urdu*, i.e. language of the camp or *Zaban-e-Urdu-e-Mulla*, i.e. the language of the state camp. With the passage of time both terms, i.e. *Mulla* and *Zaban* vanished. In this way the term 'Urdu' came to be used as a term for the dialect of a specific place. The basic foundation of Urdu is 'Khariboli' spoken around the Delhi–Meerut area. This dialect spoken in Lashkars and cantonments contained Arabic and Persian terminology and with the passage of time, came to be known as 'Urdu'.

The fact of the matter is that the language style which has been known by the name of Urdu, was not the language of the masses. That was a royal language which was learnt in royal families through coaching and which was adorned like a flower vase by the sycophantic poets of the king. The language was closer to the refined Brajbhasha of Keshav Das than to the popular Brajbhasha of Surdas. Instead of becoming the language of the toiling masses, it preferred to become the blossom of the garden of royalty. This is to say, those who termed their style of language as 'Urdu' as a matter of policy, substituted not only the prevalent terms of Hindi with the Persian words but also deliberately adopted the essence of the Persian language.[6]

In 1873, the British established the Fort William College in Calcutta (now Kolkata) and John Gilchrist was appointed Principal. Some language teachers were appointed, including Munshi Insha Allah Khan and Pandit Lallulall who were asked to write in different styles. Fort William College hatched a deep conspiracy in determining the language policy. In the name of Hindustani, Gilchrist listed three different syles in Hindustani:

(*i*) the style of the High Court, i.e. the Persian style (Urdu)
(*ii*) the style of the Munshis, which is the Middle style and
(*iii*) the rustic style, i.e. the Hindavi of the masses.

The style of the Muslims was the style of royalty or the High Court because that was the basis of their social identity. To prove themselves different from the masses they started copying the language mixed with Persian words and that is why Hindustani got moulded into Persian-mixed language. As such, when in 1872 Dawson wrote the grammar of the Hindustani language, it considered Hindustani synonymous with Urdu.

Richard Tapel did not find enough difference between Hindustani and Urdu and as the Governor of Madras, Sir William wrote in 1869, the Hindustani which thrived under the patronage of Fort William and which was adopted by the Muslims and which the students learnt in the Muslim madrasas, was not spoken in any part of India.[7]

It may be mentioned that the Muslims in different parts of the country had local languages as their languages and specifically not the languages of Hindus or other religious communities. Hence it is not correct to think that the Muslims of North India in the Hindi belt, belonged to the Persian speaking origin and that their communal attachment towards Persian was still preserved.

On the instruction of the British educationalists like John Gilchrist and George Grierson (well-known linguist) Arabic–Persian words were removed from the common language and Sanskrit words were used. It was a deliberate attempt of conspiracy to divide the common language as Hindu and Muslim. This attempt had influenced some Hindavi writers of that time to replace popular Arabic–Persian terms by pure Sanskrit terms in their writings.

This was the starting point for the claim of Hindi and Urdu as separate languages. Gradually the 'Muslim' label was put on Urdu. It is a fact that earlier (and even now) Urdu has never been the monopoly language of one community (Muslims). Thus, we see that the Fort William College hatched the deep conspiracy in dividing the then existing language, Hindavi into two different language streams.

Thus, the process of confluence got disrupted during the British period which cannot be ignored. Even though the significance of, British policy of 'divide and rule' in this context is sometimes sought to be underestimated as a stale old cliche the fact cannot be denied. That policy led to what may be called conflictual relationships between some followers of Islam and some followers of Hinduism. 'Some', because the response was confined or articulated by the elite of both communities who were concentrated in urban areas. They were interested more in getting jobs and concessions. Therefore, they were interested more in currying favour with the alien rule and it was the competition for currying favour that created the phenomena that we call communalism.

Moreover, the British deliberately and consciously did not allow the growth of fellow-feeling and goodwill among the various sections of the Indian people. Throughout their rule they articulated their imperial policy of 'divide and rule'. However, Hindu–Muslim relations underwent a great change during the British rule. Never before in Indian history had the antagonism between the two communities been so widespread and acute as it was in the last 25 years of the British rule. It extended down to mass level and manifested itself in frequent outbreaks of violence, riots and killing of innocent people. But the cause of these riots were only superficially religious, and these were engineered by 'mischief makers' enjoying political patronage.

The British rulers often generated hostility between Hindus and Muslims where it did not exist and followed policies which would further accentuate differences. During the freedom struggle Islam and Hinduism often clashed with each other. The Britishers paved the way for religious nationalism, which took an ugly shape in the course of time.

It is a fact that political unity and sense of common nationhood need not depend on religious unity but on political, historical and cultural factors. Religious nationalism is not a viable category as the same religion can be, and often is, embraced by different racial, ethnic and cultural groups. Religion, it should be remembered, is a spiritual and moral category whereas nationalism is a political-cum-territorial category. The two should not be confused together. A composite culture can be a more viable base for nationalism than religion alone. Religion provides for common spiritual experience and shared moral and ethical vision whereas nationalism provides for shared political concerns, cultural practices and historical heritage.

India had such a common heritage. Its division was brought about by extraneous factors like British imperial policies rather than by differences of religion. The British rulers encouraged communal policies in the Hindu–Muslim communities to keep them at loggerheads, as a result of which hate-campaigns started.

Raja Shivaji and Rana Pratap were the two historical personalities of eminence who had been depicted by Hindu communal politicians as great defenders of the Hindu cause and fighting treacherous Muslim rulers for saving Hinduism. Even Shivaji's fight against the Mughals was described as a conflict between Hindus and Muslims.

Shivaji, according to the Brahman historians, had allegedly taken the *Birudavali* (i.e. his descriptive title) as *Go-bramahna Pratipalaka Hindu padapatsha* (i.e. the protector of cows and Brahmanas). However, there is absolutely no historical evidence of Shivaji having taken such a *Hindutvawadi* title, including that of *Sabhasad Bakhar*. In fact, Shivaji was never against Islam or Muslims.

Shivaji's respect for Islam was deep-rooted; this was evident when he met a Muslim saint. During his visit to Khails in Ratnagiri district, he paid a personal visit to the hospice of Hazrat Yaqut Baba Sarvari and granted him a *dastaweez* of 600 acres of land. He told his followers: '*Hazrat Baba Yaqut bahut thorwale*'. He also paid reverence to Moin Baba whose hospice was situated in Maloani.[8]

Even noted historian Jadunath Sarkar testifies : 'Shivaji's religious policy was very liberal. He respected the holy places of all creeds in his raids and made endowment, for Hindu temples and Muslim saints' tombs and mosques alike. He not only granted pensions to Brahman scholars versed in the Vedas, astronomers and anchorites, but also built hermitages and provided subsistence at his own cost for the holy men of Islam. Kafikhan, a historian writes, "When Shiva gets a copy of the Koran in the loot, he returns it to its owner very respectfully. As far as government employment is concerned, both civil and military he did not discriminate between religion and castes. Hindus of all castes and Muslims living on the coasts were regularly employed in his navy. He had many Muslims in his employment.'[9] Thus, we find that the communalists' use of Shivaji for their ulterior motives is really an insult to his true personality and a vulgar degradation of his historical role.

Another historical personality used by the Hindu communalists for promoting their politics was that of Maharana Pratap, the independent king of Mewar. The Mughal emperor Akbar was then spreading his empire by adopting the stick-and-carrot policy. All other Rajput kings and princes accepted the suzerainty of the Mughal empire, while Rana, who zealously valued his independence, refused to submit to the overtures of Akbar. Akbar had sent many emissaries to Rana from 1527 to 1576, including Ajmer's prince Raja Mansingh, to prevail upon Rana to accept the position of principality under Mughal rule without even appearing in person in the court to pay respect to his throne. Rana refused to succumb to this overture too.

Ultimately Akbar sent his forces to subdue Rana and the confrontation took place at Haldi Ghati. What is important to note is that the Mughal forces were led by the Rajput Raja Mansingh. Besides, not only were Muslim forces under chieftains to be Asaf Khan, Sayyad Hasham Baraha, and Jalaluddin Kaur, but the other Rajput chieftains, Raja Jagannath Kachwah, Rana Sukaran and other relatively smaller principalities also fought on the side of Akbar. This being the real historical fact, communal politicians described the fight between Akbar and Maharana Pratap as fight between Muslims and Hindus.

In the hate campaign the name of one more personality used by the protagonists of Hindu communalism is that of Swami Vivekananda. The Hindu protagonists were spreading the canard that Swami Vivekananda was their inspiration and mentor for promoting aggression and militant Hinduism and for promoting ethnic and economic cleansing of the Muslims.[10] But in reality, Swami Vivekananda was a totally different person; the lack of correct understanding about his thoughts led to present him as a mentor for promoting aggressive Hinduism.

In reality, Swami Vivekananda was basically a preacher of the rarest distinction who gave a new dimension to Sanatan Dharma. He brought out in their broadest manifestation, the secrets of human emancipation and explored brilliantly the spiritual insights, with which the *Vedas* and the *Upanishads* were embellished. He was no sectarian; his love transcended all creeds. That is why he had an appropriate understanding of the spiritual obligations of Indian Muslims and was most sympathetic to them. He never associated himself with the campaign of hate against them.

In his letter to Sarfaraz Husain, Vivekananda wrote that love was the motivating force behind all religions. He remarked that 'without the help of practical Islam, theories of Vedantism, however, fine and wonderful they may be, are entirely valueless to the vast mass of mankind. For our own motherland a junction of the two great systems, Hinduism and Islam—Vedanta brain and Islam body—is the only hope.'[11]

He told the detractors of the Muslim rule: 'The Muhammadan conquest of India came as a salvation to the downtrodden, to the poor. That is why one-fifth of our people have become Muhammadans.' He denied that 'it was all the work of sword and fire' and said that to call it so was 'the height of madness.' Strong words, which indicated his conviction.

As Professor Bose has observed, 'To him the Muslims were as good and human, at heart Indian, the Hindus. There was affinity between Sufism and Advaita Vedanta. The distinction between them by reason of their different beliefs were subordinate to their identity as fellow countrymen.'[12]

The Swami was, no doubt, critical of some features of Islam but so was he of Hinduism. He was never dogmatic but a rationalist to the core. He always looked at the better side of every faith. He was a humanist to his fingertips, believing in the eternal values which unite all sections of the human race, emphasising that it will attain salvation only through love and compassion.

According to Professor Tapan Raychaudhari of the Oxford University, the Swami was 'among the earliest nationalist thinkers to claim the Indo-Islamic past as part of the Indian heritiage.'[13]

During the freedom movement religious nationalism took centre-stage. The Britishers were aware that one day they had to leave this country. But they were not prepared to leave an united India. Thus in 1909 the British rulers introduced separate electorate for which there was no serious movement. And it is no exaggeration to say that the separate elections was the first step in the direction of Partition of the country.

Until the advent of the British, composite culture was the ruling culture in India, particularly at the level of the masses.

Even at the level of the ruling ellites, composite culture was widely prevalent particularly during the Mughal period. With the advent of the British rule in nineteenth century a new politics of culture started. The elites of the two communities, i.e., the Hindu and Muslim communities began to assert purity of their respective culture in order to generate separate and sharply defined identities.

In India a severe conflict took place about the concept of nation-state when the colonial masters were about to leave. The Muslim League, which claimed to be the sole representative of the Indian Muslims rejected the concept of composite nationalism and advanced the theory of religious nationalism. In fact the idea of religious nationalism was mooted for the first time on the Indian *subcontinent*. It was never mooted before anywhere else in the world. Nationalism, was so far associated with shared history, culture, language and ethnicity but not with religion.

Religious nationalism finally led to the 'two-nation' theory. It is also important to note that the two-nation theory was born more out of political considerations than on grounds of religion. It was the result of competition of power between secular elites of the two communities rather than justified by theology of Islam or Hinduism. The religious leaders of Muslims opposed the theory and justified composite nationalism on religious ground. Territory and not religion forms the basis of nationalism, they argued. The most articulate theorist among religious leaders who rejected the theory of religious nationalism was Maulana Husain Ahmad Madani belonging to the Deoband school of *ulama*.

Similarly, among Hindus, it was not religious leadership which justified the two nation theory but 'secular' leadership led by Vir Savarkar and others. Neither the Muslim League nor Hindu Mahasabha was a religious party. The leaders of the Hindu Mahasabha agreed with Jinnah and his Muslim League that Hindus and Muslims were two different 'nations'. It is a different thing that the Hindu Mahasabha, unlike the Muslim League, did not demand Partition of the country. It stood for *Akhand Bharat* under the Hindu hegemony. The Hindu

Mahasabha, and later the RSS, wanted to establish the *Hindu Rashtra* wherein Muslims, Christians and Parsis would be treated as foreigners and would have no citizenship and political rights.[14]

M.A. Jinnah spoke of justice for minorities in an unjustifiably haughty tone, arrogating 'sole spokesmanship' for the Islamic community in British India, despite its many differences, at the time of the Congress governments in some provinces in 1937-39, and again during the Transfer of Power negotiations. The rhetoric of justice for entire communities was certainly based on power and vote blocks.

A man like Jinnah could not have had very much Ulama support from the great Uttar Pradesh ulama centres such as Deoband or Lucknow or Azamgarh. Maulana Husain Ahmad Madani or Tufail Ahmad Manglauri, who had written *'Hindustani Musalmanon ka Raushan Mustakbil'*, are cases in point. On the other hand, behind the Muslim League movement for Pakistan in 1940 onwards (when Jinnah led Muslim businessmen profiting from the British Indian war effort in deciding not to join the Congress in the latter's campaign not to forsake imperialist, as well as fascist, war, as a legitimate part of international relations) there was a lot of support from peasant leaders of the Indus Basin, acting as quartermasters for the British Indian Army.[14]

The two-nation theory was contested by the *Burbam,* an organ from the reformist ulama from Deoband. They indicted the Muslim League for its 'collosal blunder' which had no parallel in the history of Islam. 'The verdict of history will go against a leadership which brought ruin and destruction to the community' (*Burban,* Delhi April 1948, p.133). Muslim divines, called Jami'at-al-'Ulama-i-Hindi—were a supporters of the Indian National Congress and never budged from their position even in the heyday of the clamour for Pakistan. In fact, most of the Ulama of Deoband and of the Jamiat al-Ulama joined forces with the Congress.

In April 1940 the Jamiat sponsored an Azad Muslim Conference of nationalist Muslim parties such as the All-India Muslim Majlis, Khudai Khidmatgar, Shia Political Conference,

Majlis i-Islam, Momin Conference, Krishak Praja Party, and the Anjuman-i-Watan, which, in opposition to the Muslim League demand for a separate Muslim state, declared India as 'the common homeland of all its citizens irrespective of race and religion'. Representing at that time a substantial number of Indian Muslims, they assembled in Delhi to protest against the Pakistan idea and against the use made of the Muslims by the British government and others as an excuse for political inaction. Their views were summarised by Allah Bur Soomro, premier of Sind, and president of the conference, who said that to regard 'Muslims as a separate nation in India on the basis of their religion was un-Islamic'.

Mahatma Gandhi and Maulana Azad were unique personalities of Indian national movement. Both of them were firm believers in religion and at the same time great votaries of secularism. It was not a matter of mere strategy for them but of deep-rooted conviction. It was such a political approach, which brought the two communities together despite strong communal trend to the contrary. The spearhead of common nationhood and harmony among religions was Mahatma Gandhi. His response to religion centred on nationalism or the so-called 'two nation theory' was : 'The "two nations" theory is an untruth. The vast majority of Muslims of India are converts to Islam or are the descendants of converts. They did not become a separate nation, as soon as they became converts. A Bengali Muslim speaks the same tongue that a Bengali Hindu does, eats the same food and has the same amusements, as his Hindu neighbour. They dress alike. I have often found it difficult to distinguish by outward sign, between a Bengali Hindu and a Bengali Muslim. The same phenomenon is observable more or less in the south among the poor who constitute the masses of India.'

The idea of common nationhood was developed and shared by all Indians, irrespective of religious affiliation. Eminent Muslim scholars and divines made a significant contribution to the development of this concept even as they actively participated in the struggle against British colonialism. Hindus on the other hand shared the outrage of Muslims when

European powers meted out unjust treatment to the Muslim world. The Khilafat and non-cooperation movements are outstanding examples of that. So is the consistent Indian support to the Palestine cause.

Maulana Abul Kalam Azad, for example, held this view :

'Islam has now as great a claim on the soil of India as Hinduism. If Hinduism has been the religion of the people here for several thousands of years, Islam also has been their religion for a thousand years. Just as a Hindu can declare with pride that he is an Indian and follows Hinduism, so also can we say with equal pride that we are Indians and we follow Islam. I shall enlarge this orbit still further. The Indian Christian is equally entitled to say with pride that he is an Indian and he is following a religion of India, namely, Christianity'.[15]

In the context of Hindu–Muslim relations, he laid the greatest emphasis on harmony between the two, saying that without it all hope of independence, survival and progress of the country would be an idle dream. Without it not only will it be impossible to attain national independence but we shall fail to develop in ourselves the basic attributes and values of humanity. 'Therefore even if an angel descends from high heavens and proclaims from top of the Qutub Minar that Swaraj would come within 24 hours if we renounce the goal of Hindu-Muslim unity my response would be to renounce Swaraj but not unity. Because, if Swaraj is delayed, it would be loss only of India but if we lose unity it would be a loss for entire humanity,' he declared.[16]

As pointed out before, it is sociologically and politically wrong to consider any religious community homogenous, but 'Hindus' and 'Muslims' had become political categories since the British days in Indian political discourse as if they were monolithic blocs without any political, religious, linguistic and cultural differences. Commonality of religion, as the two-nation theory also assumed does not lead to communality of politics, nor does it lead to commonality of culture.

The Muslims of north and central India, who spoke Urdu were distinctly different from Muslims from south India who speak different South Indian languages. They had their own political inclinations and compulsions. The Muslims from south were indifferent to the question of Pakistan right from the beginning. They did not support partition with the same enthusiasm as the Urdu-speaking Muslims of north India. Communalism and communal violence remained centred right from the British days in the north.

The Indian National Congress, which was the harbinger of our freedom movement, adopted it since its foundation in 1885. The Indian National Congress was quite aware of the composite nature of our society and always tried to carry the minorities with it. The first three presidents of the Congress belonged to minority communities, i.e., W.C. Banerjee, a Christian; Badruddin Tyebji, a Muslim and Phirozshah Mehta, a Parsi. Secularism, for the founding fathers of our freedom movement meant not associating the state with any religion and also protecting the rights of minorities.

It was the philosophy of secularism which guided our freedom movement throughout and it was this philosophy which was adopted by the Constitution makers. In independent India, persons like Jawahar Lal Nehru and Abul Kalam Azad were firmly committed to this philosophy and never allowed any compromise at least in principle though in practice there were formidable challenges.

We have just seen that the British policy of 'divide and rule' finally led to partition of the country. Although the division of the country was not the common man's choosing, yet the majority of Muslims willingly chose to stay in India.

The composite culture is far more widespread even today than is generally realised. This has been vividly brought out in a recent study conducted by the Anthropological Survey of India under the 'People of India Project'. According to its findings, Indian Muslims share a very high percentage (96.77) of material and cultural traits relating to ecology, economy and occupation with Hindus. The ratio of shared traits between Muslims and Sikhs is 89.95 per cent and that between Muslims and Buddhists is 91.95 per cent.

This empirical study of our composite society clearly proves that the project of cultural nationalism is without any roots in our society and can hardly carry conviction with the common people.

Coming to our times, composite traditions are very much alive in Indian villages. We find quite illustrious examples of composite culture as far back as thirteenth and fourteenth century or even earlier. Through the following centuries, communal harmony which is the spirit of composite culture prevailed. Though during the British rule communal harmony had a severe beating, the composite culture which got deep roots in the Indian soil could not be diluted. We can give numerous examples of composite culture even in the present day Indian society, which has forged unity among the people and which is our valuable asset and heritage that will bring greater cohesion among the people of India.

To end, having gone through the foundations of the composite culture in India, we may conclude with the following message :

'Islam in India, whatever its remote past history may be, is now an integral part of the social and cultural life of the *subcontinent*. In the course of several centuries of naturalisation, it has adapted itself to the Indian environment, has developed its own characteristic quality, and has made immense contributions to the social, political and intellectual solidarity of the nation. Islamic legacy of India is as Indian as anything else that exists in this ancient land. It is certainly absurd, or perhaps mischievous to suggest that Khusrau and Ghalib were less Indian than Kalidas or Tagore, that Taj Mahal is less a national heritage than the Ajanta, or that Azad and Zakir Husain were less motivated by love for their motherland than Gandhi or Nehru.

The people of India, Hindus and Muslims, have to live and work together, build up their future destiny, and share the fruits of their achievements. They should recognise the fact that they are one unified nation composed of two major groups; they are a rich blend of two active elements, which, if dealt with properly, will complement each other. They should realise that any attempt by one group to ignore or underestimate the worth of the other, or to suppress its self-assertion, will damage the solidarity of the whole : They should love and respect each other, but at the same time they should realise the fact that mutual love and respect cannot be established if there is no mutual understanding'.

REFERENCES AND NOTES

1. Quoted by Dr.B.N. Pande in his book *Historical Distortions*, p.37.
2. Jawed, Dr. Ajeet. *Heritage of Harmony : An Insight into Medieval India*, pp. 307–309.
3. Ibid., pp. 310–311.
4. *India's Islamic Traditions, Introduction*. Ed. Richard M. Eaton, pp. 17–18.
5. *Samagira Savarkar*, in Marathi, part 4, pp. 294–295.
6. Mohamed, Dr. Malik. *The Culture of Hindi*, p. 73.
7. Ibid., p. 74.
8. Chandra, Dr. Satish. *Communalism and the Writing of Indian History*, p. 12.
9. Zakaria, Dr. Rafiq. *Communal Rage in Secular India*, p. 156.
10. Ibid., p. 157.
11. Ibid., p. 162.
12. *Swami Vivekananda and Modernization of Hindustan*. Ed. William Radice, p.290.
13. Zakaria, Dr. Rafiq. *Communal Rage in Secular India*, p. 169.
14. *Islam in India : The Imports of Civilizations*. Ed. Dr. Asghar Ali Engineer, Two Textual Paradigsm of Nationalism, Barun De, p. 97.
15. Ibid., p. 108.
16. Ibid., p. 77.

Bibliography

Abid, Hussain S. *The National Culture of India*, New Delhi : National Book Trust of India, 1978.

Aggarwal, C.M. *Akbar and his Hindu Friends*, Jullundhar : ABS 1986.

Ahmad, Aziz. *Studies in Islamic Culture in the Indian Environment*, New Delhi: Oxford University Press, 1963.

Ahmad, Imtiaz and Helmut Reifeld. *Lived Islam in South Asia: Adaptation, Accommodation and Conflict*, Delhi : Social Science Press, 2004.

Ahmad, Imtiaz. *Ritual and Religion among Muslims in India*, New Delhi : Manohar Publication, 1984.

Ali, Asad. *Bhaktikaleen, Hindi Sahitya par Mulim Sanskrit ka Prabhav*, New Delhi: AIS Publication, 1971. (Hindi)

Ali, Sirdar Ikbal. *Islamic Sufism*, Delhi : Shah Adam Publishers, 1998.

Ali, Syed Asad. *Influence of Islam on Hindi Literature*, Delhi: Idarah-i Adabiyat-i Delhi, 1998.

Ashraf, K.M. *Life and Condition of the People of Hindustan*, Delhi: 1959.

Askari, S.H. *Amir Khusrau—As a Historian*, Patna : Khuda Bakhsh Oriental Public Library, 1988.

Assayag, Jackie. *At the Confluence of Two Rivers, Muslims and Hindus in South India*, New Delhi : Manohar Publications, 2004.

Basham, A.C. *The Wonder that was India*, Sidgwick and Jackson, 1954.

Begg, Mirza W.D. *The Holy Biography of Hazrat Khwaja Muinuddin Chishti of Ajmar*, Ajmer.

Bhambhri, C.P. *Hindutva, A Challenge of Multi-cultural Democracy*, Delhi: Shipra Publications, 2003.

Bhattacharyya, N.N. *Medieval Bhakti Movements in India: Sri Chaitanya Quincentenary Commemoration*, New Delhi: Munshiram Manoharlal, 1999.

Brandon, S.G.F. *Dictionary of Comparative Religion*, London: Weidenfeld and Nicholson, 1970.

Chandra, Satish. *Communal Interpretation of Indian History*, New Delhi: 1992.

Chandra, Satish. *Mughals' Religious Policies*, New Delhi : Vikas Publications, 1993.

Choudhry, M.L. Roy. *The State and Religion in Mughal India*, Calcutta: Indian Publicity Society, 1951.

Das, N.K. *Culture, Religion and Philosophy, Critical Studies in Syncretism and Inter-faith Harmony*, New Delhi : Rawat Publications, 2003.

Day, U.N. *Some Aspects of Medieval Indian History*, New Delhi : Kumar Bros, 1971.

Devaraja, N.K. *Philosophy, Religion and Culture*, New Delhi: Motilal Banarsidass, 1974.

Devaraja. *The Philosophy of Culture*, Allahabad : Kitab Mahal, 1963.

Eaton, Richard M. *India's Islamic Traditions*, 711–1750, Oxford University Press, 2003.

Engineer, Asghar Ali. *Communal Challenge and Secular Response*, Delhi : Shipra Publications, 2003.

Engineer, Asghar Ali. *Islam in India, The Impact of Civilizations*, Delhi : Shipra Publications, 2002.

Gajendragadkar, K.V. *The Maharashtra Saints and their Teachings, Cultural Heritage of India*, IV, Calcutta.

Gottschalk, Peter. *Beyond Hindu and Muslim Multiple Identity in Narratives from Village India*, Oxford University Press, 2001.

Hameed, Syeda Saiyidian. *Contemporary Relevance of Sufism*, New Delhi : Indian Council for Cultural Relations, 1993.

Haque, Ishrat. *Glimpses of Mugal Society and Culture*, New Delhi: Concept Publishing Company, 1992.

Hasan, Ibn. *The Central Structure of the Mughal Empire*, Lahore: Oxford University Press, 1967.

Hasan, Mohibbul. *Kashmir under the Sultans*, Calcutta: Iran Society, 1959.

Hasan, Mushirul. *Legacy of a Divided Nation, India's Muslims since Independence*, New Delhi: Oxford University Press, 1997.

Hasan, Mushirul and Asim Roy, *Living Together Separately: Cultural India in History and Politics*, New Delhi : Oxford University Press, 2005.

Hasan, Mushirul. *Will Secular India Survive*? Imprint One, Gurgoan, 2004.

Husain, Yusuf. *Islam and the Cult of Bhakti, Glimpses of Medieval Indian Culture*, Bombay: 1957.

Hussain, Muzaffar. *Insight into Minoritism*, New Delhi: India First Foundation, 2004.

Hussain, Yusuf. *Glimpses of Medieval Indian Culture*, Bombay: Asia Publishers, 1957.

Jaffer, S.M. *Cultural Aspect of Muslim Rule*, Peshawar: Mohd. Sadiq, 1939.

Jawed, Ajeet. *Heritage of Harmony : An Insight into Medieval India*, New Delhi : Gyan Publishing House, 2002.

Khanam, Farida. *A Simple Guide to Sufism*, New Delhi: Goodword Books, 2006.

Khan, Rasheeduddin. *Composite Culture of India and National Integration*, Simla: Indian Institute of Advanced Study, 1987.

Khan, M. Ishaq: *Kashmir's Transition to Islam : The Role of Muslim Rishis*, New Delhi: Manohar Publication, 2002.

Kumaraswamyiji, S. *The Virasaiva Philosophy and Mysticism*, Dharwar, 1949.

Lal, K.S. *Legacy of the Muslim Rule in India*, New Delhi: Aditya Prakashan, 1992.

Latif, Abdul. *An Outline of the Cultural History of India*, Hyderabad, 1958.

Luniya, B.N. *Evolution of Indian Culture*, Agra: Lakshmi Narayan Shivlal Agarwal, 1955.

May, L.S. *The Evolution of Indo-Muslim Thought from 1857 to the Present*, New Delhi : Uppal Publishing House, 1987.

Mishra, K.C. *The Cult of Jagannath*, Calcutta, 1971.

Misra, Neeru. *Sufis and Sufism : Some Reflections*, Delhi : Manohar Publications, 2004.

Mitra, Sisir Kumar. *India's Cultural Empire and Her Future*, Madras: Aurobindo Library, 1947.

Mohamed, Malik. *The Culture of Hindi*, New Delhi : Kalinga Publications, 2005.

More, J.P. Religion and Society in South India, Institute for Research in Social Sciences and Humanities, Nirmalagiri, 2005.

Mujtabai, Fathullah. *Aspects of Hindu Muslim Cultural Relations*, Delhi: M.B.B. 1978.

Mukherjee, R.K. *History of Medieval Vaisnavism in Orissa*, Calcutta, 1940.

Nizami, Khaliq Ahmad. *The Life and Times of Shaikh Farid – Uddin Ganj-i-Shakar*, New Delhi: Oxford University Press, 1955.

Noorani, A.G. *The Muslims of India*, New Delhi: Oxford University Press, 2003.

Ohri, R.K. *Long March of Islam, The Future Imperfect*, New Delhi: Manas Publications, 2004.

Pal, Jagat. *Analysis of the Concept of Culture*, New Delhi: Indus Publishing Co., 1996.

Pande, B.N. *Islam and Indian Culture*, Part III, Patna: Khuda Baksh Memorial Annual Lecture, 1985.

Panikkar, K.M. *Essential Features of Indian Culture*, Bombay: Bharatiya Vidya Bhavan, 1974.

Panikar, K.M. *Hindu Soceity at Cross Roads*, Bombay, 1955.

Pohlong, Basil. *Culture and Religion: A Conceptual Study*, New Delhi: Mittal Publications, 2004.

Prasad, Rajendra. *The Unity of India*, New Delhi: Publications Division, Govt. of India, 1961.

Ranade, R.D. *Pathway to God in Hindi Literature*, Bombay: Published for Adhyatma Vidya Mandir, 1959.

Rashid, A. *Society and Culture in Medieval India*, Firma K.L. Mukhopadhyaya, 1969.

Rizvi, S.A.A. *Muslim Revivalist Movements in Northern India*, Agra: Balkrishna Book Depot, 1965.

Rizvi, S.A.A. *Religious and Intellectual History of India in Akbar's Reign*, Delhi: 1975.

Rizvi, Saiyad Athar Abbas. *A History of Sufism in India*, Vol. 1, New Delhi: Munshiram Manoharlal Publishers, 1978.

Sankar, D.C. *Studies in Religious Life of Ancient and Medieval India*, Delhi, 1971.Radhakrishnan. *Religion and Culture*, Delhi: Hind Pocket Books Ltd., 1968.

Sarkar, Jadunath. *India Through the Ages*, Madras University, 1928.

Sarkar, Jadunath. *The Fall of the Mughal Empire*, Vol. I.

Sastri, K.A. Nilakanta. *Development of Religion in South India*, New Delhi : Orient Longman.

Sharma, S.R. *The Religion Policy of the Mughal Emperors*, New Delhi: Oxford University Press, 1940.

Siddiqui, Iqtidar Husain. *Medieval India, Essays in Intellectual Thought and Culture*, Vol. 1, Delhi : Manohar Publications, 2003.

Sikand, Yoginder. *Hindu–Muslim Syncretic Shrines in Karnataka*.

Silakhan, Dominique. *The Pranami Faith : Beyond Hindu and Muslim*.

Singh, Purnima. *Indian Cultural Nationalism*, New Delhi: India First Foundation, 2004.

Spencer, Trimingham J. *Sufi Orders in India*, Oxford University Press, 1971.

Springsted, Eric O., T.S. Eliot and Simone Weil. *The Religious Basis of Culture in Religious Studies*, Vol. 23, No. 1-4, 1989.

Subhan, John A. *Sufism : Its Saints and Shrines*, Lucknow : Lucknow Publishing House, 1960.

Talib, Gurbachan Singh. *Baba Sheikh Farid, Life and Teachings*, Baba Farid Memorial Society, 1973.

Talib, Gurbachan Singh. *Perspectives on Sheikh Farid*, Baba Farid Memorial Society, 1975.

Tarachand, Dr. *Society and State in Mughal Period*, New Delhi: Publications Division, Govt. of India, 1961.

Tarachand, Dr. *Influence of Islam on Indian Culture*, Allahabad: Indian Press Pvt. Ltd., 1976.

Troll, Christian W. *Muslim Shrines in India: Their Character, History and Significance*, Oxford University Press, 1989.

Umar, Muhammad. *Islam in Northern India During the Eighteenth Century*, Delhi: Munshiram Manoharlal Publishers Pvt. Ltd., 1993.

Vidya, C.V. *History of Medieval Hindu India*, Vol. III, Poona: Published by C.V. Vaidya, 1926.

Waseem, M. *On Becoming an Indian Muslim : French Essays on Aspects of Syncretism*, New Delhi : Oxford University Press, 2003.

Wyatt, John Zavos Andrew and Vernon Hewitt. *The Politics of Cultural Mobilization in India*, New Delhi: Oxford University Press, 2004.

Zakaria, Rafiq. *Communal Rage in Secular India*, Mumbai: Popular Prakshan, 2002.

Zavos, John. *The Emergence of Hindu Nationalism in India*, New Delhi: Oxford University Press, 2000.

Index